T0311747

# WOMEN, MUSIC AND LEADERSHIP

*Women, Music and Leadership* offers a wide-ranging survey of women in musical leadership and their experiences, highlighting women's achievements and considering how they negotiate the challenges of the leadership space in music.

Women have always participated in music as performers, teachers, composers and professionals, but remain underrepresented in leadership positions. Covering women's leadership across a wide variety of roles and musical genres, this book addresses women in classical music, gospel, blues, jazz, popular music, electronic music and non-Western musical contexts, and considers women working as composers, as conductors, and in music management and the music business. Each chapter includes several case studies of women's careers, exploring their groundbreaking contributions to music and the challenges they faced as leaders.

Connecting management theory and leadership research with feminist musicology, this book paints a new picture of women's major contributions as leaders in music and their ongoing struggles for equity. It will be relevant to students and scholars in arts and music management, as well as all those studying music, gender or leadership, and women music professionals.

**Helen Rusak** has held high-profile positions as an arts manager and musician and was most recently Senior Lecturer and course coordinator for Arts Management at the Western Australian Academy of Performing Arts, Edith Cowan University. In 2023 she was appointed adjunct in Arts Management at the University of South Australia.

# WOMEN, MUSIC AND LEADERSHIP

*Helen Rusak*

Routledge
Taylor & Francis Group

NEW YORK AND LONDON

Designed cover image: © GeorgePeters

First published 2024
by Routledge
605 Third Avenue, New York, NY 10158

and by Routledge
4 Park Square, Milton Park, Abingdon, Oxon, OX14 4RN

*Routledge is an imprint of the Taylor & Francis Group, an informa business*

© 2024 Helen Rusak

*Library of Congress Cataloging-in-Publication Data*
Names: Rusak, Helen, author.
Title: Women, music and leadership / Helen Rusak.
Description: [1.] | New York : Routledge, 2023. |
Includes bibliographical references and index.
Identifiers: LCCN 2023008613 (print) | LCCN 2023008614 (ebook) |
ISBN 9781032025025 (hardback) | ISBN 9781032025018 (paperback) |
ISBN 9781003183631 (ebook)
Subjects: LCSH: Women in the music trade. | Leadership in women. |
Discrimination in the music trade.
Classification: LCC ML82 .R87 2023 (print) | LCC ML82 (ebook) |
DDC 780.82–dc23/eng/20220720
LC record available at https://lccn.loc.gov/2023008613
LC ebook record available at https://lccn.loc.gov/2023008614

ISBN: 9781032025025 (hbk)
ISBN: 9781032025018 (pbk)
ISBN: 9781003183631 (ebk)

DOI: 10.4324/9781003183631

Typeset in Sabon
by Newgen Publishing UK

*For my daughters Kazimiera and Margaret*

# CONTENTS

# ACKNOWLEDGEMENTS

I acknowledge the support of Edith Cowan University for the early stages of the development of this work. I am grateful that I was able to work for the institution in the namesake of Edith Cowan as the first female parliamentarian in Australia. Her achievements include significant contribution to the welfare of women and children in Western Australia. I acknowledge the support of my husband Dr Alistair Campbell who has encouraged me on my research journey.

# INTRODUCTION

I originally titled this book 'breaking the glass harmonica' as a play on the 'breaking the glass ceiling' metaphor which has become the common allusion to women breaking through the upper ranks of power and influence in business and politics. I was motivated to write this book to highlight the positive developments that are happening for women in music. As a feminist musicologist, arts manager and academic, I considered it time to celebrate the achievements of some of the women who have achieved success in musical leadership. When one of my colleagues from another discipline asked what I was writing about she remarked "that will be a very small book". I assured her not and indeed, the book is limited by the exclusion of many more remarkable women in musical leadership that are emerging each day. I had imagined a more concise book myself, but it has been difficult to select from the many talented musicians and female musical leaders whom to exclude.

The topic is problematic in itself as some might argue that once we identify our musical leaders as women, we are immediately casting them into the ghetto of a lesser minority and throughout the book there will be evidence of women claiming that they do not wish to be identified as a women composer, for example, but just as a composer. The clarification between gender and sex needs to be considered in the discussion of music and women. If it is agreed that gender is a construct and sex is biological, then music is sexually neutral. Historically choices available to women have cast them into gendered roles which have become challenged as women achieve more equity. Alongside this is the inherent paradox in the

DOI: 10.4324/9781003183631-1

use of the word woman and feminists have coined womxn or womyn to avoid the inbuilt associated binaries. Also, the rise in recognition of gender fluidity and LGBTQI+ considerations become overlooked in the male–female binary which is a limitation of any study of women exclusively. Additionally, such a feminist pursuit can be concerned with the women from privileged middle-class backgrounds, particularly when it comes to music and those with access to musical training which does not account for intersections of race, colour and class.

Chapter 1 examines the academic theory that exists on women in leadership and existing data tracking women in leadership. Commencing with a survey of the role of feminism in advancing women's struggle for economic, social and political equity, it leads to a discussion of how the burden of unpaid domestic labour increases the equity gap and how institutional structures have not been designed to accommodate women's career progress. A discussion ensues of how the COVID-19 pandemic highlighted the impact of increased care responsibilities which mainly fell to women affecting their ability to progress in their careers. It looks at women's impact upon traditional notions of leadership and as diversity in leadership increases how·the dominant leadership paradigms are being challenged. The ensuing survey of women's musical contribution throughout musical history in this chapter provides significant examples of women who have taken leading roles in a range of musical activities from composition through to performance and instrument development.

Chapter 2 provides a brief survey of some of the leading feminist musicological theorists and their contributions to feminist aesthetics, women's representation in music, analysis of musical form as gendered discourse and examining the role of women in music in relation to power and social structure.

This is followed by an analysis of some data on gender parity in the concert hall. Some of the leading women composers in the 20th century are discussed in this chapter along with some contemporary case studies of women who are taking the lead in musical composition such as Elena Kats-Chernin, Sofia Gubaidulina and Deborah Cheetham.

Chapter 3 discusses the challenges faced by women in gaining senior leadership roles as conductors of major orchestras which represents leadership at the top of the musical hierarchy. It highlights the careers of women who have been pioneers in overcoming the challenges faced by women aspiring to lead orchestras. This is followed by a survey of contemporary women who have negotiated successful careers conducting major international orchestras cataloguing their legacies.

Chapter 4 examines women's careers as classical performers on the public concert stage. It commences with a discussion of the professional public performance limitations placed on women musicians through the centuries. Some historical examples of women who undertook performing careers are provided. The role of all-women's orchestras in providing performance opportunities for women is discussed. This is followed by a survey of singers and pianists who pursued performance careers in the 19th century and, as women gained more independence, some of the leading performers of the 20th century when it became an acceptable career for women. This is followed by a survey of women maintaining professional performing careers on a range of instruments including strings, brass and percussion. It concludes with a discussion of the role of women's musical organisations in furthering the careers of women musicians.

The following chapters turn to women in popular music in a range of genres and those who have succeeded in influencing the musical genres of the 20th century. Chapter 5 surveys the contribution of leading women in the field of blues, jazz, gospel and Motown. It surveys the careers of leading women from African American roots who have capitalised on their music to gain considerable wealth and power in an industry that was previously closed to them. Blues women became successful recording artists and songwriters and were followed by successful jazz, gospel and Motown women. Their songs voiced feminist concerns which resonated with their audiences and the growing female music market. This chapter looks at women's musical contribution to these genres as singers, front women for bands, soloists and instrumentalists along with their influence on the development of styles and genres which were the precursors to the popular music industry of the 20th century.

Chapter 6 addresses leading women in popular music who have successfully negotiated their careers by taking on inspirational roles as performers, producers and songwriters. It identifies how many successful female performers have used popular musical styles to express feminist messages. It looks at women in a range of popular genres including cabaret, musical theatre, folk and protest song, civil rights and human rights activism, punk and experimental music, country music, rock and hip-hop. It also examines their legacy in empowering other women through their musical messages, financial initiatives and as role models.

Chapter 7 addresses how women have responded to the sexism of the electronic music scene, an area in which women have been particularly marginalised, to take on leadership roles as successful composers and performers. It reviews some of the women pioneers in electronic music who have responded to the new technologies as they emerged in the 20th century. It looks at some of the significant inventions and innovations that women have contributed to the development of electronic music. There is a review of women adopting electronic inventions in contemporary popular music as well as in sound production. It touches upon females progressively emerging as DJs.

Chapter 8 explores women from diverse cultural backgrounds and their leadership roles. It examines the diversity of leadership roles that women have undertaken in global music and the challenges faced by women in musical leadership in non-Western cultures. It interrogates music in cross-cultural contexts and the expressions of world and global music which became the marketing blanket term in the late 20th century. It surveys some of the most influential women in non-Western music who have gained international attention for feminist, political and social concerns of women worldwide. It also provides examples of Indigenous women involved in activating Indigenous concerns through their music.

Chapter 9 examines the data on women in the music industry providing case studies of women taking on leadership roles in the music business. It commences with the research on the gender imbalance in the music industry and the findings of that research which identifies sexism and sexual harassment as being some of the barriers for women entering the music industry. It includes examples of women who have taken on leadership roles in the recording industry, music management, music journalism, music festivals, artistic direction, curation and programming.

The book aims to cast some light on the exceptional achievements of women in music and provide a catalyst for further research into the remarkable musical achievements of women.

# 1

# THE CONTEXT FOR WOMEN
# IN MUSICAL LEADERSHIP

## Introduction

Little research exists on women in leadership as there have historically
been comparatively few women in leadership. Women's representation
in leadership increased in the 20th–21st centuries, but by no means has
gender parity been met. Indeed, in recent decades in some instances the
number of women in leadership positions has declined. This chapter
examines some of the academic theory that exists on women in leadership
from the early observations by Bass[1] to more recent explorations by
Sheridan et al.[2] and Sinclair[3] to name a few. Existing data tracking women
in leadership has been undertaken by the World Economic Forum Global
Gender Gap reports, and Catalyst. Also, more recently women leaders
have had an influence on leadership literature through documenting their
personal experience of corporate and political leadership among them
Sheryl Sandberg, Hilary Clinton, Gail Kelly, Julia Gillard, Ngozi Okonjo-
Iweala, Jacinta Ardern and Christine Nixon.[4] Issues of quotas, tokenism,
childcare and pay equity pervade the literature on women in leadership
and these will be discussed in this chapter.

## Feminism and leadership

Women engaging in leadership roles in society has been advanced by the
feminist cause. Feminism had its roots in 19th-century Europe and was
adopted by other western countries with women seeking equality of the
sexes in the areas of political, economic and social equity. The struggle for

DOI: 10.4324/9781003183631-2

equality for women in areas of education, work rights and to unionise was erupting by the end of the 19th century in Europe and various waves of activism continued throughout the 20th century. The suffragette movement sought legal rights for women through granting the right for women to vote. By the late 1880s, women were granted some rights to property, education and employment, and the right to vote in some countries. New Zealand paved the way for women to vote in 1893 followed by Finland in 1906, Australia in 1910, Poland in 1917 and Austria in 1918. British women over 30 were able to vote in 1918 and the age limit was dropped to 21 in 1928. The United States allowed women to vote in 1928. Following World War II, voting rights were granted in France, Italy, Japan and Senegal in 1945, Greece in 1952, Cambodia and Honduras in 1955. African nations that were emerging from postcolonialism gave women voting rights in the 1960s and 1970s and this expanded to the Middle East in the 1980s. Some of the most recent countries to grant voting rights include Kuwait in 2005 and Saudi Arabia in 2015. Australia was the first to give women the right to be elected to the national parliament in 1902.

In the United States, Eleanor Roosevelt worked with women activists to support women's working rights, union inclusion, wages, fair working hours, end of child labour and the right to strike. During the war, women moved into the factories, business and entertainment to assist the war effort. Following the war, men took up the positions that women were occupying and women were encouraged to return to home duties with images in the mainstream media of the domestic suburban ideal of women as stay-at-home mothers.

In the 1960s, women in some parts of the world were unable to get credit without a male underwriter, employers could advertise for men-only positions, husbands controlled their wives' property and earnings and certain bars and restaurants did not allow women unless accompanied by a man. The right to vote did not translate immediately to equality and many people of colour were deterred from voting. Women still did not have access to many education or job opportunities and this situation was even more difficult for women of colour.

French existentialist Simone de Beauvoir's *The Second Sex* (1949) is considered the starting point of the second wave of feminism challenging the historical domination of women in society by men.[5] The release of Betty Friedan's *The Feminine Mystique* (1963) reported on the psychological frustrations of US housewives who craved fulfilling careers.[6] Friedan founded the National Organisation for Women in 1966 and fought for Equal Rights for Women which it never achieved, but was instrumental in driving change to wage discrimination, women's education, domestic abuse, rape crisis support and women's shelters. In Australia Germaine

Greer's highly influential feminist text *The Female Eunuch* (1970) challenges the role of women as homemakers and the male dominance in politics, law and the media.[7] Feminist cultural theory in the second wave of feminism resulted in numerous discourses debating women's experiences, identities, empowerment and rights. Many gains were made in the second wave of feminism, but there is still ongoing debate on many issues such as legalised abortion and the limited concern for women beyond the white middle class. Also, there were women who disliked the idea of embracing patriarchal aspirations of control. Feminists were more divided on what the movement represented and second-wave feminism came to be considered as a white upper-class women's issue which did not represent issues such as race and class. Third-wave feminists also used their sexuality to empower themselves rather than view it as victimisation as can be seen in the work of Madonna, Beyonce and Miley Cyrus amongst others. Another branch was the Riot Grrl movement which addressed women's issues such as eating disorders, domestic violence and rape with driving punk music while others sought to celebrate motherhood and right to life anti-abortion movement. Diversity and international cooperation amongst feminists in organisations such as UN Women addressed concerns of women from all cultures in tackling feminist issues.

## Gender pay gap

Issues beleaguering women internationally such as participation and opportunities in the workforce, educational attainment and pay equity apply to women in music. The UN recognises the role of women in transforming economies if they are able to participate in political life and economic decision-making. The World Economic Forum Global Gender Gap, which was introduced in 2006 tracking the gender-based disparities over time, indicates that in 2022 there is an average 32% gender gap that remains to be closed. Predicting into the future the gender gap will take 136 years across 146 countries covered by the index to close. This is an increase of 36% on what was predicted pre-pandemic.[8]

The impact of COVID-19 upon women's childcare and domestic responsibilities highlighted the systematic entrenchment of the burden of care falling to women. The paid economy reduced by people losing work or having to stay home, but the care economy increased this work which includes childcare and domestic labour fell mainly to women.[9] Notwithstanding that both fathers and mothers were doing more housework and household management, the relative gender gap in these activities remained consistent with pre-COVID-19 activities.[10] Women's responsibilities in the care economy increased as did their stress due to the additional workload during COVID-19.[11] According to Catalyst.org women have been disproportionately impacted due to:

- High job loss in 'contact-intensive' industries such as Leisure and Hospitality, Education and Health Services, and Retail.
- The closings of schools and day-care centres, which put heavy childcare needs on families and particularly women.[12]

COVID-19 highlighted the already existing inequity in the institutional structures and systems that do not meet the needs of women and hinder progress in their careers.

Research by Adler and Osland indicates that most women executives create their own company, take over leadership of family companies or create and lead social enterprises.[13] It has been argued that women have been excluded from leadership positions in established companies, such as executives and boards of directors, because these positions are drawn from a pool of top executives and that women are underrepresented in these pipelines. Flabbi et al. note that only 10% of women reach executive status, despite all indications that appointing female executives has a positive impact on performance in firms where females are employed.[14] Some countries have introduced quotas for women on boards to improve their opportunities in leadership positions. Norway was the first European country to introduce quotas in 2005 requiring publicly listed companies to include at least 40% female representation on boards. Other European countries followed suit and the European Commission has considered a binding minimum quota for female board members of 40%. The effectiveness of the Norwegian experiment has been debated, but some have concluded that it has had little impact on the women in business beyond those who have made it to the boardroom.[15] Other recent research on the effect of quotas in other countries show that the threat of a gender board quota in Sweden increased the share of female board members accompanied by an improvement in firm performance.[16] However, it did not lead to the employment of female CEOs, in fact it did the opposite as female CEOs were recruited to boards but not replaced by female CEOs. An examination of gender quotas introduced in 2011 in Italy found that it led to an increased share of female board directors and overall higher levels of education of board members with no overall impact on firm performance, but a positive effect on stock market value.[17] An examination of the effects of board quotas in Belgium, France, Italy and Spain finds negative effects on firm performance in France and Belgium and positive effects on firm performance in Italy and Spain.[18] Since family consideration has an effect on the pathway for women in corporate leadership and it is more common for women to take parental leave despite the effects on their career, there is an argument that introducing quotas for men taking up parental leave could be just as important as introducing quotas for women in leadership.[19] Researchers are asking whether men will adopt the generous parental leave options available to them.[20]

## Leadership

Leadership research indicates that men and women may have different perceptions of what constitutes leadership and competitive hierarchical behaviour has been associated with what men see as effective leadership. Sinclair refers to 'The Traditional Path: Heroic Masculinity' where leadership is identified with the attributes of male warriors.[21] The 'heroic' leadership concept that has been a part of the leadership literature from the earliest times has been challenged as more women move into the leadership space. The emerging literature documenting the experience of recent women world leaders provides a broader definition of leadership which does not adhere to the traditional paradigms.[22] Also, who writes the history of women in leadership determines how culture is defined or instances that are rarely recorded. For instance, the leadership role of women in African, Pacific Island or Australian Indigenous culture is yet to be fully explored. Emerging studies of the role of women in these contexts are being addressed.[23]

Sandberg's *Lean In* (2013) influenced a debate about gender stereotypes in leadership and the systematic barriers for most women in accessing leadership.[24] Also, that privilege and access to education maintain a leadership preserve that systematically excludes representation of women of colour and even men of colour. Orr's premise in her response to Sandberg, *Lean Out* (2019), is that most arguments on women in leadership pin the blame on the gender gap on women with prescriptions for success hinging upon women's ability to adopt male leadership norms and values.[25] Women have used strategies to conceal gender by dressing in certain ways, playing along with jokes, not supporting other women or 'women's issues', and minimising or downplaying maternal responsibilities to reduce the impact of their gender or sexuality. Sinclair traces this to women working in environments in which traditional leadership is supported by and reinforces a masculine heterosexual identity where "women's sexuality has been experienced and cast as a problem – the cause of discrimination and harassment, requiring resources and legislation to control".[26]

Research on the difference between male and female leaders is mixed while some argue that current leadership theories are gender blind. More recent findings suggest that female executives tended to record significantly higher on all aspects of transformational leadership, as well as on effectiveness and satisfaction in their leadership approach. Leadership theorists argue that the transformational approach characterised as charisma, inspiration, intellectual stimulation and individual consideration can be identified with women in leadership.[27] Emerging theories on innovation leadership emphasise the role of leaders in creativity and nurturing creative efforts. According to Klenke "women leaders are often consensus builders, conciliators and collaborators; they are transformational leaders who are motivational and flexible in their leadership style who transcend their self-interests for the good of the group or organization".[28]

Women in music face similar challenges and, while the situation has slightly improved in the latter part of the 20th century, there are indications that progress is slow and sometimes retrograde. Some of the challenges facing women in music are addressed in the following chapters through both historical and empirical research. The multifaceted nature of leadership has come into question with the emergence of research into diversity in leadership. The male 'heroic' leadership paradigm is becoming increasingly challenged as we examine leadership in different contexts. Despite the challenges that women have faced in being recognised as significant contributors to music over the centuries, there are many examples of women who have contributed significantly to musical life in history, which have come to light in late 20th-century music research. Gender equity and leadership are intertwined as women have historically had limited access to leadership within traditional institutional paradigms. Whilst there is some progress for women that can be demonstrated by a few examples of women at the top of the musical hierarchy, as in other fields of endeavour women's progress is slow on the leadership ladder.

For the present, Eagly and Carli's labyrinth metaphor is pertinent:

> I used the labyrinth metaphor to underscore the image of women leaders who make some initial inroads in the labyrinth of leadership but then may not find their way out (i.e., advancing to higher levels) without the thread of Ariadne. This thread may consist of a new leadership paradigm, new organizational structures that are more congenial to women's progress as leaders or revitalized industries that offer greater gender equality.[29]

The progress into defining leadership approaches by women is generally based upon gender blind theoretical constructs of leadership. The more recent attribution of transformational leadership to women recognises that women approach leadership differently, but the new leadership paradigm is yet to be identified.

## Musical leadership

Research on women in the arts show that more women than men apply to go into arts training but their numbers at the professional level are lower.[30] As an educator of arts managers the author can confirm that the student cohort is dominated by women; however, this has not always translated to the same proportion of women in leadership roles for Alumni. The examination of boards, CEOs and managers in arts organisations indicates that men dominate, but women feature in small to medium organisations and as support staff.[31] The gender pay gap is just as apparent in the arts which has been attributed to widespread discrimination in the industry.[32]

Music performance, composition and management to this day have been dominated by men. Organisations that confront gender strereotypes 'head on' can change the system. Some argue for quotas for proportional representation to be established, enforced and tracked to change the numbers of women in top leadership. This would require implementation by current leadership which is mainly represented by men.[33]

However, it is argued that many women are unable to maintain performance careers due to the demands of child-rearing and more often than not opted to take on teaching careers which provided more flexibility than a performance career.[34] As in other professions, the institutional structures and systems do not meet the working needs of women and these systems need to change to accommodate women.

## Women in musical history

Women have always participated in music as performers, teachers, composers, professionals in management and business, but due to their restriction to the private sphere and the dominance of men in music institutions up until the early 20th century, they have been limited in their progress into leadership positions. Historically women musicians were educated and could perform on instruments and sing in spaces forbidden to other women. They were able to earn money, live independently and often move freely. The distinction between artist and courtesan was often blurred in European, Indian and Asian courts the songs and dances focused upon the erotic, were usually devised by men. Women were accomplished performers and wrote songs and poetry usually for the entertainment of men. However, women performing in the public sphere were at risk of being considered morally corrupt.

Music played an integral role in the cultures of ancient Greece and Rome and 5th- and 6th-century BCE Athenian vase paintings depict women choruses at festivals. Athenian vase paintings also depict women in scenes displaying the aulos and harp played by hetairai (courtesans), who were often slaves. These social contexts for music-making by women provoked much comment from the Greek philosophers. Both Plato and Aristotle differentiated respectable domestic female musicians from entertainer-musicians. The legendary figure of the poet-singer Sappho of Lesbos was one of the most famous musical poets in Western culture and a famous vase painting from around 460 BCE depicts her holding a barbiton.

Old Testament references describe women singing, playing instruments and dancing. It has been speculated that Miriam's Victory Song with new fragments discovered in the Dead Sea Scrolls may have been a distinctive women's genre. The participation of women in formal Jewish liturgy was prohibited in the early Rabbinic period (c. 300–600 CE) because of its association with sexual enticement and the sexes were separated during worship with prohibitions against female leadership in liturgy. Separate female choirs and separate women's synagogues voices were permitted and occasionally hymn- and psalm-chanting occurred between two such antiphonal choirs.

Based upon dictums by early Christian Church Fathers, women were silenced in secular music to avoid sexual subversion, but there is the testimony of the Spanish pilgrim Egeria of around 400 CE that nuns practiced psalmody in a church which does not rule out more widespread singing by women during this prohibition.[35] The establishment of convents in the 6th century provided musical education for women and a number of musical manuscripts from convents have been preserved up until the 15th century. The first surviving music by a female composer is a set of troparia by Kassia (b. 810), a renowned Byzantine composer of chant.

Hildegard von Bingen (1098–1179) came to the attention of medieval music scholars in the late 20th century. There is division on whether her innovations in her unique musical liturgical chants were due to her lack of musical education or a visionary approach to musical composition. Placed in a monastery at the age of eight she was a German Benedictine nun who was also a poet, musician, mystic, artist, scientist and theologian.[36] She wrote three major theological works; several treatises on natural history, medicine and the nature of the human body; over a hundred letters; several saints' lives; a complete religious drama with music and text; over 70 liturgical compositions called Symphonia armonie celestium revelationum. She recreated her visions from God in her poetry and music and was revolutionary in publishing her works which was not within the church rules of the period. She used musical innovations such as word painting, wide melodic range featuring the upper ranges of the female voice and melisma to highlight the emotional content of the texts.[37] Her texts were based upon women such as the Virgin Mary and St. Ursula and she created chants that addressed the life-giving role of women.[38] Her morality plays were the first of their kind and were characterised by personifications of vice, virtue and charity. She gave leading roles to women in these plays and wrote music that showcased women's voices. Her gender portrayals of women as co-creators were a contrast to the music that was created by men at the time. A church interdict in 1178 banned musical performance in her church just a year before her death which dealt her a great blow. Her contribution to medieval music was not recognised in the history books until the end of the 20th century.[39] It has been discovered that many nuns contributed to convent musical life, but Hildegard von Bingen was able to publish, and her preserved manuscript is now a subject of many studies.

In the medieval secular sphere love songs, songs about pregnancy and critiques of marriage are written from a woman's point of view.[40] There was a comparative growth in power and wealth amongst medieval women particularly in 12th century Occitan with the emergence of women trobairitz composers and performers. The genre of 'women's song' is also found in 15th century French and Italian chansonniers. Women were less likely to have access to training in polyphony which was becoming increasingly important in late medieval life, but their inclusion in musical performances can be witnessed by the fact that there are more women musicians than men in visual and literary references such as Boccaccio's Decameron.

Maddalena Casulana (c. 1544–1583) is credited as the first woman to have published madrigals and a rare example of a published renaissance composer.[41] In her first group of published madrigals (Primo libro de madrigali a quattro voci, Venice, 1568) she wrote the following dedication dedicated to her patron Isabella de' Medici Orsini:

> not only to give witness to my devotion to Your Excellency, but also to show to the world ... the foolish error of men who so greatly believe themselves to be the masters of high intellectual gifts that ... cannot, it seems to them, be equally common among women.[42]

It was rare for a woman to be published in this time, but her sponsor was a member of the powerful Medici family Isabelle de' Medici. Isabella did not have as happy an end as at the age of 34 she was strangled by her husband for impropriety due to her musical aspirations.[43] Casulana continued to publish after Isabella's death using musical references to Isabella's obedience. Brown questions whether she was only one of a few women who composed during this era or was it just because of her connections that she was published. Nonetheless, she was highly regarded in her time and published most of her 67 madrigals making her the first woman known in European musical history whose works were printed.[44]

Hailed as the first woman to compose an opera, Francesca Caccini (1587–1637) was employed by the Medici family. Following her father's footsteps, Francesca provided musical entertainment for the Medici court. She worked in the vibrant theatrical life of the woman's court sponsored by Christine de Lorraine involving an extensive group of aristocratic women and their attendants.[45] There was lively theatrical activity and one surviving work by Caccini for these entertainments was an early stage-musical work La liberation di Ruggiero dall'isola d'Alcina. It included operatic conventions such as recitative, aria, choruses and ritornelli and was based upon Aristo's Orlando furioso, an Italian romance epic from 1532. Composed for the 1625 Carnival and performed within the women's court, the gynocentric subject reflected the power of the women who hosted the production. The knight Ruggerio was put under a love spell of the sorceress Alcina aiming to seduce him. Melissa, another sorceress, disguises herself as a man and liberated Ruggerio from the spell after which Alcina leaves on the back of a dragon which sets fire to the island. The story appealed to the powerful ambitions of the women's court and that Caccini was given the right to compose and publish the work is no coincidence. From 1622 until 1627 she was the highest-paid musician on the staff of Grand Duke Ferdinando II.

Barbara Strozzi (1619–1677) lived a relatively secluded existence within the private and secretive world of the academy of men. It is believed that she was the biological daughter of Giulio Strozzi, a member of the very influential Academy of the Incogniti (Academy of the Unknown) and Isabella Garzoni, one of the Strozzi household servants.[46] Guilio encouraged his adopted daughter's musical career and as a woman amongst men in the academy, she was a part of the courtesan culture in Venice. The iconography in the portrait by Bernado Stozzi of Barbara as a young woman suggests both a musician and a courtesan. There has been some doubt that the painting that shows a woman with her left breast exposed holding a gamba and bow is actually Strozzi, but some indicate that the painting is actually Barbara Strozzi.[47] Strozzi was afforded the best musical education by her father and she studied composition under the leading opera composer of the time Francesco Cavalli.[48] She began performing very early in her life and her exceptional vocal ability resulted in compositions written for her by members of the academy. Her own works showcased her vocal virtuosity and her prolific compositional output resulted in publications through which she gained access to the outside world. Her talent was encouraged by her father to entertain the members of the academy and she served as host and musical entertainer. She had access to a musical and intellectual life that was not available to women of her day and she collaborated with members who espoused feminist views in a time when musical performance was a threat to women's modesty.[49] She associated with leading musicians in Venice and dedicated her music to influential musicians and nobles.[50] Her public activity, which was tightly controlled by her father, was limited to publication through her father's influence in the printing industry. Her output was prolific as one of the most published composers of her time with more than eight volumes of songs and more secular cantatas than any other composer of her era.[51] Apart from her musical activities, she was also an astute businesswoman interacting with Venetian and international businessmen and nobles as a savvy investor.[52] Strozzi rented her own dwellings and made contracts with notaries, landlords and bankers having the capacity to raise loans. She supported her father, mother and her children through her business dealings and performing.[53] She came to the musical public's attention as feminist musicology sought significant examples of women in musical history, but as a woman in her time she was subject to the dictates of the male establishment power structure.

Elisabeth-Claude Jacquet de la Guerre (1665–1729) was born into an artisan musical family of harpsichord builders, performers and teachers. She was a child prodigy on the harpsichord and came under the patronage of the French court under Louis XIV. She published her first book *Pièces de Clavecin* at the age of 20.[54] She married organist and harpsichord teacher Marin la Guerre and had a son maintaining her professional life as a composer and performer for the court off site. She was predeceased by her husband and son and with the continued patronage of Louis XIV maintained her public performing and compositional activity. Her opera *Céphale et Procris* was the first work by a woman performed that the Paris Opera. She published sets of harpsichord works along with biblical cantatas, a ballet and a Te Deum.[55]

Women have performed in classical orchestras dating back as far as the Venetian ospedali, which emerged from the hospices of earlier centuries that cared for the sick, homeless, orphaned and poor children.[56] In the mid-16th century, the ospedali trained female orphans in music, mostly by people within the intuitions that were musically proficient such as nuns or priests, to create all female ensembles called figlie del cori that provided musical support for liturgical contexts. Four women's ospedali became famous musical centres: the Incurabili, Pietà, Derelitti and Mendicanti. The female ensembles performed in raised galleries with grating that hid them from view. By the mid-17th century, the economic potential of these orchestras was realised and the governors hired professional musicians and composers to train the female students in areas of performance, music theory, aural, singing and composition. Between 1585 and 1855, the ospedali employed notable male professional musicians to teach and compose for the figlie del cori including Legrenzi, Vivaldi, Galuppi, Tartini, Vivalidi and Hasse and over 70 prestigious maestri di cappella.[57] They composed a specialised repertory of psalms, motets, liturgical dramas and oratorios, often about female saints and biblical heroines with performances supported by the citizens of Venice. Most of the cori remained as performers and teachers at the ospedali to pass on their knowledge to younger female musicians establishing a strong tradition of women performers in Venice. This model of teaching became the basis of the European Conservatory model.

The women of the ospedali were orphans who became mainly cloistered nuns and it was rare that they performed outside the confines of their restricted lives. Like courtesans they could achieve intellectual and financial independence and they could use their income to support themselves and save for a dowry should they chose to marry. If they married they had to leave the orchestra. However, overall artistic freedom and composition was not encouraged.[58] Noteworthy performers include Anna Maria della Pietà (1696–1782) who led the orchestra at the Pietà, and for whom Vivaldi wrote 28 concertos.[59] Notable performers who have successful careers outside of the ospedali were opera singers Nancy Storace (1765–1817) and Faustina Bordoni (1697–1781). Antonia Bembo (1640–c. 1720), Maddalena Lombardini Sirmen (1745–1818) and Regina Strinasacchi (1764–1839) also sustained professional careers as performers and composers outside of the ospedali.

The era of European enlightenment which is renowned for composers Haydn, Mozart and Beethoven featured many women sponsors and patrons who were also muses for the well-known composers. Artists undertaking freelance relied upon wealthy sponsors many of which were still nobility and aristocrats. Women featured amongst these and without their support it could be speculated that the careers of these composers would have struggled. Royal women were particularly well educated in the arts and music. Empress Maria Theresa (1717–1780) was highly influential in establishing Vienna central in European musical life. She commissioned numerous now famous composers such as Johann Adolph Hasse (1699–1783), Antonio Salieri (1750–1825) and Christoph Willibald Glück (1714–1787) and librettist Pietro Metastasio (1698–1782) who were some of the most significant contributors to the opera seria repertoire.[60] Her remodelling of the Schönbrunn, Hapsburg Summer Palace had a significant impact on the city's cultural life, by adding performing spaces. She also authorised the establishment of the Burgtheatre in 1841 next to her Hofburg palace which saw premièrs of works by Mozart and Beethoven.[61] She sponsored performances by numerous musicians and she directly supported women including Nannerl Mozart (1751–1829) who played for her at the age of 11 at Schönbrun.[62] Other notable women that she sponsored were composer Marianna Martinez (1744–1812) and performer and composer Maria Theresa von Paradis (1759–1824).

Marianna Martinez was one of Austria's most prolific composers who is said to have written over 200 works of which only 70 survive.[63] Following a generous inheritance from the librettist and poet Metastasio she became a sponsor with her salon becoming a leading gathering space for Viennese musicians. Composers such as Mozart and Haydn were frequent visitors. She also established a highly regarded professional singing school.

Singer and pianist Maria Theresa von Paradis was a leading female performer in Vienna and took to the new performance arena of public concerts throughout Vienna and Europe just as they were becoming established. She was sponsored by the Empress Maria Theresa, and despite losing her eyesight at the age of three she was an exceptional performer. For a female performer her tours were exceptional and her three-year multinational tour which encompassed Salzburg, Bonn, Mannheim. Geneva, Paris, Brussels, Amsterdam, Berlin, London and Prague from 1783 to 1785 attracted a huge following. She also performed at the residence of Prince of Wales and King George III at St. James Palace in London.[64] As a female performer in the male-dominated concert scene, she was an inspiration for women performers. She returned to Vienna to focus upon composition, but much of her output is lost potentially due to lack of publishing opportunities. She also was a leader in music education for girls establishing her own music school as well as the founding first school for the blind in Paris with French educator Valentin Haüy (1745–1822), where Louis Braille was a pupil and then teacher.[65]

Empress Maria Theresa's female descendants also had a significant influence on arts music and her granddaughter Marie Antoinette (1755–1793) carried her love of music to France where she married Louis XVI. Her arrival in France is associated with the building of a large opera hall at Versailles in 1770. She sponsored Glück in Paris who she discovered at her mother's court in Vienna. The Empress Maria Theresa's granddaughter and namesake was also a musician singer and collector of music. She was also one of the most important patrons of Haydn and Mozart. She is credited as influencing the creation of Beethoven's Fidelio.[66] Other notable female musicians emerging from Hapsburg include singer Maria Antonia Walpurgis (1724–1780), Electress of Saxony, and singer, opera composer and patron Maria Barbara de Braganza (1711–1758), who became Queen of Spain.[67]

The Habsburg court was not the only influence on the arts scene in Vienna and noblewomen played an important role in shaping the musical scene through their patronage, performances and commissions. Therese van Trattner was one of Mozart's students who supported Mozart's career through the commissioning and performing of his works and his Piano Sonata No. 14, K547 was dedicated to her. Mozart lived in Trattner's apartment complex where he held many of his financially successful subscription concerts.

Similarly, Regina Srinasacchi (c. 1761–1839) was a renowned Italian virtuoso violinist who inspired Mozart's Violin Sonata in B flat Major, K454. He wrote the piano concertos KV.499 and KV.543 for his student Barbara Ployer which she performed at her own residence and later in her country residence in Döbling where she also performed a work for two keyboards.[68] Similarly, the involvement of Countess Maria Thun-Hohenstein, Baroness Martha Elisabeth Waldstätten and Josepha Auernhammer in his teaching, composing and performing activities resulted in his female patrons contributing to nearly 80% of his income in 1784.[69]

The invention of the fortepiano around 1,700 revolutionised classical keyboard repertoire with its capacity for expression at different dynamic levels, loud and soft as is its namesake, because of its hammer action rather than the plucking action of its predecessor as well as the development of loud and soft pedals to dampen the strings. One of the most important individuals in leading the innovations in the development of this instrument was Nannette Streicher (nee. Stein, 1769–1833). The daughter of a German instrument maker Johann Stein (1728–1792), she was an apprentice in the factory since the age of seven. Following his death in 1792, Nanette took over the business at the age of 23. She moved the business to Vienna two years later to take advantage of the musical business opportunities. She married pianist and piano technician Johann Andreas Streicher (1761–1833) and the Streicher factory, which she managed, became one of the leading piano companies in Vienna when there were over 100 piano manufacturers. Her contribution to the development of the instrument and her work with Ludwig van Beethoven on advancing its possibilities is possibly her most influential achievement. Beethoven is known to have praised the Streicher instruments and the documented exchange of more than 60 letters between Beethoven and Streicher on instrumental specifications which Nanette hand built for customers. In 1814 she built a six-octave forte piano and in 1816 she built six and a half-octave piano exclusively for Beethoven.[70]

By 1820 the instrument grew to seven octaves and is credited for paving the way for the new romantic style of playing experiments being led by Beethoven. Apart from her talent as a piano builder Nannette was also a prodigious pianist and performed in her father's shop since the age of five. She performed throughout her life and the Streicher's factory featured one of the most eminent performance rooms in Vienna that could house over 300 people. It was a gathering place for leading performers such as Beethoven, Hummel, Nannette, her husband and their students.[71] The Streicher tradition continued following Nanette and her husband's death and her son Johann Baptist Streicher (1796–1871) took on the business. He maintained the performance space to host composers such as Brahms who was gifted the famous 1868 Streicher piano, serial number 1613. The business was sold in 1896 leaving a significant mark on the musical world having produced around 8,600 pianos.

Women from well-educated families in the 17th and 18th centuries received musical education at quite high levels to cultivate their talents in preparation for their role in the home rather than for a public career. Talented musicians and composers from musical families such as child prodigy Fanny Mendelsohn (1805–1847) are known to have withdrawn to the private domestic sphere following marriage as it would have compromised their social position to have continued to perform in public. However, Fanny Mendelssohn remained musically active and it is believed that her brother Felix Mendelssohn (1809–1847) who had a successful professional musical career was strongly influenced by his sister's musical ideas and published her work under his name as well as inspiring his writing of programmatic works.[72] She also was influential in the salon scene in Berlin and is now credited for helping ignite the 'Bach revival' often attributed to her brother.[73] She did pursue her compositional career despite the discouragement of her father and composed over 400 works which she sought to publish before she died prematurely of a stroke at the age of 41. Her mother and father encouraged her to publish and promote her work, but came into opposition with Felix who wrote to his mother discouraging the promotion of Fanny's compositions.[74] Much of her work remains unpublished in the family archives in Berlin.

Clara Wieck Schumann (1819–1896) sustained a virtuoso piano performance career as well as maintaining a prolific compositional output. A child prodigy under her father's strict guidance and control she became a renowned performer fuelling her father's fame and wealth as a piano teacher. Her marriage to fellow composer Robert Schumann (1810–1856) was, unsurprisingly, vehemently opposed by her father as he wished to maintain control over her concertising career and income. The couple eloped and Clara continued her concertising career throughout her ten pregnancies, eight live births, the death of a young child and the suicide attempt and institutionalisation of her husband. With the support of servants and students, she performed 139 public concerts during her 14-year marriage including a highly acclaimed concert tour of Russia. Her struggle with the conflicts of domestic life and professional career is evident in her letters in recognition of the emotional guilt of working mothers. Robert's early death left her supporting seven living children as a 35-year-old widow. She continued to perform throughout Europe and in her 60-year concert career undertook 38 extensive foreign tours alongside her innumerable performances in Germany.[75]

Her profile as a composer did not come to the attention of musicologists until the advent of feminist musicology in the late part of the 20th century. Her collaboration with her husband along with her profound knowledge of chamber music traditions demonstrated an ability to compose a range of works from art song to her celebrated piano concerto. Clara Schumann broke the tradition of women sacrificing their musical careers to family life to pursue a lucrative and successful performance career on the European stage. This is an exceptional departure from the expectation of middle- and upper-class women musicians of the day paving the way for the acceptance of women on the concert stage as professional artists. She became lauded for her performances and led a highly successful musical life which provided an aspirational model for female musicians despite the hardship and struggles she had endured in her early life and the mental illness of her husband Robert Schumann. Her legacy is not only in her compositions, but also her numerous students who sought out her teachings.

## Conclusion

While women have always been active as musicians, their roles as leaders have been overlooked. The advances for women in leadership in all professions are slow, but have been strengthened by the various feminist movements emerging in the late 19th century. Despite several waves of feminist activism in the 20th century, women have been unable to reach gender parity in pay and leadership. The burden of unpaid domestic labour increases this gap and institutional structures have not been designed to accommodate women's career progress. The COVID-19 pandemic highlighted the impact of increased care responsibilities which mainly fell to women affecting their ability to progress in their careers. However, regardless of the slow progress, women have emerged in the leadership space and recent research is investigating how this has impacted productivity and performance in the workplace. Leadership theorists in the late 20th century have found that as more women move into leadership roles traditional notions of leadership have been challenged. The documenting of women's leadership styles as more women enter leadership positions has provided evidence of differences in approach to leadership. As diversity in leadership increases, the dominant leadership paradigms are being challenged. The survey of women's musical contribution throughout musical history in this chapter has provided significant examples of women who have taken leading roles in a range of musical activities from composition through to performance and instrument development. Some have only recently come to the attention of scholars as feminist musicology advanced in the late 20th century and research is still yet to reveal the full extent and role of women in musical leadership across centuries and cultures.

## Notes

1 A series of research publications on transformational leadership led by Bass include the following:

Bass, B. (1954). Situational and personality factors in leadership among sorority women. *American Psychological Association*;

Bass, B. & Avolio, B. (1994). Shatter the glass ceiling: Women may make better managers. *Human Resource Management*, 33, 549–560; ___. (1994). *Improving Organizational Effectiveness Through Transformational Leadership*. Sage.

Avolio, B. & Bass, B. (2002). Developing potential across a full range of leadership: Cases on transactional and transformational leadership. Lawrence Erlbaum Associates.

Bass, B. & Stogdill, R. (1990). *Bass & Stogdill's Handbook of Leadership: Theory, Research, and Managerial Applications*. Free Press.

2 Sheridan, A., Pringle, J. & Strachan, G. (2009). Doing scholarship differently: Doing scholarship that matters: An interview with Amanda Sinclair. *Journal of Management and Organization*, 15, 549–554.

3 Sinclair, A. (1994). *Trials at the Top: Chief Executives Talk About Men, Women and the Australian Executive Culture*. University of Melbourne; ___. (1998). *Doing Leadership Differently: Gender, Power, and Sexuality in a Changing Business Culture*. Melbourne University Press; ___. (2005). Body and management pedagogy. *Gender, Work & Organization*, 12, 89–104; ___. (2005). *Doing Leadership Differently: Gender, Power and Sexuality in a Changing Business Culture*. Melbourne University Press; ___. (2007). Leadership for the disillusioned. *Melbourne Review: A Journal of Business and Public Policy*, 3, 65–71; ___. (2009). Seducing leadership: Stories of leadership development. *Gender, Work & Organization*, 16, 266–284.

4 Clinton, H. (2017). *What Happened*. Simon & Schuster; Kelly, G. (2017). *Live, Lead, Learn: My Stories of Life and Leadership*. Penguin Group; Gillard, J. & Okonjo-Iweala, N. (2020). *Women and Leadership: Real Lives Real Lessons*. Penguin Random House; Nixon, C. & Sinclair, A. (2017). *Women Leading*. Melbourne University Publishing.

5 Beauvoir, S. (1971). *The Second Sex*. Alfred A. Knopf.

6 Friedan, B. (2010). *The Feminine Mystique*. W.W. Norton.

7 Greer, G. (1970). *The Female Eunuch*. MacGibbon & Kee.

8 World Economic Forum. (2022). Global Gender Gap report.

9 Sevilla, A. & Smith, S. (2020). Baby steps: The gender division of childcare during the COVID-19 pandemic. *Oxford Review of Economic Policy*, 36(Supplement_1), S169–S186.

10 Craig, L. & Churchill, B. (2020). Dual-earner parent couples' work and care during COVID-19. *Gender, Work & Organization*, 28(1), 66–79.

11 Del Boca, D., Oggero, N., Profeta, P. & Rossi, M. (2020). Women's work, housework and childcare, before and during COVID-19. *Review of Economics of the Household*, 18, 1001–1017; Power, K. (2020). The COVID-19 pandemic has increased the care burden of women and families. *Sustainability: Science, Practice and Policy*, 16(1), 67–73.

12 Catalyst. (2020). The Detrimental Impact of COVID-19 on Gender and Racial Equality. www.catalyst.org/research/covid-effect-gender-racial-equality

13 Adler, N. & Osland, J. (2016). Women leading globally: What we know, thought we knew, and need to know about leadership in the 21st century. *Advances in Global Leadership*, 9, 15–56.

14 Flabbi, L., Macis, M., Moro, A. & Schivardi, F. (2019). Do female executives make a difference? The impact of female leadership on gender gaps and firm performance. *The Economic Journal*, 129, 390–423.

15 Bertrand, M., Black, S., Jensen, S. & Lleras-Muney, A. (2019). Breaking the glass ceiling? The effect of board quotas on female labour market outcomes in Norway. *The Review of Economic Studies*, 86, 191–239.

16 Tyrefors, B. & Jansson, J. (2017). Gender quotas in the board room and firm performance: Evidence from a credible threat in Sweden. IFN Working Paper. No. 1165.

17 Ferrari, G., Ferraro, V., Profeta, P. & Pronzato, C. (2022). Do board gender quotas matter? Selection, performance, and stock market effects. *Management Science*, 68(8), 5618–5643.

18 Comi, S., Grasseni, M., Origo, F. & Pagani, L. (2020). Where women make a difference: Gender quotas and firm's performance in three European countries. *ILR Review*, 73(3), 768–793.

19 Stoneman, T. (2017). International economic law, gender equality, and paternity leave: Can the WTO be utilized to balance the division of care labour worldwide. *Emory International Law Review*, 32, 51.

20 Pettigrew, R. & Duncan, K. (2021). Fathers use of parental leave in a Canadian law enforcement organization. *Journal of Family Issues*, 42(10), 2211–2241; Saarikallio-Torp, M. & Miettinen, A. (2021). Family leaves for fathers: Non-users as a test for parental leave reforms. *Journal of European Social Policy*, 31(2), 161–174; Tharp, D. & Parks-Stamm, E. (2021). Gender differences in the intended use of parental leave: Implications for human capital development. *Journal of Family and Economic Issues*, 42(1), 47–60.

21 Sinclair. (2005). Ibid.

22 Clinton. (2017). Ibid.; Gillard & Okonjo-Iweala. (2020). Ibid.; Nixon & Sinclair. (2017). Ibid.

23 Ryan, T. (2016) Seen but unseen: Missing visible Indigenous women and what it means for leadership in Indigenous Australia. *Platform: Journal of Media and Communication*, 7, ANZCA Special Issue, 26–34; Ryan, T. (2018). *Deadly Women: An Analysis of Indigenous Women's Leadership in Australia*. University of Canberra.

24 Sandberg, S. (2013). *Lean In: Women, Work, and the Will to Lead*. Random House.

25 Orr, M. (2019). *Lean Out: The Truth about Women, Power, and the Workplace*. HarperCollins.

26 Sinclair. (2005). Ibid., 173.

27 Bass & Riggio. (2006). Ibid.; Bass & Avolio. (1994). Ibid.

28 Klenke, K. (2011). *Women in Leadership: Contextual Dynamics and Boundaries*. Emerald Group Publishing, 7.

29 Eagly, A. & Carli, L. (2007). Women and the labyrinth of leadership. *Harvard Business Review*, 85, 62.

30 Caust, J. (2018). *Arts Leadership in Contemporary Contexts*. Routledge.

31 Ibid.

32 Throsby, D. & Shin, S. (2020, 11 November). Why is the gender pay gap in the arts so large? Widespread discrimination is the most likely cause. *The Conversation*. See also Throsby, D. & Petetskaya, K. (2017). *Making Art Work: An Economic Study of Professional Artists in Australia*. Australia Council for the Arts.

33 Arnold, K.A. & Loughlan, C. (2018). Continuing the conversation: Questioning the who what, and where of leaning in. *Academy of Management Perspectives*, 33(1), 94–109.

34 Bennett, D. (2008). A gendered study of the working patterns of classical musicians: Implications for practice. *International Journal of Music Education*, 26, 89–100.

35 Tick, J., Ericson, M. & Koskoff, E. (2001). *Women in Music*. Grove Music Online.

36 Reed-Jones, C. (2004). *Hildegard of Bingen: Women of Vision*. Paper Crane Press, 6.

37 Dunbar, J. (2021). *Women, Music, Culture: An Introduction*, 3rd ed. Routledge, 30.

38 Ibid., 28.

39 Ibid., 25.

40 Bogin, M. (1980). *The Women Troubadours*. W.W. Norton.

41 Pescerelli, B. (1979). I madrigali di Maddalena Casulana. *LS Olschki*.

42 Bridges, T. (2001). *Casulana [Mezari], Maddalena*. Grove Music Online.

43 Kisby, F. (2001). Urban history, musicology and cities and towns in renaissance Europe. In *Music and Musicians in Renaissance Cities and Town*. Ed. Kisby, F. Cambridge University Press, 1–13.

44 Brown, H.M. (1986). Women singers and women's songs in fifteenth-century Italy. In *Women Making Music: The Western Art Tradition, 1150–1950*. Ed. Bowers. J. & Tick. J. University of Illinois Press, 62–89.

45 Cusick, S. (2004). Francesca Caccini. In *New Historical Anthology of Music by Women*. Ed. Briscoe, J. Indiana University Press, 41.

46 Rosand, E. (1978). Barbara Strozzi, 'virtuosissima cantatrice': The composer's voice. *Journal of the American Musicological Society*, 31(2), 241–281.

47 Ibid.

48 Beer, A. (2016). *Sounds and Sweet Airs: The Forgotten Women of Classical Music*. Oneworld Publications, 81.

49 Glixon, B. (1999). More on the life and death of Barbara Strozzi. *The Musical Quarterly*, 83, 134–141.

50 Kendrick, R. (2002). Intent and intertextuality in Barbara Strozzi's sacred music. Recercare. *Rivista per lo Studio e la Practica della Musica Antica*, 14, 65–98.

51 Glixon. Ibid. 135.
52 Rosand. Ibid.
53 Rosand, E. & Glixon, B.L. (2001). *Strozzi, Barbara*. Grove Music Online.
54 Dunbar. Ibid. 108.
55 Ibid.
56 Baldauf-Berdes, J.L. (1996). *Women's Musicians of Venice: Musical Foundations, 1525–1855*. Clarendon Press, 47.
57 Arnold, D. (1988). Music at the ospedali. *Journal of the Royal Musical Association*, 113(2), 159.
58 Baldauf-Berdes. Ibid.
59 Rosand, E. (2001). Vivaldi's stage. *Journal of Musicology*, 18(1), 8–30.
60 Grout, D.J. & Palisca, C. (2009). *A History of Western Music*, 8th ed. W.W. Norton, 498.
61 Dunbar. Ibid. 116.
62 Ibid.
63 Pendle, K. (2004). Mariana von Martines. In *New Historical Anthology of Music by Women*. Ed. Briscoe, J.R. Indiana University Press, 113.
64 Matushita, H. (2004). Maria Theresa von Paradis. In *New Historical Anthology of Music by Women*. Ed. Briscoe, J.R. Indiana University Press, 121.
65 Dunbar. Ibid. 124.
66 Rice, J. (2003). *Empress Marie Therese and Music at the Viennese Court, 1792–1807*. Cambridge University Press.
67 Dunbar. Ibid. 117.
68 Einstein, A. (1962). *Mozart, His Character, His Work*. Oxford, 303.
69 Solomon, M. (1995). *Mozart: A Life*, reprint ed. Harper Collins, 522.
70 Dunbar. Ibid. 127.
71 Dunbar. Ibid.
72 Kimber, M.W. (2004). Felix and Fanny: Gender, biography and history. In *The Cambridge Companion to Mendelssohn*. Ed. Mercer-Taylor, P. Cambridge University Press, 44.
73 Dunbar. Ibid. 146.
74 Neuls-Bates, C. (Ed.) (1996). *Women in Music: An Anthology of Source Readings from the Middle Ages to the Present*, revised ed. Northeastern University Press, 49.
75 See Reich, N. (2001). *Clara Schumann: The Artist and the Woman*. Cornell University Press.

# 2

# WOMEN AND MUSICAL COMPOSITION

## Introduction

Studies of women composers of classical music emerged with the second and third wave of feminism driven by the desire to address the imbalance of women's representation in the musical literature and on the concert stage. The influential work of leading women musicologists who spearheaded scholarship in the area of women in music resulted in an apparent increase in the performance and commissioning of music by women. It has been argued that the victories for women in the concert hall, broadcasting and recording won by the resurgence of research into women's composition have been diluted with a backlash against feminist musicology in the early part of the 21st century along with a consequent drop in women's representation in the concert hall. The following provides a brief survey of some of the leading feminist musicological theorists and their contributions to the discourse on women in music. This is followed by an analysis of some data on gender parity in the concert hall. Some of the leading women composers in the 20th century are discussed in this chapter along with some contemporary case studies of women who are taking the lead in musical composition.

## Feminist musicology

Since the period that has been termed the second wave of feminism or the reawakening of feminism, there was a growth in feminist scholarship. This was the period following World War II when the UN affirmed

DOI: 10.4324/9781003183631-3

the equal rights of men and women in its 1945 charter followed by the establishment of the UN Commission on the Status of Women. Shortly after French philosopher Simone de Beauvoir's *The Second Sex* (1949)[1] was translated and widely read, the rate of growth of publications relating to the feminist movement increased steadily. There was a musical response to this growth in feminist literature with a proliferation of historical studies on women composers during the latter part of the 20th century which includes dictionaries, discographies, editions, catalogues, collected essays, as well as biographies on individual composers. This endeavour was often undertaken with the aim of redressing the imbalance of women's representation in music history. The later manifestation of this movement is feminist musicological scholarship that incorporates intellectual ideas derived from interdisciplinary studies in feminism.

In the 1970s the feminist revival resulted in revisionist history powered by women who were receiving professional academic training in musicology. Elizabeth Wood's 1980 survey is a useful measure of the number of pre-1980s studies of women in music, as well as being a springboard for further research in this area. She notes that among the various sources available in the past there has been a lack of cross reference to interdisciplinary women's studies.[2] It is mainly through the studies of women in music in non-Western cultures that such interdisciplinary discourses are located, since ethnomusicology takes its lead from anthropology that itself derives ideas from a range of social sciences. Wood finds that cross-disciplinary discourses also enter into American studies and 19th-century research into music. In these areas she refers to the emergence of a new scholarship that "identifies patterns of discrimination in the past and analyses how this has curtailed women's career patterns".[3] These approaches take their methodology from early feminist activists who advocated equal opportunities for women. The obstacles for women in general are applicable to women in music and the recognition of women's creative contribution to music has been thwarted by entrenched social systems. In the compositional sphere, women suffered considerable discrimination due to historical attitudes surrounding class propriety and the roles of women in public. Academic and political distinctions between 'public' and 'private' has relegated women and their creative efforts to the private less recognised sphere. Wood argues for new directions in musical scholarship that take on the challenge of political activism as well as for analysis that is linked to developments in feminist scholarship. For its time, this survey provides a concise overview of the research to date on women in music and challenges musicology to review its approach in the discussion of women in music calling for "... theoretical analyses that link the work of feminists in music to what is emerging elsewhere in the new feminist scholarship".[4]

By 1990, feminist musicologists found plenty of examples of women performers throughout musical history with ample evidence of the contribution of women to all areas of music-making throughout the centuries. Valuable collections of source readings emerged on women musicians and composers that provide concise surveys of women's historical role in music composition and performance.[5] This distinction of sex and gender is central to the academic feminist debate that distinguishes between the biological 'male and female' and social 'masculine and feminine'. The feminist critique is therefore based upon the social role and options for women and, where this is applied to creativity, it refers to the creative response to these options. Also, diverse feminist approaches that include liberal, radical, lesbian, poststructural, psychoanalytic and Marxist are neither mutually exclusive nor necessarily in agreement with each other.[6] However, they are more significant for their contribution to the rewriting and re-reading of women's history by including the other half of the relevant data into the dominant discourses. The influence of poststructural and deconstructionist theory upon academic feminism allows for multiple approaches to the critical reading of culture and inverts our notions of cultural absolutes in musical analysis. Other ideas that are enlivening the feminist debate are those of sex, gender, sexuality, race, ethnicity and social class.

While earlier work on women in music focused mainly upon the historiography of women's contribution to musical composition through the documentation of life and works, towards the end of the 20th century there was an increase in feminist criticism in musicology alongside the proliferation of feminist theories in cultural criticism. The outcome is not only the continued documentation of women's musical activities with feminist theories in mind, but also the application of feminist analysis to the established musical canon. Feminist musicologists addressed feminist aesthetics, women's representation in music, undertook the analysis of musical form as gendered discourse and examined the role of women in music in relation to power and social structure.

Rieger was one of the earliest to discuss the notion of feminine aesthetics in music and attributes the systematic exclusion of women from composition in history to the patriarchal structure of the institutions that have supported high art over the centuries: the churches, academies and courts.[7] Rieger deconstructs the masculine worldview of German idealism and deduces that it impinges upon notions of genius and creation resulting in the exclusion of women. Rieger contends that the subversion of women can be identified in historical discussions of Sonata Form where its dual themes are described in gendered terms. This is exemplified by citing Hugo Reiman's definition in 'Form', from the 1956 Music Dictionary Music in

Geschichte und Gegenwart, which states: "Two basic human principles are expressed in each of these two main themes; the thrusting, active masculine principle (first theme) and the passive, feminine principle (second theme)".[8] Rieger argues that Reiman's binary analysis of Sonata Form, wherein the 'art of a woman' which is overpowered in the development section of the sonata, is given resonance and life by 'the art of man' in the recapitulation when he takes up her voice, or her theme. Rieger extends this analogy to social attitudes of the time about the natural passivity and subordination of women. Drawing upon established musicological texts to provide examples of the masculine association with forceful, loud and strong music and the feminine association with lyrical, delicate and soft music, she considers a reflection of the beliefs of the time regarding the natural passivity and weakness of women, while the secondary status of women as both performers and composers is attributed to ideological and institutional barriers. While women have accessed training in many areas of music-making such as singing, piano playing and other instrumental tuition, the most elusive area of training for women has been theory and composition.

Rieger takes a more empirical approach in attempting to define a feminine aesthetic based upon sociological arguments indicating that gender is one of the most important determinants of human behaviour.[9] She argues that the existence of feminine aesthetics does result from sex role differences. This is supported by pedagogical studies which show that the musical preferences of girls and boys are different, as is their choice of instruments. Rieger maintains that theoretical constructions are difficult to ignore and, rather than redefining past traditions, women should build upon them and reconstruct them for the present. For example, Rieger's first point is: "Many women have a special ability to create a maximum amount out of a minimum amount of material, a sort of 'restricted aesthetics'".[10] Rieger is referring more to the types of forms women use than to the musical ideas within highlighting the historically limited access women had to large-scale forms. The argument is that they have made the most of what has been available to them and while they have had restricted access to say the symphony or the opera, they have certainly been prolific in other areas. Unfortunately, any attempt to find particular characteristics in the music of half of the world's population does fall into the trap of essentialism as the above statement demonstrates. Historically, women have had restricted access to large-scale musical composition. It is also true that women have been socially restricted.

This contribution to the broader field of feminist aesthetics in musicology led the way for the feminist musicology that emerged in the 1990s, with cross reference to postmodern discourses. At the forefront is the work of Susan McClary, Renée Cox, Ruth Solie, Marcia Citron and Jill Halstead.

McClary argued that female subversion is symbolically implied in classical music and became the basis for descriptions of Sonata Form as referred to previously by Rieger.[11] McClary engages with discourses on academic feminism including marginalisation, professionalism, gender encoding, aesthetics, feminine embodiment in musical texts and representation of women in music. She argues that Western history does not offer a separate women's culture, complete with styles or performing institutions of its own, denying a position for a female composer to bargain or negotiate.[12] McClary's re-examination of some 'masterworks' from a feminist perspective using sexual analogies resulted in criticism from the musicological establishment. The response at the time ranged from applause to outrage and condemnation along with a significant backlash in musicology against feminist approaches.[13]

Feminist aesthetics emerging from the writings of French feminists Julia Kristeva, Luce Irigaray and Hélène Cixoux entered the musicological discourse in the writings of Renée Cox, Catherine Clement and Susan McClary. Cox champions the idea of feminist aesthetics in music and aligns her with the exponents of l'écriture feminine in literature.[14] Alongside Eva Rieger's call for conditions enhancing women's independent musical development and McClary's seeking a woman's voice in music, Cox argues that dramatic music, song and programmatic music are ripe for gender analysis, but that it may be more difficult with abstract music. Critics of feminist aesthetics in music argue against essentialism and the difficulty of prescribing feminine characteristics to abstract musical forms.

Citron deconstructs the notions of musical genius responsible for systematically excluding women from the musical canon.[15] She ascribes the problem partly to women's lack of access to learning and the achievement of professional status in music in the same way as occurs in other professions and the arts. With a focus upon the obstacles to professionalism for women in music, and drawing upon feminist discourse, Citron examines socialisation, training, mentoring and reception of women's music concluding that the same social forces that shape canon formation also construct societal expectations for women and have limited their participation in the process. Feminist arguments on the obstacles to professionalism that apply to music include women's socialisation, child-rearing, domestic roles and cultural perspectives. She returns to the significance of public/private dichotomy in notions of professionalism of women's experience. Given that home-life forms a large part of women's identity due to their domestic responsibilities they become removed from the public arena demanded by a typical career path. However, rather than take the burden from women's domestic responsibilities, Citron suggests a paradigm shift in societal attitudes, namely, to accept women will take on domestic responsibilities and can compose good music in the meantime. Unfortunately, this assumes that time is a plentiful commodity in women's lives. Citron also highlights the significance of reception in the recognition and survival of women's composition and censures the discipline of musicology for disregarding women musicians and composers. The wider issue of societal construct and aesthetic values are central to the reception of women's music and Citron argues for the development of feminine aesthetic values on the basis that women assume creativity from different social positions and are therefore capable of offering different aesthetic solutions. Thus, what is really required is not a process for the recognition of their value within the current aesthetic system, but rather the development of an alternative system that recognises feminine aesthetic values. Citron engages in the discussion of feminine aesthetics but, like McClary and other feminist aestheticians, warns against any essentialism which diminishes the importance of social context and individual difference. Whilst the problems of essentialism are taken into account, sociological research indicates that cultural factors do lead to some form of gendered style. Citron's arguments are systematically based upon ideas drawn directly from academic feminism and the application of these ideas to musical thinking is timely. She addressed many of the concerns relating to barriers for women entering into the musical canon and questioned the absolutes of musical greatness.

Citron finds one thing remains unchanged, despite awarding a number of significant rights to women, women still provide the mainstay of domestic and childcare work. This constant in women's lives, particularly those who choose to have families, is the main contributing factor to inequality in status and opportunities. The common themes emerging from the study are that the women composers come from middle-class families, marriage in all cases led to reduce compositional output and in some cases ceasing to compose altogether. The recurring issue reinforced in her study of women composers is the unequal distribution of domestic responsibilities and 'invisible' work wedged around paid employment. Whilst it has been traditionally accepted that women support men in their creative endeavours, or any other ambitions for that matter, men tend to face emasculation and denigration when they try to assist their wives by taking on domestic responsibilities. Gendered social roles imply that women who become wives and mothers have a prime function as housewives and can only be part-time composers relegated to composing in the kitchen.

Poststructuralist writing became the philosophical point of departure for 'new' musicology represented in *Musicology and Difference* (1995), a diverse collection of essays informed by Derrida's *Writing and Difference* (1978).[16] The essays address music within discourses of 'the Other' that have emerged with reference to gender, sexuality, race, social class and any combination of these factors which distinguish expressions of difference. Postmodern feminist ideology is closely related to poststructuralist critiques of dominant, totalising structures and theories of difference. This notion of women as 'the Other' preoccupied Simone de Beauvoir in *The Second Sex* and has become central to feminist discourses on difference and marginalisation.[17]

Halstead adopts a sociological approach in her discussion of women composers in England.[18] Arriving at similar conclusions to Citron, namely that the obstacles for women composers are a societal condition and opportunities for women composers will only increase if societal attitudes change. Halstead adds another dimension to the discourse by documenting research into scientific studies on women and musical creativity in the areas of psychology and neuropsychology. During her discussion on music and aptitude she asserts that scientific research in the past has set out to prove why women are less creative and intelligent than men. One of the oldest arguments for lack of female intelligence has been based on brain size. However, Halstead cites research that proves that previous methods for measuring brain size are not entirely accurate and such data is generally used to support theories of sex difference which disadvantage females. In drawing a distinction between biology and psychology, based upon the theories of Freud and Chodorow, Halstead finds no conclusive evidence on whether musical creation is in any way affected by the gender of the creator.

Halstead also examines whether sex differences in personality affect women as composers and the theories on personality traits outlining commonly perceived male/female personality characteristics. The commonly identified masculine traits are aggressive, unemotional, brave, decisive, independent, strong, assertive, analytical, dominant and initiative, whereas the feminine traits are identified as passive, sympathetic, nurturing, friendly, yielding, shy, childlike, nurturing, submissive and sensitive. However, the data cited proves that masculinisation, as defined by these characteristics, occurred in the personalities of both males and females as a direct result of higher education. Also, the data proves that occupational interest has an effect on sex typing. While musicians generally proved to exhibit feminine personality traits one could conclude that women are best suited by nature to excel in music. Further studies demonstrate that composers required masculine-identified behavioural characteristics such as self-belief, confidence, conviction, self-reliance and conceit. For women who enter music, by the time they reached the stage of becoming professional, there is an increased need to exert more masculine behaviour in order to succeed, but at this same stage females are limited in their choice of female role models capable of reinforcing the gender-appropriateness of professional musicianship.

Like Citron, Halstead examines why women have not been prolific in the professional sphere of music despite traditionally having access to music education. Unlike other professions, which have denied women training, music has been one of the few accessible areas of tuition for middle-class women. She traces the historical position of women in relation to education and evidence that the biological argument has been used as justification for the unsuitability of women for education. Historically, the employment of middle- and upper-class women was considered socially unacceptable, so an education for women was basically in artistic skills and hobbies to be carried out in their spare time. Vocal and instrumental proficiency has been a significant part of women's education for centuries, but not theoretical and compositional studies.

Halstead's analysis of statistics on women in music employment reveals that there continues to be a gulf between women in low-paid musical work and men in high-paid musical jobs. Women are predominantly involved in early music education with only a small number taking on full-time professional employment in music. Their access to high-paid jobs in music has been limited and the apex of the musical hierarchy remains male-dominated. The analysis of examination trends in Britain over 30 years concludes that women have been predominant at a secondary level throughout the period and only began to dominate at the tertiary level in the 1980s, indicating that discrimination barriers in education may be waning. However, Halstead's research in the 1990s still shows little change in the top ranks of the music profession, indicating that increased opportunities in education have not led to corresponding success in achieving higher-paid, higher-status employment in the music arena.

The influence of political bias and discriminatory motivations surrounding musical composition creates serious obstacles for women and like Citron, Halstead emphasises the importance of the reception in the acceptance of women's music. She notes that the rise of feminism in music has not really resulted in major advances since it causes discomfort to those committed to the musical establishment and its attitudes. Also, the fact that most of the discourses about women in music are by women has enabled the establishment to dismiss them on the grounds that they are the work of a minority self-interest group. Women composers have found benefits from joining together in leagues and actively promoting the work of the group including the Society of Women Musicians founded in Britain by Marion M. Scott in 1911, which was only disbanded in 1972. Nicola Le Fanu set up the Women in Music Organisation in 1987. In America, the International League of Women Composers was formed in 1975. Many women composers feel uncomfortable about such associations because they may risk relegation to a culturally inferior group and reinforce prejudice about their work. The study group and examples from other women composers' statements provided by Halstead all demonstrate that women feel more comfortable if they can view themselves as token men and do not wish to be burdened with the negative implications by being labelled a 'women composer'.[19]

Halstead argues that a compositional genre can be a powerful indicator of that place of composers in musical life and access to institutions that can bring their music to public attention. The idea of music as cultural capital and its place in the construction of value systems which privilege cultural superiority through music is drawn from the cultural theorist Pierre Bourdieu placing symphonic and instrumental music at the top of the hierarchy and folk and popular song, along with domestic and small-scale music at the bottom.[20] Despite these difficulties women did produce large-scale compositions towards the end of the 19th century. Halstead, like Citron, highlights the role of the printed score as having significant influence in the realisation of large-scale works. To secure repeated performances of works and to provide the opportunity for works to be programmed repertory requires that publishing contracts are secured. Women have historically been limited in securing publishing contracts.

Common to the discussions to date on women's musical creativity are similar conclusions about the negative effects of female socialisation on their music compositional endeavours, particularly in the Western world. In the words of Cixous: "woman has never (had) her turn to speak".[21] Institutional barriers, male dominance of the musical hierarchy, lack of meaningful reception and reproduction of women's music and restriction to creativity in the domestic sphere of small-scale forms have all been located as the causes for women's limited success in musical composition. Women who have been successful as composers or choose composition as a career path find themselves struggling against these, as well as all of the other obstacles associated with being a composer. Where the question of feminine aesthetics enters the debate the problems of essentialism cause not only the composer, but also commentators to become highly sensitive. To label anything as 'women's music' immediately establishes a binary opposition which implies a secondary status for women. Denial of women's experience and history has obvious advantages in women's attempts to gain recognition by so-called universal principles and to achieve success as a woman composer. However, in doing so women composers deny not only the significance of feminine inscription, but also the opportunity to express difference in creativity.

## Gender parity in commissioning and performance

The work of feminist musicology in the 1990s resulted in a reaction which at the time generated a flurry of scholarship, debate, women's music festivals along with lobbying commissioning, performing and broadcasting bodies to include compositions by women. The result was positive for some women composers, but scholars have bemoaned that research on women in classical music began to disappear by 2010 and, with it, the associated gains for women composers.[22] Support for women in the concert hall and success with commissions has been directly associated with research activity, thus the decline in research activity on women composers in the early part of the 21st century has led to a corresponding decline in support for women composers.[23] Analysis of the statistics on women's access to commissions for large-scale works, which feminist musicology found an area that women had limited access, remains an area that is elusive to women.[24] Surveys of major classical international concert programmes indicate that less than 4% of 15 major orchestras worldwide in 2020 included compositions by women.[25] Data gathered on classical music commissions by Women in Music UK women still lag behind men and generally are commissioned to write shorter works. In 2019 works by living women composers were featured at just 22% of concerts.[26] The inequality in the commissioning and programming of music composed by women continues to reflect gender inequities that result in a gap in pay, employment and education. Research into the effects of the COVID-19 pandemic on the gender pay gap where women have borne the burden of unpaid domestic labour has exacerbated the inequities for women in general.[27]

The findings of research into women composers' lived experiences are that they feel gender negatively impacts their career.[28] Themes that recur are that they feel discouraged, isolated, discriminated against and sexually harassed. Motherhood results in their being taken less seriously and affects their self-confidence. The lack of role models and women composition teachers, as well as lack of study of music by women in their composition training at the tertiary level compounds their insecurity. Networking opportunities outside of women's support networks are limited. Despite the efforts of feminist musicology and women in the musical academy by the early part of the 21st century, women composers remain marginalised in their efforts to gain equal distinction on the concert platform.

Despite this, there are a number of extremely successful women composers who have managed to win valuable commissions, high-profile performances and recordings.

Efforts made by educational institutions, concert music programmers, broadcasters and funding bodies to redress the balance include positive discrimination in the form of women composers' celebrations, inclusion of women on funding boards and increasing quotas of compositions by women in on-air broadcasts. As the number of women conductors reaches the podium of high-profile orchestras, efforts are made to programme women's music. Notwithstanding these efforts, progress for women composers is glacially slow.

### Leading 20th-century women composers

Chapter 1 provided many examples of women in history who successfully took the lead in performance and composition. While the previous section indicates that women have struggled to win high-profile commissions and performances of their music, the 20th century provided new freedoms with increasing social emancipation for women. Creative possibilities such as music composition became available, but established attitudes remained patronising. In the early part of the century, women began to engage with the modern styles that were emerging winning success on the concert stage. Leading figures include Dame Ethyl Smyth (1858–1944), Nadia Boulanger (1887–1979) and her sister impressionist composer Lili Boulanger (1893–1918), modernist Ruth Crawford Seeger (1901–1953), serialist Elisabeth Lutyens (1906–1983), neoclassicists Germaine Tailleferre (1892–1983) and Louise Talma (1906–1996). Post-tonal dissonance is expressed in the compositions of Elizabeth Maconchy (1907–1994), Grażyna Bacewicz (1909–1969) and Miriam Gideon (1906–1996).

Dame Ethyl Smyth was critically acclaimed for her music, writing and militancy in advocating for the rights of women. Born into an upper middle-class family Smyth studied music and despite her father's objection to her pursuing a professional career as musician, she entered the Leipzig Conservatory to study composition. She became involved in musical circles that included Brahms, Grieg, Joachim and Clara Schumann. After successful débuts in Germany, she returned to England which resulted in Smyth receiving a successful orchestral début in London with her *Serenade* and *Antony and Cleopatra* overture at Crystal Palace in 1890 to favourable reviews.[29] Her *Mass in D* (1893), inspired by her relationship with devout Catholic Pauline Trevelyan, was less favourably received.

Her ambition to compose opera was fulfilled by her collaboration with Harry Brewster with whom she co-wrote librettos for three operas: *Fantasio* (première 1898, Wiemar), *Der Wald* (première 1902) in Berlin and London, and *The Wreckers* (première 1906, Leipzig). Her exposure to Parisian musical circles through her infatuation with the influential patron, the Princess de Polignac (nee. Singer; 1865–1943) brought about a shift in her musical style. She found it difficult to secure performances in her home country due to the conservatism of the British musical establishment and *The Wreckers* had to wait until 1909 for a London performance.

Smyth met Emmeline Pankhurst in 1910 and began two years of dedication to the women's suffrage campaign. Her *Songs of Sunrise* featuring the rousing anthem, 'The March of the Women', premièred in 1911 at a concert of her music given by the LSO and Crystal Palace Choir under Smyth herself. Her involvement in the suffrage movement intensified her politicised awareness of her own position as a woman and her next opera, *The Boatswain's Mate* (1913–1914), whose feisty heroine outwits her bumbling suitor, is her most overtly feminist work. Composed to her own libretto after a short story by W.W. Jacobs, it is a light-hearted comedy and, though not performed until 1916, became the most frequently staged of her six operas. Her final major work was the hour-long choral symphony *The Prison* (1930) setting a text by her long-time collaborator Harry Brewster. She worked as a radiologist in France during World War I and became devastated to experience hearing loss. She found a new interest in literature and, between 1919 and 1940, she published ten highly successful, mostly autobiographical, books.[30]

Whilst not pursuing a career solely in composition, Nadia Boulanger (1887–1979) was a leading composition teacher and a successful conductor. She was born into a musical family and her father won the highly coveted Prix de Rome aged 20 later becoming the professor of singing at the Paris Conservatoire.[31] Nadia entered the conservatoire aged nine and when her father died at a young age she trained to become a teacher to help support her family. She began teaching from her family apartment and holding her Wednesday afternoon group class in analysis and sight-singing which she continued throughout her life.[32] She was a keen composer with the goal of winning the Prix de Rome and for the 1908 competition she submitted an instrumental fugue in the vocal fugue category which caused a stir in the international press when the French Minister of Public Information decreed that her work be judged on musical merit alone awarding her Second Grand Prix for her cantata *La Siréne*.[33] Still hoping to win she entered the competition again in 1909, but failed to reach the final round. Her sister Lili announced her ambitions to compose and win the prize.

Lili Boulanger was beset with ill health and could not attend the conservatoire to study instead taking private tuition at home. When her sister gave up trying to win the Prix de Rome, Lili entered the competition in 1912 which was unsuccessful, but upon her second attempt in 2013 she won and as the first woman ever to do so the news hit international headlines. Her residency at Villa Medici in Rome was cut short by the outbreak of World War I, but she managed to complete several compositions and returned in 1916. Her health deteriorated and she returned to France to dictate her last works to her sister in early 2018. Her final work *Pie Jesu* incorporated experimental orchestral colours and polytonality which was ahead of its time and influenced the following generation French composers.[34] A prize was established in her name by her sister Nadia and her American friends to perpetuate her memory. In 2018 in Washington, DC, women musicians started the Boulanger Initiative to support music composed by women.

Following Lili's death Nadia worked as a performer of her own and Lili's works. She continued to compose and teach, as well as conduct. Her success in the salon life of Paris in the early part of the 20th century was cultivated by her powerful sponsor Princess Winaretta de Polignac. Polignac was an American by birth and an heiress to the Singer sewing machine fortune. Raised in England and France her second marriage was a lavender union with Prince Edward de Polignac (1834–1901). Both were accomplished musicians, Winaretta an organist and pianist and Edward a composer. They sponsored performances in their salon of early music with rare performances of Rameau's work as well as modern compositions by Fauré and Debussy. Following Prince Edward's death Winaretta continued to sponsor performances by composers such as Stravinsky, Milhaud, de Falla and Tailleferre. She was also a sponsor of Diaghilev's Ballet Russes and after his death Nadia Boulanger became her chief music counsellor. They became close friends and the Princess supported her conducting career. The Polignac salon afforded Boulanger opportunities in presenting concerts and developing her conducting skills with no financial risk and was essential to Boulanger's public success which later transferred to the concert hall.

In the US, Ruth Crawford Seeger (1901–1953) led the way in avant-garde music with her compositions employing free atonality and serialism. She faced considerable discrimination, but her music was published in the high-profile journal *New Music Quarterly*, performed in Chicago at the International Society for Contemporary Music and in New York at the Copland-Sessions Concerts.[35] She was the first woman to receive the Guggenheim Fellowship in composition to study in Berlin and Paris. Following her marriage and the birth of her first child in 1933, she moved away from composing serialist works. The family moved to Washington, DC, and she began working at the Archive of American Folk Song transcribing field recordings. Her treatise on how American traditional music should be performed and notated began as an introduction to the collection 'Our Singing Country' (1941) and was published 60 years later as 'The Music of American Folk Song' (2001).[36] In 1941 she became involved in teaching music at her daughter's pre-school beginning her successful career as a music educator and resulted in the publication of 'American Folk Songs for Children' (1941). Seeger resumed her compositional activities in the late 1940s winning the Washington chapter of the National Association for American Composers and Conductors with her Suite for Wind Quintet (1952). Unfortunately resuming her composition career was cut short by her death in 1953 aged 52. Apart from her influence on traditional music and serial composition she was a role model for her children Pete(r), Mike and Peggy who became prominent professional folk musicians.

English composer Elizabeth Lutyens studied at the Ecole Normale, Paris and the Royal College of Music. She developed an innovative style and personal brand of serialism but found herself spurned by the British establishment. She turned to composing film and television music to support her children due to the precarious nature of her husband's employment, which she considered a distraction from her serious composition, a situation lasting more than 20 years.[37] She continued to develop her style using 12-note technique and an individual approach to harmony. In her autobiography Lutyens reported that her use of 12-note technique seemed to be considered morally reprehensible leading to neglect of her work, but by the 1950s there was more acceptance of her approach which brought increased recognition of her work.[38] Her works were often based upon texts from Donne and Conrad to Islam and her early chamber operas dealt with social issues: *The Pit* (1947) a story about miners trapped in a mine and *Infidelio* (1954) a story about a broken love affair leading a woman's suicide. Her first full opera *The Numbererd* (1965–1967) addresses the problems of society and her third opera *Isis and Osiris* (1969–1970) addresses rituals of life and death. She ultimately received recognition with the award of the City of London Midsummer Prize (1969) and in the same year a Commander of the Order of the British Empire (CBE).

In 1904 French composer Germaine Tailleferre entered the Paris Conservatoire against her father's wishes prompting her to change the spelling of her surname from Taillefesse in protest. A formidable pianist and talented composer she won numerous awards being well regarded for her neo-classical compositional style. She was accepted as the only female member of the French composers' circle Les Six. Princesse de Polignac became one of her sponsors and Tailleferre became a close colleague of Maurice Ravel.[39] Her two unhappy marriages caused financial problems and led her to taking commissions which she hastily produced. During

World War II she emigrated to America and after four years returned to France in 1942. She resumed composing major works including operas, orchestral works, chamber music and French folksong settings. Her skilful and accessible style led to a demand for her music for film, radio and television. She remained a prolific composer and teacher late into her life with her last major work composed at the age of 89, *Concetto de la fidélité*, for coloratura soprano, which premièred at the Paris Opera a year before her death. Amongst her awards were Medal of the City of Paris and the Prix Italia.[40]

French-born Louise Talma moved to New York aged eight with her American mother who was a professional soprano. She studied piano and composition at Julliard and chemistry at Columbia after which she returned to France to study composition with Nadia Boulanger. Her early style focused on neo-classicism and in her later work introduced serial elements developing her own unique compositional voice.[41] Her opera *The Alcestiad* (1962) was premièred by the Frankfurt Opera as the first opera by an American woman to be performed in a major European theatre. Talma's extensive compositional output comprises more than 40 major works with *The Tolling Bell* (1969) nominated for a Pulitzer Prize. Her music has been widely acclaimed, and she has been awarded three honorary doctorates from Hunter College (1983), Bard College (1984) and St. Mary-of-the-Woods (1991). She was the first woman to be awarded the Sibelius Medal of Composition (1963) and became the first woman in the National Institute of Art and Letters (1974).[42]

Dame Elizabeth Maconchy was born in Ireland and moved to London aged 16 to study composition at the Royal College of Music. She won scholarships to further her studies in Prague. One of her early successes was the performance of her cantata *The Land* performed at BBC Proms in 1930 and in 1948, she was awarded the Edwin Evans Prize for her String Quartet No. 5. In 1953, her *Proud Thames* overture won the London County Council Competition as Coronation Overture for the new Queen of the United Kingdom. She was active in organising concerts for female composers and in 1959 was appointed first female Chair of the Composers Guild of Great Britain, along with being President of the Society for the Promotion of New Music where she worked to improve opportunities for composers. Her activism extended to political activism amongst other causes.[43] In 1960, she was awarded the Cobbett Medal for chamber music. She was made a CBE in 1977 and elevated to Dame Commander (DBE) in 1987.

Grażyna Bacewicz graduated from the Warsaw Conservatory in violin and composition. She continued her studies in Paris under Nadia Boulanger and returned to Poland to be principal violinist with the Polish

Radio Symphony Orchestra. She composed numerous works and had the opportunity to perform them in her orchestral role. During World War II she continued to compose and give underground concerts, but moved to Lublin during the Warsaw uprising. Following the war, she took up the position of professor at the State Conservatoire of Music in Łódź. Her prolific compositional output includes numerous solo, chamber, orchestral, concerto, vocal, choral and stage works in post-tonal style. She also provided incidental music for film and radio broadcasts. Apart from the many prizes she received for her compositions she has received lifetime achievement awards including the Order of the Banner of Work Class II (1949) and Class I (1959), Order of Polonia Restituta Cavalier (1953) and Commander's Cross (1955), and the 10th Anniversary Medal of the Polish People's Republic (1955).

Miriam Gideon was an American composer who began her studies with her uncle and went on to private studies in harmony, counterpoint and composition. Her studies with Roger Sessions saw her abandoning tonality and writing in a more extended post-tonal style.[44] Apart from her prolific compositional output, she was an influential music educator with posts at Brooklyn College, City University of New York (1944–1954; 1971–1976), the Jewish Theological Seminary of America (1955) and the Manhattan School of Music (1967–1991). She was the second woman inducted into the American Academy and Institute of Arts and Letters in 1975, following Louise Talma.

In the second half of the 20th century and into the 21st century, women gained increased access to music theory and compositional training, but still remain the exception. However, for those who succeed in the academy there are many examples of distinguished women composers acclaimed for their pioneering exploration of idiom, form, style and technology.

Among the many established composers working today are the American-born Nancy Van de Vate (b. 1930) known for her large-scale works. Her début was with the *Adagio for Orchestra* (1958). She taught at various North American universities and has worked professionally as a violist and pianist. Apart from her many vocal and instrumental compositions, she has also produced a number of electronic compositions for tape.[45] In 1975 she founded the League of Women Composers to provide opportunities for female composers and served as chairperson until 1982. In 2010 she became a composer in residence at the Institute for European Studies in Vienna.

English composer Nicola LeFanu (b. 1947) belongs to an established musical family as daughter of the afore-mentioned Dame Elizabeth Maconchy. LeFanu became a talented composer who studied at Oxford and Harvard, before taking a position as Professor of Music at the University of

York. While opera and musical theatre have been central to her output, she also achieved critical success for her orchestral and ensemble works. She is particularly successful at conveying natural landscapes through innovative orchestral textures and communicating social issues through storytelling in her operas.[46] She was one of the founding members and helped launch Women in Music along with being a long-standing member of professional musical bodies. She has been awarded a DMus from London University (1993) and an honorary DMus from Durham University (1995).

Judith Weir (b. 1954) began performing as an oboist with the National Youth Orchestra of Great Britain and went on to Kings College, Cambridge, to study composition. She won high-profile scholarships to study composition at Tanglewood (1976–1979), Glasgow University (1979–1982) and was a creative arts fellow at Trinity College, Cambridge (1983). She then became composer-in-residence at the Royal Scottish Academy of Music and Drama, Glasgow (1988–1991), and Fairbairn Composer in Association with the CBSO (1995–1958). Weir was made a CBE in 1995, and in the same year she received an honorary doctorate in music from the University of Aberdeen. She was the artistic director of the Spitalfields Festival in London from 1995 to 2000. She received first prize at the international Opera Screen Festival in Helsinki (1991) for *Heaven Ablaze in His Breast*, a dance-opera collaboration with the dance company Second Stride based on E.T.A. Hoffmann's *Der Sandmann*. Weir was Hambro's Visiting Professor in Opera Studies at Oxford University (1999) and became an Honorary Fellow of St Hilda's College, Oxford, in 2000. In 2007, she was the third recipient of The Queen's Medal for Music. She was Visiting Distinguished Research Professor in Composition at Cardiff University from 2006 to 2009. She won ISM's Distinguished Musician Award in 2010. In 2014, she was appointed the Master of the Queen's Music, a fixed-term appointment for ten years, the first woman to be awarded this role.[47] In May 2015, Weir won The Ivors Classical Music Award at the Ivor Novello Awards and in 2018 she was elected an Honorary Fellow of the Royal Society of Edinburgh.

Betsy Jolas (b. 1926) grew up in Paris surrounded by artistic and literary influences in France through her family associations and after her family moved to New York in 1940 she transferred to musical studies after discovering Renaissance music through the Dessoff Choirs.[48] In 1946 she returned to Paris and resumed studies at the Paris Conservatoire where she became inspired by avant-garde approaches to counterpoint and rhythm. Her experimentation with the expressive qualities of the voice led to wordless settings blurring the distinction between instruments and voice. She has been commissioned by leading international musical companies and composed opera, orchestral, solo, ensemble, chamber choral and vocal works. She has also had a distinguished career as a teacher, including as visiting professor in numerous American universities, and assisting and then succeeding Messiaen as professor of analysis (1975) and professor of composition (1978) at the Paris Conservatoire. She has received numerous prestigious awards including Commandeur des Arts et des Lettres (1985), Prix International Maurice Ravel (1992), Grand Prix de la Ville de Paris (1981), Officier de l'Ordre du Mérite (2003), Berlin Prize (2000), Officier de la Légion d'honneur (2006) and Prix de l'Académie Charles Cros pour l'ensemble de son œuvre (2015). Jolas is a member of the American Academy of Arts and Letters (1983) and of the American Academy of Arts and Sciences (1995).[49]

Swedish composer and conductor Karin Rehnqvist (b. 1957) studied at the Royal College of Music in Stockholm and continued her studies in composition. From 2000 to 2003 she was composer in residence for the Scottish Chamber Orchestra and the Svenska Kammarorkestern for which she wrote a number of works. She composes instrumental works and music for the stage and is noted for incorporating folk material and kulning (Scandinavian cattle calling) particularly into her vocal music.[50] In 2008 she was appointed the first female professor at the Royal College of Music in Stockholm. She has received numerous awards along with the honour of a major retrospective of her works by the Royal Stockholm Philharmonic Orchestra in 2006. In 2022 the Nordic Council Music Prize was awarded to Rehnqvist for the ecological crisis oratorio Silent Earth (libretto by Kerstin Perski), which received its première on January 29, 2022, after postponements in the two previous years.[51]

American composer Joan Tower (b. 1938) spent her childhood in South America which familiarised her with percussive rhythm that characterises her compositions.[52] She studied at Columbia University and was awarded a Masters in Composition (1965) and a Doctorate of Musical Arts (1978). She was a founding member of the Da Capo Chamber Players leading the group to wining a Naumburg Award (1973). Her music is based on serialist tradition but as her compositional voice developed more impressionistic colour entered her musical palette. She has composed ballet, orchestral, choral, ensemble and solo works. Tower has won major awards including Guggenheim Fellowship (1977), composer-in-residence with the St. Louis (1985–1987) and Pittsburgh Symphonies (2010–2011), the 1988 Kennedy Center Friedheim and 1990 Grawemeyer Awards (for Silver Ladders, 1986), membership in the American Academy and Institute of Arts and Letters (1998), composer-in-residence with Orchestra of St. Luke's (1997–2007), Chamber Music America award identifying Petroushskates (1980) as among the 101 most significant compositions for small ensemble, the Medora King Award for Musical Composition (2006) and honoree distinction at the Kennedy Center Gala for Women in the Arts (2009). Her *Made in America* project (2004), to date the nation's largest multi-orchestra consortium, provided 65 smaller-budget American symphonies the opportunity to commission a work by a major composer, with the goal of increasing audiences for contemporary music. In 2008, the recording of Tower's *Made in America* by the Nashville Symphony won three Grammy Awards in the categories Best Orchestral Performance, Best Classical Album and Best Classical Contemporary Composition.[53]

Ellen Taafe Zwilich (b. 1939) is an American composer who became the first female composer to win the Pulitzer Prize for Music (1983) for her Symphony No. 1. She earned her bachelor of music degree with a violin major from Florida State University (1960) and joined the American Symphony Orchestra in New York. She enrolled in Julliard and in 1975 she became the first woman to earn a Doctor of Musical Arts in composition. Her 1982 Pulitzer Prize win increased her profile and led to major commissions which allowed her to devote herself to full-time composition. She was the first occupant of the Composer's Chair at Carnegie Hall where she established the 'Making Music' concert series devoted to living composers. Her style is characterised by building a work from developing and generating ideas from an initial motive.[54] She has composed large-scale orchestral works, concerti, choral works and song cycles. She has received a number of other honours, including the Elizabeth Sprague Coolidge Chamber Music Prize, the Arturo Toscanini Music Critics Award, the Ernst von Dohnányi Citation, an Academy Award from the American Academy of Arts and Letters, a Guggenheim Foundation Fellowship and four Grammy nominations. She was elected to the American Academy of Arts and Letters and the American Academy of Arts and Sciences, and in 1999, she was designated Musical America's Composer of the Year. She has been a professor at Florida State University and has served for many years on the advisory panel of the BMI Foundation, Inc. In 2009, she became the chair of the BMI Student Composer Awards following Milton Babbitt and William Schuman. She has received six honorary doctorates.

Since the end of the Cold War, composers from Eastern Europe and Russia have gained international recognition; among them are prominent women composers, including Russian-born Sofia Gubaidulina, who is discussed in the following contemporary case studies. Polish composer and percussionist Marta Ptaszyńska (b. 1943) has become one of the best known contemporary Polish women composers through her performances of contemporary music on percussion. In 1968 she earned three Master of Arts degrees in composition, music theory and percussion at the Academy of Music in Warsaw and Poznán. In the 1970s she continued her composition studies with Nadia Boulanger and studied electronic music at the ORTF Centre in Paris. She then studied percussion at the Cleveland Institute of Music in the United States where she was awarded an Artist Diploma Degree (1974). She has since taught composition and performed percussion in the United States, Poland and Europe. She has been on many international panels for composer and percussionist competitions and has received numerous grants, awards and commissions She has been honoured with many prizes and awards including Simon J. Guggenheim Foundation Fellowship, the Danks Award of the American Academy of Arts and Letters, the Fromm Music Foundation Award, the Award at the International Rostrum of Composers at the UNESCO in Paris, several ASCAP Awards and many more. In 1995, she received the Officer Cross of Merit of the Republic of Poland. Her music has been performed by leading orchestras and premièred by major international musicians. In 1998, she was appointed a Professor of Music and the Humanities at the University of Chicago. Since 2005 she holds an endowed chair of Helen B. and Frank L. Sulzberger Professor in Composition.

## Contemporary case studies

The following provides a selected sample of women composers who have established successful careers and have broken through the barriers to achieve success in the concert hall and in recordings.

### Elena Kats-Chernin

My research into the music of women composers resulted in my PhD thesis on the music theatre works of Australian composer Elena Kats-Chernin (b. 1957) influenced by the 1990s musicological pursuits into feminist aesthetics.[55] Born in Tashkent in the time of Soviet rule, Kats-Chernin studied at the Yaroslavl Music School and the Gnessin State Musical College in Moscow. In 1975 she migrated with her family to Australia, continuing her studies at the Sydney Conservatorium of Music where she won two composition prizes. During this time, she participated in the Darlinghurst underground theatre scene, with groups such as Cabaret Conspiracy, Fifi Lamour and Boom La Bern. In 1980 she won a postgraduate scholarship to study in Germany where she was active in theatre and ballet, composing for state theatres in Berlin, Vienna, Hamburg and Bochum. In 1993 she wrote 'Clocks' for Ensemble Modern which received international attention.

Upon returning to Australia in 1994, Kats-Chernin received high-profile commissions with major Australian and international symphony orchestras, opera companies and ensembles. For the 2000 Sydney Olympic Games, she collaborated with choreographer Meryl Tankard to create *Deep Sea Dreaming* which was broadcast to millions worldwide as a part of the Olympic opening ceremony. *Lotus (Water) and Fire* (2003) was another high-profile commission for the 2003 Rugby World Cup opening ceremony. She collaborated again with Tankard on the Australian Ballet Commission *Wild Swans* (2003) which had an afterlife when the 'Eliza Aria' became the theme for a bank television advertisement in the UK, which went viral and a remix hit the UK Dance charts.[56] The original 2004 recording of the suite from the ballet was re-released following the UK success of the 'Eliza Aria' by ABC records and became an instant bestseller.

Kats-Chernin has written a number of ragtime pieces for piano with her 'Russian Rag' (1996) used in two different instrumental ensemble arrangements; as the theme of Late Night Live on ABC Radio until 2010 and featured as the theme for Max in the film *Mary and Max* (2008) by Adam Elliot introducing her to new audiences. Her success continued with major commissions in various genres into the next decade amongst them *Symphonia Eluvium* (2012) for organ, choir and orchestra, commemorating the devastating Queensland floods of January 2011, for the 2011 Brisbane Festival which was voted by the readers of the Australian monthly arts magazine *Limelight* as the best composition of the year. Her adaptation of Monteverdi's operas for Komische Oper Berlin in 2012 resulted in a 12-hour marathon performance with live telecast on 3sat TV. In 2015, her music for the television opera *The Divorce* (2015) was nominated for ACCTA (The Australian Academy of Cinema and Television Arts Awards) in the category Best Music for Television. Produced by Opera Australia, ABC TV and Princess Pictures and broadcast in December 2015 on ABC TV the musical mini-series had over one million views.[57]

In 1998 following her son's diagnosis of schizophrenia aged 14, Kats-Chernin became involved in mental health support and her chamber work 'Blue Silence' (2006) was devoted to artists suffering from mental illness. It was composed for an art exhibition in New South Wales called 'For Matthew and Others' that included artworks by her son. In 2011 'Vocalise' was commissioned for the Melbourne Mental Health Research Institute's 19th Annual John Cade Lecture. Between 2013 and 2018 she was commissioned several times by the Hush Foundation on the National Composers-In-Residence project, an initiative of Dr Catherine Crock AM aiming to use new Australian music to calm young patients with chronic illness and mental health entering the health system.

In 2020 she created the soundtrack for the TV channel Ten documentary *Lindy Chamberlain, the True Story* which chronicled the wrongful infanticide committal of Chamberlain whose baby was taken by a dingo. Kats-Chernin's support for women in music is represented in *Jubilissima* (2022) commissioned in collaboration with the Australian Brandenburg Orchestra's Principal Trumpet, Leanne Sullivan for the Australian Women in Music Awards. It received the AWMA award for artistic excellence. The title is her own invented word to celebrate the brave, honest and supportive work of women in the music industry.[58]

She has won numerous music composition prizes and her work is performed and broadcast regularly. In 2019 Kats-Chernin was appointed an Officer of the Order of Australia (AO) for distinguished service to the performing arts, particularly to music, as an orchestral, operatic and chamber music composer.

### Sofia Gubaidulina

Soviet-Russian composer Sofia Gubaidulina (b. 1931) studied at the Kazan Conservatory during a time when contemporary Western music was banned. However, the students managed to smuggle scores and secretly studied them despite the raids conducted to search for illicit material.[59] She went on to study at the Moscow Conservatory completing postgraduate studies in 1963. She worked at the Moscow experimental studio for electronic music (1969–1970) and in the 1970s was a member of the Astrea improvisation group which often drew on Eastern folk traditions. Her works draw from both Western and Russian Orthodox traditions along with her Tartar extraction and she often incorporates texts and titles from Latin, Italian and German with symbolic references to mystical spiritualism. She also incorporates techniques from electronic music and novel instrumentation including traditional Russian folk instruments, Japanese instruments and innovative percussion combinations. She became known internationally in the 1980s through Gidon Kramer's performances of her violin concerto *Offertorium* (1980). She also became well known through her film scores for over 30 films. In 1992 she moved to Germany where she earned major commissions. Her 2000 commission to write a piece for the Passion 2000 project in commemoration of J.S. Bach by the international Bachakademie Stuttgart resulted in her work Johannes-Passion. This along with her 2002 Johannes-Ostern, commissioned by Hannover Rundfunk, formed a 'diptych', her largest work to date. In 2003 she was the first female to be invited to feature in the annual Rheingau Musik Festival.

She has won numerous prizes from Russia, Germany, Japan and Sweden including the Europäischen Kulturpreis (2005), the Russian Cultural Prize 'Triumph' (2007) and the International Council of Russian Compatriots 'The Compatriot of the Year – 2007'.

Her many honours include foreign honorary member of the American Academy of Arts (2005), Dr honoris causa of Yale University (2009), honorary Doctor, University of Chicago (2011), Golden Lion for Lifetime Achievement in music Venice Biennale (2013), honorary doctorate New England Conservatory, Boston (2017) to name a few. In October 2021 her 90th birthday was celebrated with performances of her works by Gewandhaus Orchestra, on BBC Radio 3 amongst other celebrations.

### Deborah Cheetham Fraillon

Deborah Cheetham Fraillon (b. 1964) is a Yorta Yorta soprano, actor, composer and playwright. As a member of the Australian stolen generations, she was taken from her mother when she was three weeks old to be raised by a white Baptist family. She graduated from the New South Wales Conservatorium of Music with a Bachelor of Music Education Degree. She has performed internationally as a soprano and has sung at major Australian events including the opening of the 2000 Summer Olympics and the 2003 Rugby World Cup. In 1997 she wrote the play *White Baptist Abba Fan* which draws upon her own experiences of coming to terms with her racial identity and sexuality whilst seeking to reunite with her Aboriginal family. In 2009 Cheetham Fraillon established the opera company 'Short Black Opera' devoted to the development of Indigenous singers. In the following year the company produced the première of her opera *Pecan Summer* (2010) which was based on the 1939 Cummeragunja walk-off, one of the first protests by Indigenous Australians against treatment at the mission reserve. It is Australia's first Aboriginal opera.

Cheetham Fraillon wrote Australia's first requiem *Eumeralla*, a war requiem for peace (2019) based upon the frontier wars between First Nations people in South Western Victoria and settlers between 1840 and 1863. It is sung entirely in the Gunditjamara language and premièred to sell out audiences on-country at the Port Fairy Spring Festival in October 2018. This was followed by a performance in June 2019 in Melbourne by the Melbourne Symphony Orchestra and Chorus and the Dhungala Children's Choir and a national tour. Cheetham Fraillon has been commissioned by major Australian orchestras and ensembles.

Cheetham Fraillon refused to sing the Australian national anthem at the Australian Football League's 2015 Grand Final and advocated for a change in the lyrics for the anthem putting forward new lyrics composed in 2009 by Judith Durham in consultation with Muti Muti singer-songwriter Kutcha Edwards.[60] These lyrics were never adopted, but a small change in the wording of the anthem was introduced by the government of Australia in 2021 with the second line of the Australian National Anthem changed from 'For we are young and free' to 'For we are one and free' in an effort to reflect greater unity.

In the 2014 Queen's Birthday Honours List, Cheetham Fraillon was appointed as an AO, for distinguished service to the performing arts as an opera singer, composer and artistic director, to the development of Indigenous artists, and to innovation in performance. In 2019 she was appointed Professor of Practice at the School of Music, Monash University, and was the 2020 composer in residence at the Melbourne Symphony Orchestra. In April 2018, the University of South Australia awarded Cheetham Fraillon an honorary doctorate. Amongst her accolades are two Australian Women in Music Awards (2018, 2021), National Live Music Awards (2019), Sir Bernard Heinz Memorial Award (2019) and Helpman Award (2020).

## Conclusion

The studies and debates that emerged from the feminist musicological arena in the late 20th century highlighted the significant barriers that women faced in achieving recognition in the field of musical composition. This resulted from women's exclusion from the dominant musical discourses and texts. Feminist musicology has examined these barriers and, informed by feminist debates in other disciplines, has identified significant obstacles to women negotiating careers in musical composition. Socialisation has been, and still is, a substantial obstacle to women's compositional achievements. Institutional barriers have been an obstacle to women's professional development in composition. Networking has a significant role to play in the acceptance of women's composition as does mentoring and role models which have been limited in the past. Women's choice of compositional genres were dictated by different opportunities offered to them as women impacting their critical recognition. Women may have different aesthetic approaches to creativity due to their different experience from men which has impacted their reception. Notwithstanding, many women have achieved significant success as composers in the 20th century and into the 21st century as educational opportunities for women have increased along with networking opportunities in the public sphere. The women discussed in this chapter have demonstrated that women can negotiate successful careers in music composition. Those who have taken the lead in musical composition provide significant examples of possibilities for women composers into the future.

## Notes

1  De Beauvoir, S. (1971). *The Second Sex*. Alfred A. Knopf.
2  Wood, E. (1980). Women in music. *Signs: Journal of Women in Culture and Society*, 6, 283.
3  Ibid. 290.
4  Ibid. 296.
5  These include Bowers, J. & Tick, J. (1987). *Women Making Music: The Western Art Tradition, 1150–1950*. University of Illinois Press; K. Pendle (Ed.) (1991). *Women and Music: A History*. Bloomington; Jezic, D. & Wood, E. (1994). *Women Composers: The Lost Tradition Found*. Feminist Press at CUNY.
6  Solie, R. (2001). *Feminism*. Grove Music Online.
7  Rieger, E. (1985). 'Dolce semplice'? On the Changing Role of Women in Music. In *Feminist Aesthetics*. Ed. Ecker, G. Beacon Press, 135–139.
8  Ibid. 139.
9  Rieger, E. (1992). 'I recycle sounds': Do women compose differently? *Journal of the International League of Women Composers*, March 1992, 22–25.
10  Ibid. 147.
11  McClary, S. (1991). *Feminine Endings: Music, Gender, and Sexuality*. University of Minnesota Press.
12  Ibid. 119.
13  Van den Toorn, P. (1991). Politics, feminism, and contemporary music theory. *The Journal of Musicology*, 9(3), 275–299; Solie, R. (1991). What do feminists want? A reply to Pieter van den Toorn. *The Journal of Musicology*, 9, 399–410. Van den Toorn, P. (1996). *Music, Politics, and the Academy*. University of California Press; Higgins, P. (1993). Women in music, feminist criticism, and guerrilla musicology: Reflections on recent polemics. *19th Century Music*, 27(2), 174–192; Sayrs, E. (1993). Deconstructing McClary: Narrative, feminine sexuality, and feminism in Susan McClary's feminine endings. *College Music Symposium*, 33, 41–55.
14  Cox, R. (1991). Rediscovering jouissance: An introduction to feminist musical aesthetics. In *Women & Music: A History*. Ed. Pendle, K. Indiana University Press, 331–340.
15  Citron, M. (1993). *Gender and the Musical Canon*. University of Illinois Press.
16  Solie, R. (Ed.) (1995). *Musicology and Difference: Gender and Sexuality in Music Scholarship*. University of California Press; Derrida, J. (1967. Reprinted 2001). *Writing and Difference*. Routledge.
17  De Beauvoir. Ibid.
18  Halstead, J. (1997. Revised 2017). *The Woman Composer: Creativity and the Gendered Politics of Musical Composition*. Routledge.
19  This echoes the earlier findings of both Barkin, E. (1980–1981). Questionnaire. *Perspectives of New Music*, 19, 460–462 and Citron. (1993). Ibid.
20  Shepherd, J. (1993). Power and Difference in Music. In *Musicology and Difference: Gender and Sexuality in Music Scholarship*. Ed. Solie, R. University of California Press.
21  Cixous Hélène, Cohen K. & Cohen P. (1976). The laugh of the medusa. *Signs* 1(4), 875–893.
22  Adkins Chiti, P. (2003). Cultural diversity-musical diversity: A different vision – Women making music, 1–9 www.imc-cim.org/mmap/pdf/prod-chiti-e.pdf; Macarthur, S. (2010). *Towards a Twenty-First-Century Feminist Politics of Music*. Ashgate.

23 Macarthur, S., Bennett, D., Goh, T., Hennekam, S. & Hope, C. (2017). The rise and fall, and the rise (again) of feminist research in music: What goes around comes around. *Musicology Australia*, 39(2), 73–95.
24 Adkins Chiti. (2003). Ibid. Rusak, H. (2010). Operas by women in Australia: Some data. *Asia Pacific Journal of Arts and Cultural Management*, 7(1), 557–568.
25 Tilden, I. (2021, 20 August) Blistering and virtuosic, depth and wisdom … women composers we should listen to. *The Guardian*.
26 Women in Music (2020). Retrieved from womeninmusic.org.uk/proms-survey.htm
27 Ibid. Del Boca et al. (2020), Power, K. (2020).
28 Macarthur et al. (ibid).
29 Fuller, S. (2001). *Smyth, Ethel*. Grove Music Online.
30 Ibid.
31 Rosenstiel, L. (1998). *Nadia Boulanger: A Life in Music*. W.W. Norton, 13.
32 Monsaingeon, B. (1985). *Mademoiselle: Conversations with Nadia Boulanger*. Carcanet Press, 26.
33 Potter, C. (2001). *Boulanger, (Juliette) Nadia*. Grove Music Online.
34 Fauser, A. (2004). Lili Boulanger. *New Historical Anthology of Music by Women*, 1, 275.
35 Hisama, E.M. & Tick, J. (2001). *Crawford (Seeger), Ruth*. Grove Music Online.
36 Seeger, R.C., Crawford, R. & Polansky, L. (2001). '*The Music of American Folk Song' and Selected Other Writings on American Folk Music*. Vol. 17. University Rochester Press.
37 Payne, A., & Calam, T. (2001). *Lutyens, (Agnes) Elisabeth*. Grove Music Online.
38 Lutyens, E. (1972). *A Goldfish Bowl*. Cassell.
39 Orledge, R. (2001). *Tailleferre, Germaine*. Grove Music Online.
40 Shapiro, R. (2011). *Les Six: The French Composers and Their Mentors, Jean Cocteau and Erik Satie*. Peter Owen.
41 Leonard, K. (2014). *Louise Talma: A Life in Composition*. Ashgate.
42 Ibid.
43 Beer, A. (2016). Maconchy. In *Sounds and Sweet Airs: The Forgotten Women of Classical Music*. Simon and Schuster, 286–330.
44 Hisama, E. M. (2006). *Gendering Musical Modernism: The Music of Ruth Crawford, Marion Bauer, and Miriam Gideon*. Cambridge University Press.
45 See Foulkes-Levy, L. & Levy, B. (2005). *Journeys Through the Life and Music of Nancy van de Vate*. Scarecrow Press.
46 Fuller, S. (2001). *LeFanu, Nicola*. Grove Music Online.
47 Booth, R. (2014, 29 June). Judith Weir to be appointed first female master of Queen's music. *The Guardian*.
48 Thurlow, J. (2001). *Jolas, Betsy*. Grove Music Online.
49 Briscoe. J. (2011/2012). *Jolas, Betsy*. *Grove Dictionary of American Music*, 2nd ed. 2012. Oxford Music Online.
50 White, J.D. & Christensen, J. (2002). *New Music of the Nordic Countries*. Pendragon Press, 503.
51 Lebrecht, N. (2022, 3 November). Climate Catastrophe Oratorio wins 40k Nordic Prize. Slipped Disc.
52 Grolman, E. (2014). *Tower, Joan*. Grove Music Online.
53 Ibid.
54 Schwartz, K.R. (2001). *Zwilich, Ellen Taaffe*. Grove Music Online.

55 Rusak, H. (2005). Simply Divine: Feminist aesthetics in three music theatre works of Elena Kats-Chernin. Phd Dissertation, University of Adelaide.

56 Rusak, H. (2019). Wild Swans by Elena Kats-Chernin: The journey from the Australian Ballet to the UK dance charts. *Sound Scripts*, 6(1), 17.

57 Rusak, H. (2020). The Divorce: A soap opera. In *Opera, Emotion, and the Antipodes*, Volume II. Ed. Davidson, J., Halliwell M. & Rocke, S. Routledge, 90–112.

58 Robertson, H. (2022, 8 March). New Elena Kats-Chernin piece announced for International Women's Day. Limelightmagazine.com.au

59 Lukomsky, V. (1999). 'Hearing the subconscious': Interview with Sofia Gubaidulina. *Tempo*, 209, 27–31.

60 Cheetham, D. (2015, 20 October). Young and free? Why I declined to sing the national anthem at the 2015 AFL Grand Final. *The Conversation*.

# 3

# WOMEN CONDUCTORS

## Introduction

It is rare to find women on the conducting podium of the world's great orchestras. However, it is not unusual for women to dominate the podium of community choirs, school orchestras and ensembles. Despite this, the world's leading opera houses and concert halls remain the domain of men with the majority of senior conducting posts held by men. Notwithstanding, some women have managed to negotiate successful careers as conductors of major orchestras and opera companies. This chapter discusses the challenges faced by women in gaining senior leadership roles as conductors of major orchestras.

## Women's access to the podium

Conducting orchestras may represent musical leadership at the top of the musical hierarchy. The orchestral podium in the late 19th and early 20th centuries was dominated by men and was a demonstration of masculine power and authority over the orchestra to command the musical resources in a display of musical genius mainly represented by men. Women have entered this space in the professional sphere but researchers such as Bartleet and Lazarou[1] observe that the obstacles faced by women still remain in this profession as in other professions. Women are still outnumbered, discrimination, bias, appearance, dress, motherhood, and all the issues beleaguering women in professional life apply to this profession.

DOI: 10.4324/9781003183631-4

Lazorou's investigation of women conductors finds that discrimination, bias, sexist and misogynist comments are prevalent against women in her interviews with conductors and analysis of media surrounding women conductors.[2] Lazarou also raises the issue of limitations of these studies that do not even discuss discrimination in areas such as LGBTQI+ and people of colour in this profession. While Bartleet's earlier examination of women conductors examines the dichotomy of motherhood and guilt that plagued women conductors in the latter part of the 20th century, particularly where extensive travelling is involved, she argues that women do not have the institutional support required for their careers as professional conductors. Despite the inroads that women are making into the highest level of classical musical hierarchy they are still the minority.

Openings in professional orchestras have always been a covert activity with positions often not advertised and 'boy club' tendencies in the hiring of musicians by section leaders and conductors. By far the most influential decision-makers in the orchestra are conductors, a profession dominated by men. Renowned conductor Zubin Meta, who led the New York Philharmonic until 1990, is noted as saying "I just don't think women should be in an orchestra".[3] As recently as November 2017 renowned conductor of the Concertgebouw Mariss Jansons stated "Women on the podium ... it's not my cup of tea".[4] The Vienna Philharmonic also controversially did not accept female membership up until 1997 which was later than most orchestras and faced protests from the International Alliance of Women in Music at their US tour agreeing to admit a woman harpist for the tour. It sparked a controversy that led to blind auditions to remove the bias against females and ethnic minorities.

Blind or screened auditions introduced between 1980 and 2000 resulted in the increase in hires of women in orchestras. Sometimes carpeted floors had to be introduced to avoid the gender betrayal of women's shoes tapping on the floor. These extra measures allow some kind of fair playing field for women. The bias in the profession against women is evident from the few examples of women on the podium listed in the literature and women conductors are still the exception.

## Pioneering women conductors

Early exceptions did begin to emerge as women began to assert their rights towards the end of the 19th century. The following discussion looks at the challenges faced by women aspiring to lead orchestras and some of the successful pioneers who opened opportunities for women on the podium by accessing conducting training that was generally not available to women at the time.

Ethel Leginska (Liggins; 1886–1970) started her influential career as concert pianist and she also studied composition at an early age. She was born in Hull, England, and studied in Vienna with Polish pianist and Professor Theodor Leschetizky. She adopted a Polish-sounding name as most of the best musicians of the day were Polish and her socialite friends considered this would be a marketing advantage.[5] She was hailed at her US début as a young Paderewski.[6] Her personal style and flair was enhanced by her focus upon stage design and masculine concert dress which influenced her many women fans. She took composition studies with Ernest Bloch in 1914 and produced a body of works in various genres.[7] She took orchestral conducting studies in her late 30s in London. In 1924 she guest-conducted the Paris Conservatory Orchestra, the Munich Konzertverein, the London Symphony and the Berlin Philharmonic, all of which were all-male orchestras. In 1925, she made her début as a conductor in the United States with the New York Symphony Orchestra in Carnegie Hall making her the first woman conductor on the Carnegie Hall podium. She went on to conduct the Boston People's Symphony Orchestra, Cleveland Orchestra and the Los Angeles Symphony Orchestra at the Hollywood Bowl with an audience of 30,000 people.[8] In 1926 she founded the Boston Philharmonic Orchestra and led its performances and in the late 1920s she founded and led women's orchestras in Boston, Chicago and New York. In 1929 Leginska founded and directed the Boston English Opera Company and made guest appearances with the Montreal Opera Company. She was the first woman to conduct her own opera in the Chicago Opera House, one of several notable 'firsts'. In 1939 Leginska settled in Los Angeles where, as a music teacher, she built up a large circle of talented students, continuing in this role right up to her death in 1970. She outwardly expressed feminist sentiments questioning why women shouldn't pursue careers, why women performers had to dress in uncomfortable gowns and why women should have to spend all their time occupied with the frivolity of their appearance. She stated "Most women consider that their duty in life is to please men and, with this object in view, they waste hours every day caring for their complexions, their figures, their hair, their clothes. Clothes!"[9] She can be credited for her pioneering efforts in women's leadership in music performance, composition and conducting.

Influential composition teacher Nadia Boulanger was also a successful conductor who was the first woman to conduct many high-profile orchestras including the Royal Philharmonic in 1937 where she conducted Fauré's Requiem.[10] She was also the first woman to conduct the BBC Symphony, Boston Symphony, New York Philharmonic and Philadelphia Orchestra. She preferred not to discuss gender issues in music and in her response to the reporters who quizzed her about what she thought about being the first woman to conduct the Boston Symphony Orchestra she said "I've been a woman for a little over 50 years, and I've gotten over my initial astonishment. As for conducting an orchestra, that's a job. I don't think sex plays much part".[11] Boulanger's revival of the works of Bach and Monteverdi fixed her position as leader of the early music revival fostering the careers of contemporary composers both French and American many of which she premièred in the salon of Princess Polignac as discussed in Chapter 2.[12]

Antonia Brico (1902–1989) was a Dutch-born conductor and pianist who migrated at an early age with her foster parents to the United States. Her early studies in music led to conducting studies at the University of California, Berkley, and an assistant position to the director of the San Francisco Opera. In 1927 she entered the Berlin State Academy of Music and became the first American to graduate from the master class in conducting in 1929. Despite her successful career in Europe in the early part of the 1920s and 1930s she faced discrimination upon her return to the United States.[13] She ended up forming her own women's orchestra to which she later added men. However, this collapsed in the Great Depression.[14] In July 1938 she was the first woman to conduct the New York Philharmonic. Brico performed and conducted a successful European tour before settling in Denver Colorado in 1942 where she founded a Bach Society, a women's string ensemble as well as conducting the Denver's Businessmen Orchestra, which later became the Brico Symphony Orchestra. She later went on to conduct the Denver Community Symphony which became the Denver Philharmonic and the Boulder Philharmonic Orchestra. In the 1974 documentary film about her life, she describes her career-long struggle with gender bias that limited her opportunities to conduct.[15] A Dutch movie, *De Dirigent* (2018), and a children's picture book, *In One Ear and Out the Other: Antonia Brico and Her Amazingly Musical Life* (2020), celebrate her career as a pioneering women conductor.[16]

Margaret Hillis (1921–1988) entered the world of conducting through the pathway of choral conducting. Born in Kokomo, Indiana, she studied music and had her conducting début with her high school student orchestra. She studied music composition for her bachelor of music degree from Indiana University. She became active as a choral conductor following her graduation in 1947 founding the Tanglewood Alumni Chorus which became the New York Concert Choir and Orchestra. She was choral conductor for the New York City Opera, the American Opera Society and taught choral conducting. Following her successful establishment of the Chicago Symphony Chorus she was provided with conducting opportunities with the orchestra becoming the first woman to conduct the Chicago Symphony Orchestra maintaining a 40-year career with the orchestra. She also worked with major American orchestras as guest conductor and won a series of Grammy Awards for her choral performances.[17]

Veronika Borisovna Dudarova (1916–2009) was a Soviet and Russian conductor born in Baku, the capital of the now independent republic of Azerbaijan, on the Caspian Sea. She received her early training in her hometown and later at the Leningrad Conservatoire, where she studied the piano. Drawn towards conducting, an activity not then regarded as the domain of women, she then studied at the Moscow Conservatoire graduating in 1947. She immediately became associate conductor of the Moscow State Symphony Orchestra and, although she encountered a degree of male opposition, her talents soon swept aside any reservations. In 1960, she took over as the principal conductor becoming the first woman in Russia to hold such a post. Occasionally she led the orchestra in tours to Europe and South America, becoming recognised for introducing the works of contemporaneous Russian composers.

In 1989, Dudarova left Moscow for Istanbul, but when the Soviet Union fell two years later, she was back and, although well into her 70s, formed a new orchestra, the State Symphony Orchestra of Russia which featured young musicians. She also was a regular visiting conductor in Europe and South America, Panama. She retained the role of artistic manager of the orchestra until her death in Moscow in January 2009 at the age of 92. She is listed in the Guinness Book of Records as the only woman in the world to have headed large Philharmonic orchestras for over 50 years and the main-belt asteroid 9737 Dudarova was named after her.

## Principal women conductors taking the lead

Whilst appointing women to leading major orchestras remains marginal, it is not insignificant that they are emerging in the field providing examples of leadership and role models for aspiring musicians. More women conductors have entered the world of directing orchestras in the 21st century and have claimed numerous 'firsts' and while less than 10% of conductors are women, it is becoming more common to see women leading major orchestras. The following provides some examples of women leading orchestras internationally and how they have shaped their own pathways and influenced the role of women in classical music.

## European and UK women taking the podium

In Europe more women are taking to leading positions in major orchestras. Sylvia Caduff (b. 1937) is a Swiss orchestral conductor who in the 1960s was assistant to Leonard Bernstein at the New York Philharmonic, one of the first women to conduct this orchestra. In the late 1970s she became the first woman to hold a post of principal conductor for a German orchestra, when she took up a post in Solingen. On October 15, 1978, she conducted the Berlin Philharmonic, as a guest conductor substituting for Herbert von Karajan who was unwell. She was the seventh woman to conduct the orchestra since its foundation, and the only one between 1930 and 2008. As a teenager, Caduff decided that she would later study music and become a conductor. Although she met with a lack of understanding from teachers and parents, she pursued this goal with passion. While at school, Caduff met Herbert von Karajan at a conducting course and he encouraged her conducting aspirations. She studied piano and music theory at the Lucerne Conservatory graduating in 1961. She also attended master classes with Rafael Kubelík, Lovro von Matačić, Franco Ferrara and Willem van Otterloo. In 1962 she completed a three-year conducting internship with Karajan at the Berlin Conservatory. In 1965 she reached the final of the Guido Cantelli Conducting Competition in Stresa and received an honourable mention in 1966 at the Nikolai Malko Competition in Copenhagen. In 1966 she became the first woman to win the Dimitri Mitropoulos International Music Competition in New York. She prevailed against 34 conductors from 23 countries. This achievement enabled her to spend a year as an assistant to Leonard Bernstein and the New York Philharmonic. During this time she also conducted the orchestra several times. The statutes of the Philharmoniker had to be changed specifically for this: they excluded the presence of women up to this point in time. In 1967 she made her UK début with the Royal Philharmonic Orchestra. From 1972 to 1976 she was a professor of conducting at the Bern Conservatory Music School. In 1973 she received the Art and Culture Prize of the City of Lucerne. She led her first 'own' orchestra from 1977 to 1986 as general music director (GMD) in Solingen (Germany). She travelled the world as a guest conductor and in 1978 became the first woman to conduct the Berlin Philharmonic after World War II. She also conducted the Zurich Tonhalle Orchestra, the Munich Philharmonic, the Berlin Radio Symphony Orchestra, the Bavarian Radio Symphony Orchestra and the Cologne Gürzenich Orchestra.

Alicja Mounk (b. 1947) grew up in Łódź, Poland, received piano lessons at an early age and made her first public appearance as a pianist at the age of eight. After graduating from the State Music High School in Warsaw, she began studying sound engineering and music direction at the Warsaw University of Music in 1966. After two years she had to break off this training; anti-Semitic campaigns in Poland in 1968 led to her expatriation. After a semester in 1969 at the Musikhochschule in Vienna, she continued her studies in the same year at the Musikhochschule in Detmold where she received her diploma in sound engineering and piano in 1971. She then studied conducting at the Berlin University of the Arts and at the Cologne University of Music. Further studies followed with Nadia Boulanger in Paris and with Michael Gielen in Basel. She began her professional career in 1975 as a repetiteur, first at the opera studio of the Cologne Opera and from 1976 with a conducting engagement at the Municipal Theatres of Krefeld, Mönchengladbach. In 1979 she became Kapellmeister at the Gärtnerplatztheater in Munich. This was followed by further positions as first conductor from 1984 at the Municipal Theatre in Freiburg, from 1987 at the State Theatre in Kassel and from 1989 at the Stuttgart State Opera. In 1991 she became GMD at the Ulm Theatre, making her one of the first women in this position in Germany, after Sylvia Caduff and Romely Pfund. There she became a respected interpreter of contemporary music premièring György Ligeti's opera *Le Grand Macabre*, Peter Michael Hamel's song opera *Radio-Sehnsucht* and Wolfgang Rihm's *The Conquest of Mexicocause* (1992). She made her US début in 1994 at the Spoleto Festival in Charleston. In 1997 Mounk became head of the opera school at the Hochschule für Musik Karlsruhe. Mounk had a formative effect on subsequent generations: Julia Jones was her assistant and second conductor in Ulm, Anna Skryleva her student in Karlsruhe.

English born Julia Jones (b. 1961) studied conducting at the University of Bristol and the Guildhall School of Music and Drama. She moved to Germany in her 20s to pursue her conducting career and from 1998 to 2002, she was principal conductor of the Basel Theatre/Basel Opera. In 2008, Jones became principal conductor of the Orquestra Sinfónica Portuguesa at the Teatro Nacional de São Carlos and held the post until 2011. Jones made her first guest conducting appearance at the Royal Opera, London, and her first professional guest conducting engagement in the UK, in January 2010. In April 2016, she was named the next GMD (Generalmusikdirektorin) of the Wuppertal Symphony Orchestra (Sinfonieorchester Wuppertal), which also encompasses the music directorship of the Wuppertal Opera (Wuppertaler Bühnen), the first female conductor ever appointed to the Wuppertal posts. In December 2020, Jones announced her intention to stand down from her posts in Wuppertal at the close of the 2020–2021 season.

Nathalie Stutzmann (née Dupuy; b.1965) is a French contralto and conductor. Born in Suresnes in France, Stutzmann first studied with her mother, soprano Christiane Stutzmann, then at Nancy Conservatoire and later at the École d'Art Lyrique of the Paris Opera, focusing on lieder, under Hans Hotter's tutelage. Stutzmann débuted as a concert singer at the Salle Pleyel, Paris, 1985, in Bach's Magnificat. Her recital début was the following year in Nantes. In addition to her concert work, Stutzmann has taught at the Geneva University of Music. She began performing and recording with Inger Södergren in 1994. She took part in the project of Ton Koopman and the Amsterdam Baroque Orchestra and Choir to record Bach's complete vocal works. Stutzmann developed an interest in conducting and in 2009, Stutzmann founded the chamber orchestra Orfeo 55, where, as artistic director, she performed as both soloist and conductor until the ensemble disbanded in 2019. In September 2017, Stutzmann became principal guest conductor of the RTÉ National Symphony Orchestra in Dublin, Ireland. In 2018, she was appointed chief conductor of the Kristiansand Symphony Orchestra, in Kristiansand, Norway, the first woman chief conductor in the orchestra's history. In the United States, the Philadelphia Orchestra announced the appointment of Stutzmann as its next principal guest conductor in December 2020, the first woman conductor ever named to this post. In 2020 and 2021, Stutzmann was guest conductor of the Atlanta Symphony Orchestra. In October 2021, the Atlanta Symphony Orchestra announced the appointment of Stutzmann as its next music director being the first woman conductor to hold this position. She has made numerous prize-winning recordings and won significant awards from the French government.

Finnish conductor Susanna Ulla Marjukka Mälkki (b. 1969) was appointed to lead both the Gulbenkian and Helsinki Philharmonic orchestras. In May 2013, Mälkki was appointed principal guest conductor of the Gulbenkian Orchestra. In September 2014, she was named chief conductor of the Helsinki Philharmonic Orchestra, effective autumn 2016. She is the first woman conductor to be named to this post and her contract has been extended twice through to 2023 after which she takes the title of chief conductor emeritus with the orchestra. She studied violin, piano and cello in her youth, eventually focusing her studies on the cello. She studied at the Sibelius Academy and later at London's Royal Academy of Music. In 1994, Mälkki won the first prize in the Turku National Cello Competition and from 1995 to 1998, she was principal cellist in the Gothenburg Symphony Orchestra. She participated in a Sibelius Academy Conductor's Workshop at Carnegie Hall in 1998 and left her Gothenburg position to devote herself to conducting. From 2002 to 2005, she was artistic leader of the Stavanger Symphony Orchestra. Her début with the Ensemble InterContemporain (EIC) was in August 2004, in a programme of Harrison Birtwistle at the Lucerne Festival. She became the EIC's music director in 2006, the first woman to hold the post, and served as the EIC's music director until 2013.

Mälkki is known as a specialist in contemporary music with several world premières and opera productions. Her conducting début at the BBC

Proms was in July 2007 and she conducted the world première of Luca Francesconi's opera *Quartett* at La Scala in Milan in 2011, becoming the first woman ever to conduct an opera production in the history of the house. Outside of Europe, Mälkki made her New Zealand conducting début in November 2006 with the New Zealand Symphony Orchestra. Her North American conducting début was in February 2007 with the St. Louis Symphony Orchestra (SLSO). She first guest-conducted the Los Angeles Philharmonic in 2010. In April 2016, the orchestra announced her appointment as its next principal guest conductor. Mälkki is the first woman conductor to be named to the principal guest conductorship of the Los Angeles Philharmonic. In December 2016, she made her Metropolitan Opera conducting début in the company's first-ever production of L'Amour de loin of Kaija Saariaho, the fourth woman conductor to lead a production at the Metropolitan Opera, and the first woman conductor to be featured in the Metropolitan Opera Live in HD series. Mälkki has conducted recordings for the Kairos label and in 2017 she won the Nordic Council Music Prize.

Joana Carneiro, born Joana Maria Amaro da Costa da Luz Carneiro (b. 1976), is a Portuguese conductor. In the United States, in January 2009, Carneiro was named the third music director of the Berkeley Symphony. The first woman to hold this post and the position marks Carneiro's first music directorship. In May 2018, the Berkeley Symphony announced the conclusion of Carneiro's music directorship of the orchestra at the end of the 2017–2018 season, at which time she took the title of music director emerita. In her youth, Carneiro played the viola. In Portugal, Carneiro studied music at the Academia Nacional Superior de Orquestra in Lisbon. She moved to the United States and earned a master's degree in music at Northwestern University, continuing graduate studies in music for a doctorate at the University of Michigan, where she also served as the conductor of the University Symphony Orchestra and University Philharmonia Orchestra.

Carneiro first gained attention as a finalist in the 2002 Maazel-Vilar Conductor's Competition at Carnegie Hall. She then served as Music Director of the Los Angeles Début Orchestra from 2002 to 2005. She has worked as an assistant conductor with the Los Angeles Chamber Orchestra. She was an American Symphony Orchestra League Conducting Fellow with the Los Angeles Philharmonic from 2005 to 2008. In Portugal, Carneiro became principal guest conductor of the Metropolitan Orchestra of Lisbon as of the 2005–2006 season. In the 2006–2007 season, she became principal guest conductor of the Gulbenkian Orchestra, and held the post through the 2012–2013 season. In September 2013, Carneiro was announced as the next principal conductor of the Orquestra Sinfónica

Portuguesa at the Teatro Nacional de São Carlos. Carneiro made her Edinburgh International Festival début in August 2019, leading the BBC Scottish Symphony Orchestra.

In September 2019, the Lahti Symphony Orchestra announced the appointment of German-born conductor Anja Bihlmaier (b. 1978) as its next principal guest conductor. She is the first woman conductor named to the Lahti post. Bihlmaier graduated from the Staatliche Hochschule für Musik Freiburg in 2003 earning a conducting diploma in 2006. From 2004 to 2005, she held a conducting scholarship at the Mozarteum Salzburg. From 2005 to 2008, she was part of the Conductors' Forum of the German Music Council.

Following a series of posts as repetiteur and assistant conductor at theatres in Görlitz, Coburg, Hildesheim and Chemnitz, Bihlmaier moved to the Hanover State Opera in 2013, where she held the position of second conductor. Bihlmaier was appointed first conductor at the Staatstheater Kassel. After Alicja Mounk (1987–1989), Bihlmaier is the second woman to hold the position of first conductor at the Kassel State Theatre.

In July 2017, Bihlmaier conducted the St. Margarethen Opera Festival production of *Rigoletto*, the first woman conductor in the festival's history. In November 2018, Bihlmaier first-guest conducted the Residentie Orchestra (Residentie Orkest). She first guest-conducted the Lahti Symphony Orchestra in December 2018. In May 2019, the Residentie Orkest announced the appointment of Bihlmaier as its next chief conductor, effective with the 2021–2022 season. This appointment marks her first chief conductorship. Bihlmaier is the first woman conductor to be named chief conductor of the Residentie Orkest, and the second woman conductor to be named chief conductor of any Dutch orchestra.

In 2019 Finnish conductor Eva Ollikainen (b. 1982) was appointed chief conductor and artistic director of the Iceland Symphony Orchestra. This appointment marked Ollikainen's first chief conductorship, and she is the first woman conductor to be named to this post. She studied piano, violin and French horn as a child and commenced conducting studies by age 12 at the Sibelius Academy from 1994 to 2002 and graduated at the age of 20 with a Masters of Music. She studied conducting with Jorma Panula and Leif Segerstam and was a member of the Finnish contemporary ensemble. In 2003, Ollikainen won the second Jorma Panula Conductors' Competition. She first guest-conducted the Iceland Symphony Orchestra in 2005. In the summer of 2006, she was a Tanglewood Music Centre conducting fellow. She returned as guest conductor with the Iceland Symphony Orchestra on three occasions between 2007 and 2010, and once again in February 2019. In November 2019, the Orchestra della Toscana also announced the appointment of Ollikainen as its next principal conductor, the first woman conductor to be named to the post, effective with the 2020–2021 season.

Dalia Stasevska (b. 1984) is a Ukrainian-born conductor who received her musical training in Finland. She is currently the principal guest conductor of the BBC Symphony Orchestra (BBC SO), and chief conductor of the Lahti Symphony Orchestra. Born in Kyiv, Ukrainian SSR, Soviet Union, Stasevska and her family subsequently moved to Tallinn, and later to Finland. Stasevska studied violin and composition at the Tampere Conservatory and the Sibelius Academy, Helsinki. In her 20s, she developed a new interest in conducting and pawned her violin to finance education in conducting. Stasevska studied conducting at the Royal Swedish Academy of Music and at the Sibelius Academy earning a diploma from the Sibelius Academy in 2012. From 2010 to 2015, Stasevska was artistic director of the Kamarikesä Festival. From 2014 to 2016, Stasevska was an assistant conductor to Paavo Järvi at the Orchestre de Paris. In 2015, Stasevska first guest-conducted the Lahti Symphony Orchestra (Sinfonia Lahti). On December 10, 2018, she conducted the Royal Stockholm Philharmonic Orchestra at the Nobel Prize Award Ceremony 2018, the second woman conductor ever to conduct the orchestra at the Prize Award Ceremony.

Stasevska made her UK guest-conducting début in 2018 with the orchestra of Opera North. In May 2018, Stasevska first guest-conducted the BBC SO at a Maida Vale studio concert. On the basis of this appearance, in January 2019, the BBC SO announced the appointment of Stasevska as its next principal guest conductor, effective July 2019. Stasevska is the first woman conductor ever to be named principal guest conductor of the BBC SO, and the second woman conductor to have a titled post with a BBC orchestra. She made her public début with the BBC SO at The Proms in July 2019. She conducted the Last Night of The Proms in September 2020, under social distancing conditions and without an audience in the wake of the COVID-19 pandemic, the second woman conductor to conduct the Last Night and the third Last Night to feature a woman conductor following Marin Alsop. In July 2021, she conducted the First Night of The Proms, the second woman conductor ever to conduct the First Night.

In May 2020, Lahti Symphony Orchestra announced the appointment of Stasevska as its next chief conductor, effective from the 2021–2022 season, with an initial contract of three seasons, and making her the first woman conductor to be named chief conductor of the Lahti Symphony Orchestra. This appointment marks her first chief conductor post. In November 2020, the Royal Philharmonic Society announced Stasevska as the recipient of its 2020 Conductor Award.

Joana Mallwitz (b. 1986) is the first woman conductor to be named chief conductor of the Berlin Concert House Orchestra (Konzerthausorchester

Berlin). Mallwitz studied violin and piano at an early age and continued her music studies at the Hochschule für Musik und Theater Hannover. She made her début professional conducting appearance at Theater und Heidelberg Orchestra in 2006 three months into her tenure on six hours' notice at the first night of the company's new production of Madama Butterfly.[18] In 2013, Mallwitz was named GMD of the Theater Erfurt, the first woman conductor named to the post in the institution's history and the youngest GMD of a German opera house. In October 2017, the Nurnberg State Theatre (Staatstheater Nürnberg) appointed Mallwitz as its new GMD. She is the first woman conductor to be named to the Nurnberg post. In August 2020, Mallwitz made her début at the Salzburg Festival with Così fan tutte, the third woman conductor ever to conduct an opera production at the Salzburg Festival, and the first woman conductor directly scheduled in advance by the Salzburg Festival for an opera production. Mallwitz was guest-conductor of the Concert House Orchestra Berlin during the 2020–2021 season and in August 2021, the orchestra announced the appointment of Mallwitz as its next chief conductor and artistic director. In 2019, *Opernwelt* (Opera world) magazine voted Mallwitz its Dirigentin des Jahres ('Conductor of the Year'). In November 2020, Mallwitz received the Sonderpreis (Special Prize) of the Bavarian Culture Prize.

Corinna Niemeyer (b. 1986) was appointed artistic and music director of the Luxembourg Chamber Orchestra (Orchestre de Chambre du Luxembourg) in September 2020. This follows a two-year tenure as assistant conductor with the Rotterdam Philharmonic Orchestra in 1918–1920. Niemeyer completed her training as a conductor at the Hochschule der Künste Zürich and previously studied orchestra conducting, cello and musicology at the conservatories of Munich, Karlsruhe and Shanghai. She has won awards from a number of international conducting competitions, including Tokyo International Conducting Competition in 2015, and Talent Chef d'orchestre in Paris in 2014. During her studies, she was artistic director of the Orchestre Universitaire de Strasbourg, establishing the orchestra as one of the most active university orchestras in Europe. She was awarded the 'Prix de l'Amitié franco-allemande' in 2018 by the German Consulate General in Strasbourg for her cross-border cultural commitment. She also regularly conducts the children's orchestra at the Philharmonie de Paris. From 2016 to 2018, she was lecturer and principal conductor of the orchestra at the Sorbonne University in Paris. Apart from her role as director of the Orchestre de Chambre du Luxembourg she regularly makes guest appearances with major European orchestras.

Lithuanian conductor Mirga Gražinytė-Tyla (b. Mirga Gražinytė, 1986) is currently musical director of the City of Birmingham Symphony

Orchestra (CBSO). Gražinytė-Tyla was born into a musical family, but received her initial education in French and painting, and studied at the National M. K. Čiurlionis School of Art in Vilnius. At age 11, she decided that she wanted to study music, and the one remaining musical programme option was choral conducting. She subsequently received musical training and education without ever playing a musical instrument. She first conducted a choir at age 13. She subsequently continued music studies at the University of Music and Performing Arts Graz, graduating in 2007. She then studied conducting at the Music Conservatory Felix Mendelssohn-Bartholdy in Leipzig and the Music Conservatory in Zurich.

Gražinytė-Tyla became Second Kapellmeister at the Theater Heidelberg in the 2011–2012 season and in 2012, she won the Nestlé and Salzburg Young Conductors Competition. With the 2013–2014 season, she became First Kapellmeister at the Bern Opera. Gražinytė-Tyla became music director of the Salzburger Landestheater with the 2015–2016 season, with an initial contract of two seasons. She concluded her music directorship of the Salzburger Landestheater after the 2016–2017 season. In the United States, Gražinytė-Tyla was a Gustavo Dudamel Fellow of the Los Angeles Philharmonic for the 2012–2013 season. In July 2014, she was named the orchestra's assistant conductor, on a two-year contract. In August 2015, the orchestra named her its new associate conductor, effective with the end of the 2015–2016 season, contracted through 2017.

Following guest appearances with the CBSO in 2015 and 2016 she was named as its next music director and first woman conductor of the CBSO. She made her first appearance at The Proms on August 27, 2016. Gražinytė-Tyla is to conclude her tenure as CBSO music director after the 2021–2022 season, and subsequently to take on the post of principal guest conductor of the CBSO. In February 2019, Gražinytė-Tyla signed an exclusive long-term recording contract with Deutsche Grammophon (DG). She is the first woman conductor ever to sign an exclusive recording contract with DG. Her first DG recording, issued in 2019, was of symphonies of Mieczysław Weinberg, with the CBSO. In October 2020, it won the 'Album of the Year' prize at the annual Gramophone Awards. Her following DG albums include works by Raminta Šerkšnytė, Benjamin Britten, Ralph Vaughan-Williams and William Walton.

## American women on the podium

The United States has seen more women conductors that have emerged to hold senior positions in major orchestras into the 21st century stemming from a range of cultural backgrounds as opportunities for training have opened for women and as more women become involved in the training of music and conducting.

Marsha Eve Mabrey (b. 1949) is the first African American woman to be appointed and serve as the conductor of a major American orchestra. She received a Bachelor of Music in 1971 and a Master of Music in 1972 from the University of Michigan. She went on to complete her Doctor of Musical Arts in orchestral conducting at the University of Cincinnati. She continued to conduct and teach in the United States and was guest conductor for orchestras in the United States and Germany. In 1996 she was appointed as conductor of the Seattle Symphony orchestra where she distinguished herself as both an advocate for community outreach and for programming lesser-known American composers.

JoAnn Falletta (b. 1954) was raised in the borough of Queens in an Italian-American household. She was educated at the Mannes College of Music and The Juilliard School in New York City. Falletta entered Mannes in 1972 as a guitar student, but began conducting the student orchestra in her freshman year, which initiated her interest in a conducting career. While the Mannes administration at that time expressed doubts about the ability of any woman to gain a music directorship, it consented to an official transfer of emphasis for Falletta. After graduation, she pursued further study at Queens College (MA in orchestral conducting) and the Juilliard School of Music (MM, DMA in orchestral conducting). Falletta studied conducting with such conductors as Jorge Mester, Sixten Ehrling and Semyon Bychkov and also participated in master classes with Leonard Bernstein.

Falletta's first permanent engagement was as music director of the Jamaica Symphony Orchestra, a position she held from 1977 to 1989. She subsequently served as music director of the Denver Chamber Orchestra, associate conductor of the Milwaukee Symphony Orchestra, music director of the Bay Area Women's Philharmonic and music director of the Long Beach Symphony Orchestra. She was also called upon by orchestras to perform mandolin and guitar in works that called for these instruments.

In 1991, Falletta was appointed the 11th music director of the Virginia Symphony Orchestra and remained in the position until the 2021 season. During her tenure, the Virginia Symphony performed at Carnegie Hall in New York and the Kennedy Centre in Washington, DC, and released 18 recordings including discs on the Naxos label, Albany Records, NPR and the orchestra's own Hampton Roads label.

In May 1998, Falletta was named music director of the Buffalo Philharmonic Orchestra and held this position up until their 2021 season. During her tenure in Buffalo, the orchestra has made recordings for Naxos Records and returned to Carnegie Hall after a 20-year absence. In 2004, the orchestra and television station WNED established the JoAnn Falletta International Guitar Concerto Competition. In 2011, she was appointed the principal guest conductor of the Brevard Music Institute, serving through the 2013 season.

Outside of the United States, Falletta first guest-conducted the Ulster Orchestra in August 2010 and returned for further concerts in January 2011. In May 2011, Falletta was named the 12th principal conductor of the Ulster Orchestra, effective with the 2011–2012 season, with an initial contract of three years. She was the first American and the first woman conductor to be appointed the orchestra's principal conductor. She concluded her Ulster Orchestra tenure after the 2013–2014 season. She was also the first woman to conduct the orchestra of the National Theatre Mannheim.

Falletta served on the National Council on the Arts from 2008 to 2012, following her appointment by President George W. Bush. In the 1987 Swedish documentary *A Woman Is a Risky Bet: Six Orchestra Conductors*, directed by Christina Olofson, JoAnn Falletta appears conducting the Queens Philharmonic in Stravinsky's *The Rite of Spring* in rehearsal and performance.

Falletta is a strong advocate and mentor for young professional and student musicians, and she has remained a strong advocate for the role of women in music. She champions women composers through performances and recordings, she mentored women musicians and considered the development of women conductors crucial providing mentoring opportunities. She has led seminars for women conductors for the League of American Orchestras and established a unique collaboration between the Buffalo Philharmonic and the Mannes College of Music to give up-and-coming conductors professional experience with a leading American orchestra. In 2018, she served on the jury of the Malko Competition in Denmark. She has had great success working with young musicians, guest conducting orchestras at top conservatories and summer programmes such as the National Repertory Orchestra, National Orchestral Institute, Interlochen, and Brevard Music Center, and as Artistic Advisor at CIM.

Falletta has recorded over 70 albums for such labels as Naxos, featuring works by Brahms, Barber and Schubert, and women composers such as Fanny Mendelssohn, Clara Schumann, Lili Boulanger and Germaine Tailleferre, in addition to contemporary composers such as John Corigliano. She won a Grammy Award in 2019 for her work as a conductor in the category of Best Classical Compendium for the Naxos recording of 'Fuchs: Piano Concerto "Spiritualist"; Poems of Life; Glacier; Rush' with the London Symphony Orchestra. Her recording with the Buffalo Philharmonic Orchestra of John Corigliano's *Mr. Tambourine Man: Seven*

*Poems of Bob Dylan* won two Grammy Awards in 2009. Falletta has won a number of conducting awards, including the Seaver/National Endowment for the Arts Conductors Award in 2002, the Bruno Walter Conducting Award in 1982, First Prize in the Stokowski Competition in 1985, the Toscanini Award in 1986 and the Ditson Conductor's Award for the Advancement of American Music in 1998. She has also received 11 awards from the American Society of Composers, Authors and Publishers for creative programming, as well as the American Symphony Orchestra League's John S. Edwards Award. Falletta has championed the work of several contemporary American composers throughout her career, with an extensive repertoire of new works and over 100 world premières to her credit. In 2016, Falletta was elected to the American Academy of Arts and Sciences. In Virginia, she was honoured as one of the Library of Virginia's 'Virginia Women in History' and has also been named 'Norfolk Downtowner of the Year' in 2011, received a star on the Norfolk Legends of Music Walk of Fame and received the '50 for 50 Arts Inspiration Award' from the Virginia Commission for the Arts in 2018. In 2019, the classical music network, Performance Today, named Falletta Classical Woman of the Year.

In January 2018 Marin Alsop (b. 1956) was the first woman to be named chief conductor of the Vienna Radio Symphony Orchestra (Vienna RSO). She had previously conducted the orchestra in 2014 and her appointment follows an illustrious international career with numerous 'firsts'. She is also music director of the Baltimore Symphony Orchestra, as well as chief conductor of the Ravinia Festival (2020). In 2020 she was elected to the American Philosophical Society.

Alsop was born in New York City to professional musician parents. She studied violin at Juilliard's Pre-College Division and later earned her master's degree in violin at Juilliard. Following an early career as a performer and orchestral leader she won the Koussevitzky Prize as outstanding student conductor at the Tanglewood Music Centre in 1989, where she met her hero and future mentor Leonard Bernstein. Her early stellar conducting career led to becoming the first conductor ever to receive a MacArthur Fellowship commonly known as the 'Genius Grant'.

In September 2007, Alsop was appointed the 12th music director of the Baltimore Symphony Orchestra, having been named Music Director Designate for the 2006–2007 concert season. Alsop is the first woman to hold this position with a major American orchestra which caused significant controversy and resistance from the orchestra, but upon meeting her the members were satisfied to the point that her contract was repeatedly extended until February 2020, when the Baltimore Symphony announced that Alsop was to conclude her music directorship of the orchestra at the close of the 2020–2021 season and to take the title of Music Director Laureate. Alsop's initiatives with the Baltimore SO have included the 'Webumentary Film Series', a free iTunes podcast, 'Clueless About Classical', and the 'OrchKids' programme, the last directed at underprivileged Baltimore children and based on Venezuela's El Sistema programme. Alsop was elected a Fellow of the American Academy of Arts and Sciences in 2008. In August 2015, Alsop was appointed Director of Graduate Conducting at the Peabody Institute of the Johns Hopkins University, succeeding one of her mentors, Gustav Meier.

In the UK, Alsop has served as principal guest conductor with numerous orchestras in the UK as the first woman conductor and in 2003 she was voted *Gramophone* magazine's Artist of the Year. In April 2007, Alsop was one of eight conductors of British orchestras to endorse the ten-year classical music outreach manifesto, 'Building on Excellence: Orchestras for the 21st Century',[19] to increase the presence of classical music in the UK, including giving free entry to all British schoolchildren to a classical music concert. Alsop received an honorary degree of Doctor of Music from Bournemouth University on November 7, 2007. Alsop served as an Artist-in-Residence at the Southbank Centre, London, for the 2011–2012 season.

In 2012, Alsop became principal conductor of the São Paulo State Symphony Orchestra (OSESP), the first woman principal conductor of OSESP. In July 2013, OSESP granted her the title of music director and in April 2015 it extended her contract to the end of 2019. Alsop led the orchestra on a European tour, including its first appearance at the Proms in August, the first Proms appearance by any Brazilian orchestra. They returned to Europe in October 2013, with concerts in Berlin, London, Paris, Salzburg and Vienna and to the Proms in August 2016. In December 2017, OSESP announced that Alsop would stand down as its music director in December 2019, and subsequently to take the title of honorary conductor. In 2010, 2013, 2015 and 2016, Alsop conducted the Belgian National Orchestra at the Queen Elizabeth Competition. On September 7, 2013, Alsop became the first woman conductor of the Last Night of The Proms, and returned to conduct the Last Night on September 12, 2015. On September 4, 2014, at the Proms, she was awarded Honorary Membership of the Royal Philharmonic Society.

Alsop was a recipient of one of the 25th Annual Crystal Awards for 2019 at the World Economic Forum Annual Meeting in Davos, Switzerland. Since 2020 she is Artist in Residence at the University of Music and Performing Arts Vienna. Alsop was commencement speaker at Juilliard's 116th Commencement Ceremony on June 18, 2021, in Damrosch Park, where she was awarded an Honorary Doctor of Music. She recorded the works of Samuel Barber for Naxos Records and the work of Leonard Bernstein with her 2005 fully staged production of Bernstein's Candide winning an Emmy Award. She has recorded the works of Brahms, Stravinsky, Dvorak, Mahler, Copland to name a few.

Karina Canellakis (b. 1981) is an American conductor and violinist, born in New York City, of Greek and Russian background. She is the first woman conductor to be named chief conductor of the Radio Filharmonisch Orkest (RFO), and the first woman conductor to be named chief conductor of any Dutch orchestra. Canellakis grew up in a family of musicians. She studied violin at the Curtis Institute graduating in 2004. As a violinist, she played in the Chicago Symphony Orchestra and was guest leader with the Bergen Philharmonic Orchestra at the Berlin Philharmonic Orchester-Akademie where Simon Rattle encouraged her growing interest in conducting. She subsequently studied conducting at the Juilliard School from 2011 to 2013 and at the Pacific Music Festival. In 2013, she was the winner of the Taki Concordia Conducting Fellowship. From 2014 to 2016, she was the assistant conductor of the Dallas Symphony Orchestra, where she stood in as an emergency substitute for Jaap van Zweden with the Shostakovich 8th Symphony without rehearsal.

Canellakis made her European conducting début in 2015 with the Chamber Orchestra of Europe, as an emergency substitute for Nikolaus Harnoncourt. In 2016, she won the Georg Solti Conducting Award. She has also conducted the International Contemporary Ensemble notably the première of David Lang's chamber opera *The Loser* in September 2016. Her conducting début at The Proms in September 2017 was also her début with the BBC SO and in September 2017, Canellakis made her first guest-conducting appearance with the Berlin Radio Symphony Orchestra.

In March 2018, Canellakis first guest-conducted the RFO, with concerts in Utrecht and Amsterdam. On the basis of this series of concerts the RFO announced the appointment of Canellakis as its next chief conductor, the first woman conductor to hold the post. This appointment marks her first orchestral post. In December 2018, Canellakis conducted the annual Nobel Prize concert with the Royal Stockholm Philharmonic Orchestra, the first woman conductor to do so. She was subsequently announced as the Orchestra's next principal conductor. On July 19, 2019, Canellakis became the first woman conductor to conduct the First Night of The Proms, at the Royal Albert Hall, London. In April 2020, the London Philharmonic Orchestra announced the appointment of Canellakis as its new principal guest conductor, the first woman conductor to hold the post.

Carolyn Kuan (b. 1977) is a Chinese-American conductor. Carolyn Kuan's family is originally from Guangzhou, China, though Kuan was born in Taipei. When she was five years old, her older brother received a piano as a birthday gift. Kuan convinced her parents to allow her to play the piano. She sang in choirs and had an appreciation for opera, and initially wanted to be an opera singer.

Kuan's middle school had an American sister school, Northfield Mount Hermon School, where Asian students from outside of the United States could study. At age 14, she travelled by herself to the United States to attend Northfield Mount Hermon. Kuan subsequently studied economics (at her parents' request) and music, graduating cum laude from Smith College. At Smith College, she first conducted an orchestra. She continued her music education at the University of Illinois, where she earned a Master of Music degree, and at the Peabody Conservatory, where she earned a performance diploma. Her conducting mentors have included Gustav Meier.

In 2003, Kuan was the first woman to be awarded the Herbert von Karajan Conducting Fellowship, which resulted in a residency at the 2004 Salzburg Festival. She won the first Taki Concordia Fellowship. She began work as a conducting assistant to Marin Alsop at the Cabrillo Festival of Contemporary Music in 2003 and continued to work regularly at Cabrillo through 2012. In 2006, Kuan became assistant conductor of the Seattle Symphony, with a contract of two years. In 2007, the orchestra promoted her to associate conductor.

Kuna's first music directorship was her appointment in 2011 with the Hartford Symphony Orchestra as its tenth music director. She is the first woman and the first Asian-American conductor to hold the post. During a labour dispute between Hartford Symphony Orchestra musicians and management, Kuan offered to reduce her salary commensurate with the pay reductions that management requested of the musicians.

Kuan released her début album with the Naxos label in 2012, in works by various Chinese composers, featuring the New Zealand Symphony Orchestra. Her other work in contemporary music has included conducting the North American premières of Huang Ruo's Dr. Sun Yat-sen at Santa Fe Opera in 2014, and of Philip Glass and Christopher Hampton's The Trial at Opera Theatre of St. Louis in June 2017.

Jessica Bejarano (b. 1980) is the founder and conductor of the San Francisco Philharmonic. Bejarano grew up in Bell Gardens southeast of Los Angeles, California, raised by a single mother. When Bejarano's older brother Rigoberto brought his trumpet home in middle school, Bejarano would sneak into the case and play the instrument. She taught herself to play for two years before joining her middle school band. She continued in marching bands and later auditioned for the Troopers, a prestigious competitive drum and bugle corp. In return for a two-summer commitment to the corp, the Troopers would help Bejarano get a full scholarship to Casper College in Wyoming.

> I was working on my degree in music education, and I did residencies where I had to go into a middle school or high school, just to get the hands-on experience of working with children. And one of my mentors looked at me and said, "How are you going to stand in front of children, looking the way you do?" At that point, aside from having tattoos, I had 13 piercings on my face, she chuckles. I said, "it doesn't matter what I look like, I know the material, and I know how to educate, motivate, and inspire music in those kids".[20]

Bejarano transferred with a full scholarship to the University of Wyoming in Laramie to complete her BA in music education. Classical music was not a part of her childhood growing up in a low-income minority community and she did not discover classical music until her first year in college. In order to fulfil the requirements of her trumpet music scholarship, Bejarano had to play in a few ensembles. When she did, she said "It was like that music was already ingrained in my body, but it just needed to be activated".[21] Bejarano's initial degrees were in music education as she had aspired to be a music educator at a prestigious high school or college. When she decided to change her focus to conducting, she said she probably would have been dissuaded if she had realised how complicated it is for women and how much more complicated it would be for a woman with her background and ethnicity. She was told many times that she would never be a successful conductor in the United States due to her looks and background.

After graduating from the University of California, Davis, Bejarano was accepted into a doctoral programme in orchestral conducting at the University of South Carolina. She was also offered a position as assistant conductor of the Peninsula Symphony in Los Altos, California. Bejarano chose to conduct instead of pursuing her doctorate. Bejarano started her conducting career as an assistant conductor of the Peninsula Symphony. Later she became the principal conductor of the San Francisco Civic Symphony, the oldest symphony west of the Mississippi. Bejarano is also assistant conductor of Opera Parallele in San Francisco, California, and a guest conductor for the Bay Area Rainbow Symphony. She has been a guest conductor in Russia, Bulgaria, Italy, Romania, Spain, Venezuela and the Czech Republic, and with orchestras in the United States from Santa Cruz to Baltimore. She is a regular guest conductor with Camerata Antonio Soler Orchestra in San Lorenzo de el Escorial, Spain. Bejarano was the first woman to conduct L.A.'s American Youth

Symphony in 2019. In the same year Bejarano founded the San Francisco Philharmonic, an 80-piece symphony created to "be reflective of the diversity of our community, both as an orchestra and in the music that we champion".[22]

Laura Jackson (b. 2009) is an American conductor who serves as the music director and conductor of the Reno Phil. In addition to concerts with the Reno Phil, Ms. Jackson guest conducts nationally and internationally. She has performed with the symphonies of Alabama, Atlanta, Baltimore, Berkeley, Charlottesville, Detroit, Hartford, Hawaii, Orlando, the Philippines, Phoenix, Richmond, San Antonio, Toledo, Toronto, Windsor and Winnipeg in addition to concerts with the Philly POPS and L'orchestre symphonique de Bretagne in France. Jackson served as the first woman assistant conductor of the Atlanta Symphony Orchestra from 2004 to 2007. Prior to her appointment in Atlanta, she studied conducting at the University of Michigan and spent summers as the Seiji Ozawa Conducting Fellow at the Boston Symphony Orchestra's Tanglewood Music Center in 2002 and 2003.

Jackson spent her early childhood in Virginia and Pennsylvania before moving at age 11 to Plattsburgh, NY, where she grew up waterskiing, swimming and sailing on Lake Champlain. She fell in love with the violin in public school, later attending the North Carolina School for the Arts to finish high school. She pursued an undergraduate degree at Indiana University where she studied both violin and conducting before moving to Boston in 1990 to freelance as a violinist and teach at Phillips Exeter Academy in New Hampshire. Jackson recorded Michael Daugherty's Time Cycle on Naxos with the Bournemouth Symphony in partnership with Marin Alsop and served as the first American to guest conduct the Algerian National Orchestra in 2013.

### Australian women on the podium

Nicolette Ella Fraillon AM (b. 1960) is an Australian conductor, who was chief conductor of The Australian Ballet from 2003 until 2022 and the only woman conductor of a ballet company in the world as of 2016.[23] Fraillon grew up in a musical household in Melbourne, a child of immigrant parents of Huguenot-Sicilian and Austrian Jewish origins. She started violin and piano studies as a child and performed with the Victorian Youth Symphony Orchestra and the Melbourne Youth Orchestra.

Fraillon studied conducting at the Hochschule für Musik in Vienna, Austria, from 1984, and later in Hanover, Germany. She moved to the Netherlands in 1990 and her professional conducting début was with the Nederlands Dans Theater, when she deputised for another conductor who had fallen ill. Later she was appointed music director and chief conductor of the Dutch National Ballet.

In 1995 she was engaged by the Tasmanian Symphony Orchestra, becoming the first Australian woman to conduct an Australian symphony orchestra. She later conducted the West Australian Symphony Orchestra. In 1998 she commenced at the Australian Opera and Ballet Orchestra. In 2003 she was appointed chief conductor of The Australian Ballet. She was their first woman conductor in 2016. In November 2021, Fraillon announced that she would leave that position in 2022. Her views on sexism in the classical music industry were reported in an interview with Australia's national broadcaster ABC Radio national where she stated that "I've had managers of orchestras say to me, 'We love your work, but we can't employ you because you're a woman', as though that was an explanation in itself".[24]

In Australia, of the eight major state orchestras two have appointed chief women conductors: Simone Young AM (b. 1961), chief conductor of the Sydney Symphony Orchestra (SSO), and Jessica Cottis (b. 1979), artistic director and chief conductor of the Canberra Symphony Orchestra.

Simone Young is a pioneer as a woman conductor and represents a number of notable firsts for women in conducting. She was the first woman to conduct the Vienna Philharmonic. She made her first appearance at the Metropolitan Opera while she was five months pregnant and conducted at the Vienna State Opera one month prior to giving birth in 1997.

Of Irish and Croatian descent, Young studied composition, piano and conducting at the Sydney Conservatorium of Music. In 1983, Young commenced working at Opera Australia as a répétiteur under various conductors, including Charles Mackerras, Richard Bonynge, Carlo Felice Cillario and Stuart Challender. She started her operatic conducting career at the Sydney Opera House in 1985 and in 1986 she was the first woman and youngest person to be appointed a resident conductor with Opera Australia. She received an Australia Council grant to study overseas and was named Young Australian of the Year. In her early years, she was assistant to James Conlon, and Kapellmeister, at the Cologne Opera, and assistant to Daniel Barenboim at the Berlin State Opera and the Bayreuth Festival. Young was the first woman conductor at the Vienna State Opera in 1993. From 1998 until 2002, Young was principal conductor of the Bergen Philharmonic Orchestra in Norway. She conducted the SSO when they performed Elena Kats-Chernin's 'Deep Sea Dreaming' at the 2000 Summer Olympics opening ceremony in Sydney. From 2001 to 2003, Young was chief conductor of Opera Australia in Sydney. Her contract was not renewed after 2003, with one given reason being the excessive expense of her programming ideas.[25]

Having previously made her first conducting appearance at the Hamburg State Opera in 1996 in May 2003 she returned to Hamburg to be named both chief executive of the Hamburg State Opera and chief conductor of the Philharmoniker Hamburg, posts which she assumed in 2005. In 2006, she became Professor of Music and Theatre at the University of Hamburg. It was in November 2005 that she became the first woman conductor to conduct the Vienna Philharmonic. Critics of the magazine *Opernwelt* selected her in October 2006 as the Dirigentin des Jahres (Conductor of the Year). Alongside this in August 2008, Young appeared as part of the judging panel in the reality TV talent show-themed programme Maestro on BBC Two. In December 2011, it was announced that Young would conclude her tenures with both the Hamburg State Opera and the Hamburg Philharmonic after the 2014/2015 season. In December 2012, she was voted *Limelight* magazine's Music Personality of the Year.

Her discography includes the complete symphonies of Anton Bruckner and the complete Ring Cycle of Richard Wagner, where she was the first woman conductor to have recorded either of these cycles. She has also recorded the complete cycle of Brahms' symphonies.

In 2013, in commemoration of the bicentenaries for Richard Wagner and for Giuseppe Verdi, Young conducted the entire 'Bayreuth canon' of ten Wagner operas in Hamburg, along with three rarely performed Giuseppe Verdi operas. In March 2016, Young was appointed a member of the board of the European Academy of Music Theatre. Young had first guest-conducted the SSO in 1996. In December 2019, the SSO announced the appointment of Young as its next chief conductor, effective in 2022, with an initial contract of three years. Young is the first woman conductor to be named chief conductor of the SSO.

Young has received honorary doctorates from the Universities of New South Wales, Sydney and Melbourne. She has been appointed a Chevalier des Arts et des Lettres of France. Young was inducted into the Victorian Honour Roll of Women in 2001. On January 26, 2004, in the Australia Day Honours, Young was named a Member of the Order of Australia (AM). She received the Sir Bernard Heinze Memorial Award in 2011. In 2021 Young was named the Advance Awards Global Icon.

Jessica Cottis (b. 1979) is an Australian-British woman conductor who is currently artistic director and chief conductor of the Canberra Symphony Orchestra in Australia. As the daughter of an Australian Defence Attaché and Royal Australian Air Force officer the family lived around the world, including the United States, England and New Zealand. In school she played trumpet, French horn and piano and went on to study organ, piano and musicology at the Australian National University, graduating with first-class honours. With support from the Royal Philharmonic Society and Australian Music Foundation, she continued her studies as an organist in Paris with Marie-Claire Alain. She was a prize winner in the 2000 Australian Young Performers' Competition and made her European début as an organist at London's Westminster Cathedral the following year. A wrist injury halted her playing career. Cottis read law at the University of London and in 2006 she began conducting studies at the Royal Academy of Music where her teachers included Colin Metters and Sir Colin Davis. She also spent time at the Accademia Musicale Chigiana in Siena. She graduated from the Royal Academy of Music in 2009, with distinction, and was appointed RAM Manson Fellow in Composition.

Upon graduation from the Royal Academy of Music, in September 2009, she became the first Postgraduate Conducting Fellow of the Royal Conservatoire of Scotland and was appointed assistant conductor with the BBC Scottish Symphony Orchestra. In 2012 the SSO appointed Cottis its assistant conductor, where she worked closely with the orchestra's then-chief conductor, Vladimir Ashkenazy. In 2014, Cottis was appointed principal conductor of the Glasgow New Music Expedition, where she curated notable projects alongside visual artists and film-makers. During her time at the Royal Academy of Music, Cottis founded a new opera company, Bloomsbury Opera. Cottis has also commissioned new operas, including Anna Meredith's *Tarantula in Petrol Blue* and *The Mirror* by Martin Georgiev and has conducted the premières of new operas including Na'ama Zisser's *Mamzer Bastard* for the Royal Opera House. In 2014, Cottis became a visiting professor in conducting at the Royal Conservatoire of Scotland. She is a regular contributor to BBC radio and television programmes. She has also served as chair of the Tait Memorial Trust Music Board. She was made an associate of the Royal Academy of Music in 2015.

Cottis conducted her first commercial recording, *Gallipoli Symphony*, in 2015, a tri-nation project of cultural diplomacy between Australia, New Zealand and Turkey, for ABC Classics. In 2021, Cottis became artistic director and chief conductor of the Canberra Symphony Orchestra, the first woman conductor to hold the post.

## Canadian women on the podium

Amongst a list of more than 20 Canadian orchestras three have appointed women music directors: Elisa Citterio (b. 1975), Gemma New (b. 1986) and Holly Mathieson (b. 1981). Elisa Citterio joined Tafelmusik as Music Director in 2017. She moved to Toronto from her native Italy, where she divided her artistic life between orchestral work and an intense schedule as a chamber musician. In 2000, Elisa was selected as concertmaster and soloist with the orchestra of the Accademia del Teatro alla Scala di Milano, where she received intensive professional training in orchestral and chamber music repertoire, as well as violin technique. Soon after graduating, she began studying baroque violin, taking part in masterclasses with Enrico Onofri and studying with Chiara Banchini at the Schola Cantorum Basilensis, and with Luigi Mangiocavallo in Rome. Elisa played with Stefano Montanari in Estravagante Ensemble, and from 2014 to 2016 she worked alongside Stefano as co-chair of the baroque violin studies programme at the Civica Scuola di Musica Claudio Abbado in Milan. She has recorded and toured, often as leader or concertmaster, with such ensembles as Dolce & Tempesta, Europa Galante, Accademia Bizantina, Accordone, Zefiro, la Venexiana, La Risonanza, Ensemble 415, Concerto Italiano, Orquestra del Monsalvat, Il Giardino Armonico, Orchestra Academia 1750 and Balthasar-Neumann Choir & Ensemble. From 2004 to 2017 she was a member of the Orchestra del Teatro della Scala di Milano. Elisa Citterio's discography includes more than 35 recordings. Eighteen months into her position at Tafelmusik, she was awarded 2019 Leonardo Award for Arts, Science and Culture by the Italian Chamber of Commerce for her contribution to the cultural and intellectual life of Canada. North American orchestras have taken notice with invitations as guest director with the Seattle Symphony, and Québec's Les Violons du Roy.

Gemma New who is Musical Director of the Hamilton Philharmonic Orchestra is a New Zealand-born conductor. In May 2015, the Hamilton Philharmonic Orchestra appointed New as its next music director, the first woman conductor ever to hold the post and her first music directorship. Her contract has been extended twice until 2024. New studied violin and piano from an early age and conducted the Christchurch Youth Orchestra. She undertook undergraduate study at the University of Canterbury and graduate studies in Baltimore at Maryland's Peabody Institute. After founding and directing the Maryland music collective Lunar Ensemble she became assistant conductor at the New Jersey Symphony Orchestra from 2011 to 2016 and in 2014, she was Dudamel Conducting Fellow with the Los Angeles Philharmonic Orchestra under Kurt Masur.

In June 2016, she was appointed resident conductor of the SLSO and music director of the St. Louis Symphony Youth Orchestra. In September 2018, she was the first woman conductor ever to direct the opening concerts of the SLSO's 2018–2019 season. New stood down from her St. Louis posts at the close of the 2019–2020 season. In October 2018, the Dallas Symphony Orchestra announced the appointment of New as its next principal guest conductor, the first woman conductor to hold the title, effective with the 2019–2020 season. She was reappointed to this position for the 2022–2023 season. In March 2021, the Solti Foundation United States announced New as the 12th recipient of The Sir Georg Solti Conducting Award.

Holly Mathieson is the first woman conductor to be named music director of Symphony Nova Scotia. This appointment marks her first orchestral music directorship. Also born in New Zealand, Mathieson started out as a dancer, but due to injury and illness she turned to music study. She held several significant early-career positions, including the Leverhulme Fellowship in Conducting at the Royal Conservatoire of Scotland, Assistant Conductor of both the Royal Scottish National Orchestra and BBC Scottish Symphony Orchestras, and Resident Conductor within the National Youth Orchestras of Scotland. Prior to that, she was chosen as one of only four young conductors from around the world to participate in the Interaktion Dirigentenwerkstatt des Kritischen Orchesters with players from the Berlin Philharmonic and other top-tiered German orchestras. She enjoyed a critically acclaimed London début with Opera Holland Park as part of the 2015 Christine Collins Young Artist Programme and was a conducting fellow at Dartington International Summer School and Taki Alsop Conducting Fellowship Prizewinner in 2013. She holds a PhD in Music Iconography, during which she was awarded the global Sylff Fellowship, and in 2016 Zonta New Zealand named her one of New Zealand's Top 50 Women of Achievement. In 2018, Mathieson first guest-conducted Symphony Nova Scotia, as one of two finalist candidates for the post of music director with the orchestra. She returned in November 2019 for a further guest-conducting engagement. In December 2019, Symphony Nova Scotia announced the appointment of Mathieson as its next music director, effective January 2020, with an initial contract of three years. In 2021 she conducted the New Zealand Symphony Orchestra for the first time in concerts with the metal band Alien Weaponry.

In 2019 Mathieson launched her own blog and podcast, Scordatura, which explores ideas around digital developments, musical culture, advocacy and arts governance. Here she expresses views on conducting and collaborative musical leadership that she is exploring through the Nevis Ensemble which she formed with her husband as co-artistic director.[26]

## Women taking the podium in Asia

Women conductors are emerging in China and Hong Kong-born Synthia Ko (b. 1973) was appointed Music Director and Chief Conductor Guangxi Symphony Orchestra in 2010. She studied conducting in the United States and Europe and in 2008 Ko took part in the Aberdeen International Youth Festival and Festival of British Youth Orchestras where her concerts all had tremendous success. Under Ko the Guangxi Symphony Orchestra has toured the National Centre for the Performing Arts in Beijing, the Shanghai Expo 2010, Guangzhou, Xiamen, Vietnam, Singapore and Taiwan. She collaborated with the Slovak State Philharmonic Orchestra and was guest conductor of the Kunming Symphony Orchestra in China and the Hong Kong Children Symphony Orchestra. Apart from her professional work, Ko is also engaged in strongly promoting classical music in the community. Not only is she a guest speaker for the Hong Kong Philharmonic Orchestra and presenter for RTHK Radio 4, but she is also the artistic director and chief conductor of one of Asia's top youth orchestras, the Metropolitan Youth Orchestra of Hong Kong.

Shi-Yeon Sung (b. 1975) is the only South Korean woman to hold a classical conductor post in South Korea. In 2006, she became the first woman to win first prize in the Sir Georg Solti International Conductors' Competition. In 2007, she won second prize in Bamberg's Gustav Mahler Conducting Competition (no first prize was given that year). That year, she became the first woman assistant conductor of the Boston Symphony Orchestra, a post she held through 2010. Among the orchestras she has conducted are the Los Angeles Philharmonic, Royal Stockholm Philharmonic Orchestra, Swedish Radio Symphony Orchestra and the US National Symphony Orchestra. She was the associate conductor of the Seoul Philharmonic from 2009 to 2013. She has served as the artistic director and chief conductor of Gyeonggi Philharmonic Orchestra since January 2014.

Han-Na Chang (Chang Han-Na; b. 1982) is a South Korean conductor and cellist. Chang began studying piano and cello at an early age. In 1993, her family moved to the United States, where she was enrolled in the pre-college division of the Juilliard School. In addition to studies at Juilliard, Chang read philosophy at Harvard University. In 1993, she attended Mischa Maisky's masterclasses in Siena, Italy, and continued to study with him privately. In 1994, she competed in the Fifth Rostropovich International Cello Competition and was awarded both the First Prize and the Contemporary Music Prize. Chang studied privately with Mstislav Rostropovich and in 1995, she made her début recording of Tchaikovsky's Variations on a Rococo Theme and Saint-Saëns' Cello Concerto No. 1 with Rostropovich conducting the London Symphony Orchestra.

Chang subsequently developed an interest in conducting and studied conducting with James DePreist. She made her professional conducting début in Korea in 2007. In 2009, she founded the Absolute Classic Festival, based in Gyeonggi Province, Korea, with a focus on young musicians and served as its artistic director. Chang made her UK conducting début with the Philharmonia Orchestra in January 2012 and conducted the Royal Liverpool Philharmonic for the first time in February 2012. By this time she shifted her musical focus to conducting, away from cello performances.

Following a guest-conducting engagement with the Qatar Philharmonic Orchestra 2012 the orchestra named her its next music director. She led the orchestra in its first-ever appearance at The Proms on September 7, 2014. The next day Chang resigned the music directorship of the orchestra, with immediate effect, citing "persistent administrative difficulties and irreconcilable artistic differences with the management".[27] Chang was then appointed principal guest conductor of the Trondheim Symphony Orchestra as of the 2013–2014 season and in March 2016, the orchestra announced the appointment of Chang as its next chief conductor. She is the first woman conductor to be named chief conductor of the Trondheim Symphony Orchestra.

## South American women taking the podium

Cuban-born Tania León (b. 1943) also enjoys an international conducting career alongside her high-profile composing career and music advisor to major arts organisations. She earned her musical qualifications in Cuba and settled in New York in 1967 to continue her studies at New York University. She became founding member and musical director of Arthur Mitchell's Dance Theatre of Harlem for which she composed a series of ballet compositions. She co-founded the Sonidos de las Americas Festivals and served as Latin American Music Advisor to the New York Philharmonic and American Composers orchestra. She has been a guest conductor with the Beethovenhalle Orchestra, Bonn, the Gewandhausorchester, Leipzig, the Santa Cecilia Orchestra, Rome, the National Symphony Orchestra of South Africa, Johannesburg, the Netherlands Wind Ensemble, the Netherlands, and the New York Philharmonic, among others.

Odaline de la Martinez (b. 1949) is a Cuban-American composer and conductor, currently residing in the UK. She is the artistic director of Lontano, a London-based contemporary music ensemble which she co-founded in 1976 with New Zealand flautist Ingrid Culliford. Martinez was the first woman to conduct at the BBC Promenade Concerts (the Proms) in 1984. As well as frequent appearances as a guest conductor with leading orchestras throughout Great Britain, including all the BBC orchestras, she has conducted several leading ensembles around the world, including the Ensemble 2e2m in Paris, the New Zealand Symphony Orchestra, the Australian Youth Orchestra, the OFUNAM and the Camerata of the Americas in Mexico and the Vancouver Chamber Orchestra. She is also known as a broadcaster for BBC Radio and Television and has recorded extensively for several labels. After the Bay of Pigs Invasion in 1961 her parents decided to send her and her sister to live with their aunt and uncle in the United States. She enrolled at Tulane University, New Orleans, where she studied both music and mathematics, graduating summa cum laude in 1972 and receiving several awards upon graduation – a Marshall Scholarship from the British government, and a Danforth and Watson Fellowships – which allowed her to continue her studies at the Royal Academy of Music where she founded Lontano Ensemble in 1976 with Ingrid Culliford. With Lontano she conducted the première of Judith Weir's The Consolations of Scholarship at the University of Durham in 1985.

Martinez received her MMus in composition from the University of Surrey in 1977. This was followed by composer awards from the American National Endowment for the Arts (1979) and a Guggenheim Fellowship (1980), supporting the composition of her first opera *Sister Aimee: An American Legend* (1984). In 1987 Marinez was awarded the Villa Lobos medal from the Brazilian government for her championing of the music of Heitor Villa Lobos and other Brazilian composers. Her continuing commitment to showcase the music of Latin America for UK and European audiences led her in 1989 to co-direct with Eduardo Mata VIVA! – a festival of Latin-American music – at London's South Bank Centre. In 1990 she was made a fellow of the Royal Academy of Music and in 1992 she founded LORELT (Lontano Records Limited) with the intent of promoting the work of living composers, women and Latin American composers from all periods. The label has since released over 30 CDs to critical acclaim.

### Podium leadership styles

On the matter of transformational leadership, women conductors are divided. Some consider that they are more collegial in their approach while others state that this is impossible within the orchestral construct.

Simone Young expressed her views to the author on these theories about women being more consultative and empathetic in their approach to their followers. She stated that she had a real problem with this because it is not possible in the role of a conductor which is a 19th-century construct based upon a vertical hierarchy with conductor at the top of that hierarchy. Her response was that gender did not come into the discussion of the conductor's leadership role:

> I have real problems with this because I see the role of the conductor is yes the role of leadership, but I see no delineation between the role

of male and woman work in the area. I define myself as a conductor certainly not as a woman conductor. I happen to be a woman who conducts but I am a conductor and there is nothing inherently gender oriented in my work.[28]

However, in an interview she conducted in March 2016 for the Sydney Morning Herald she did acknowledge that leadership has become more horizontal in orchestras stating: "Leadership in all circles has become more horizontal and orchestras have more say these days".[29]

This opinion on the difference between male and woman conductors is echoed by Julia Jones who took to the podium at the Royal Opera House in January 2010 to conduct Mozart's 'Così fan tutte' in an interview with *The Independent* "How come we're even having this conversation?" Jones protested. "It's 2010! Women conductors should not be the issue – it's the musicianship that counts, it's what you can bring to the work that is important, and for that gender is completely unimportant". This was Jones' first performance in her home country at the age of 48 following a traineeship in Germany during her 20s and working overseas since then. Jones says that she was actively discouraged from her aims by her professor at music college: "He was worried that I wouldn't get a job". But she stayed determined and won through. "I've never encountered any issues or any prejudice from musicians because I'm a woman", she insists. "On the contrary, I was elected to my job by the musicians of the orchestra. What other proof do we need?".[30]

On the issues of mentorship, specialist women's training, quotas, championing women's music and childcare, Young is vehement that these were retrograde steps:

> I see my responsibility to be the best I possibly can in my profession and that in itself will champion the cause for younger women because it gives them a role model. I didn't have any role models who were women. My role model was fabulous musicians. I think that is probably a positive. I didn't try to be like anybody else, I just tried to be the best musician I could be. So gender did not come into it.[31]

Regarding her role she said:

> There was another woman who said very interesting things that I resonated with which was that women who are pioneers in any industry, it is not their job then to then reach down as assist the next lot. It is simply their job to be so good at what they do that they have opened the door. They then don't have to stand there to hold it for the

next lot, they have to open the door by proving the door shouldn't be there in the first place.[32]

Sinclair refers to the added responsibility of the associated burden of becoming a role model for other women when taking on leadership positions. Women who have been strong role models for other women become exhausted by the extra visibility and workload. Leading women are not only expected to do their job, but to do it in a way which supports and empowers other women.[33]

In another contrasting context, Marin Alsop is keen on mentoring women having mentored US composer Anne Clyne and commissioned 'Masquerade' for Alsop's appearance at the last night of the BBC Proms in 2013. She was the first woman conductor of the Proms in 2013 and at her closing speech for the 2015 Proms, she said:

When I was last with you for this amazing and wonderful celebration, I shared how proud I was to be the first woman to conduct the LNOP. I have to share though that I am even more proud to be the first second woman – or maybe it's the second first woman. What excites me is that now we're going to see the third, the fifth, the tenth, the one hundredth woman to follow me because we have to work towards a more just and equal playing field for women. I think it's clear that inequality is one of the greatest challenges facing us today – whether it's gender, racial, economic or ethnic inequality.[34]

While conductors such as Alsop, Worby and Bond have expressed that their approach is more team oriented, both Young and Jones claim that gender is completely unimportant in the orchestral hierarchical construct.

### Conclusion

As more women earn positions as leaders of major classical orchestras and opera companies the possibilities for women to follow are revealed. The women discussed in this chapter are achieving stellar heights in some of the finest international musical institutions which are renowned for the dominance of male leaders. Women are still very much in the minority in these roles and some have overcome considerable obstacles to achieving success in this field, but it is not a complete rarity to see a woman conducting a major orchestra today. Some are of the view that women are more collaborative in their approach to leadership whilst others argue that it is not possible within the context of the orchestral hierarchy. Some consider mentoring other women significant and redressing the gender imbalance in the profession while others consider providing the role model allows women musicians to identify the possibilities for themselves.

## Notes

1 Bartleet, B. has produced a number of publications on this topic including:

(2002). Re-embodying the 'Gendered Podium'. *Context: Journal of Music Research*. 49–57;

(2005). 18 Reflections on females conducing. *Aesthetics and Experience in Music Performance*, 235–242;

(2006). Conducting motherhood: The personal and professional experiences of women orchestral conductors. *Outskirts: Feminisms along the edge*, 15;

(2008a). Women conductors on the orchestral podium: Pedagogical and professional implications. *College Music Symposium*, 48, 31–51. College Music Society.

(2008b). You're a woman and our orchestra just won't have you: The politics of otherness in the conducting profession. *Hecate*, 34, 6–23.

2 Lazarou, L. (2017). *Women Conductors: A Qualitative Study of Gender, Family, 'the Body' and Discrimination*. Durham University.

3 Quote found in Goldin, C. & Rouse, C. (2000). Orchestrating impartiality: The impact of 'blind' auditions on woman musicians. *American Economic Review*. 90(4), 719.

4 Hewett, I. (2017, 27 November). Mariss Jansons: Women on the podium are not my cup of tea. *The Telegraph*.

5 Sicherman, B. & Green, C. (1980). *Notable American women: The Modern Period: A Biographical Dictionary*. Belknap Press of Harvard University Press, 416.

6 Broadbent, M., & Broadbent, T. (n.d.) Leginska: Forgotten Genius of Music. The Story of a Great Musician. Leginska.org. Leginska.org.

7 Griffin, M. (n.d.). Ethel Leginska: Pianist, Feminist, Conductor Extraordinaire, and Composer. Sail.cnu.edu. CNU.

8 Ibid.

9 *Minneapolis Journal*. (1915, 11 October) as cited by Griffin Ibid. 11.

10 Rosenstiel, L. (1982). *Nadia Boulanger*. W.W. Norton, 292.

11 Ibid. 293.

12 Potter, C. (2001). *Boulanger, (Juliette) Nadia*. Grove Music Online.

13 Macleod, B. (2000). *Women Performing Music: The Emergence of American Women as Classical Instrumentalists and Conductors*. McFarland, 124–139.

14 Neuls-Bates, C. (1987). Women's orchestra's in the United States 1925–1945. In *Women Making Music*. Ed. Bowers, J. & Tick, J. University of Illinois Press, 253.

15 *Antonia: A Portrait of the Woman* (1974) director Jill Godmilow, with help from Brico's former student Judy Collins.

16 *De Dirigent* (The Conductor) director Maria Peters, starring Christanne de Bruijn as Antonia Brico released in 2018. Worthey, D. & Wallace, M. (2020). *In One Ear and Out The Other: Antonia Brico And Her Amazingly Musical Life*. Penny Candy Books.

17 Frazes Hill, C. (2022). *Margaret Hillis: Unsung Pioneer*. Carroll Lee Gonzo.

18 Detlef Krenge (2017, 24 October). 'Neue Generalmusikdirektorin in Nürnberg–Joana Mallwitz: "Ich fühle mich hier wirklich wohl"'. BR-Klassik.
19 Building on Excellence: Orchestras for the 21st century published by the eight British publicly funded orchestras. See also Higgins, C. (2007, 26 April). Orchestras urge free concerts for children. *The Guardian.*
20 Kallis, J. (2020, 1 February). Conductor Jessica Bejarano makes her own magic happen. *San Francisco Classical Voice.*
21 Meline, G. (2018, 13 August). *Bay Brilliant: Jessica Bejarano.* KQED.
22 Friedman, R. (2020, 21 January). Latin lesbian conductor takes podium. *The Bay Area Reporter/B.A.R. Inc.*
23 Carter, J.S. (2016, 13 June). Australian Ballet music director calls out sexism in classical music world. ABC Radio National.
24 Ibid.
25 Strickland, K. (2005, 27 May). OA turns corner on debt. *The Australian.*
26 Mathieson, H. scordiatura.io
27 Ashley, T. (2014, 9 September). Prom 67: Qatar Philharmonic/Chang/Matsuev review – a full-throttle performance. *The Guardian.*
28 Young, S. (2017, 2 July). Rusak Interview with Simone Young.
29 Wheatley, J. (2017, 25 March). Conductor Simone Young: 'You're not gesturing with the music, you're instigating it'. *Sydney Morning Herald.*
30 Duchen, J. (2010, 22 January). A glass ceiling for women in the orchestra pit. *The Independent.*
31 Young. Ibid.
32 Young. Ibid.
33 Sinclair, A. (1998). *Doing Leadership Differently: Gender, Power, and Sexuality in a Changing Business Culture.* Melbourne University Press, 127.
34 Alsop, M. (2015). 'Marin Alsop's Last Night of the Proms speech'. In *Proms Last Night Celebrations.* Ed. www.bbc.co.uk/programmes/p032nw0w/player. UK: BBC www.bbc.co.uk/programmes/p032nw0w/player

# 4

# WOMEN IN CLASSICAL INSTRUMENTAL AND VOCAL MUSIC PERFORMANCE

## Introduction

Women have performed music throughout history, but professional roles such as orchestral musicians have been limited. As women gained more independence into the 19th century, women were still not permitted to play in orchestras alongside men. They did appear on harp or as soloists on violin, voice or piano, but their appropriateness on stage was questioned for years. Women were allowed to play piano as it represented the domestic sphere and often women were encouraged to develop it as an accomplishment with the aim of attracting a suitable husband. It was also a private outlet for their pent-up emotions. The all women orchestras of the late 19th and early 20th centuries were a new phenomenon resulting from the exclusion of women in traditional orchestras. Women performing alongside men in professional orchestras has been a slow process since the mid-20th century and the Vienna Philharmonic famously banned women until 1997. To redress the imbalance of women in orchestras, blind auditions were held in the 1970s–1980s which has caused an increase in the number of women in professional orchestras in the late 20th century.

It is well known that in 1970 about 10% of orchestra members were women; by the mid-1990s it was 30% due to the introduction of so-called blind auditions. Orchestra applicants auditioned behind a curtain so the people judging competence could no longer filter their hiring decisions through a gender lens. Goldin and Rouse found that this practice increased the probability of women advancing from preliminary selection rounds by 50% and concluded that blind audition did increase the number of women

DOI: 10.4324/9781003183631-5

undertaking orchestral position by at least 30%.[1] Sergeant and Himonides argue that this only applies where orchestras fully adopt the blind audition process and the trials that often follow up the blind audition process do not conceal the sex of the applicant which defeats the original purpose.[2] Similarly, Phelps argues that in spite of blind auditions in US orchestras gender constructions surrounding instrument choices for women exclude them from the higher-paying positions in the orchestra.[3] This is endorsed by the aforementioned study by Sergeant and Himonides who provide convincing data on female instrument choices and section leadership that supports the argument that there is overall higher representation of men in the higher-paying orchestral positions.[4]

## Women as instrumental performers

Economic and social changes of the 19th and 20th centuries opened possibilities for women musicians. The various feminist movements emerging from the late 19th century sought access to musical education and demanded admission to orchestras, and competitions such as Prix de Rome. Women began to receive musical posts, awards and high-level musical qualifications from Conservatoires. However, not even by the end of the 20th century were women taking equal part in musical leadership.

The secularisation of the conservatories in the late 19th century led to the provision of musical training but women generally had limited subject choices such as the Paris Conservatoire originally offering classes in singing and keyboard, or only offering shorter courses for women as was the case at the Leipzig Conservatory. Women were trained to exercise their musical talents in the private sphere and not the public sphere which was the domain of men. Only later in the century did the barriers for women's musical education begin to fall allowing women to study theory, harmony or composition. American composer Clara Rogers was barred from studying composition at Leipzig in the 1860s, but in 1877 Ethel Smyth was able to enrol. Jeannette Thurber founded the National Conservatory in New York (1885), admitting black as well as white students and letting her female student violinists play in the orchestra. By the early 1900s, women began to outnumber men in musical training much to the consternation of men. Women quickly dominated music teaching as a profession in the course of the 20th century, but rarely in Conservatoires until the middle of the century where all senior positions remained in the hands of men. Rather than taking roles such as composer, conductor or professors, women's options were as accomplished ladies at home, private studio teachers or performers. Some women sustained careers in their home studios such as Nadia Boulanger.

## Women in orchestral performance

Despite these new music educational advances that women were making they were still finding themselves excluded from professional orchestras, conducting posts, positions in conservatoires and the church. In response women formed all-women chamber groups and 'lady orchestras' to provide employment opportunities for women. This initiative took off in Europe and the United States. In 1887, violinist Marie Soldat-Roeger (1863–1955) was one of the first to form the all-female Soldat Quartet in Berlin. Dutch composer Elisabeth Kuyper (1887–1953) founded four women's symphony orchestras first in Europe, then in the United States. Women's orchestras flourished in the United States in the 1920s through to the 1940s and in 1937 the Cuban composer Ernestina Lecuona Casado (1882–1951) founded a Cuban women's orchestra that toured Cuba, Mexico, Chile and Argentina. These orchestras petered out in the 1950s, but a revival occurred in the 1980s with the aim of championing women's music such as the Women's PO (formerly Bay Area Women's PO; founded 1982), directed for many years by JoAnn Falletta and now by Apo Hsu, and the European Women's Orchestra, founded by Odaline de la Martinez in 1990.

As in other industries, World War II accelerated change for women due to men being sent to battle. More women joined mainstream orchestras, but upon the return of men from the frontline women were replaced by their male counterparts. Women still lobbied for inclusion and the Civil Rights Act of 1964, and laws dealing with gender discrimination in other English-speaking countries resulted in more opportunities for women musicians. The introduction of blind auditions had some effect on the gender balance, but the continent was still resistant to females in orchestras. It was not until 1982 that the Berlin Philharmonic Orchestra employed its first female player and in 1997 protests against the Vienna Philharmonic led to admission of women to its membership. It was only in 1998 that the Czech Philharmonic removed its men-only policy.

## Women singers

The survey of women's achievements as performers outlined in Chapter 1 indicates that women have participated in musical life from early times. Options for women musicians did improve in the 19th century to perform as soloists, but mostly as singers and pianists. By the 19th century, women singers represented the liberation of women's power and authority through the voice. Women had great success as singers with leading artists Angelica Catalani (1780–1849), Henriette Sontag (1806–1854), Maria

Malibran (1908–1836), Pauline Viardot (1821–1910), Jenny Lind (1820–1887), Dame Nellie Melba (1861–1931) and Mary Garden (1874–1967).

Angelica Catalani was from an impoverished background and joined the convent of Santal Lucia at Gubbio, near Rome when she was 12 years old. Her soprano voice was recognised for its power and range and she became a famous and highly paid bravura opera singer. Her training at the convent left her with some poor vocalisation habits, but her intonation and expressive style were highly suited to bravura singing. Upon leaving the convent she commenced her professional career in Venice at the age of 16. Her success took her to Milan, Florence, Trieste, Rome and Naples. She was invited by the Prince Regent of Portugal to sing at the Italian opera.[5] There she met her husband whom she married in 1804, but his role in the marriage appears to have been securing the highest possible fees for her performances and spending a large portion of them on gambling. Together they went to Madrid and then to Paris where her concerts earned vast sums of money and enormous recognition. In 1807, she was engaged by King's Theatre in the Haymarket, London, to perform in a series of operas for which she was handsomely paid. However, her riches were quickly dissipated by her servants and husband. In 1813 following her failed attempt to buy the theatre in order to become the sole proprietor, manager and singer she quit the King's Theatre and left the stage to only perform in Paris. There she took over the management of the Théâtre Italien, but left Paris when Napoleon returned in 1815 and toured Hamburg, the Netherlands, Denmark and Sweden. She later returned to Paris to manage the Théâtre Italien, but her cost-cutting efforts resulted in the operas artistic values so poorly represented that she left the company to her managers. In 1816, she resumed touring the continent and England until 1828 when she retired from singing in public due to her voice losing some of its quality. She moved to a villa in Florence where she established a singing school for young girls and later died of cholera in Paris.[6]

Henriette Sontag was one of the most successful sopranos in the first half of the 19th century. She was accepted at an early age into the Prague Conservatory to study voice and piano. She moved to Vienna in 1822 where she performed in German and Italian operas. She triumphed in Weber's Euryanthe in 1823 and in 1824 she sang in the premières of Beethoven's Ninth Symphony and Missa Solemnis. Following a brief season in Leipzig in 1825 she went to Paris to début at the Théâtre Italien in 1826. She also maintained her German performances and made her début in England at the King's Theatre in 1828. She renounced the stage when she married diplomat Count Carlo Rossi, but performed privately at the cities where he was posted. Financial difficulties resulting from the loss of Rossi's position following the abdication of the King of Sardinia saw Henriette return to the stage. She toured England, Paris, Germany and Mexico and following her last appearance as Lucrezia Borga on June 11, 1854, she took ill and died of cholera.

Maria Malibran was a Spanish contralto and soprano with a remarkably wide tessitura and was known for her dramatic intensity and stormy personality. Her parents were also famous singers and her father was an influential composer and teacher. From a young age she performed alongside her father and at the age of 17 she sang in the choir at King's Theatre London. She performed in her family's troupe in New York where Italian opera was performed for the first time. Her vocal range and emotional intensity on stage made her a popular choice for composers in particular Rossini. She premièred many works in the leading opera houses in Europe and England. Following a fall from a horse, she died at the age of 28. Her legacy includes patroness of the Teatro Malibran in Venice where her cameo hangs above the stage, and the Maria Malibrand Fund in the Library of the Royal Conservatory of Brussels which is a collection of scores, documents and objects from the diva.

Pauline Viardot was the younger sister of Maria Malibran and studied singing and piano from a young age with her father. She travelled with her family on their musical tours in Europe, the United States, Mexico and England. By the age of six she was fluent in a number of languages and was an outstanding pianist. She had lessons with Franz Liszt, Anton Reicha and Hector Berlioz. Her mother forced her to focus on her singing, but her début was on piano and she regretted not being able to focus on piano. She made her operatic début in 1839 in London and was engaged at the Théâtre Italien in Paris.[7] She was a good friend of Chopin and his partner renowned writer George Sand, who based her novel *Consuelo* (1843) on Viardot. Viardot was the muse for the leading composers of the time and she composed songs, operas, choral works and instrumental works in a range of national styles. She was married to Louis Viardot (1800–1883) who became her manager, but was to have a string of male admirers during her marriage. She was also adored by the Russian novelist Ivan Turgenev who left Russia to follow her and installed himself in her home with her children. She taught at the Paris Conservatory and a part of her legacy was her many high-profile students and their influence upon following generations of musicians.

Jenny Lind was a Swedish-born soprano who from humble beginnings went on to train at the Royal Opera School, Stockholm, to become known as 'the Swedish Nightingale'.[8] At the age of 18, she made her operatic début in Sweden followed by a highly successful operatic career on the European stage. She began to suffer vocal damage from overuse and sought help from vocal coach Manuel Garcia who helped her preserve her voice through rest and correcting her vocal technique. She returned to the stage with an improved voice and continued touring Sweden, Germany, England following which she announced her retirement from opera at age 29. In 1850 upon the invitation of P.T. Barnum, Lind undertook a highly lucrative tour of the United States where she visited 93 cities.[9] She donated much of her earnings to establish schools in Sweden and other Swedish charities. Following her final public performance in 1883 at the age of 63 she became professor of singing at the Royal College of Music.

Dame Nellie Melba (the pseudonym taken from her hometown Melbourne) was an Australian soprano who became one of the most famous singers of the late Victorian era. During an early and short-lived marriage troubled by domestic abuse, she moved to Europe to pursue her singing career and studied in Paris after which followed a career as a leading singer with Covent Garden. She had international triumphs and numerous recordings. She made her first recordings around 1895, which she did not release as she did not like the sound quality. Later between 1904 and 1926, she made gramophone recordings of operatic arias which have been rereleased on CD. She was the first artist of international reputation that performed in direct radio broadcasts and participated in a pioneering broadcast from Chelmsford in June 1920 that was heard across the United States. Her Covent Garden farewell performance in September 1927 was broadcast throughout the British Empire.

She returned frequently to Australia for performances and teaching at the music school she set up which she later merged into the Melbourne Conservatorium. It was renamed Melba Memorial Conservatorium of Music in 1956. She undertook extensive tours of Australia including remote towns. During World War I she was in Australia and performed to raise large sums of money for war charities which earned her the honour of Dame Commander of the Order of the British Empire (DBE) which was later upgraded to Dame Grand Cross of the Order of the British Empire. Amongst many other honours the music hall at the Conservatorium is named the Melba Hall and the Canberra suburb Melba is named after her. She is one of only two singers with a marble bust on the grand staircase of the Royal Opera House, Covent Garden. She supported the careers of Australian singers alongside many younger European protégées. She provided financial assistance and artistic connections for Australian painter Hugh Ramsey who was living in poverty in Paris. Her name is associated with food created in her honour by the French chef Auguste Escoffier: Peach Melba, Melba Sauce, Melba Toast and Melba Garniture. She is featured on the Australian $100 note. There have been numerous films, plays, television representations and biographies of Melba.[10]

Mary Garden was a Scottish soprano whose family moved to the United States when she was nine years old and she became an American citizen.[11] She studied singing in Chicago and took further studies in Paris. Her operatic career commenced in Paris as the lead soprano at the Opéra-Comique where she was noted for creating the lead role for Debussy's *Pellás and Mélisande* amongst her other roles. Oscar Hammerstein invited her to join the Manhattan Opera House in 1907 and her success led to invitations from other leading American opera houses. She joined the Chicago Opera Association in 1915 and became the director in 1921. This was followed by a directorship of the Chicago Civic Opera. She appeared in two silent films produced by Samuel Goldwyn and in 1934, after retiring from the opera stage, she worked as a talent scout for MGM. Her gramophone recordings preserve her performances along with some of her radio broadcasts. According to her biographer, she was an archetypal diva who lived a flamboyant personal life and took control of the Chicago opera scene where she dominated the stage.[12] She lived her final 30 years in retirement in Inverurie, Scotland, where she is buried.

In the 20th century, women singers continued to achieve great international success and iconic status, including Marian Anderson (1897–1993), Elena Gerhardt (1883–1961), Kirsten Flagstad (1895–1962), Ernestine Schumann-Heink (1861–1936), Renata Tebaldi (1922–2004), Maria Callas (1923–1977), Joan Sutherland (1926–2010), Leontyne Price (b. 1927), Beverly Sills (1929–2007), Kiri Te Kanawa (b. 1944) and Jessye Norman (1945–2014).

American contralto Marian Anderson was a significant leader in the struggle for African American artists to overcome racial prejudice. She personally suffered direct discrimination in her youth and her impoverished family could not provide support for her musical ambitions. Her early music experience was gained in the Union Baptist Church in Philadelphia. Under her aunt's influence, she experienced musical life through church and community events and her aunt brokered early performances. Her father died when she was in her early teens and her single mother could not afford singing lessons. She applied to the Philadelphia Music Academy, but was turned away for being coloured. She remained heavily involved in the church choirs that raised funds for singing lessons for Marian. Her first big break was at a singing competition sponsored by the New York Philharmonic which she won providing the opportunity to sing with the orchestra. The concert was a success, but her subsequent career was hindered by racial prejudice. She won a scholarship to study in Berlin and launched her singing career there.

Anderson performed opera through to spirituals in recitals across the United States and Europe. In 1939, following the refusal by the Daughters of the American Revolution to allow her to perform in Washington, DC, First Lady Eleanor Roosevelt supported her performance to an open-air concert on Easter Sunday (April 9, 1939) on the Lincoln Memorial steps to an audience of 75,000 people and a radio audience in the millions.[13] In 1955 she became the first African American singer to perform at the Metropolitan Opera. Alongside her singing career, she was a delegate to the United Nations Human rights Committee and Goodwill Ambassador for the US Department of States. She participated in the civil rights movements in the 1960s and sang at the March on Washington for Jobs and Freedom in 1963. She won numerous state and national awards honouring her contribution to music and leadership in the civil rights movement. Her legacy included being an inspiration to African American singers such as Jessye Norman and Leontyne Price, along with the establishment of the Marian Anderson Award which was originally to support singers, but was restructured to award any artist who shows leadership in a humanitarian cause. She made numerous recordings in a variety of genres and published her autobiography in 1956.[14]

Leontyne Price was also an African American soprano who achieved international fame born into a racially segregated segregated community in Mississippi. The church was the centre of her early musical exposure where her parents were musically active. She showed an early aptitude for music and sang at the home of Alexander and Elizabeth Chisholm, a wealthy white family for whom Leontyne's aunt worked as a laundress.[15] Her first exposure to classical music was a school trip at the age of nine to hear Marian Anderson sing a recital in Jackson. The occasion deeply moved her and it is believed that this event inspired her to pursue a musical career. With the only option as a black woman at the time to study teaching she enrolled in music education at the Central State University, but her performances in the Glee Club so impressed the university president that she was enrolled in a music major and participated in singing. Her singing coach and the school hosted a benefit to support her studies at Julliard along with the Chisholms. There she experienced performances at the Metropolitan Opera, attended Julliard's Opera Workshop and enrolled in the Berkshire Music Centre at Tanglewood. Virgil Thompson chose her for his 1952 revival of his all-black opera *Four Saints in Three Acts* after which she was engaged as Bess in a new Broadway production of Gershwin's musical *Porgy and Bess* (1935). Her concert career featured premières of new works by leading composers, but it was her highly successful television appearance as *Tosca* (1955) that was a defining point in her career. She auditioned for Austrian conductor Herbert von Karajan who was touring with the Vienna Philharmonic and he asked to direct her European career. Her first performance in a major opera house was in San Francisco and her

European début as Aida was with von Karajan at the Vienna State Opera. She was the first African American to sing a prima donna role as Verdi's *Aida* at La Scala, Milan.[16] In 1961 she made a successful début at the Metropolitan Opera with the company booking her for five prima donna roles that season. She became one of the highest paid singers of her era and a box-office success. As she began to step back from the operatic stage in the late 1960s she was increasingly called upon to sing at important national occasions. In her later years, she made a number of comeback appearances, but turned her attention to masterclasses and recitals. She has received many honours and awards including the Presidential Medal of Freedom and a Grammy Lifetime Achievement Award.

Norwegian soprano Kirsten Flagstad was born into a musical family becoming widely known for her interpretations of Wagner and was feted in London and New York where she had successful careers. She was still singing in major roles in London at the age of 55 and retired in 1952. Following a successful and sustained concert career she continued to be active as a director of the newly formed Norwegian State Opera and in the recording studio where she later turned to recordings of Greig and Sibelius. Her legacy is her 30 recordings which were reissued in 1995 to mark her centenary.

Austrian-born contralto Ernestine Schumann-Henk made her début in Dresden in 1878 into a successful career interpreting the works of Wagner, Mahler and Richard Strauss. She appeared in a number of seasons at Covent Garden under Gustav Mahler and by the turn of the 20th century she made regular appearances at the Metropolitan Opera in New York as well as tours across America. In 1905 she became an American citizen ultimately settling in San Diego where she raised funds in support of injured war veterans.[17] During World War I she supported the US troops touring the United States to raise funds for the war effort and the wounded. During a visit to San Diego, she began giving benefit concerts for undernourished children. At the age 65 she began a weekly programme singing on radio. After her 50th Jubilee in 1927 she gave a series of farewell concerts, but when she lost most of her assets in the Wall Street Crash of 1929, she continued to sing at the age of 69.[18] She appeared in radio broadcasts, joined a vaudeville troupe, continued to give concerts and announced plans to teach 40 American girls. She performed at the Metropolitan Opera as Erda in Wagner's *Das Rheingold* and in concerts along with working for President Franklin D. Roosevelt's National Recovery Administration. She denounced the Nazi regime for its treatment of the Jews and publicly rebuked members of an audience for protesting the appearance of Chinese and African American children at a dedication ceremony in Sacramento.[19] With her voice beginnning to fail she decided to embark on a career as a motion picture actress and signed a three-year contract with MGM, but she became gravely ill with leukaemia and died in her Hollywood home at the age of 76. Her passing was mourned internationally except in Germany and she was given a full military funeral escorted by the American Legion and Disabled War Veterans.

Maria Callas was one of the most renowned singers of the 20th century praised for her bel canto technique and wide vocal range haled as La Divina ('the Divine one'). She was born in New York to Greek parents. Her personal life and tragedy were documented in the popular press, but her achievements as a singer influenced music long after her death. She was pressed into singing by her mother with whom she had a difficult relationship. Following her studies at the Greek National Conservatoire and Athens Conservatoire, she began appearing in secondary roles at the Greek National Opera. She quickly gained recognition for her dramatic skills and exceptional voice and appeared in a number of leading roles for which she received critical acclaim. She made a return visit to the United States where she auditioned for the Metropolitan Opera, but declined the roles that were offered as she did not think they were suitable.[20] She made her Italian début as Turandot in Verona and there she met her first husband Giovanni Battista Meneghini, a wealthy, older, industrialist who provided the support she needed to establish her career in Italy. During the ten years of their marriage (1949–1959) he assumed control of her career. She conquered all the stages of the great Italian opera houses and, despite the resistance of the most prestigious Teatro alla Scala at Milan whose manager had taken dislike to her, she eventually dominated that stage throughout the 1950s. She performed in the United States and South America, but in 1958 her feud with the manager of the Metropolitan Opera in New York led to her contract being cancelled. They were reconciled and in 1965 she returned to perform several leading roles. She also launched her career in England and performed between 1952 and 1965. She struggled with weight and fitness issues and after finding it difficult to perform some roles, she went on a weight loss programme. This increased her casting options and resulted in praise from critics and impresarios. However, it has been said that it had a damaging effect on her voice and led to vocal strain, but there is debate on whether it had to do with other factors and the findings of Italian researchers at the University of Bologna proposed that she had a rare illness that affected her vocal chords which may have been the cause of her death.[21] Her influence on other singers resulting from her leadership of the bel canto repertoire has been praised by the generations of singers that followed her. She was both praised and derided for her acting, but her overall artistry as a performer was never questioned.

Beverly Sills, born Belle Miriam Silverman, was an American soprano who was a child of Jewish immigrants, her mother being a musician. As a child she spoke Yiddish, Russian, Romanian, French and English. At age three she won a singing contest and at age four she had a professional engagement on a Saturday morning radio programme under the name 'Bubbles' Silverman. She began singing lessons at the age of seven and sang in the short film where she adopted her stage name Beverly Sills. In 1945 she made her professional stage début in a tour of seven Gilbert and Sullivan operas to 12 cities in the United States and Canada. In 1947 she made her operatic stage début with the Philadelphia Grand Opera Company. She performed in the major opera houses of Europe and the Americas in principal soprano roles alongside leading tenors such as Pavarotti. She also made television appearances on talk shows and was a huge hit popularising opera amongst television audiences. She hosted her own talk show Lifestyles with Beverly Sills in the late 1970s on NBC which won an Emmy Award. She turned to recital singing in the final decade of her singing career while still adopting new operatic roles right up to her retirement. Gian Carlo Menotti was commissioned to write *La Loca* in honour of her 50th birthday and her final performance was in 1980 at San Diego Opera in a performance of Die Fledermaus alongside Joan Sutherland. She became co-director of the New York City Opera and later sole general director until 1989 during which time she turned the struggling company into a viable enterprise. She stayed on the board until 1991. She devoted herself to arts causes and charities and regularly was called upon to speak at fundraisers and college campuses. From 1994 to 2002 she was chair of the Lincoln Centre and from 2002 to 2005 she served as chair of the Metropolitan Opera. She continued to make television appearances and during HD transmissions in movie theatres live from the Met in on-screen interviews during intermissions. She received many awards and honorary doctorates in recognition of her talent and contribution to opera.

Kiri Te Kanawa was born in New Zealand to a Māori father and an Irish mother. She was given up for adoption because her father was already married. Following performances and some success on stage she won the Mobil Song Competition which provided funds to study at the London Opera Centre. She won some minor roles in London and a contract at the Royal Opera House as a junior principal. Thereafter she successfully undertook principal roles in major opera companies and festivals internationally. Her appearances in film boosted her international fame and she played Donna Elvira in Joseph Losey's 1979 film adaptation of Mozart's *Don Giovanni*. In 1981 she sang at the wedding of Charles, Prince of Wales and Lady Diana Spencer which is said to have attracted an estimated audience of 600 million people. Leonard Bernstein cast her as Maria in the recording of his musical *West Side Story* which he conducted. It was said to be the operatic version of the musical and featured internationally acclaimed opera singers winning a Grammy Award for Best Cast Show Album in 1985. The recording process was filmed as a documentary which was also viewed widely. Apart from her now highly successful opera career where she appeared in many principal roles she performed at popular events. In 1991 she premièred the theme song 'World in Union' at the World Cup which reached No. 4 on the UK Singles chart. In 2006 she sang 'Happy Birthday' and 'God Save the Queen' to Queen Elizabeth II at the Commonwealth Games in Brisbane, Australia, and in 2013 she performed at Harusha Handa's inaugural Tokyo Global Concert in Nakano, Tokyo. Also, in October 2013 she appeared in the role of Nellie Melba in the television series *Downton Abbey*. Her numerous awards include Dame Commander of the Order of the British Empire, for services to opera (1982), Honorary Companion in the Order of Australia (1990), Order of New Zealand (1995) and honorary degrees to universities in the UK, United States and New Zealand. In 2019, to mark her 75th birthday the Aotea Centre in Auckland was renamed the Kiri Te Kanawa Theatre and the Kiri Te Kanawa Retirement Village in her birthplace of Gisborne is named after her. She established the Kiri Te Kanawa Foundation with the aim of supporting talented New Zealand singers through financial scholarships. In 2010 the Kiri Prize competition was launched by BBC Radio 2. Finalists attended masterclasses with Te Kanawa and other artists and semi-finalists were broadcast on BBC Radio 2's 'Friday Night Is Music Night'. The winner of this competition Shuna Scott Sendall performed with Te Kanawa and José Carreras at the BBC Proms in Hyde Park, London, in September 2010 and won the opportunity to attend a three-week residential course at the Solti Kanawa Academia in Italy. Her discography includes recordings of major operatic roles, oratorios, musicals, popular song and Maori song, many topping international charts. She was honoured with *Gramophone* magazine Artist of the Year (1982), Golden Plate Award for the American Academy of Achievement (2006), Edison Classical Music Award (2008), Brit Award for Outstanding Contribution to Music (2010) and World Class New Zealand Award (2012).

American opera singer Jessye Norman was born into a family of amateur musicians. Her talents as a singer were displayed as a young child singing gospel at Mount Calvary Baptist Church. She undertook singing training during her high school years and fell in love with opera through the broadcasts of the Metropolitan Opera. She won a scholarship to study at Howard University in Washington, DC. After graduating in 1967 with a degree in music she went on to earn a master's degree in 1968 at the

University of Michigan School of Music. She moved to Europe to establish her career and after winning an international competition in Munich she took a contract with the Deutsche Oper Berlin. She was a guest with other German, Italian and English opera houses with many significant return visits to the United States. Between 1975 and 1980 she stopped performing opera and dedicated herself to recital and soloist work. She returned to the opera stage in 1980, but also programmed recitals often incorporating new works and commissions. She commissioned a song cycle woman.life.song (2000) by composer Judith Weir to texts by Toni Morrison, Maya Angelou and Clarissa Pinkola Estés, premièred at Carnegie Hall. She sang La Marseillaise to celebrate the 200th anniversary of the French Revolution (July 14, 1989) at the Place de la Concord which inspired the South African poet Lawrence Mduduzi to write the poem 'I shall be heard' dedicated to Norman. She was awarded the Légion d'honneur, France, in 1989 adding to her previous French award in 1984, Commandeur de l'ordre des Arts et des Lettres.

Norman didn't want her voice to be classified because she liked so many different styles of music.[22] She was noted for her versatility in singing from grand operatic roles such as Verdi's Aida and Wagner's Isolde, to baroque roles such a Purcell's Dido through to Duke Ellington swing and contemporary song by Michal Legrand. She explored less familiar repertoire from the early 20th century works by Poulenc, Stravinsky, Bartók and Schoenberg. She also collaborated with jazz musicians, dance choreographers and film-makers.

She sang at two presidential inaugurations for Ronald Reagan and Bill Clinton and Queen Elizabeth II's 60th birthday celebration. Her friend President Barack Obama awarded her the National Medal of Arts in 2009 and she has won five Grammy Awards. She established the Jessye Norman School of Performing Arts in her hometown Augusta Georgia and was prominent as an African American voice in the arts. She was active on numerous arts and charitable boards such as Carnegie Hall, Dance Theatre Harlem, and Elton John Aids Foundation to name a few. She performed into her 70s at significant events such as the opening of the Esplanade – Theatres on the Bay, Singapore, 2002, and the unveiling of the two columns of light at the World Trade Center memorial service on March 11, 2002. In 2009 she curated Honour! a celebration of the African American cultural legacy in a festival featuring African American trailblazers and artists. Her final public appearance and one of her many in Carnegie Hall met with mixed reviews as she combined jazz, musical and art song.[23] She died of complications with spinal surgery aged 74 in 2019 and was memorialised with a gala tribute in the Metropolitan Opera House.

## Women pianists

The piano was an acceptable instrument for women to study in the 19th century and in fact it was considered an asset in attracting prospective husbands. However, women were confined to performing in the private sphere and were not encouraged to perform publicly particularly after marriage. Nonetheless, there were a number of women who became virtuosi on the piano such as Clara Schumann, who was discussed in Chapter 3, having an international performing career as well as being a highly successful composer and teacher. Other pianists who had highly successful careers in the nineteenth century include Marie Pleyel (1811–1875), Annette Esipova (1851–1914) and Teresa Carreño (1853–1917).

Maria Pleyel was born in France to a Belgian father and a German mother and became one of the most admired pianists of her time. As a prodigy she made her début at Théâtre de la Monnaie in Brussels at the age of 14. She was teaching piano at a French girls' school by 1830 and in 1848 he became chair of the piano department at Brussels Conservatoire.[24] After her marriage to Camille Pleyel, heir to the piano manufacturing business, she continued her teaching career, but stopped performing publicly. Following her separation from her husband in 1835 she resumed her performing career across Europe and in London to great critical acclaim. She also composed several piano works which she performed on her tours.[25]

Annette Esipova was a Russian pianist who made her début in Saint Petersburg in 1871 at the age of 20 to critical acclaim. Her concert tours took her to the United States and Portugal. In 1885 she was appointed Royal Prussian Court Pianist and from 1893 to 1908 she was appointed professor of pianoforte at the Saint Petersburg Conservatory. In the early 1900s, she made a number of recordings on piano rolls.

Teresa Carreño was a Venezuelan internationally renowned pianist, singer and composer. She was known as 'The Valkyre of the pianoforte'.[26] Following her début at the age of eight she performed in the Americas, Europe, Russia, England, Australia, New Zealand, North and South Africa. As one of the first women to tour the United States she was a role model for future female musicians. She also was an impresario of her own opera company in Venezuela for a short time in 1887 which was difficult to sustain due to political unrest.[27] Alongside this she was a prolific composer of approximately 80 works for piano, voice, choir and orchestra with Venezuelan musical influences. She also studied singing and while touring as a pianist she appeared as the Queen in *Les Huguenots* at short notice in Paris in 1875. She recorded more than 40 master piano works on piano roll including some of her own. She also published many of her compositions.

In the United States notable figures in the late 19th century include Julie Rivé-King (1854–1937) and Fannie Bloomfield-Zeisler (1863–1927). Julie Rivé-King born in Cincinnati was the first American-born woman to achieve a concert career. As a child she was taught by her mother who was also a musician. She appeared in recitals from the age of eight and went on to study at the Cincinnati Conservatory. In 1870 she studied with major pianists in New York and later in Europe.[28] She made her début in Leipzig in 1873 and embarked on a concert tour of Europe which was cut short following the death of her father. In 1874 she made her début in Cincinnati and following her marriage to her manager in 1877 embarked on a composing career. Her husband published his works under her name to ostensibly enhance her reputation.[29] She performed throughout United States and Canada and her extensive solo repertory included over 300 works by more than 75 composers many of them American.[30] She moved to Chicago following her husband's death in 1900 and took a teaching position at the Bush Conservatory. Fannie Bloomfield-Zeisler was born in Austria to Jewish parents who emigrated to the United States when she was four years old. She studied piano as a child and made her début at the age of 11. She returned to Vienna at the age of 13 to study piano and five years later returned to Chicago. In 1885 she made her début in New York and like other pianists around the turn of the century turned to producing piano rolls. In 1888 she joined the recently formed musical women's fraternity Alpha Chi Omega. Through her success and artistic example, she contributed to the rising standards of pianism in America and changing the identities of women pianists.[31]

Notable keyboard performers of the 20th century include the harpsichordist Wanda Landowska (1879–1959) and the pianists Marguerite Long (1874–1966), Myra Hess (1890–1965), Clara Haskil (1895–1960), Guiomar Novaes (1895–1979), Eileen Joyce (1908–1991), Rosalyn Tureck (1913–2003), Annie Fischer (1914–1995), Moura Lympany (1916–2005) and Alicia de Larrocha (1923–2009). Wanda Landowska was born in Warsaw to Jewish intellectuals and began playing piano at the age of four. As a child prodigy she studied at the Warsaw Conservatory and later studied composition and piano in Berlin and Paris. Her interest in the work of J.S. Bach led to her devoting her career to the harpsichord and paved the way for authentic performances on original instruments. In Berlin she met Polish ethnomusicologist Henry Lew who became her husband in 1900. He encouraged her research and interest in early music assisting her with the writing of her book *Musique Ancienne* (1909).[32] She toured Russia (1908–1909) with a Pleyel harpsichord.[33] She established a harpsichord class at the Berlin Hochschule für Musik in 1913. Following World War I, she settled in Paris and was a frequent guest at Barney's renowned lesbian salon. She toured America in 1923 with Pleyel concert harpsichords. Her interest in performing early keyboard music on original instruments resulted in her visiting European museums to study original keyboard instruments, acquiring early instruments and having reproductions made by Pleyel. New works for harpsichord were written for her by Manuel de Falla (*El retablo de maese Pedro, Master Peter's Puppet Show*, 1923 and *Harpsichord Concerto*, 1926) and Francis Poulenc (*Concert champêtre*, 1927). Landowska's fame and success continued in the 1930s until the Nazi invasion of France in 1940 when her library and instruments were seized.[34] She escaped as a refugee to New York with her partner Denise Restout and re-established her career as a performer and teacher. There she made her landmark recording of Bach's *Goldberg Variations* along with her many other recordings. Landowska was decorated by the governments of France and Poland and her pioneering efforts in the championing of the harpsichord established its revival in the historically informed approaches to the performance of early music in the 20th century.

Marguerite Long was a French pedagogue and champion of French piano music. She was encouraged by her elder sister who was a Professor of Piano when Marguerite entered her piano class at Nîmes conservatory. Marguerite made her successful début at the age of 11 and was invited to attend the Paris Conservatoire in 1889 where in 1891 she took the Premier Prix at age 17. She became close friends with Fauré early in his career premièring new works by him and he appointed her professor of piano at the Paris Conservatoire while he was director. However, the relationship turned sour and it has been speculated that it had to do with rivalries at the Conservatoire.[35] In 1920 she was granted full professorship at the Paris Conservatoire being the first woman appointed to this position. She studied the works of Debussy and Ravel and promoted their works on tours. She performed and toured regularly with Ravel performing his G major Piano Concerto while he was at the podium. She established a friendship with Darius Milhaud who, following her successful tour of Ravel's piano concerto, asked her to première and be the dedicatee for his first piano concerto. She also programmed the works of Schumann, Franck and Chopin. She embarked on a tour to South America in 1937 and in Brazil she established her role as ambassador of French music.[36]

She received many national honours including Commandeur de la Légion d'Honneur which was rarely given to performers and indeed women. Long resigned from the Conservatoire to establish a school with Jacques Thibaud and Marcelle Lyon dedicated to teaching violin and piano sonata playing. Her concert career continued, but she dedicated her time to cultivating young artists in her later life and her masterclasses attracted pianists from around the world. Thibaud and Long established an international competition for violinists and pianists in their name which became recognised as one of the major European competitions of its kind. In 1956 the French government sponsored a concert at the Sorbonne in honour of her contribution to French musical life where at age 81 she performed Fauré's Ballade, Op. 19. A tribute in her honour was the première of a suite by eight French composers titled Variations sur le nom de Margeurite Long.[37] She published her own piano book in 1959 featuring the pedagogy that she had developed over 60 years of teaching. Shortly before her death she received the Grand-croix de l'ordre national du Mérite.

English pianist Myra Hess was of Jewish descent and established her international career in 1907 at her début at the age of 17 performing Beethoven's Piano Concert No. 4 under the baton of Sir Thomas Beecham. She toured Britain, the Netherlands and France and following her début in America in 1922 she became a favourite on the concert circuit. She distinguished herself by organising over 2,000 lunchtime concerts during World War II when all concert halls in London were blacked out at night to avoid bombing by the Nazis during the Blitz. The concerts were held at the National Gallery and in Trafalgar square daily from Monday to Friday and moved to safer locations if required. They continued for over six years without fail and provided the opportunity for young performers and established musicians with a set fee of five guineas for all performers except for Hess herself who never took a fee.[38] She presented 1,698 concerts attended by 824,152 people and performed herself in 150 concerts.[39] Due to her contribution to maintaining the morale of the people of England during the war King George VI promoted her 1936 Award of Commander of the British Empire to Dame Commander of the Order of the British Empire in 1941. Her post-war career was distinguished by the interpretations of a wide-ranging repertoire of classical and baroque masterworks through to premièring of new works by Howard Ferguson. She championed the piano duet and two piano repertoire of Schubert and famously arranged selected Bach cantatas for piano and two pianos. Her legacy is marked by the Dame Myra Hess Memorial Concerts series of free lunchtime concerts at the Chicago Cultural Centre established in 1977, The Myra Steinway at Bishopsgate Institute, her great nephew composer Nigel Hess and his music publishing company Myra Music, and the plaque marking her residence at 48 Wildwood Road, London.

Clara Haskil was born into a Jewish family in Bucharest. Following studies in Vienna she moved to France where she studied at the Conservatoire de Paris and graduated at the age of 15 with a Premier Prix. She embarked on a concert career, but her physical ailments and extreme stage fright prevented her from gaining financial success. She did perform as a soloist under the baton of many great conductors and alongside leading chamber musicians and received critical acclaim. At age 65 she died from injuries sustained from a fall on the staircase at the Brussels-South railway station a day before a concert was scheduled. The Clara Haskil International Piano competition is held biennially in her memory in Switzerland where she resided from 1942 until her death in 1960. Her recordings have received critical acclaim for their expression and technique. She was awarded Chevalier of the Légion d'Honneur in 1951. In August 2017 a 70-minute documentary about her life and work was released.[40]

Guiomar Novaes distinguished her career as a Brazilian pianist who was awarded one of two places at the Conservatoire de Paris in 1909 at the age of 14. She won first place among 387 applicants and the formidable jury included Debussy, Fauré, Moszowski and Widor.[41] She became one of the most admired pianists on the European and American concert circuits and was renowned for her interpretations of Chopin and Schumann. Her recordings span the 1920s to 1950s and remain as some of the most highly rated interpretations of the Classical and Romantic repertoires.

Eileen Joyce was born in Tasmania and moved with her family to Boulder, a gold mining town in Western Australia at the age of 11. Boulder and its adjacent mining town Kalgoorlie were multicultural communities whose music traditions reflected their diversity through choirs, bands and orchestras. She studied piano working through a system of examinations organised by London academies and her talent was discovered by a visiting examiner when she was 15 years old. Money was raised in the goldfields to provide her with the funds to move to Perth to study at Loreto Convent school. In her final year of study at the Convent further funds were raised for her to study at the Hochschule für Musik in Leipzig. She moved to London to undertake further study and made her London début in September 1930 playing Prokofiev's third piano concerto at the BBC Proms. In 1933 she embarked on her first Australian tour organised by the newly established Australian Broadcasting Commission. During World War II she performed alongside other musicians to help raise morale amongst citizens in England. In the 1940s she formed a relationship with Christopher Mann, a theatrical and film agent who was an agent for some of the leading stars of Britain and the United States. Mann managed her career and she gained star status on her intranational tours through Europe, the United States, South America and Asia including Australia in 1948. Her image was highly glamorous enhanced by lavish gowns created by leading designers such as Norman Hartnell. Her star status led to considerable wealth which allowed the couple to buy property in Mayfair and country properties including one formerly owned by Winston Churchill who became their neighbour.[42]

In 1949 she took up the harpsichord and clavichord joining the early music revival taking place in Britain. She also extended her career into film and television performing and acting on screen and on soundtracks.[43] Joyce was both generous to her fans and her causes and she performed in schools, asylums, hospitals and prisons. Her gruelling performance schedule included tours, broadcasts, recording sessions and lengthy stage performances resulted in a nervous breakdown in 1953. She effectively retired from performing in 1960, but maintained her support of musical causes. She returned to Perth in 1979 to adjudicate the National Eisteddfod and donated $37,600 to the University of Western Australia (UWA) music fund, plus a clavichord, an antique French music chair, a portrait of herself by Augustus John and a bronze bust by Anna Mahler. In 1981 she attended the opening of the Eileen Joyce Studio at UWA which she financed. She was awarded honorary doctorates by the universities of Cambridge (1971), Western Australia (1979) and Melbourne (1982).

Rosalyn Tureck was an American pianist of Jewish descent who also excelled on harpsichord, clavichord and organ. Her early interest in the music of Bach drew her to playing the harpsichord and she was influenced by the work of Wanda Landowska. Her first teacher was Russian pianist Sophia Brilliant Liven a former pupil of Anton Rubenstein who introduced Tureck to Russian composers and musicians who passed through Liven's household on their visits to Chicago. Notable was the inventor Léon Théremin, famous for musical invention the Theremin. She later applied to study with him and her New York début was a performance of a Bach concerto on Theremin in Carnegie Hall on April 1, 1932. She also took lessons from Javanese-born Dutch pianist Jan Chiapusso who introduced her to Javanese gamelan. At age 16 she won a full scholarship to Julliard School of Music where her audition included 16 of Bach's preludes and fugues. After graduating with distinction in 1935 she made her piano début at Carnegie Hall.[44] In 1937 she performed six weekly all-Bach Town Hall recitals. She remained in New York teaching and performing and her first European tour was in 1947, with her London début in 1953. She moved to London in the mid-1950s and formed the Tureck Bach Players. She performed regularly in Europe and America as well as touring South America, Israel, Turkey, South Africa, Australia and the Far East. Apart from her interest in programming the works of Bach she broadened her repertoire to include Classical and Romantic masterworks as well as contemporary works by composers such as Aaron Copland, Charles Ives, Arnold Schoenberg, David Diamond, Luigi Dallapiccola and William Schumann. In 1966 she set up the International Bach Society as a forum for musicologists and performers. Upon returning to the United States she set up the Tureck Bach Research Institute in New York. In 1994 she founded the Oxford Tureck Bach Research Institute and her publications include a three-volume introduction to the *Performance of Bach* (1960) alongside articles on performing and teaching. She has edited a number of works by Bach and her playing has been captured in recordings on a variety of mediums including LPs, CDs, television and film. She received numerous awards and five honorary doctorates, including one from Oxford University in 1977. She advocated for women in leadership roles and was one of the first women to conduct the New York Philharmonic (1958) as well as the London Philharmonic (1958) from the keyboard whilst performing Bach concerti.

Annie Fischer was born into a Jewish family in Budapest and studied at the Franz Liszt Academy winning the International Franz Liszt Piano Competition in 1933. She was greatly admired by her contemporaries for her interpretations of great piano work, but her greatest influence has been through her recordings and in particular her studio recordings of the complete piano sonatas of Beethoven.

Dame Moura Lympany was an English Concert pianist who made her concert début at the age of 12. She studied at the Royal Academy of Music in London and went on to study in Vienna. She was one of the most popular pianists in the UK by the end of World War II. She was the first British musician to perform in Paris after the liberation and became widely known through her touring of Europe, the United States, Canada, Australia, New Zealand and India. She performed before Charles the Prince of Wales in 1979 and was appointed a Commander of the Order of the British Empire in that year. In 1981 she established the annual Rasiguères Festival of Music and Wine near Perpignan, France, which she ran for ten years and she also helped Prince Louis de Polignac to establish the Festival des Sept Chapelles in Guidel, Brittany, in 1986. In 1992 she was made Dame Commander of the Order of the British Empire. She also received honours from the French and Belgian governments.[45]

Alicia de Larrocha was considered one of the greatest Spanish pianists in history.[46] She championed the music of Spanish composers and brought popularity to the works of Isaac Albeniz and Enrique Granados. Born into a family of pianists she began the study of piano at the age of three. She gave her first public performance at the age of five at the International Exhibition in Barcelona and performed her first concert at the age of six at the World's Fair in Seville. Her orchestral début was at the age of 11. Her performances in Spain were winning large audiences and she began touring internationally. In 1954 she toured to North America with the Los Angeles Philharmonic and in 1966 she toured to South Africa which was so successful that three more tours were completed. In 1969 she performed in Boston for the Peabody Mason Series. She also was a prolific composer, but she did not perform her works publicly. She gave her family the choice of making them available which they did and now have been recorded.[47] She made numerous recordings of Spanish repertoire which won a series of awards including Edison, Grand Prix do Disque, Grammy Awards, Records of the Year (London), Deutsche Schallplattenpreis and Japan Record Academy Award. She also was awarded Musician of the Year – Musical America Magazine (1978), Commander of the Ordre des Artes et des Lettres (1988), Prince of Asturias Award for the Arts (1994), UNESCO Prize (1995) and Paderewski Memorial Medal, London (1961).

The more recent generation of leading women pianists includes Martha Argerich (b. 1941) and Mitsuko Uchida (b. 1948). Martha Argerich is an Argentinian pianist with maternal Russian-Jewish grandparents with paternal ancestors from Spain. Her talent was identified at an early age and she began piano studies at the age of three giving her début concert at the age of eight. Her family moved to Vienna after her winning major international piano competitions as a teenager. Following these early successes she had a personal and artistic crisis looking to other career choices. Her teacher's wife Anny Arkenase is credited with encouraging her return to the piano.[48] She went on to win the VI International Chopin Competition in 1965 at the age of 24 which won her international prominence. She received critical acclaim for her performances and recordings including a number of Grammy Awards, but found the concert stage lonely and turned to chamber music performances.[49] To support younger musicians she established an annual festival, has sat on the Jury of many international piano competitions, is President of the International Piano Academy Lake Como and General Director of the Argerich Music Festival and Encounter in Beppu, Japan. She also performs regularly at the Lugano festival performed at the Proms in 2016 and 2019. She has an aversion to publicity the press despite being recognised as one of the world's greatest pianists.

Dame Mitsuko Uchida is a Japanese-born pianist and conductor who moved to Vienna with her diplomat parents when she was 12 years old. She studied at the Vienna Academy of Music and gave her first recital at the age of 14 at the Vienna Musikverien. She won first prize in the Beethoven Competition in Vienna (1969), second prize in the VIII International Competition in Vienna (1970) and second prize in the Leeds Piano Competition (1975). She has won Gramophone Awards for her interpretations of Mozart's piano sonatas (1989) and Schoenberg's piano concertos (2001) and a Grammy Award (2011) for her recordings of Mozart's piano concertos. She took on a role as senior artist with the Marlborough Music Festival since 1974 and has continued in various roles with the Festival including as sole director until 2018. She is a founding trustee of the Borletti-Buitoni Trust which helps and supports young artists' careers. She was also awarded an honorary Doctor of Music from Oxford University (2009) and Dame Commander of the Order of the British Empire (2009).

## Women violinists

Other instruments, particularly the violin, soon found their champions as well in the 19th century. Wilma Neruda (1838–1911), Camilla Urso (1840–1902) and Maud Powell (1867–1920) set important precedents. Wilma Neruda was born in Morovia when it was a part of the Austrian Empire. She came from a highly musical family and began studying piano, but preferred the violin which was not encouraged as it was considered an unsuitable instrument for women. However, she showed a natural ability for the violin and her father allowed her to study the instrument. She became a child prodigy alongside her siblings and the family moved to Vienna where she pursued her study of violin. Following her début at the age of 11 with the London Philharmonic Orchestra she pursued an international career. Her success led to an explosion in the number of female violinists and compositions dedicated to her.

Camilla Orso was a French-born violinist from a musical family. She was admitted to the Paris Conservatory at the time when women were not admitted to study violin, but won a spot for her audition at the age of eight becoming the first female student to win a violin prize in the 1852 annual student competition.[50] In 1852 she made her début in the Metropolitan Hall, New York City, to much critical acclaim and followed up with tours to Boston, Philadelphia and other American cities. In 1855 her family established residence in Nashville, Tennessee. In 1863–1865 she toured New England and Canada, and in 1865 she returned for well received performances in Paris. She continued to tour America, Australia and South Africa until her retirement from the stage in 1895. She then taught at the National Conservatory of Music in New York.[51]

Maude Powell was the first American violinist to achieve international status. Born in Chicago suburb Peru, Illinois, she studied violin from the age of seven and was soon recognised as a prodigy. Her parents sold the family home to move to Europe where she could take studies at the Leipzig Conservatory, The Paris Conservatory and the Berlin Hochshule. In 1885 she had her début with the Berlin Philharmonic and with the New York Philharmonic when she returned to the United States. She became an advocate for music by American composers, women musicians and composers and black composers as well as British composer Samuel Coleridge-Taylor.[52]

In the 20th century, celebrated violinists include Erika Morini (1904–1995), Gioconda De Vito (1907–1994), Ginette Neveu (1919–1939) and Ida Haendel (1928–2020). Erika Moroni was a Jewish Austrian violinist from a family of intellectuals. Her father was a director of his own music school and taught her from an early age. She entered the Vienna Conservatory at the age of eight and made her début in 1916 at the age of 12 with the Leipzig Gewandhaus Orchestra. She travelled first class to New York performing for the first-class passengers on the ship and made her début in New York at the age of 17 (January 26, 1917). Shortly after her début in New York she was gifted the Guadagnini violin which had been owned by Maude Powell. She made a number of recordings in the United States and in 1923 she made her first visit to London. She moved permanently to the United States in 1938 making regular concert appearances and teaching at the Mannes College of Music. During her career she performed with an impressive list of high-profile orchestras and conductors. She took a ten-year break from performing and returned in 1976 to give a final recital at Hunter College after which she retired. She received many awards including honorary doctorates from Smith College, Massachusetts (1955), New England Conservatory of Music, Boston (1963) and a lifetime achievement gold medal in New York City. She repeatedly claimed that due to narrow mindedness and prejudice of many managers women had much more difficulty in achieving success and rejected the labelling of 'female violinist'.[53] Sadly her belongings including her violins, paintings, letters and marked up scores were stolen from her Fifth Avenue apartment while she lay in a hospital before her death. They were intended to fund several Jewish charities, but have never been recovered.

Gioconda De Vito was an Italian-born violinist who taught herself violin until her uncle a professional violinist in Germany heard her play and began teaching her. At age 11 she entered the Rossini Conservatory and graduated at the age of 13 commencing her professional career as a soloist. At the age of 17 she became professor of violin at the newly established Bari Conservatory. In 1932 she won the international Violin Competition in Vienna. She taught at Palermo and Rome, but the war interrupted her burgeoning career. After the war she made a small number of recordings and made her London début in 1948. She retired in 1961, aged 54, from performing and teaching. She never appeared in the United States despite performing in Australia (1957 and 1960), Argentina, India, Israel, Europe and the Soviet Union.

Ginette Neveu was born in Paris to a musical family making her solo début at the age of seven and at the age of nine winning first prize at the École Supérieure and the City of Paris Prix d'Honneur. She studied at the

Conservatoire de Paris with one of her teachers being Nadia Boulanger. At the age of 15 she won worldwide celebrity after winning the Henryk Wieniawski Violin Competition resulting in the signing of an extensive international touring contract. World War II interrupted her international touring and she performed mainly in France. She made her London début in 1946 and recorded with Abbey Road Studios in the same year. Her few commercial recordings still remain in the catalogue. Her post-war activities included touring with her brother in Europe and visiting Australia and South America, as well as return engagements in the United States and England. Her career was cut short when she died in a plane crash on her flight from Paris to New York. Her brother was on board and also died along with all 48 passengers. Tributes poured in from royalty and the musical establishment and she was posthumously awarded the Cross of the Legion d'Honneur. A street in the Montmartre region of Paris is named after her and a plaque in her honour is situated at the Salle Pleyel, Paris.

Ida Haendel was born in Polish to a Jewish family and as a child prodigy she had major success in violin competitions from an early age. In 1933, aged five, she won the Warsaw Conservatory's gold medal and the first Huberman Prize. In 1935 she competed against David Oistrakh and Ginette Niveu becoming a laureate of the first Henryk Wieniawski Violin Competition in 1935. She studied in Paris and England and during World War II she played in factories for British and American troops and in Myra Hess's National Gallery concerts. She toured regularly internationally and worked with leading international conductors and musicians. Haendel lived in Montreal from 1952 to 1989 and performed with Canadian orchestras. She was the first Western soloist invited to perform in China following the Cultural Revolution.[54] In 1993 she made her concert début with the Berlin Philharmonic and in 2006 she performed for Pope Benedict XVI at the former Nazi concentration camp Auschwitz-Birekenau. Her recordings have earned critical acclaim and she was awarded the Sibelius medal in 1982 by the Sibelius society for her interpretation of the Sibelius violin concerto which the composer himself applauded.[55] She was a regular adjudicator for international competitions and inspired the new generation of violinists. In 1991 she was appointed Commander of the Order of the British Empire and received honorary doctorates from the Royal College of Music, London (2000) and McGill University (2006).

More recently, Kyung-Wha Chung (1948), Viktoria Mullova (b. 1959), Anne Sophie Mutter (b. 1963) and Midori (b.1971) have emerged on the international violin scene. Kyung-Wha Chung was born in Seoul and commenced piano and violin studies at an early age becoming recognised as a prodigy at the age of nine when she played the Mendelssohn Violin Concerto with the Seoul Philharmonic Orchestra. All of her siblings played classical instruments and three of them became professional musicians. As the children became famous in Korea performing as soloists and in ensembles their mother decided to move them to the United States to further their careers. Chung arrived in the United States at the age of 13 and attended Julliard. In 1967 she was the joint winner of the Edgar Leventritt Competition, being the first time for this outcome. This led to engagements with Chicago Symphony Orchestra and the New York Philharmonic. She was also substituted at late notice for the White House Gala. In 1970 she substituted for Itzhak Perlman with the London Symphony Orchestra which led to many other invitations in the UK. Her début album with the London Symphony Orchestra brought her international attention and she has since made recordings of core repertoire of violin concerti. She temporarily halted her career due to illness in 2008 and in 2014 she returned for a performance in London at the Royal Festival Hall. She controversially complained to a mother of a child who was persistently coughing in her line of vision which was widely reported.[56] She remains one of the most accomplished violinists and interpreters of the classical violin repertoire.

Viktoria Mullova was born in Soviet Russia but defected during a concert tour of Finland in 1983. She was a product of the Soviet state-sponsored music system which she found stressful and hierarchical. She enjoys an international career as a soloist and has had performances with major international orchestras. Her recordings have been nominated and won numerous awards and her interpretations of popular and jazz compositions by Miles Davis, Duke Ellington and the Beatles amongst others have had wide appeal.[57]

Anne-Sophie Mutter was born in Germany and studied violin at the Winterthur Conservatory. She came to Herbert von Karajan's attention who, in 1976, arranged for her to play with the Berlin Philharmonic when she was 13 years old at the Lucerne festival. In 1977 she performed at the Salzburg Festival with the English Chamber Orchestra under Daniel Barenboim and at the age of 15 she made her first recording of the Mozart Third and Fifth violin concerti with Karajan and the Berlin Philharmonic. In 1980 she made her US début with the New York Philharmonic and in 1985, aged 22, she was made an honorary fellow of the Royal Academy of Music London. In 1988 she toured Canada and the United States including a performance at Carnegie Hall. In 1998, she recorded the complete set of Beethoven's Violin Sonatas on CD and DVD which were broadcast on international television and radio. Her repertoire includes many classical works as well as championing contemporary music. Her world premières of around 30 works composed for her by Unsuk Chin, Sebastian Currier, Henri Dutilleux, Sofia Gubaidulina, Witold Lutoslawski, Norbert Moret, Krzysztof Penderecki, Sir André Previn, Wolfgang Rihm, Jörg Widmann and John Williams.[58] She was awarded a Grammy (2005) for her recording of the violin concerto written for her by her ex-husband André Previn. Academy Award winner John Williams also composed original music for her and she appeared as a soloist in his début concert with the Vienna Philharmonic (January 2020) which was recorded and became the best-selling orchestral album of 2020. She set up the Anne-Sophie Mutter Foundation in 2008 to provide scholarships to support young musicians and in 2022 she joined the foundation board of the Lucerne Festival. Alongside her musical philanthropy she supports other social concerns as President of a German cancer charity and in 2022 she participated in benefit concerts for victims of Russia's aggression in Ukraine.[59]

Midori Goto, who performs under the mononym Midori, is a Japanese-born American violinist. She gave her first public performance at the age of six in her native Osaka and in 1982 she moved to New York City with her violinist mother to study at Julliard and the Aspen Music Festival and School. In 1982 at the age of 11 she made her début with the New York Philharmonic as a surprise at the New Year's Eve Gala. In 1986 she performed at the Tanglewood Music Festival with Leonard Bernstein conducting his own work Serenade. The performance reached the front page of the *New York Times* on account of Midori breaking the E string of her violin, then again on the concertmaster's Stradivarius and finishing the performance on the associate concertmaster's Guadagnini for which she received a standing ovation.[60] She became a professional violinist at the age 15 and made her Carnegie Hall recital début just before her 19th birthday.

In 1994 she withdrew from public life and in her 20s she was hospitalised and officially diagnosed with anorexia and depression. After recovering she continued to perform and studied psychology and gender studies. In 2000 Midori graduated from New York University with a degree in Psychology and Gender Studies. In 2005 she earned a master's degree in Psychology with a thesis on pain research. She returned to the stage and took a teaching position at the Manhattan School of Music. She received the Avery Fisher Prize in 2001 and established the Partners in Performance programme to assist classical music organisations in smaller communities. Midori formed Midori and Friends a non-profit organisation that aims to bring music education to children in New York. She established Music Sharing in 2002 an organisation that aims to bring Western classical and Japanese traditional music into the lives of young people in Japan including instrument instruction for differently abled children. In 2004 she instituted the Orchestra Residencies programme for US youth orchestras which expanded to include youth orchestra outside the United States. In 2004 she was named professor at the University of Southern California's Thornton School of Music. She has won numerous accolades including artist of the Year by the Japanese government (1988) and the recipient of the 25th Suntory Music Award (1993). Midori has won the Avery Fisher Prize (2001), Musical America's Instrumentalist of the Year award (2002), the Deutscher Schallplattenpreis (2002, 2003), the Kennedy Centre Gold Medal in the Arts (2010) and the Mellon Mentoring Award (2012). In 2007 Midori was named a United Nations Messenger of Peace. In 2012, she received the prestigious Crystal Award by the World Economic Forum in Davos for 20-year devotion to community engagement work worldwide. In May 2021 she was an honouree of the 43rd Kennedy Centre Honours.

Candida Thompson is a British violinist and has been Amsterdam Sinfonietta's artistic director and leader since 2003. Under her leadership the group has performed both in the Netherlands and actively commissions new work. Thompson was born in Glasgow, Scotland, and has been living in Amsterdam since 1992. She was at the Guildhall School of Music and Drama in London, where she received her soloist's graduation diploma with honours and went on to study at the Banff Centre for the Arts in Canada. She also participated in various national and international competitions and received several awards. Her career as a chamber musician has seen her performing alongside major international artists at festivals including Kuhmo (Finland), Gubbio (Italy), International Chamber Music Festival Utrecht (the Netherlands) and La Musica (the United States).

Thompson has been a regular guest artist at La Musica Chamber Music Festival in Florida and she appeared at the Boston Chamber music festival in July 2007 and participated in the Finnish Kuhmo Chamber Music Festival and at the Gubbio Chamber Music festival. Thompson performed as a soloist with orchestras such as Moscow Chamber Orchestra, English String Orchestra, Netherlands Radio Chamber Orchestra, Holland Symfonia and Camerata Nordica, one of Sweden's leading chamber orchestras. She gave solo concerts in England, Germany, Denmark, Italy, Finland, Sweden, Czechoslovakia, Florida and Hong Kong. Most recently she performed in the prestigious Saturday Matinee series at the Concertgebouw in Amsterdam. Her recordings, for which she has received numerous awards, range from Dutch violin sonatas, the Bohemian Album with Amsterdam Sinfonietta, string quartets by Beethoven, Schubert, Shostakovich Shönberg and Brahms as well as music from Argentina.

## Women cellists

Notable cellists include May Mukle (1880–1963), Guilhermina Suggia (1885–1950), Beatrice Harrison (1892–1965), Zara Nelsova (1918–2002) and Jacqueline du Pré (1945–1987). May Mukle was a British cellist and composer who was a feminist[61] and encouraged other women cellists. She studied at the Royal Academy of Music and had a successful concert career including tours to Australia, Africa and Asia. She was a member of the all-women English Ensemble and with her pianist sister Anne Mukle she was a member of the Maude Powell Trio. Her apartment near Wigmore Hall was a meeting place for musicians and she convinced the landlords to rent other apartments in the building to musicians to avoid complaints about noise. During World War II she founded the Mainly Musicians Club and was an original member of the Society of Women Musicians established in 1911. The May Mukle Prize was founded in her honour in 1964.[62]

Guilhermina Suggia was a Portuguese cellist who by the age of 12 was appointed principal cellist at the local orchestra. In 1904, under the patronage of the Queen of Portugal she went to study in Leipzig where she established an international reputation. She lived in the UK for most of her career where she was highly celebrated. Her portrait by Augustus John is considered one of his best and promoted her rarity as a female cellist. She arranged for most of her assets to be used to support future generations of cellists including her Stradivarius and her Montagnana cellos, plus two bows.[63] She established scholarships at the Royal Academy of Music in London and at the Porto Conservatory. In 2010 the scholarship was run in association with the Suggia Festival held in her native city of Porto. The Suggia Trust was set up from the proceeds of her bank account to support young cello players aiming for a solo career.

Beatrice Harrison was a British cellist born in Roorkee, British India. Her family returned to England when she was a child and she studied at the Royal College of Music London. She became a cellist of renown and an inspiration for composers Edward Elgar and Frederick Delius whose cello works she premièred and recorded. She apparently practiced in the outdoors in her Surrey garden and on hearing a nightingale sing back to her convinced the BBC to make a recording of this interaction. On May 19, 1924, she performed a live duet with a wild nightingale in one of the world's first outdoor performances which captivated the nation with more than one million listeners and tens of thousands of letters of appreciation. The concerts were repeated every year until 1942. It was later found that her initial recording involved a nightingale substitute because the bird did not come out to sing at the allotted time and a professional bird song imitator was engaged.[64] Despite the initial fraud the recordings represent a seminal moment in outdoor broadcasting.[65]

Zara Nelsova was born in Canada of Jewish-Russian descent. She was a child prodigy and she moved to England to study at the London Cello School. She gave her London début at the age of 13 as a soloist with the London Symphony Orchestra. During World War II she returned to Canada where she was principal cellist for the Toronto Symphony Orchestra and in 1942 she made her solo début in the United States. Upon her return to London in 1949 she introduced English audiences to new works and premièred new English compositions. In 1955 she became an American citizen and toured extensively in the United States and Canada. In 1966 she was the first US cellist to perform in the Soviet Union.

Jacqueline du Pré was a British cellist who achieved mainstream success at a young age. Her career was cut short by multiple sclerosis. She studied cello from an early age with initial lessons from her mother a talented concert pianist. At the age of 11 she won the Guilhermina Suggia Award which was renewed each year until 1961 allowing her to study at the Guildhall School of Music in London.[66] She entered and won music competitions which brought her to the attention of leading musicians and invitations to perform. In March 1961 she made her début at the age of 16 at Wigmore Hall in London. Her concerto début took place on March 21, 1962 at the Royal Festival Hall with the BBC Symphony Orchestra. In the same year she made her début at the Edinburgh Festival, followed by débuts in Berlin and Paris. Supported by the Suggia Award she took lessons at the Paris Conservatoire. In 1963 she performed at The Proms and her performances of the Elgar Cello Concerto were so popular that she became a regular favourite in the series returning each year until 1969. Her recording of the Elgar Cello Concerto at the age of 20 brought her international recognition and she became recognised as the foremost interpreter of the work. She performed the work at her Carnegie Hall début in 1965. In 1966 she studied in Russia with Rostropovich who declared her his potential successor. Her international performing career resulted in commissions and engagements with leading orchestras. She converted to Judaism to marry her husband Daniel Barenboim in 1967 at the Western Wall in Jerusalem and they gave concerts around Israel for its troops and citizens. Their musical collaborations during the 1960s and early 1970s resulted in recordings and performances which were considered some of the finest of the time. Her playing declined as her illness progressed in the early 1970s and her final performance was in New York in February 1973. She is the subject of several biographies,[67] several documentaries,[68] a film,[69] a ballet[70] and an opera[71] and has received many honours including Officer of the Order of the British Empire (1967), fellow of St Hilda's College, Oxford, and voted into the first Gramophone Hall of Fame (2012).

## Women breaking music instrumental boundaries

Sex-typing of other orchestral instruments such as timpani, horn and saxophone still prevailed up until the end of the 20th century. The virtuoso percussionist Evelyn Glennie (percussion), Alison Balsom (trumpet) and Velvet Brown (tuba) are exceptions. Evelyn Glennie (b. 1965) is a Scottish percussionist and the Indigenous musical traditions of north-east Scotland were integral to her development as a musician. She studied at the Ellon Academy in Scotland and the Royal Academy of Music, London. She was a member of the National Youth Orchestra of Scotland and formed the Cults Percussion ensemble in 1976. She tours internationally with orchestras and a range of eclectic musicians. She is a leading commissioner of new works for percussion. She also plays the Great Highland Bagpipes and has her own registered tartan known as 'The Rhythms of Evelyn Glennie'.[72] At the Opening Ceremony of the 2012 Olympic Games in London 2012, she led a thousand drummers in the opening music and during the lighting of the Olympic Cauldron. She began losing her hearing at the age of eight and has been profoundly deaf since the age of 12 which has not inhibited her performing. She regularly plays barefoot as she maintains that she feels the music and hears it with other parts of her body. She has published 'Hearing Essay' on her website explaining the nature of her condition and how she hears and performs music. Her TED talk of 2003 and her published essays in her book *Listen World!*[73] discuss her approach to hearing and performing music. She has collaborated with contemporary musicians including Björk, Bobby McFerrin, Mark Knopfler, The King's Singers and professional Japanese taiko drumming ensemble Kodō. She has composed music for the Royal Shakespeare Company, collaborated with experimental Jazz Ensemble Trio HLK and composed for Audio Network. She is a patron of the music charity Sound World and composed a new work for the Coronavirus Fund for Freelance Musicians which was recorded in 2021. She has won numerous awards including 28 honorary doctorates for UK Universities and became Dame Commander of the Most Excellent Order of the British Empire (2007).

Alison Balsom (b. 1978) is an English classical trumpet player who began her studies in her youth. In 2001 she graduated from Guildhall School of Music and Drama with first-class honours. She has performed major trumpet concerti with BBC Orchestras and released her début album in 2002. Her awards include three Classic Brit Awards and three German Echo Awards. She was a soloist at the 2009 Last Night of the Proms and principal trumpet of the London Chamber Orchestra. In 2013 she collaborated and performed with actors and The English Consort to produce Gabriel at Shakespeare's Globe. She performs Baroque music on natural trumpet and has given world premières of contemporary compositions. She has also directed the Kent Festival (2015) and Cheltenham Music Festival (2019). She was awarded Officer of the British Empire (2016) along with honorary doctorates and Fellowships in the UK.

American-born Velvet Brown has distinguished herself on the Tuba and has an international professional career as a soloist, chamber musician, recording artist and orchestral player. She has also performed with some of the leading contemporary jazz and commercial artists and has performed in Europe, Russia, Japan, Cuba, Canada and the United States. She is a passionate educator and is Distinguished Professor of Music at the Pennsylvania State University. She is also associate director of the School of Music, Equity, Diversity and Inclusion. She wrote the forward to *The Horizon Leans Forward* (2021) which contains insights and first-hand experiences of people of colour, women and LGBTQI+ individuals working in the wind band field addressing racism and the black experience in America and band music; the intersection of Asian culture and a career in music; experiences and insights of esteemed female band directors; queer identity and visibility in the wind band; encouragement, wisdom and advice for empowering women in music; unique approaches to programming diverse works by diverse composers. The book also features an annotated bibliography of works by underrepresented composers.[74] She is the co-founder of MOJATUBA: Tuba and Dance Fusion Project and leads tuba with Howard Johnston's 'Gravity' Tuba Ensemble. She is a founding member of Stiletto Brass Quintet, Monarch Brass Quintet and Brass Ensemble, the Quintet of Americas and the Pennsylvania Brassworks. She is a founding board member of the International Women's Brass Conference.

## Professional women's musical organisations

All-women's instrumental ensembles and all-female professional societies were formed in reaction to discrimination. In Britain, barred from the Royal Society of Musicians (founded in 1838), women founded the Royal Society of Female Musicians in 1839. In 1865, the two societies merged. The pattern repeated itself in the 20th century when, in 1905, the newly founded Society of British Composers included no women among its 48 members. In 1911 the Society of Women Musicians was founded in London, with Liza Lehmann as its first president (it disbanded in 1972). In 1925 Amy Beach was elected president of the Society of American Women Composers, a group that lasted only a few years. Few other such organisations were formed in the middle decades of the century.

In the activist years of the 1970s and 1980s women's music organizations re-emerged on the cultural horizon: at least 13 were founded between 1975 and 1990. In 1975 Nancy Van de Vate (b. 1930) founded the (International) League of Women Composers, in response to the impact of International Women's Year in 1975; this was followed in 1976 by American Women Composers, Inc. In 1978 two German organisations, the Frau und Musik-Internationaler Arbeitskreis and Musikfrauen Berlin, supported primarily by musicologists and conductors, were founded, with additional archival goals. The 1980s saw the foundation of the Association of Canadian Women Composers (1980–1988), Frauenmusik-Forum in Switzerland (1982), the Stichting Vrouw en Muziek (Foundation for Women in Music) in the Netherlands (1987) and the re-emergence of British Women in Music (1988), as well as other organisations founded in Denmark, Spain and Japan. The Finnish association Nainen ja Musiikki ry (Woman and Music) began in 1995. In the same year, a merger of two American organisations – the International League of Women Composers and American Women Composers, Inc. – with the International Congress on Women in Music (1982) produced the International Alliance of Women in Music (IAWM); the IAWM acts as a clearing house for many individual national societies and internet research websites (it helped to support demonstrations against the admissions policy of the Vienna PO in New York in 1998).

Festivals and thematic concerts devoted to music exclusively by women emerged in the late 19th century. Concerts and events for the Women's Building at the World's Columbian Exposition in Chicago in 1893 set important precedents in the United States. Many annual festivals in the late 20th century continue this tradition. Of note is the Donne in Musica festival founded by Patricia Adkins Chiti in 1982, in collaboration with the Unione Donne Italiane, the oldest and most militant feminist organisation in Italy. Important Women in Music festivals were held in Bonn and Cologne in 1980. The International Congress of Women in Music began its Annual Festivals in New York in 1981. The Frau Musica Nova conference in Cologne in 1998 brought together composers from Asia, Europe and the United States.

## Conclusion

The opportunities for women singers and instrumentalists have increased along with the access to training. It is now common to see women performing alongside their male peers on the concert stage sometimes leading sections. Women soloists have achieved enormous success on the concert platform paving the way for future generation of female musicians. However, barriers still exist for women as instrumental sections are still often led by men and artistic leadership remains largely in the hands of men. Blind auditions introduced in some orchestras have highlighted the unconscious bias that has predominated in orchestras over time, but some have identified that there are still barriers for women in orchestras. As the gender balance in artistic leadership becomes more equal there is increased potential for this to be reflected on the concert stage.

## Notes

1 Goldin, C., & Rouse, C. (2000). Orchestrating impartiality: The impact of 'blind' auditions on female musicians. *American Economic Review*, 90, 715–741.
2 Sergeant, D. & Himonides, E. (2019). Orchestrated sex: The representation of male and female musicians in world-class symphony orchestras. *Frontiers in Psychology*, 10, 1760.
3 Phelps, A. (2010). Beyond auditions: Gender discrimination in America's top orchestras. DMA dissertation, University of Iowa, USA.
4 Sergeant, D. & Himonides, E. (2019). Ibid.
5 For more information about her stay in Lisbon, see Cranmer, D. (July 1996). Madame Catalani em Lisboa: a mulher e a suafamília. Arte Musical IV, série I, 163–168, or in the biographic entry of this singer by the same author in 'Angelica Catalani', Dicionário BiográficoCaravelas www.caravelas.com. ptldicionario_bio grafi co-caravelas.html
6 Cranmer, D. Ibid.
7 Kendall-Davies, B. (2012). The Life and Work of Pauline Viardot-Garcia. Vol. 2, The Years of Grace, 1863–1910. Cambridge Scholars.
8 Denny, G. (1962). *Jenny Lind, the Swedish Nightingale*. Lippincott.
9 Block, A.F. (1992). Two virtuoso performers in Boston: Jenny Lind and Camilla Urso. In *New Perspectives on Music: Essays in Honor of Eileen Southern*. Ed. Wright, J. & Floyd, S.A. Harmonie Park Press, 355–372.
10 These include Melba, N. (1925/2011). *Melodies and Memories*. Cambridge University Press; Hetherington, J.A. (1967/2013). *Melba*. Melbourne University Publishing; Moran W.R. (Ed.) (1984). *Nellie Melba: A Contemporary Review*. [with bibliography and discography]. Greenwood Press; Radic, T. (1986). *Melba: The Voice of Australia*. Springer.
11 Garden is sometimes referred to as solely 'American', as she had lived in America since the age of six, however she did not even apply for American citizenship until April 8, 1924 and lived in Europe thereafter. Turnbull, M. (1997). *Mary Garden*. Scholar Press, 159.
12 Ibid.
13 Arsenault, R. (2010). *The Sound of Freedom: Marian Anderson, The Lincoln Memorial, and the Concert that Awakened America*. Bloomsbury Publishing USA.
14 Anderson, M. (1956/R. 2002). My Lord, What a Morning with Intro. by J.A. DePriest. Urbana.
15 Story, R.M. (1990). *And So I Sing: African American Divas of Opera and Concert*. Amistad.
16 Blyth, A. (2001). *Price, (Mary Violet) Leontyne*. Grove Music Online.

17 Amero, R. (1991). Madame Schumann-Heink: San Diego's Diva. *Southern California Quarterly*, 73(2), 157–182.

18 Shawe-Taylor, D. (1997). Schumann-Heink, Ernestine. In *The New Grove Dictionary of Opera* (Vol.4). Ed. Stanley, S. Oxford University Press, 255.

19 Amero, R. Ibid.

20 Petsalis-Diomidis, N. (2001). *The Unknown Callas: The Greek Years* (Vol. 14). Hal Leonard Corporation.

21 Fussi, F., & Paolillo, N. (2011). Analisi spettrografiche dell'evoluzione e involuzione vocale di Maria Callas alla luce di una ipotesi fisiopatologica. *La voce del cantante*, 7, 33–51.

22 Gruen, J. (1983, 18 September). An American Soprano Adds the Met to her Roster. *The New York Times*.

23 Braun, W. (2015, May). Jessye Norman & Mark Markham; New York City, Carnegie Hall, 2/14/15. *Opera News*. 79(11).

24 Schonberg, H. (1987). *The Great Pianists*. Simon & Schuster, 204.

25 Fétis, F. (1860–1868). *Biographie universelle des musiciens et bibliographie générale de la musique*, vol VII. Firmin-Didot.

26 (1917, 13 June). Mme. Teresa Carreno, Famous Pianist, Dies. Artist, Who Also Had a Career in Opera, a Victim of Paralysis at 63. *The New York Times*.

27 Pita, L. (2015). *Carreño, (María) Teresa*. Grove Music Online.

28 Fillmore, J.C. (1877). Piano teachers and concert pianists. *Dwight's Journal of Music*, 37, 84–85.

29 Macleod, B. (2001). Women performing music: The emergence of American women as instrumentalists and conductors. *McFarland*, 167.

30 Petteys, M. (2001). *Rivé-King [née Rivé], Julie*. Grove Music Online.

31 Hallman, D. (2001). *Bloomfield Zeisler [née Blumenfeld], Fannie*. Grove Music Online.

32 Smith, P. (2002). Juliana Landowska profile, GLBTQ.com.

33 Kottick, E. (2003). *A History of the Harpsichord*, Vol. 1. Indiana University Press, 426.

34 Shapreau, C. (2020, 8 February). The Nazi Confiscation of Wanda Landowska's Musical Collection and Its Aftermath. In *Polin: Studies in Polish Jewry*, the Littman Library of Jewish Civilization in Association with University of Liverpool Press. 32, 429–449 – via Project Muse.

35 Dunoyer, C. (1993). *Marguerite Long: A Life in French Music, 1874–1966*. Indiana University Press, 37–41.

36 Ibid. 92–99.

37 Ibid. 186.

38 Myers, R. (1947). Music in battle-dress. In *Music Since 1939*. British Council, 9–30.

39 Lassemonne, D., & Ferguson, H. (1966). *Myra Hess, by Her Friends* (First American ed.). Vanguard Press, 99.

40 Pascal Cling, Prune Jaillet and Pierre-Olivier François, Clara Haskil, le mystère de linterprète, www.radiofrance.fr/francemusique/podcasts/l-inv ite-du-jour/pierre-olivier-francois-realisateur-du-documentaire-clara-has kil-le-mystere-de-l-interprete-3599932

41 Schonberg, H. Ibid.

42 Tunley, D. (2014). Joyce, Eileen Alannah (1908–1991). *Australian Dictionary of Biography*. National Centre of Biography, Australian National University.

43 *A Girl in a Million* (1946) and *Man of Flowers* (1983). In 1945 Joyce played Rachmaninoff's second piano concerto on the soundtrack in two feature films, *Seventh Veil* and *Brief Encounter*.

44 Feinberg, H. (2021). Rosalyn Tureck, December 14, 1914–July 17, 2003. Jewish Women's Archive. jwa.org.
45 Dame Moura Lympany. (2005, 31 March). *The Telegraph.*
46 Webb, J. (2009, 26 September). Renowned Spanish pianist de Larrocha dead at 86. *Reuters.*
47 Distler, J. (2016). Alicia de Larrocha, Composer, Classics Today.
48 Elder, D. (1979). The Mercurial Martha Argerich. In *Clavier.* Instumentalist Co.
49 According to an archived YouTube interview.
50 Kagan, S. (1977). Camilla Urso: A nineteenth-century violinist's view. *Signs: Journal of Women in Culture and Society,* 2(3), 727–734.
51 Schiller, J. (2006). *Camilla Urso: Pioneer Violinist (1840–1902).* University of Kentucky.
52 Shaffer, K. & Greenwood, G. (1988). *Maud Powell: Pioneer American Violinist.* Maud Powell Foundation.
53 Ostleitner, E. & Morini, E. (n.d.). Maude Powell. In *The Shalvi/Hyman Encyclopaedia of Jewish Women.* Jewish Women's Archive. jaw.org
54 Siskind, J. (1973, 14 April). Ida Haendel – Reflections on music in the land of Mao. *The Montreal Gazette.*
55 Smith, H. (2020, 3 July). Ida Haendel, Polish-born musician known as 'grande dame of the violin', dies at 96. *Washington Post.* Washington.
56 Jeal, E. (2014, 3 December). Kyung Wha Chung review – A legend makes a tense return. *The Guardian*; Hewett, I. (2014, 5 December). Kyung-wha Chung was right to shush a toddler. *The Daily Telegraph*; Chung, K. (2014, 9 December). I have always welcomed children to my concerts. *The Guardian.*
57 Chapman, E. (2012). *From Russia to Love: The Life and Times of Viktoria Mullova.* Robson Press, UK.
58 www.anne-sophie-mutter.de/en/page/biography/a-biographical-timeline/
59 Ibid.
60 Rockwell, J. (1986, 28 July). Girl, 14, Conquers Tanglewood with 3 Violins. *The New York Times.*
61 Caldwell, J. (2010). *Essays on the History of English Music in Honour of John Caldwell: Sources, Style, Performance, Historiography.* Boydell & Brewer, 251.
62 Campbell, M. (2011). *The Great Cellists.* Faber & Faber.
63 Mercier, A. (2017). *Guilhermina Suggia: Cellist.* Routledge, 116.
64 Alberge, D. (2022, 8 April). The cello and the nightingale: 1924 duet was faked, BBC admits. *The Guardian.*
65 Baird, I. (2015, 19 October). Capturing the song of the nightingale. *Science Museum Group Journal,* 4(4).
66 Easton, C. (2000). *Jacqueline du Pré: A Biography.* Da Capo Press, 31.
67 Easton. (2000). Ibid; Wilson, E. (1999). *Jacqueline du Pré: Her Life, Her Music, Her Legend.* Faber and Faber; Du Pré, P. & Du Pré, H. (1997). *A Genius in the Family: An Intimate Memoir of Jacqueline du Pré.* Sinclair-Stevenson.
68 *Remembering Jacqueline du Pré* (1994), directed by Christopher Nupen; *Jacqueline du Pré in Portrait* (2004), directed by Christopher Nupen; *The Trout* (1970 documentary released on DVD in 2005), directed by Christopher Nupen; *Jacqueline du Pré: A Celebration of Her Unique and Enduring Gift* (2007), directed by Christopher Nupen.
69 *Hilary and Jackie* (1998), dramatised portrait directed by Anand Tucker.
70 Choreographer Cathy Marston choreographed a one-act ballet titled *The Cellist,* based on du Pré's life, for The Royal Ballet. The ballet premièred in

2020 at the Royal Opera House, with Lauren Cuthbertson as 'The Cellist', Matthew Ball as 'The Conductor' and Marcelino Sambé as 'The Instrument'.
71 Jacqueline, by Luna Pearl Woolf (music) and Royce Vavrek (libretto) had its world première at Canada's National Ballet School's Betty Oliphant Theatre in Toronto, in a production by Tapestry Opera, on February 19, 2020.
72 Tartan Details – The Scottish Register of Tartans. February 5, 2009. Tartanregister.gov.uk.
73 Glennie, E. (2019). *Listen World!*. Balestier Press.
74 In Leung, E., Brown, V., Blackshaw, J., Shapiro, A., Snyder, C., Taylor, R. & Watkins, A.L. (2021). *The Horizon Leans Forward: Stories of Courage, Strength, and Triumph of Underrepresented Communities in the Wind Band Field: With an Annotated Bibliography of Works by Underrepresented Composers*. GIA Publications Inc.

# 5

# WOMEN IN BLUES, JAZZ, GOSPEL AND MOTOWN

## Introduction

Women from African American slave roots expressed the concerns of women through the blues. In the tradition of the African lament, women sang of oppression, love, pain and suffering. The blues was also an outlet for expressing resistance and empowerment. The recording industry paved the way for black female musicians in an industry that was previously closed to them. Gospel pulpits provided women with the opportunity to participate in musical performance and develop their musical skills providing black women a springboard for their musical careers through the church. The record promoters glamorised and sexualised the lives of blues and gospel singers to capitalise on their talent and cater to the male gaze. Women also took on prominent positions in jazz and many early jazz pianists and composers were women. Similar to other musical genres, their role has generally been largely non-instrumental throughout the 20th century, but in the latter part of the century with access to more musical educational opportunities women took to the jazz instrumental stage. Notwithstanding early barriers there was an emerging trend of women jazz instrumentalists and all-women jazz ensembles. Women began to gain considerable wealth for their performances and the ability to capitalise on their music, but it was rare that they earned appropriate royalties for their recordings and publications were often ruthlessly exploited by the recording industry. Some gained financial independence and creative control, but many spent their final years in poverty. The following surveys the careers of some of the leading women in blues, jazz, gospel and Motown.

DOI: 10.4324/9781003183631-6

## Blues

Music emerging from African American slave roots was a means of expressing social messages. The musical pulpit of gospel was a powerful way in which women could convey their concerns and needs. In the tradition of the West African lament, the blues was also a way in which women could use music to deliver the message of oppression. Blues for these female vocalists was a vehicle for the expression of black righteousness, female sexuality and resistance to racial oppression. Gertrude 'Ma' Rainey (1886–1939) and Bessie Smith (1894–1937) were some of the leaders of this movement and the recordings of Mamie Smith (1891–1946) paved the way for black women's music in an industry that was previously closed to them. At the time women on the stage earning an income was possible, but they were considered no more than prostitutes and it was not until the rise of the recording industry that women broke through.

Ma Rainey was a hard-headed businesswoman who paved the way for female blues artists that became more successful than their male counterparts in the 1920s. However, not all were as astute in the management of their finances as Rainey and artists such as Ethyl Waters (1896–1977), Ida Cox (1888 or 1896–1967), Alberta Hunter (1895–1984) and Bessie Smith who were some of the highest-earning artists at the time did not invest and died penniless and almost forgotten along with many women in music had it not been for the research into reviving their work. Black American singers such as Bessie Smith, Ma Rainey, Billie Holiday (1915–1959) and Nina Simone (1933–2003) have been models of empowerment in contemporary black American literature.[1]

Mammie Smith entered blues history as the first African American artist to make vocal blues recordings. She was a vaudeville singer, dancer, pianist and actress who performed in multiple styles including jazz and blues. She was born in Cincinnati and started performing white vaudeville acts at the age of 10 moving to New York to sing in clubs in Harlem. The early 20th century saw a mass migration of post-Slavery Southern African Americans to Harlem in New York City. The so-called Harlem Renaissance became a centre for black art and culture with an emphasis on new ideas and social experimentation in an atmosphere of social permissiveness. In 1920 Smith's first recording was the first recording by an African American blues singer, but the backing musicians were all white men. The producer received death threats for recording a black artist, but this was overridden by its enormous success.[2] In 1920 she recorded her greatest hits in a set of songs that sold a million copies in less than a year.[3] Many copies were bought by African Americans which represented the new market for race records. Smith's success led recording producers to seek out other female blues singers beginning the era of classic female blues. Smith toured the United States and Europe with her band Mamie Smith & Her Jazz Hounds and was billed as the 'Queen of the Blues'. As radio emerged as a mass medium Smith saw this as an opportunity to increase her fan base and her reach in cities with predominantly white audiences who were increasingly developing an appetite for the new blues sounds. She also saw opportunities in the early sound film medium and appeared in a number of early motion pictures. She reportedly died penniless and in an unmarked grave until 2013 following a successful crowdfunding campaign which bought a four-foot-high etched granite headstone bearing her image.[4] In 1994 her recording of 'Crazy Blues' was inducted into the Grammy Hall of Fame and selected for preservation due to its historical significance to the Library of Congress in 2005.

Ma Rainey began performing as a teenager at a talent show in Georgia as Gertrude Pridgett. She became known as 'Ma' Rainey following her marriage to Will 'Pa' Rainey in 1904. They toured with the Rabbit's Foot Minstrels where they were billed as 'Black Face Song and Dance Comedians, Jubilee Singers [and] Cake Walkers'.[5] In 1914 they formed their own group Rainey and Rainey, Assassinators of the Blues. She claimed to be the originator of the term 'blues' in her description of her songs.

Ma Rainey benefited from the high demand for recordings of black musicians or race records and made around a hundred recordings commencing with the signing of a Paramount contract in 1923 who marketed her as 'Mother of the blues' and 'Songbird of the South'.[6] In 1924 she also recorded with Louis Armstrong and toured the Midwest and South of the United States performing to both black and white audiences. Her songs centre around both heterosexual and lesbian or bisexual love and, unlike many of the blues singers of the day, she wrote at least a third of the songs in her repertoire.[7] Her songs spoke of her experiences and those of other black women including anguish, rage, love, sexual desire and life. She portrayed women as independent, sexually liberated, challenging norms of respectability and heteronormative standards of women's behaviour.

Ma Rainey was one of the first businesswomen to capitalise on the black music market. Her legendary extravagant performance attire along with her bulging eyes and gold teeth captivated audiences and she paved the way for the popularity of the blues. She capitalised on the rising recording industry as did other blues singers, but many of the early women blues artists died in poverty due to lack of business acumen. Ma Rainey was the exception. When she was fired from Paramount in 1928 it is not known whether she received the royalties for her work, but she pivoted into another kind of leadership buying two movie halls, the Lyric and Airdrome theatres in Columbus, Georgia. This foresight into investing in the new ventures of cinema theatres lead to a comfortable retirement for Ma Rainey.

While Ma Rainey and other female blues artists did earn a reasonable amount of money as race records flourished in the 1920s, they didn't receive the amount they deserved. The record executives exploited them at every step and coerced them into signing away royalties and sometimes ownership of their songs.

Bessie Smith was born in Tennessee and became known as 'The Empress of the Blues'. As a child she busked on the streets of Chattanooga to support her existence as a young impoverished orphan in the care of her older sister. In 1912 she auditioned for a travelling troupe featuring Ma Rainey and Smith started performing as a dancer. She began forming her own act and by 1920 she had established a career in the South and on the East Coast of America. She was signed to Columbia Records to the race records series which was gaining popularity. Her first record was a hit and she became a success on the performance circuit. Columbus records haled her as 'Queen of the Blues', but the national press upgraded this to 'Empress of the Blues' to trump the former title held by Mammie Smith. She became one of the highest-paid black performers and began travelling in her own 72-foot-long railroad car.[8] Her touring exploits involved drinking, partying, drug taking and orgies with her dancers, musicians and worshiping drag queens who followed her.[9] Smith's bisexuality was well known and there were rumours circulating that she was involved with Ma Rainey. Ma Rainey was famously arrested for attending a lesbian orgy and it was Bessie who collected her from prison. It was a period of social upheaval and experimentation where queer artists were able to express their sexuality in an atmosphere of social permissiveness. Smith sang about independence, fearlessness and sexual freedom for working-class women. Some scholars consider many of her songs to be a form of African American protest music.[10] She advocated for empowerment for African American women and their right to express their independence.[11] She made 160 recordings for Columbia with some of the finest musicians of her time and many became best-selling hits. She made her only film appearance in *St Louis Blues* (1929), but the musical and narrative of the film is a departure from her recordings portraying her as a pitiful woman scorned rather than an independent black woman. However, it did bear some resemblance to her marriage to her manipulative husband and self-styled manager who abused her while taking gifts and money from her at one point using it to produce a show for one of his lovers. This provoked Bessie into tracking her down and beating her unconscious resulting in a police fine. The Great

Depression and the decline in interest in the blues recording industry put an end to elaborate vaudeville shows, but Smith continued to tour and party. She diversified her style appeared on Broadway and her last recordings were made in 1933 reflecting the emerging swing sounds. She was critically injured in a car crash in 1937 and died the following day. Her funeral was attended by over 7,000 people, but her grave remained unmarked as her husband pocketed her remaining money. It was not until 1970 that she received her tombstone funded by a younger generation blues singer Janis Joplin. Her legacy includes recordings inducted into the Grammy Hall of Fame, her recording of 'Downhearted Blues' is selected for preservation by the Library of Congress and is included in the list of Songs of the Century by the Recording Industry of America and the National Endowment of the Arts in 2001 and the Rock and Roll Hall of Fame's 500 songs that shaped rock 'n' roll. In 1984 Smith was inducted into the National Women's Hall of Fame. She has been the subject of short stories, movies, biographies and tribute songs.

Ethel Waters began her career by singing the blues. Following a troubled background and an itinerant upbringing she began singing professionally at the Lincoln Theatre in Baltimore at the age of 17. She toured the vaudeville circuit and joined a carnival before moving to Atlanta where she worked alongside Bessie Smith. Around 1919 she moved to Harlem to join the 1920s Harlem Renaissance and became involved in a romantic relationship with dancer Ethel Williams to become dubbed as 'The Two Ethels'. She was the fifth black woman to be recorded by the new race records producers and became one of the highest-paid black recording artists of the time. She joined a vaudeville circuit performing to white audiences and accompanying screenings of silent movies. In 1933 she began appearing in films as an actress, the first being an all-black satire *Rufus Jones for President*. She was a star at the Cotton Club. She became the first black woman to perform regularly on Broadway becoming the highest-paid performer of her time.

In 1939 she became the first African American to star in her own television show, The Ethel Waters Show, a variety special. In 1942 she moved to Los Angeles to appear in Hollywood movies and was nominated for an Academy award for her performance of the song 'Happiness is Just a Thing Called Joe' in the movie *Cabin in the Sky*. In 1949 she was nominated for an Academy Award for best supporting actress for the film *Pinky*. In 1950 she won the New York Drama Critics Circle Award for the performance in *The Members of the Wedding*, which was made into a film in 1952. Also, in 1950 she became the first African American to star in a television series Beulah which aired on ABC until 1953. She left the role in 1952 finding the role degrading to blacks.[12] She became increasingly devout as a Christian in her later years and bad tempered on film sets if she felt that the scripts went against her spiritual beliefs. She became closely associated with American Christian evangelist Billy Graham and found it increasingly difficult to find work as an actress.[13] Although she made several fortunes over her career of six decades, she died in near poverty with her only income being a Social Security check. Three recordings by Waters have been inducted into the Grammy Hall of Fame Award (1973) and her recording of 'Stormy Weather' (1933) has been listed for preservation by the Library of Congress in 2003. She has also been approved for a star on The Hollywood Walk of Fame in 2004.

The prospect of educational and employment opportunities for black children born on wealthy Plantations was limited as they were for Ida Cox, who was born in Georgia on the wealthy Prather Riverside Plantation. She joined the local African Methodist Choir and developed an interest in gospel music and performance. At the age of 14 she left home to tour with the African American travelling minstrel shows on the vaudeville circuit. Her stint with the Rabbit's Foot Minstrels was important to her career as it provided her with a nurturing environment to develop her stage presence. It was also responsible for launching the careers of her idols Ma Rainey and Bessie Smith. In 1920 she left the vaudeville circuit to headline at the 81 Theatre in Atlanta. She was scouted by race music producers and secured a contract with Paramount who promoted her as 'The uncrowned Queen of the Blues'.[14] Between September 1923 and October 1929, she recorded 78 titles for Paramount. With the waning of interest at the end of the 1920s in blues singers she formed the tent review show Raisin' Cain with her husband Jesse 'Tiny' Crump. They toured into the early 1930s to black theatres across the Southeast and west towards Texas with Cox as the act and Crump as the accompanist and manager. The shows had chorus girls, comics and backup singers.[15] In 1935 they reorganised the troupe and named it Darktown Scandals. Following the Great Depression, she was invited to sing at Carnegie Hall which was a boost to her career and continued to make recordings in the late 1930s. She also continued to perform until 1945 when she was forced into retirement with a debilitating stroke during a performance at a nightclub in Buffalo, New York. She was recalled to the recording studio in 1961 for her final album *Blues for Rampart Street*.

Cox's fierce independence learned at an early age characterised her approach to her career. She was an astute businesswoman and she was central to the management of her troupe Raisin' Cain. She wrote songs that address female independence, sexual liberation and the social-political struggles of black women. Her song 'Wild Women Don't Have the Blues' is considered to be one of the first feminist anthems.[16]

Like many of the blues women before her Alberta Hunter was born into difficult circumstances in Memphis, Tennessee, to a single mother who worked as a maid in a Memphis brothel. This did provide her with the opportunity to attend school until the age of 15, but when her mother remarried Hunter left for Chicago as she heard that she would be able to get work as a paid singer. She sang at various brothels and eventually at Chicago bars. Her career began to take off as she received engagements at clubs with white audiences. Her big break was in 1917 where she was booked for a five-year engagement at Dreamland Café. She first toured Europe in 1917 performing in Paris and London and where she was treated as an artist with respect which made a great impression on her.[17] She married in 1919, but it was short-lived as she discovered that she was a lesbian. She kept her subsequent relationships low-key and her career as a songwriter and performer flourished in the 1920s with performances in both New York and London. She recorded for the labels that were promoting race music and her songs such as 'Downhearted blues' which Bessie Smith covered, became a big hit for her producers. However, the deals that were made did not benefit her as well as it did her producers.

Her styles included blues, jazz and popular music and during the Great Depression, she moved to Europe. In 1928 she appeared in the first London production of *Showboat* at Drury Lane and subsequently performed in nightclubs throughout Europe. She later appeared at the Dorchester, London during which time she made several recordings and featured in the British film *Radio Parade of 1935* (1934).[18] She continued to perform both in London and the United States during the late 1930s and early 1940s, but upon returning to the United States in the late 1930s her recording career went into decline. During the war, she headlined the first black show for the United Service Organisation Inc. which provided entertainment for the United States Armed Forces. Her tours with USO took her to Casablanca and Korea.

Hunter left her performing career after 1956 reinventing her age and qualifications to study and practice nursing in New York. During this career, she returned to performing only once in 1961 to record with her friends Lovie Austin and Lil Hardin Armstrong. She retired from nursing in 1977 when she was 81 at the request of her employers who thought she was 70 and too old to continue. She made four more albums before her death in 1984.

## Jazz

As the blues became less popular jazz and swing bands took over. Arguably the greatest exponent of the emerging trend was Billie Holiday (1915–1959) with her emphasis on improvisation and manipulation of rhythm. However, with a life born in poverty and abuse she was wracked with drug addiction and alcoholism, and she faced exploitation and racial stigma. Nonetheless, her musical legacy has profoundly influenced generations of female performers. Holiday was influential in the development of the blues through the introduction of the sounds of swing and her distinctive style of improvisation. She was engaged to perform with the great blues and jazz legends of the era and profited from the new jukebox revolution.

Holiday began her career singing in nightclubs in Harlem and made her recording début at the age of 18. In 1935 she made her first film appearance in *Symphony in Black–A Rhapsody of Negro Life*, a nine-minute early cinematic musical exploration of African American popular culture featuring Duke Ellington performing his first extended swing composition and Billie Holiday singing the blues. She was represented in the common narrative of the time of a black women abused and discarded by her lover.

In 1935 Holiday began to record pop tunes in swing style for jukebox trade. Her unique improvisations set her apart from her contemporaries and she brought financial success mainly to her producers and drug dealers. In late 1937 she began touring with Count Basie choosing songs that portrayed her as unlucky in love. She came into competition with Ella Fitzgerald (1917–1996) who was having success with the Chick Webb Band, but they became good friends.[19] Holiday left the Basie band in 1938 possibly because she was complaining of working conditions, pay and repertoire.[20] She joined the Artie Shaw's band as one of the first black women to work with a white orchestra in the segregated US South which resulted in racially motivated attacks. Shaw came to her defence, but was pressured to hire a white singer to replace her. The racial discrimination that Holiday faced during this time with Shaw's band became unbearable and she eventually found it difficult to continue. However, her popularity resulted in bestselling recordings of what became jazz standards. Commencing in 1938 her performances and recordings of the song 'Strange Fruit' that signified lynching, became a huge success and a hit on the record charts. A string of hits followed and by the mid-1940s she was one of the highest-earning artists of her time. Much of her income was spent on her drug addiction despite her high earnings in the 1940s. She was arrested for narcotics possession in New York in 1947 for which she was convicted causing her to lose her cabaret performance rights after which she only performed in concert venues and theatres. This had a considerable effect on her earning capacity and her confidence that her audiences would accept her. However, at her comeback concert on March 27, 1948, she played to a sold-out crowd. Following another arrest in

January 1949 she continued to record and in October 1949 recorded one of her most successful hits 'Crazy He Calls Me' which was induced into the Grammy Hall of Fame in 2010. By the late 1940s her songs were receiving less airplay and by the 1950s her records went out of print. Her royalty arrangements were unfavourable and her loss of her club licence affected her earnings. Her tragic life circumstances, narcotic and alcohol addiction damaged her health and career. The men in her life abused her and the record industry exploited her. This experience became common to women in popular music such as Anita O'Day and Judy Garland. Holiday died with US$0.70 in the bank and a US$1,000 estate. Her commercial success in performances and recordings was enormous and she has been the subject of movies, plays and books. Her distinctive singing style and idiosyncratic improvisations influenced the path of the blues and popular song and her legacy remained long after her death.

Holiday's direct competitor at the time Ella Fitzgerald was referred to as 'the Queen of Jazz' and became particularly famous for her improvisations and scat singing. Born in Newport News, Virginia, her early years were disrupted by the death of her mother when she was 15 years old. She was a talented and accomplished student and her early experiences of music were through the church and recordings of jazz. After her mother's death, she lived with her stepfather for a year before moving to live with her aunt in the Bronx. Her schooling was disrupted by this move and she survived by singing in the streets of Harlem. At age 17 she won first prize in amateur night at the Apollo Theatre and a year later she joined the Chick Webb's orchestra to perform at the Savoy Ballroom, Harlem. She recorded several hit songs with the orchestra and in 1938 she co-wrote and recorded the nursery rhyme 'A-Tisket, A-Tasket' which became a major hit and one of the biggest selling records of the decade. Webb died in 1939 and the band was renamed Ella and Her Famous Orchestra which she led for several years before it disbanded. She also recorded with the Benny Goodman Orchestra and led her own group Ella Fitzgerald and Her Savoy Eight. For a period, she worked as lead singer with The Three Keys and in the mid-1940s she began singing for Jazz at the Philharmonic. During this time, she recorded a number of hits with Decca.

The advent of bebop led to a decline in swing and Fitzgerald adapted her style introducing scat singing to her repertoire. She started working with Dizzy Gillespie's big band and her scat recording of 'Flying Home' (1945) was considered one of the most influential vocal jazz records of the decade.[21] Similarly her bebop recording of 'Oh, Lady Be Good' (1947) increased her reputation as the leading jazz vocalist of the time.[22] Fitzgerald toured to Australia in 1954 and set new box office records in that country, but a racial discrimination incident which saw her and her band removed from their first-class seats in Honolulu causing her to miss the first two concerts in Sydney. The band sued the airline and won with a sizeable settlement.

In 1955 Fitzgerald's manager started Verve records to produce crossover non-jazz recordings with a spotlight on American composers and lyricists. The first was released in 1956 titled *Ella Fitzgerald Sings the Cole Porter Songbook*. The songbook series recordings continued until 1964 and represent a significant and critically acclaimed contribution to American culture. She continued to record albums devoted to significant songwriters Cole Porter (1972) Antônio Carlos Jobim (1981) and George Gershwin (1983). She made numerous live recordings on Verve which were also critically acclaimed hits. She continued to record on other major labels until 1991.

Fitzgerald toured regularly in the United States and internationally and bought a house in Denmark after she began a relationship with a Danish man. She considered buying a jazz club there, but eventually sold her house and moved permanently back to the United States. She won 14 Grammy Awards, the National Medal of the Arts, the NAACP's inaugural President's Award and the Presidential Medal of Freedom. Fitzgerald was a civil rights activist and insisted on non-segregated performance venues. She was awarded the National Association for the Advancement of Coloured People Equal Justice Award and the American Black Achievement Award. Fitzgerald established a charitable foundation focussing upon providing opportunities for children, music education, care for the less fortunate and medical research into diabetes. Fitzgerald also supported other charitable organisations with a similar focus. She appeared on popular television and in movies and collaborated with major artists of the time and her last public performance was in 1993 at the age of 76 before her death aged 79. There have been numerous tribute albums recorded by leading singers and musicians along with documentaries featuring rare footage of her life.

Nina Simone's (Eunice Kathleen Waymon) leadership in civil rights activism was also voiced in her songs, performances and public endorsements for outspoken campaigners. She demonstrated talent in playing the piano from a young age and being from a poor family her music teacher helped raise funds for her tuition. Her early consciousness of civil rights was demonstrated at her concert début at her local church at the age of 12 where she insisted that her parents sit in the front row which was reserved for white audiences.[23] In 1950 she studied at Julliard to prepare for audition at the Curtis Institute of Music, Philadelphia, but her application was rejected. She was sorely disappointed and attributed this to racism. She took private lessons which she paid for by working as a photographer's assistant, an accompanist at a vocal studio and private piano teaching. She also performed at the local bar and grill. She took on the stage name Nina Simone knowing that her mother didn't approve of her playing 'the Devil's music' and her identity could be protected. Her recording of Gershwin's 'I Loves You Porgy' became a Billboard top 20 success in the United States. Her début album *Little Girl Blue* (1959) was a huge success, but because she sold her rights for US$3,000 she lost millions in royalties. She continued to record, but insisted on contracts that allowed her to have creative control over what was recorded and included material that addressed her African American heritage. Her response to the murder of civil rights activist Medgar Evers by white supremacists and the bombing of the 16th Street Baptist Church in Birmingham Alabama was to record the protest song 'Mississippi Goddam' (1964). It was boycotted in some southern states and promotional copies were destroyed at some radio stations. She began to perform and speak at civil rights meetings and supported the views of her neighbour Malcolm X for black nationalism and violent revolution. In the late 1960s, her social-political consciousness was expressed in her recordings and performances including at the Harlem Cultural Festival (1969). She felt punished by the music industry for boycotting her records and left the United States in 1970 for Barbados where she avoided paying tax in the United States as a protest against the Vietnam War. In the 1980s she toured for performances in London, Liberia, Barbados and Switzerland eventually ending up in Paris. In 1987 the re-release of her 1959 recording 'My Baby Just Cares for Me' as a result of being used in a Chanel No. 5 commercial resulted in a huge European hit and a brief resurgence in popularity. In 1988 she moved to Nijmegen in the Netherlands to get back on track as her temper and aggression on stage were affecting her career. At this time, she was diagnosed with bipolar disorder and with medication, and the ability to live fairly anonymously, her life improved. She won a legal battle with Chanel for the use of her song and in 1991 moved to the livelier city, Amsterdam. In 1993 she settled in Aix-en-Provence in Southern France, returning to Newark for a final performance in the United States in 1998. After suffering from breast cancer for several years, she died in 2003.

She earned the title 'The High Priestess of Soul' as a pianist, singer, songwriter and performer.[24] She moved between gospel, blues, jazz, folk, pop and classical. Her classical training and understanding of counterpoint from her study of the works of J.S. Bach infused an innovative approach to jazz making her one of the most influential improvisers of her time. Her social commentary went beyond her civil rights activism to challenging Eurocentric notions of women's beauty imposed on black women to inspire black women to define their beauty and identity beyond the stereotypes that had been imposed on them. She composed and recorded *Four*

*Women* (1965–1966) to challenge African American women stereotypes. Her role in supporting the civil rights movement led her to be one of the first black entertainers to 'rediscover' her African heritage influencing the generations of black women musicians that followed her.

Women vocalists carried on the revolutionary work of Ma Rainey include Billie Holiday, Nina Simone and Ella Fitzgerald. Similar to other musical genres, their role has generally been focussed on voice and piano with other instruments dominated by men.[25] However, in the latter part of the century with access to more musical educational opportunities women took to the jazz instrumental stage. In examining the differences in confidence, anxiety and attitudes towards learning jazz improvisation, Wehr-Flowers found that these social-psychological issues were a negative influence on women in jazz. Notwithstanding there was an emerging trend of women jazz instrumentalists and all-women jazz ensembles.[26]

## Jazz instrumentalists

Women instrumentalists and composers were prominent in the jazz and swing era and influenced the new styles that were emerging. Due to the social acceptability of the piano, there are many examples of women blues and jazz pianists such as Lillian Hardin Armstrong (1898–1971), Lovie Austin (1887–1972), Mary Lou Williams (1910–1981), Marian McPartland (1918–2013) and Hazel Scott (1920–1981). This group of talented women instrumentalists had a large role to play in the early years of the blues and jazz, but associations such as marriages to jazz musicians and reflected glory overshadowed their achievements. The names of their male counterparts became renowned and celebrated in perpetuity while the outstanding contribution of these women to jazz has been largely overlooked. The resurgence of research into women's contribution to blues and jazz in the second wave of feminism has redressed the balance somewhat, but their leadership role in the development of musical style, feminist and civil rights activism, and business is still obscured. Women formed jazz bands in response to the difficulty of gaining access to the male-dominated jazz world, but women such as clarinettist Ann Dupont (1915–1998) moved into leading all male bands after 1939 as a way to gain increased professional recognition. Sarah McLawler (1926–2017) was a piano child prodigy whose mission was to inspire other women led some of the finest female jazz combinations in New York in the late 1940s and 1950s and was a pioneer in championing women, but at great cost to her physical health. Some women did manage to break into the business, but generally the higher-selling artists were male.

Lillian Hardin Armstrong was a brilliant jazz pianist as well as composer, arranger, singer and bandleader. She mentored her son Lester Young and her husband Louis Armstrong and led many male and female bands. She had a postgraduate degree from the New York College of music and composed over 150 pieces of music. She studied music from a young age at school and then Fisk University College for African Americans in Nashville. In 1918 she moved to Chicago with her family and became a sheet music demonstrator at Jones Music Store. She was enamoured with jazz and rebelled against her mother's wishes for a career as a concert pianist. She was offered a job in a band performing at De Luxe Café and Dreamland where she accompanied Alberta Hunter. She joined King Oliver's Creole Jazz Band which had a six-month engagement with Pergola Ballroom, San Francisco, after which she returned to Chicago. In 1929 she earned a postgraduate diploma at the New York College of Music. She married Louis Armstrong and mentored him in his career by assisting him in learning classical music, helping him to dress more fashionably for the stage, encouraging him to manage his own money and convincing him to assert himself on the bandstand as well as during recording sessions. She also persuaded him to go out on his own. They collaborated on numerous recordings in the 1920s but they grew apart and eventually divorced in 1938. After the divorce she remained dedicated to him and when he died in 1971 she travelled to New York to the funeral and rode in the family car. Their relationship and her adopting his surname caused some confusion about the authorship of many of the songs that she arranged and wrote. Hardin successfully sued Armstrong over the false attribution of Armstrong as songwriter for the song 'Struttin' with Some Barbecue' (1927) recorded by OKeh by the Louis Armstrong: Hot Five. Examination of the chord structure and the inclusion of the dominant seventh point to a classically trained songwriter which Hardin was. There is also the view that her compositions contributed to the invention of the Chicago sounds that were distinct from the New Orleans tradition.[27]

Hardin Armstrong led two all-women bands through the 1930s including one of the first all-female swing bands, The Harlem Harlicans which featured Leora Mieux on trumpet, Alma Long Scott on reeds and Dolly Jones (1902–1975) on trumpet.[28] In 1936 she became the house pianist for Decca leading many all-star recording sessions. In the late 1940s and 1950s, she worked mostly as a soloist, singing and playing piano around Chicago. In 1952 she moved to France for four years during which time she toured Europe. When she returned to Chicago, she continued to play extended engagements for the next 30 years.

She also pursued other creative projects. In the late 1940s, she decided to take a course in tailoring which was a male-dominated profession and her graduation project was a tuxedo for Louis Armstrong. She opened a restaurant called the Swing Shack, which used musical themes in the menu listings, designed clothes and taught music and French. In 1961 she appeared as accompanist for Alberta Hunter in the recording project Chicago: The Living Legends and was subsequently included in the 1961 NBC network special Chicago and All That Jazz, along with its follow-up album. In 1971 she died of a heart attack following collapsing at that piano during a televised memorial concert for Louis Armstrong whilst playing 'St Louis Blues'.

Cora 'Lovie' Austin was an American bandleader, session musician, singer and arranger and was considered one of the best blues and jazz pianists of her time along with Lil Hardin Armstrong. Born to Cora Taylor in Chattanooga, Tennessee, she took the surname of her second husband and her nickname 'Lovie' was given by her grandmother who raised her. She studied theory at Knoxville College, Tennessee, but like classically trained Lil Hardin she was drawn to jazz. She was childhood friends with Bessie Smith and they used to sneak out together to watch Ma Rainey perform. From 1912 Austin toured the vaudeville circuit but tired of touring and due to the associated poor conditions for black musicians she moved to Chicago. There she led her own band the Blues Serenaders which accompanied many of the Classic Blues singers of the 1920s, including Ma Rainey, Ida Cox, Alberta Hunter and Ethel Waters. Lovie Austin's song 'Down Hearted Blues' (1922) was a big hit for Bessie Smith. When the classic blues craze began to wane in the early 1930s Austin became music director for the Monogram Theatre, Chicago. Following World War II, she recorded and performed occasionally and played for a local dance school. In 1961 she made a comeback to record one more album with Alberta Hunter after which she retired. Her influence has been documented in the interviews with Mary Lou Williams who attributed her career to this role model.

Mary Lou Williams grew up in Pittsburgh, Pennsylvania, and was a child prodigy who taught herself to play the piano. She began supporting her family at the age of 6 by playing at parties and was a fully professional musician by the age of 15 citing Lovie Austin as her greatest influence.[29] In 1922 she joined the Orpheum Circuit. In 1927 following her marriage to saxophonist John Overton Williams, she accompanied him as a composer, arranger and performer. She was the arranger and pianist for recordings in Kansas City (1929), Chicago (1930) and New York City (1930) which sold quickly and she rose to national prominence. She worked as a freelance composer and arranger for leading jazz musicians during the 1930s. In 1942 she divorced her husband and stopped performing with him and his band. She continued as composer, arranger and performed with bands including Duke Ellington and her second husband Harold 'Shorty' Baker who she left after a year of marriage. She took a job with the Café Society in New York and began a radio show called the Mary Williams's Piano Workshops. She also began mentoring and composing for younger generations of bebop musicians. She composed the *Zodiac Suite* (1945) dedicated to musical colleagues including Billie Holiday. Williams recorded it and performed it at the Town Hall in New York City. In 1952 she toured the UK and Europe for two years returning to the United States physically and mentally exhausted. She took a three-year break from performing and converted to Catholicism devoting her time to worshipping at Mass and her charitable work in assisting the poor as well as musicians grappling with addiction. She was convinced to return to performing by her priest mentors and she returned to performing in 1957 at the Newport Jazz Festival. She returned full time to performing in the 1960s and formed her own record label and publishing companies. She also founded the Pittsburgh Jazz Festival and appeared regularly on television. Throughout the 1960s she concentrated on composing sacred music and became the first jazz composer commissioned to write a Mass in jazz idiom. Her mass *Music for Peace* was choreographed by Alvin Ailey and performed as Mary Lou's Mass by Alvin Ailey Dance Theatre (1971). She worked with youth choirs and musicians to perform her works and her performance of Mary Lou's Mass at St. Patrick's Cathedral in New York City in April 1975 was a gathering of over 3,000 people marking the first time a jazz performance had taken place in a cathedral. Her career continued to flourish in the 1970s with successful recordings and performances at Monterey Jazz Festival (1971), Greenwich Village plus a recorded performance with avant-garde pianist Cecil Taylor at Carnegie Hall (April 1977). She taught jazz to schoolchildren and was artist-in-residence at Duke University (1977–1981). In 1978 she performed at the White House for President Jimmy Carter. Her final solo recital at the Montreux Jazz Festival, 1978, which included spirituals, ragtime, blues and swing was recorded three years before her death in 1981. She received a number of significant honours including Guggenheim Fellowship (1972, 1977), Grammy nominations and honorary degrees. Her legacy includes the Duke University Centre for Black Studies in her honour, Kennedy Centre annual Jazz Festival in her name, to name a few.

Marian McPartland OBE was an English-American jazz pianist, composer and writer. She studied violin and singing, but was denied lessons on piano despite her early aptitude on the instrument until she was 16. She applied to the Guildhall School of Music and Drama in London and was accepted in 1935 based upon her enthusiasm rather than technique.[30] She studied classical piano and voice, but her real talent was in improvisation and composition. She became enamoured of American jazz much to the dismay of her parents and in 1938 she joined Billy Mayerl's School of Modern Syncopation. She left Guildhall promising her parents that she would return and joined Mayerl's Claviers a four-piano vaudeville act. Performing under the stage name Marian Page, she joined the Entertainment National Service Association to play for Allied troops and in 1944 she joined the United Service Organisations because they paid more and played with American men. She was assigned to a group called the Band Wagon which followed the Allied forces after the D-Day invasion and learned the accordion in case there were no pianos available. She joined a sextet put together by Chicago cornetist Jimmy McPartland who she married in 1945 and gained US citizenship. In January 1946 they made their first recording together before returning to Chicago later that year. Together they played the major clubs in Chicago and New York and toured to France in 1949 for the Paris Jazz Festival where she launched her writing career reporting on the festival for DownBeat. In 1949 they settled in Manhattan and she formed her own trio which was engaged at the newly opened 54th Street club, The Embers. She continued to write for DownBeat and in the late 1950s she began writing about the issue of being a woman in jazz. Following many years of recording for major record labels she founded her own label Halcyon Records. She suffered physical and emotional strain in the early 1960s and sought psychotherapy which resulted in her ending a long affair with her drummer and divorce from her husband. Despite their divorce, they remained close friends and remarried before Jimmy's death in 1991.[31] She was not able to connect with the 1960s avant-garde jazz styles and continued her individual style of improvisation which drew on bebop and jazz. She also maintained that she visualised keys in colours which is a phenomenon shared by some musicians called synaesthesia and saw her improvisations within a colour palette. She became interested in writing and education. She wrote reviews of new releases for DownBeat, and hosted a weekly radio show called A Delicate Balance which was a precursor to her highly successful Marian McPartland's Piano Jazz series which became the longest-running jazz programme ever on public radio. The broadcasts increased her profile and she became highly sought after for performances and recordings. She championed women and young musicians and conducted jazz workshops at major music institutions and festivals. Towards the end of the 1970s, McPartland was a public advocate for women in jazz and headlined the first Women's Jazz Festival in Kansas City, March 17–19, 1978. She won a grant to write a book about women in jazz, but never completed it due to the rise in publications on women in jazz in the 1980s reducing the novelty of her research and interviews. She continued to perform internationally including tours to Asia, Europe, South America and the United States. Just before her 90th birthday, she composed the symphonic composition, *A Portrait of Rachel Carson*, marking the centennial of the environmental pioneer. She won numerous awards including DownBeat's Lifetime Achievement Award (1994), a Grammy Award (2004) and Order of the British Empire (2010). She died aged 95 in 2013.

Hazel Scott belonged to a newer generation of jazz pianists and was the daughter of Alma Long Scott who was an established blues and classical musician. Hazel Scott was born in Trinidad and moved to New York with her mother aged 4. She received a scholarship to study at Julliard at the age of 8 and started performing in her teens in Greenwich Village and on radio. Throughout the 1930s and 1940s, she became a leading attraction and was one of the highest-earning artists in New York. She also performed in musicals and gained respectable roles in major Hollywood motion pictures. She was the first person of African descent to have her own television show in America which premièred on July 3, 1950, changing the way that black women were viewed through the television format.[32]

She was a civil rights activist and refused to perform in segregated venues and successfully brought a suit against a Washington restaurant for refusing to serve her and her travelling companion because they were black which inspired other civil rights activists and organisations. In 1950 she appeared before the House of Un-American Activities to clear her name during the era of McCarthyism. Her suggestions and comments led to the cancelling of her television show after which she suffered a nervous breakdown. When she recovered she continued to perform and tour in the United States and Europe and appeared on television. She persisted with her public opposition to McCarthyism and racial segregation and in 1957 she moved to Paris to evade political fallout. She performed regularly and even appeared in a French film whilst maintaining her activism. In 1981 she died aged 61 and is remembered for her success as a jazz virtuoso as well as a celebrated television personality, actor on screen and classical musician.

Little research exists on the all-female swing band members such as members of Hardin Armstrong's The Harlem Harlicans, but Alma Long Scott was recognised as a classically trained musician and mother of Hazel Dorothy Scott. Dolly Jones was also considered one of the best trumpeters of her time and was the first female jazz trumpeter to be recorded.[33] She learned trumpet from her mother and worked in the family band as a teenager. She formed her own band the Three Classy Misses in Kansas City and then toured as a trombonist with Ma Rainey. She toured with Ida Cox in 1928 and with Lill Hardin Armstrong's Harlem Harlicans in the early 1930s. In 1932 she formed her own band The Twelve Sprits of

Rhythm and was part of the New York multiracial band the Disciples of Swing. Her first recording in 1926 was with Albert Wynn's Gut Bucket Five and she also recorded in 1941 with the Stuff Smith Sextet. She also performed in the 1936 musical film *Swing!* She taught Valaida Snow (1904–1956) who became internationally celebrated as 'Little Louis' and the 'Queen of the Trumpet'.

Snow came from a musical family. Her mother was an educated music teacher and her father was the leader of the Pickaninny Troubadours. She was raised on the road and began performing in her father's group. She learned to play multiple instruments as well as singing and dancing. Her solo career began in Harlem cabarets where she began focussing on the trumpet. Her performances sometimes involved dancing and singing, but despite her talent she had few opportunities to hold residencies in New York or Chicago. She toured throughout the United States, Europe and South East Asia, and in the 1930s she became a hit in London. While touring Denmark in 1941 she was arrested by Nazis, only being released in 1942 on a prisoner's exchange.[34] It is believed that she never recovered from this experience and was unable to regain her former success.[35] In 1956 he died of a brain haemorrhage aged 51 during a performance at the backstage in Palace Theatre, New York. Despite being a major influence in the development of the jazz trumpet style, she also contributed to the spread of jazz in Europe and South East Asia.

In the UK, bandleader Ivy Benson (1913–1993) was a multi-instrumentalist who led all-female bands to promote professional opportunities for women musicians. She was a piano prodigy but on hearing jazz music took up the clarinet and saxophone and dropped out of school to join dance bands in her teens. Her break came as it did for other women in professional life during the Blitz when men were conscripted. She mentored women musicians and led women bands forming Ivy Benson and her Rhythm Girls in 1939. The band was top billed at Palace Theatre Manchester, and the London Palladium.[36] Her band was appointed resident house band in the BBC during the war. She was popular with the general public, and continued to lead the band into the 1980s giving women the opportunity to become professional musicians. Benson retired in the 1980s to Clacton-on-Sea and continued to entertain holiday guests on the coast.

Emerging from the internationalization of Jazz is Toshiko Akiyoshi (b. 1929) a Japanese-American jazz pianist who led jazz big bands and ensembles, performing her unique progressive arrangements and compositions. She was born in Manchuria to Japanese emigrants, but the family returned to Japan following World War II. She studied jazz from recordings and was discovered playing in a club on the Ginza by Oscar

Peterson whilst visiting Japan which led to a recording contract in 1953 with Norman Granz.[37] She applied to study at the Berklee School of Music in Boston and in 1956 she became the first Japanese student to study at the school. The school was in its early days and she received a lot of media interest because of her background and gender, but she felt that the school capitalised on that and that there was resentment from some quarters that she was getting so much attention. She also felt that the school did not really teach her anything new so she headed for New York to try to make a name for herself.[38] She struggled through these years and formed several bands with her first husband during the early 1960s. Following her divorce in 1967, she remarried and moved to Los Angeles where she composed and arranged the music for her first album *Kogun* (1974). She began to infuse traditional Japanese musical elements into her jazz and her albums were a huge success in Japan. In 1982 they moved back to New York and assembled the Toshiko Akiyoshi Jazz Orchestra featuring her husband on saxophone and continued to release her big band recordings in Japan. She did release recordings in the United States of her small combo settings and piano solos, but was unable to obtain recording contracts for the big band. She was well schooled and accomplished in all jazz styles and her unique inclusion of traditional Japanese musical instruments and themes resulted in an innovative new brand of progressive jazz. However, perhaps because of gender and race she was frustrated in receiving recording contracts for her big band in the United States, The Tokshiko Akiyoshi Orchestra, played their last show at Birdland New York City in 2003 after performing there every Monday night for more than seven years. She remains active in music but performs less in her later years.

While women pianists achieved success during the classic era of the blues and jazz due to the piano being more socially acceptable, women guitarists were much more uncommon. Memphis Minnie (1897–1973) was a guitarist, vocalist and songwriter born in Mississippi (although she claimed to be born in New Orleans). Her family moved to Memphis, Tennessee, when she was seven and she received her first guitar in the following year. By the age of 10 she learned banjo and guitar. In 1910 aged 13, she ran away from home to live on Beale Street, with its thriving blues scene and played on street corners supplementing her income with sex work. She joined a tour with the Ringling Brothers Circus from 1916 to 1920 and returned to Beale Street. In 1929 she was discovered by a record talent scout outside a barber shop playing for dimes with her second husband.[39] They went to record in New York City under the names Kansas Joe and Memphis Minnie. Their recording partnership continued until their divorce in 1935. By 1935 Minnie was established in Chicago and recorded regularly for the major labels. She also toured extensively in the southern states. In 1938 she began recording with her third husband and they continued to record and perform together throughout the 1940s. Minnie took up electric guitar and recorded some of her biggest hits on that instrument. In the late 1940s, the taste for blues was changing and clubs were hiring younger and cheaper musicians. She continued to record and perform in the 1950s but her health was waning and she retired in 1957. Occasionally she appeared on Memphis radio stations to encourage young blues musicians. Her influence on the blues from her vaudeville roots to the Chicago-style electric blues of the 1930s and 1940s was coupled with her radical rejection of feminine expectations. She was hard-drinking, drove flashy cars, and was highly competitive with her male counterparts. Unfortunately, she did not reap the benefits of her recording success and died penniless.

In the male-dominated field of jazz, horn player Melba Liston (1926–1999), the soprano saxophonist Jane Ira Bloom (b. 1955), Marilyn Mazur (b. 1955) and Melissa Aldana (b. 1988) have made a significant impact on the genre.

Melba Liston was an American jazz trombonist, composer and arranger who began playing trombone aged 7. She was largely self-taught and was mentored by her guitarist grandfather learning spirituals and folk songs. She was born in Kansas City and aged 10 she moved to Los Angeles. She began performing in youth bands and began recording with saxophonist Dexter Gordon in 1947. She joined Dizzy Gillespie's big band in New York for a time and later toured with Count Basie and Billie Holiday in 1949. She found the gruelling existence on the road unfulfilling and turned to teaching and extras work in Hollywood. She returned to touring with Gillespie in 1956 and 1957, recorded with Art Blakey's Jazz Messengers and formed an all-women quintet in 1959. She toured and recorded with Quincy Jones and in the late 1950s she took on numerous collaborations arranging for jazz and Motown artists. In 1964 she helped establish the Jazz Orchestra. She continued her career as an arranger in the late 1960s and 1970s before moving to Jamaica to teach music. She returned to the United States in the late 1970s to lead her own bands and retired due to a stroke in 1985. She was a female in a very male-dominated profession and was a trailblazer as a woman trombonist. She also articulated the struggles of African American women in the music business and on the road.

Jane Ira Bloom moved to soprano saxophone as her primary instrument after studying piano and drums and her compositions represent avant-garde jazz styles. She was born in Boston, Massachusetts, and her music studies earned her a degree in liberal arts and a master's degree in music from Yale University. Her pathway into jazz diverts from the experience of the black descendants of the blues tradition, but she has made a contribution to the genre as a pioneering brass instrumentalist in the male-dominated field. She has composed for soprano sax and electronics for the first musical commission from NASA and has founded two record labels releasing several of her own recordings. In 2007 she was awarded a Guggenheim Fellowship and is a tenured professor at The New School of Jazz and Contemporary Music in Greenwich Village, New York. Her compositions have won numerous awards including a Grammy (2017).

Marilyn Mazur was born in New York to Polish and African American parents who moved with her to Denmark when she was aged 6. She was largely self-taught learning to play the piano and at age 19 she turned to playing drums. She earned a degree in percussion from the Royal Danish Academy of Music. She started her first band Zirines in 1973 and in 1978 she formed the all-women band Primi. She was invited to join Miles Davis's big-band concept album *Aura* after which returned to New York to perform on tour with Davis. In 1989 she returned to Denmark forming the band Future Song in 1989. She continued to perform with leading jazz musicians and in 2001 she won the Jazzpar Prize, the world's largest international jazz prize.[40] She has championed the progress of women in jazz and her all-woman album *Shamania* (2019) featured musicians from the avant-garde Scandinavian jazz scene.[41] She has featured on numerous recordings and is consistently recognised by Down Beat as the No.1 Jazz Performer.[42]

Melissa Aldana is a Chilean tenor saxophone player who performs both as a soloist and with her trio Melissa Aldana & Crash Trio. Her father was a professional saxophonist who taught her from a young age. She performed in Santiago jazz clubs in her teens and in 2005 she was invited to perform in the Panama Jazz Festival.[43] She successfully auditioned for Berklee College of Music in Boston and graduated in 2009 after which she relocated to New York City. She performed at the Blue Note and Monterey Jazz Festival during this period and at the age of 24 was the first female and the first South American to win the Thelonious Monk International Jazz Saxophone Competition (2013). She has recorded six albums as of 2022, one being with the Crash Trio.[44] She has also won several prestigious awards including the Altazor National Arts Award of Chile and the Lincoln Centre's Martin E. Segal Award.[45]

## Gospel

Gospel featured many successful women and this form stemmed from church congregations that largely featured women. As a strand of rhythm and blues originating in devotional music of the southern states of the United States, it produced artists such as 'Diamond Teeth' Mary McClain (1902–2000), Big Mama Thornton (1926–1984), Mavis Staples (b. 1939), Aretha Franklin (1942–2018) and Etta James (1938–2012) manifesting in the music of Tina Turner (b. 1939) and Patti LaBelle (b. 1944).

'Diamond Teeth' Mary also known as 'Walking Mary McLean' was the half-sister of Bessie Smith and started out her career in vaudeville and blues. She left home aged 13 to avoid beatings and joined a circus. She joined the vaudeville circuit working as a singer and dancer through the 1920s and 1930s. She performed in the major nightclub and theatre circuits, toured with the US organisations and performed with the major blues performers of the time. Her stage name resulted from the setting of diamonds in her front teeth in 1940. She was often billed as 'Queen of the Blues'. She continued to perform with touring shows and was the lead blues singer for the Rabbit's Foot Minstrels in 1954.[46] In 1960 she settled in Florida, gave up her nightclub work and began singing gospel music becoming a star at local church events. In 1986 she became one of the first recipients of the Florida Folk Heritage Award and in 1993 she recorded her first album. She toured Europe in the 1990s and continued to sing at blues festivals until shortly before her death at age 97.

Big Mama Thornton (Willie Mae Thornton) was introduced to music in a Baptist church in Alabama where her father was a minister and her mother was a singer. She left home after her mother died and with the help of 'Diamond Teeth' Mary joined Sammy Green's Hot Harlem Revue. She moved to Houston where a new blues sound was emerging and she recorded 'Hound Dog' (1952) which ushered in the era of rock 'n' roll selling more than half a million copies. The song was recorded three years later by Elvis Presley and sold ten million copies despite the fact that the song was an anthem for female power. In the early 1960s Thornton recorded her own song 'Ball 'n' Chain' but since she did not own the copyright missed out on publishing rights when Janis Joplin recorded it as a major hit later in the decade. The song is included in the Rock and Roll Hall of Fame list of the 500 songs that shaped rock and roll.[47]

Mavis Staples had her early experience of music in gospel which carried through her career as a singer, actress and civil rights activist. She was born in Chicago and began singing with her family group in 1950 performing in local churches and on radio. The group became highly influential as the voices of the civil rights movement endorsed by Martin Luther King Jr. Their recordings hit the charts regularly in the 1970s. Staples began to forge her solo career releasing the single 'Crying in the Chapel' (1968) which received little attention and it wasn't until her solo album *Mavis Staples* (1969) that she received any recognition outside of her family group. Her collaboration with Prince in the late 1980s on her albums was highly successful as was her collaboration with Lucky Peterson for her 1996 release *Spirituals and Gospels: A tribute to Mahalia Jackson*. She has shared the stage with many great artists including Bob Dylan, Prince, Mahalia Jackson and Janis Joplin, and has performed at the White House for numerous presidents of the United States.[48] Her freedom songs have been recorded on her solo albums and with her numerous collaborators and songwriters. She has appeared at major international festivals and rallies including Rally to Restore Sanity and/or Fear (2010), Chicago's Annual Blues Festival in Grant Park (2012), Glastonbury, Somerset UK (2015 and 2019) and recorded many benefit albums. In May 2019 she celebrated her 80th birthday with a concert at the Apollo Theatre where she first performed as a teenager 63 years before. She has also appeared on television and in film throughout her career and won numerous awards including Grammys (2010, 2015, 2022), a Grammy Lifetime Achievement Award (2005), Blues Music and Americana Music Awards. She has received honorary doctorates from Berklee College of Music in Boston, Massachusetts (2011), Columbia College, Chicago (2012) along with being recognised as a Kennedy Centre Honouree (2016), inducted into the Blues Hall of Fame (2017), Laureate at the 57th Laureate Convocation of the Lincoln Academy of Illinois, and the Order of Lincoln.

Aretha Franklin's hit 'Respect' became the anthem for feminism and racism and her high-profile career resulted in her earning the label 'Queen of soul' and one of the best-selling artists of all time. She was born and raised in Memphis, Tennessee, in the gospel tradition. Her mother was an accomplished pianist and singer and her father was a Baptist preacher whose emotionally driven sermons were famous across the country. Franklin began singing solos in church as a young girl and her father began managing her when she was 12-years-old and took her on the road with him. He helped her sign her first recording deal and assisted in her first recording at the age of 14. Her tours on the gospel circuit brought her into contact with many major producers and musicians. At the age of 16, she went on tour with Dr Martin Luther King Jr., and she ultimately sang at his funeral in 1968. She turned to pop music at the age of 18 and signed with Columbia Records to produce her first single 'Today I Sing the Blues' (1960) which reached the top 10 of the Hot Rhythm and Blues Sellers chart. She began to perform in diverse genres and was crowned 'The Queen of Soul'. By 1964 she was recording more pop music and earning a high income performing in clubs and theatres. Her record sales did not meet expectations with Columbia Records and her contract ended with her owing money.[49] Her next contracts were mildly successful with her recording of 'I Never Loved a Man (The Way I Love You)' (1967) reaching number one on the Billboard Hot 100. Her recording of Otis Redding's 'Respect' (1967) became hailed as a civil rights and feminist anthem. By 1968 she became one of the most successful performers with top-selling albums and singles. In May 1968 she toured outside of the United States and her appearance at the Concertgebouw in Amsterdam drew a hysterical response with the audience covering the stage with flower petals.

During the 1970s her success continued to expand. She received numerous awards and in January 1972 she returned to Gospel music to record the album *Amazing Grace*. It became one of the best-selling gospel albums of all time. Her popularity began to wane and by 1975 her albums and songs were no longer best sellers. She had some success with the soundtrack to the film *Sparkle*, however, her follow-up recordings were less successful. Her 1980 performance at London's Royal Albert Hall in front of Queen Elizabeth II along with her appearance in a guest role in the *Blues Brothers* comedy movie caused a revival in interest in her performances. A string of hit albums and appearances followed encompassing soul, rhythm and blues, and gospel. Her success rate declined somewhat in the late 1980s, but was revived by her appearance in the Apollo Theatre's revival of *The Wiz* (1995). Her final top 40 single was 'A rose is still a rose' (1998) and the album of the same name was released after the single selling over 500,000 copies earning gold certification. In 1998 she stood in for her friend Luciano Pavarotti at the Grammys to perform 'Nessun Dorma' in an acclaimed performance for which she received a standing ovation. This became one of her signature performances in her repertoire and the last time she sang it live was in 2015 for Pope Francis at the World Meeting of Families.[50] She continued recording and performing at celebrity events until her final public performance at the Cathedral of St John the Divine in New York City for Elton John's 25th anniversary gala for the Elton John AIDS Foundation on November 7, 2017.

Franklin was inducted into numerous halls of fame and won high-ranking awards such as The Presidential Medal of Freedom (2005) and a Pulitzer Prize (2019), not to mention her numerous honorary degrees. She immersed herself in the struggle for civil rights and women's rights which she funded through personal donations and performances at benefits and protests. She also funded Native American people's rights and First Nations cultural rights. Her influence extended to other women of soul such as Dionne Warwick and Cissy Houston.

Etta James (b. Jamasetta Hawkins) began singing at the age of 5 at the St. Paul Baptist Church in South-Central Los Angeles. She suffered abuse from her choir masters and foster fathers. In 1950 she moved to San Francisco with her mother and formed the girl group the Creolettes. The group changed their name to Peaches and in 1954 recorded her song 'The

Wallflower' which reached number one on the Hot Rhythm and Blues chart. She left Peaches and set out on a recording career which earned her success on the pop charts, becoming known as 'Miss Peaches'.[51] She began adding gospel elements in the early 1960s and continued to achieve success on the R&B charts. In the 1970s she began to incorporate the new styles of rock and funk and was a headliner at Montreux Jazz Festival and opener for the Rolling Stones in 1978. Her career in the 1980s continued with guest appearances at major music events as well as recording hit albums. After nearly 30 years of recording and performing she began to receive recognition for her contribution to rock and blues receiving more than 30 significant awards. She was inducted into the Rock and Roll Hall of Fame (1993), the Blues Hall of Fame (2001) and the Rockabilly Hall of Fame (2001) and was awarded a Grammy Lifetime Achievement Award (2003). She received a star on the Hollywood Walk of Fame (2003) and received the Billboard R&B Founders Awards (2006). She continued to perform in major Festivals and record into the early 2000s releasing her final album in 2011. She is considered a major influence upon the singers Amy Winehouse and Adele.[52]

Patti LaBelle began singing at the Beulah Baptist Church, Philadelphia aged 10 and turned to singing secular music in her teens. She began her career in the 1960s as lead singer for the group Patti LaBelle and the Bluebelles which became Labelle in the 1970s. Their hit 'Lady Marmalade' (1970) went to number one after which the group split and LaBelle went solo. Her début album 'You Are My Friend' (1976) was critically acclaimed and set her on her successful career path resulting in numerous hits and accolades. In 1992 she won the Grammy for Best Female R&B Vocal Performance for her 1991 album *Burnin'*. She won her second Grammy for her *Live! One Night Only* (1999) and in 2003 she was inducted into the Grammy Hall of Fame. She has sold over 50 million recordings over her career that has spanned seven decades and along with being inducted into the Grammy Hall of Fame, she has been honoured with lifetime achievement awards including the Apollo Theatre Hall of Fame(2009) and the Black Music & Entertainment Walk of Fame (2022). She has a strong LGBTQI+ following and was the poster girl for an AIDS/HIV campaign in the 1980s.

## Motown

There was a prevalence of women in Motown, but the managers and producers were predominantly men. Motown did provide a voice for black civil unrest and despite the exploitation of women by the producers like the blues, it was a conduit for upward mobility. Diana Ross (b.

1944) emerged from one of the most successful Motown acts of the 1960s The Supremes who were the best-selling all-girl group of all time. After her departure from the group in 1970 she embarked on a successful solo career on stage, film and television. She has achieved numerous global top ten hit singles and albums, appeared on prime-time television specials and in a number of successful movies. Her first movie role was the portrayal of Billie Holiday in *Lady Sings the Blues* (1972) which was nominated for an Academy Award and won a Golden Globe Award. The soundtrack became a number one hit in the US album chart. In 1976 she was named 'Female Entertainer of the Century' by Billboard. She was inducted into the Rock and Roll Hall of Fame (1988) as a member of the Supremes, was a recipient of a Special Tony Award (1976), a Kennedy Centre Honours (2007), the Grammy Lifetime Achievement Award (2012) and the Presidential Medal of Freedom (2016). Her releases continue to top the charts and her high-profile appearances continue with a performance at Glastonbury (June, 2022) and as the finale act at the Platinum Party at the Palace in celebration of the Platinum Jubilee of Elizabeth II.

## Conclusion

Women in jazz, blues, gospel and Motown have had a defining influence on these genres and in many instances music has been the vehicle for empowerment and emancipation for these women. Some have emerged as leading influences commenting on women's issues, racism, sexism, diversity and social justice. Their songs voiced feminist concerns which resonated with their audiences and the growing female music market. Not all retained the wealth that they generated as exploitation continued in the industry still mainly dominated by men. Those who inadvertently sold the rights to their music and recording income may have lived comfortably while they were performing, but were often left destitute at the end of their careers. Sexualisation of women was central to their marketing and while their music resonated for women maintaining their glamorous appearance set unrealistic standards dictated by the men in the industry. Those who were preyed upon by dealers of illicit drugs and alcohol found their addictions draining their fortunes which for some led to an untimely death. Nonetheless, women's musical contribution to these genres as singers, front women for bands, soloists and instrumentalists influenced the development of styles and genres which were the precursors to the popular music industry of the 20th century.

## Notes

1 Tick, J., Margaret E. & Koskoff, E. (2001). Women in music. Grove Music Online.
2 Oakley, G. (1997). *The Devil's Music*. Da Capo Press, 83.
3 Schuller, G. (1986). *Early Jazz: Its Roots and Musical Development*. Oxford University Press.
4 A Headstone for Mamie Smith Campaign Has Ended. (2013, 22 August).1World-1Family.me.
5 Abbott, L. & Seroff, D. (2009). *Ragged but Right: Black Traveling Shows, Coon Songs, and the Dark Pathway to Blues and Jazz*. University Press of Mississippi, 261.
6 Lieb, S. (1983). *Mother of the Blues: A Study of Ma Rainey* (3rd ed.). University of Massachusetts Press, 25.
7 Friederich, B. (2017, 7 June). *Ma Rainey's Lesbian Lyrics: 5 Times She Expressed Her Queerness in Song*. Billboard.
8 Albertson, C. (2003). *Bessie*. Yale University Press, 80.
9 Devi, D. (2012, June 25). *Bessie Smith: Music's Original, Bitchinest Bad Girl*. HuffPost.
10 Rabaka, R. (2012). *Hip Hop's Amnesia: From Blues and the Black Women's Club Movement to Rap and the Hip Hop Movement*. Lexington Books.
11 George, A., Weiser, M.E. & Zepernick, J. (2013). *Women and Rhetoric between the Wars*. Southern Illinois University Press, 143–158.
12 Bourne, S. (2007). *Ethel Waters: Stormy Weather*. Scarecrow Press.
13 Bogle, D. (2011). *Heat Wave: The Life and Career of Ethel Waters*. HarperCollins.
14 Harrison, D.D. (1988). *Black Pearls: Blues Queens of the 1920s*. Rutgers University Press.
15 Bogle, D. (2007). *Brown Sugar: Over One Hundred Years of America's Black Female Superstars*. Continuum International Publishing Group, 31.
16 Harrison, D.D. Ibid.
17 Barlow, W. (1989). *Looking Up at Down: The Emergence of Blues Culture*. Temple University Press, 134–135.
18 Russell, T. (1996). *The Blues: From Robert Johnson to Robert Cray*. Carlton Books, 120–21.
19 Gourse, L. (2000). *The Billie Holiday Companion: Seven Decades of Commentary*. Schirmer Trade Books, 40.
20 Nicholson, S. (1995). *Billie Holiday*. Victor Gollancz Ltd, 96.
21 Holden, S. (1996, 16 June). Ella Fitzgerald, the Voice of Jazz, Dies at 79. *The New York Times*.
22 Gioia, T. (2012). *The Jazz Standards: A Guide to the Repertoire*. Oxford University Press, 307.
23 Cohodas, N. (2010). *Princess Noire: The Tumultuous Reign of Nina Simone*. Pantheon Books, 37.
24 Henley, J. & Campbell, D. (2003, 22 April). Nina Simone, high priestess of soul, dies aged 70. *The Guardian*.
25 McKeage, K. (2014). Where Are All the Girls? Women in Collegiate Instrumental Jazz. GEMS (Gender, Education, Music, and Society), the on-line journal of GRIME (Gender Research in Music Education), 7(3).
26 Wehr-Flowers, E. (2006). Differences between male and female students' confidence, anxiety, and attitude toward learning jazz improvisation. *Journal of Research in Music Education*, 54(4), 337–349.

27 Tirro, F. (2007). Historia del jazz clásico. American Bar Association.
28 Dickerson, J.L. (2002). *Just for a Thrill: Lil Hardin Armstrong, First Lady of Jazz*. Cooper Square Press, 171.
29 Dahl, L. (2000). *Morning Glory: A Biography of Mary Lou Williams*. Pantheon Books, 29.
30 de Barros, P. (2012). *Shall We Play That One Together?*. St. Martin's Press, 16.
31 Gourse, L. (1995) Marian McPartland:...Something you really need in life, someone to encourage you. In *Madame Jazz: Contemporary Women Instrumentalists*. Oxford University Press, 197.
32 Bogle, D. (2001). The Hazel Scott Show. In *Primetime Blues: African Americans on Network Television*. Farrar, Straus and Giroux, 15–19; Armstrong, J. (2021). *When Women Invented Television: The Untold Story of the Female Powerhouses Who Pioneered the Way We Watch Today*. Harper Collins.
33 Dahl, L. (1984). *Stormy Weather: The Music and Lives of a Century of Jazzwomen*. Hal Leonard Corporation, 28.
34 Rye, H. (2001). Snow, Valaida. Grove Music Online.
35 Yanow, S. (2003). *Jazz on Record: The First Sixty Years*. Backbeat Books, 228.
36 Chilton, J. (2004). *Who's Who of British Jazz* (2nd ed.). Continuum, 32.
37 NEA Jazz Masters–Toshiko Akiyoshi. (2015). [US] National Endowment for the Arts (NEA).
38 In Conversation with Toshiko Akiyoshi and Lew Tabackin (2008, 5 December). www.jazz.com
39 Garon, P. & Garon, B. (1992). *Woman with Guitar: Memphis Minnie's Blues*. Da Capo Press, 24.
40 Marilyn Mazur on JAZZPAR Artists.
41 Tucker, M. (2019, 25 April). Marilyn Mazur's Shamania: Shamania. *Jazz Journal*. jazzjournal.co.uk.
42 See Marilyn Mazur's official website.
43 Jurek, T. (n.d.). Melissa Aldana–biography and history. AllMusic.
44 Panken, T. (2016, July). 25 for the future / Melissa Aldana. *DownBeat*, 83(7), 30.
45 Jurek. Ibid.
46 Abbott, L. & Seroff, D. Ibid. 288.
47 Gaar, G. (1992). *She's a Rebel: The History of Women in Rock & Roll*. Seal Press, 4.
48 Remnick, D. (2022, 27 June). The Gospel According to Mavis Staples. *The New Yorker*.
49 DeCurtis, A., Henke, J. & George-Warren, H. (1992). *The Rolling Stone Illustrated History of Rock & Roll*. Random House, 339.
50 Feeney, N. (2018, 16 August). Grammys Producer Ken Ehrlich on Aretha Franklin's Last-Minute, Showstopping 1998 Opera Moment: 'She Was Incomparable'. Billboard.
51 James, E. & Ritz, D. (1998). *Rage to Survive: The Etta James Story*. Da Capo Press.
52 Jonze, T. (2012, 20 January).Etta James, blues icon, dies aged 73. *The Guardian*.

# 6

# WOMEN IN POPULAR MUSIC

## Introduction

This chapter examines how leading women in popular music have successfully negotiated their careers by taking on inspirational roles as performers, producers and songwriters. It identifies how many successful female performers have used popular musical styles to express feminist messages. Their approach has ranged from controlling their own output and managing their careers to achieving independent financial success. It looks at women in a range of popular genres including cabaret, musical theatre, folk and protest song, civil rights and human rights activism, punk and experimental music, country music, rock and hip-hop. It also examines their legacy of empowering other women through their musical messages, financial initiatives and as role models.

## Women in cabaret

Cabaret takes many forms and is generally associated with social activity featuring musical performances in places of entertainment involving food and drink. Cabarets had been in existence in Paris by the late 15th century and were frequented by writers, actors, poets, musicians and painters. In November 1881 the famous Chat Noir opened in Paris to become a place where bohemian poets, musicians and artists gathered alongside wealthy Parisians. The entertainment combined music and poetry with political commentary and satire. The Chat Noir experience was replicated through North Africa and Germany. Cabaret clubs began to proliferate in Paris

DOI: 10.4324/9781003183631-7

alongside music halls from London towards the end of the century, and the Moulin Rouge opened in 1889 to become a prominent cabaret venue distinguished by its large red imitation windmill on its roof and as the birthplace of Cancan dance. Yvette Guilbert (1865–1944), Mistinguett (1873–1956) and Édith Piaf enjoyed great success in cabaret during the Belle Epoque.

Guilbert became a famous diseuse in cabaret venues throughout France for her highly entertaining wit and animated delivery. She established her career in the late 1880s at the Eldorado café-concerts and by the end of 1894 she had established herself in music halls in Europe and London.[1] Her tours to England (1893) America (1896, 1906, 1909) and Germany (1902) stimulated the developing cabaret styles featuring political, sentimental, realist and comic themes that were emerging in intimate entertainment venues. Her association with the artistic scene at Le Chat Noir resulted in friendships with leading personalities of the time and she was the muse for well-known artists including Toulouse Lautrec and Picasso. Guilbert became disenchanted with being typecast as a singer of bawdy songs continuing her career after World War I singing repertoire from medieval to 19th century songs.[2] She devoted herself to researching and publishing old French chanson repertoire and performed them on her self-promoted international tours to Europe, Egypt, United States and Canada. From 1915 to 1919 she lived in New York establishing her École des arts du théâtre for young women which was a financial failure leading to her financial ruin. Her other ventures included appearing in several movies, publishing novels, writing and directing a musical comedy, performing in Brecht's *Threepenny Opera*, broadcasting and recording her chansons. She was awarded the Legion of Honour as Ambassadress of French Song in 1932. The German invasion of Europe resulted in her selling her letters and stage costumes and in 1941 the Germans confiscated her Paris apartment. She died penniless in 1944 but had a lasting influence on the genre.

In France Édith Piaf (1915–1963) established her career in cabaret and German-born Marlene Dietrich (1901–1992) achieved huge success in the genre. Piaf became one of France's widely known international singers with a legacy that has endured long after her death. She had a successful film career and achieved international recording success during World War II. Following World War II, she became known internationally and toured Europe, the United States and South America. Critical acclaim in the United States led to television appearances and two performances in Carnegie Hall (1956 and 1957).[3] Piaf collaborated with composer Luiguy on her signature song 'La vie en rose' (1947) which won a Grammy Hall of Fame Award in 1998. Despite illness, drug addiction and alcoholism along with several well-publicised marriages and affairs her fame continues beyond her untimely death. She developed the tradition of the French chanson into international popular musical vernacular that was adopted by many of her followers. She has been recognised in numerous books, films, plays, television specials and memorial concerts. A museum in Paris dedicated to Piaf and a small planet 3772 Piaf was named in her honour.[4]

Marlene Dietrich studied violin and piano at the Berlin Hochschule für Musik, but abandoned her instrumental career to join the Berlin cabaret circuit. She entered the Max Reinhardt theatre school and her first major role was in the 1928 musical *Es liegt in der Luft*, in which she sang and recorded her first hit 'Wenn die beste Freundin'. Her breakthrough role was in the film *Der blaue Engel* (1930) cast as the cabaret singer Lola-Lola where she performed her signature song and recording hit 'Falling in love again'. Her German accent and contralto voice made her the first and lasting voice of the femme fatale.[5] She then appeared in a number of Hollywood films where she sang in cabaret settings with a provocative Academy Award nominated performance in *Morocco* (1930) where she performs a French song in a man's tuxedo and kisses another woman. Her public image continued to defy sexual norms and she was well known for her androgynous film roles and bisexuality.[6] She claimed her singing in men's clothes was for singing songs by men and it was more her initial interest in American popular song that drew her to America than Hollywood.[7] She renounced her German citizenship in 1939 due to her anti-Nazi political convictions and became an American citizen. During World War II she performed for allied troops where her signature song was an English version of the German classic 'Lilli Marlene'. She was decorated by American and French governments for her war efforts, which included supporting exiles, but she declared herself to be a pacifist ending recitals with Pete Seeger's anti-war ballad 'Where have all the flowers gone'. From the 1950s to 1970s she worked almost exclusively as a cabaret singer commencing in the Sahara Hotel in Las Vegas notably appearing in the daringly sheer 'nude dress' with a swansdown coat, changing into gender defying circus master's costume or top hat and tails. She toured internationally including returning to a mixed reception in Germany where she was previously shunned as a traitor.[8] She also toured to Israel around this time and breaking the unofficial taboo of singing songs in German. She became one of the highest paid cabaret performers and most influential and imitated singers of the 20th century. Her final poignant performance was at the age of 77 singing the title song for the film *Just a Giglio* (1978). She famously withdrew from public life for the final 13 years of her life to her apartment in Paris during which time only a select few were allowed to visit her. During this time she devoted herself to phone calls and letter writing. In 1982 she participated in an award winning documentary about her life *Marlene* (1984) where the film director Maximilian Schell was only allowed to record her voice. Dietrich's legacy includes being referenced in a number of popular 20th and 21th century songs, the subject of documentaries and film biopics, a style icon and a LBGTQI+ celebrity.

## Musical theatre

Musical theatre like opera combines music with theatrical performance that includes songs and spoken dialogue and, in the 20th century has become known simply as musical. What distinguishes musicals from opera is that they usually include more dancing, are generally performed in the language of the audience, use more popular music styles and opera singers are primarily singers not actors and dancers.[9] Also opera tends to be performed in opera theatres and musicals in theatres. Since the advent of musical theatre, women have taken on a significant role as performers such as with Ethel Merman, Angela Lansbury, Tyne Daly, Bernadette Peters, Barbara Streisand, Julie Andrews and Patti LuPone. Few have emerged as composers and producers of musicals.

The first Broadway musical to be created and directed entirely by women was *The Secret Garden* (1991).[10] Based on the novel by Frances Hodgson Burnett, the book and lyrics are by Marsha Norman and the score is by Lucy Simon. The sets were created by Heidi Landsman and direction by Susan H. Schulman. Composer Lucy Simon (b. 1940) began her professional singing career aged 16 with her younger sister Carly Simon. Her first solo albums were *Lucy Simon* (1975) and *Stolen Time* (1977) and she received a Grammy Award for her Sesame Street album of children's songs, *In Harmony* (1980). Her collaboration on *The Secret Garden* won her a Tony Award nomination for Best Original Score and Drama Desk Award for Outstanding Music. She also composed the music for the musical *Doctor Zhivago* (2006) and contributed to the Off-Broadway musical *Mama and Her Boys* (2011).

In 2013 Cyndi Lauper (b. 1953) was the first female composer to win a Tony Award for the best score without a male collaborator for the music and score for the Broadway musical *Kinky Boots* (2012). At the 2013 Tony Awards the musical was awarded five other awards including Best New Musical. In 2014 Lauper won a Grammy Award for Best Musical Theatre Album for the cast recording and in 2016 the West End production won Best New Musical at the Olivier Awards.[11] Lauper was already an established singer, songwriter, actress and activist when she engaged with Broadway. Her début album *She's So Unusual* (1983) was the first début album by a female artist to achieve four top-five Billboard Top 100 hits and earned her the Grammy Award for Best New Artist (1985). She rewrote the original lyrics to the song 'Girls Just Want to Have Fun' intending it to be an anthem for women and the video was rated the best one of all-time by Rolling Stone, MTV and VH1. Since Lauper has released 11 albums selling over 50 million worldwide and participated in projects including films and musicals. Her 2010 album Memphis Blues won her Billboard's most successful blues album of the year. Her numerous awards include Grammys, Emmys, Tonys, New York's Outer Critic's Circle, MTV, Billboard and American Music Awards. She is an inductee to the Songwriter's Hall of Fame and Hollywood Walk of Fame. Her song 'True Colors' (1986) is a gay anthem, after which the humanitarian organisation True Colors United founded by Lauper in 2008 is named, which advocates for runaway and homeless LGBTQI+ youth. Her distinctive hybrid punk image featuring a variety of hair colours and eccentric clothing along with her powerful four-octave singing range have contributed to her recognition. She has also been celebrated for her humanitarian work and advocacy for LGBTQI+ rights in the United States which were acknowledged at President Obama's second term inauguration in 2013. Her first foray into musical theatre for *Kinky Boots* has brought her considerable success despite it not being her primary musical medium. She admitted to finding the process challenging as she drew on a range of styles from musical, pop, funk and new wave.[12]

Jeanine Tesori (b. 1960) is probably the most prolific and honoured female musical theatre composer in history with a string of Broadway successes over her 30-year career. She started out studying medicine, but changed her major to music.[13] Her early Broadway experience was working on the aforementioned first all-women Broadway production *Secret Garden* (1991) where she was involved in dance arrangements, as associate conductor and on keyboards. In 1995 she arranged the dance music for the revival of *How to Succeed in Business Without Really Trying*. In 1997 she composed the score for the Off-Broadway musical *Violet*, for which she won an Obie Award, the New York Drama Critics Circle Award for Best Musical, and the Lucille Lortel Award for Outstanding Musical, and in the same year she arranged the dance music for the Johnny Mercer revue *Dream*. She went on to arrange the music for the revival of *The Sound of Music* (1998) and wrote original incidental music for *Twelfth Night* (1998). She arranged the music for the revue *Swing!* (1999) and created new music and vocal arrangements for *Thoroughly Modern Millie* (2002), *Caroline, or Change* (2004), *Shrek The Musical* (2008), *A Free Man of Color* (2010), *Violet* (2014), *Fun Home* (2015) and *Kimberly Akimbo* (2022).

Tesori's scores have won her five Tony Award nominations and with her lyricist Lisa Kron became the first all women team to win a Tony Award for the Best Musical and Best Original Score for *Fun Home* (2013) along with a Pulitzer Prize nomination in 2014.[14] Tesori has eight Drama Desk Outstanding Music nominations for which she won Outstanding Music for *Twelfth Night* (1999) and *Caroline, or Change* (2004).

She has also written operas including *A Blizzard on Marblehead Neck* (2011), *The Lion, The Unicorn, and Me* (2013) and *Blue* (2019). Her involvement in film includes being credited as voice coach on the Steven Spielberg film of *West Side Story* (2019) and she has composed music for a number of films including *Nights in Rodanthe* (2008), *The Loss of a Teardrop Diamond* (2008), *The Little Mermaid: Ariel's Beginning* (2008), *Shrek the Third* (2007), *Mulan II* (2004) and *The Emperor's New Groove 2: Kronk's New Groove* (2005).[15]

*9 to 5: The Musical* (2008) features the lyrics and music of country music star Dolly Parton (b. 1946). It is based upon the 1980 film of the same name which featured Parton with a storyline based around three working women who seek to overthrow their company's autocratic sexist and lecherous boss. It premièred in Los Angeles in 2008 and opened on Broadway in 2009. Following a short season on Broadway it toured the United States (2010) and premièred in the UK (2012) with a tour of Australia (2021–2022) and a return to the UK (2021–2022). Parton won the Los Angeles Drama Critics Award for the musical score, which also received positive reviews on Broadway.[16]

In the genre of Jukebox musical based on music that is already written British playwright Catherine Johnson (b. 1957) wrote the book for the ABBA-inspired musical *Mamma Mia!* (2008) and co-wrote the sequel *Mamma Mia! Here We Go Again!* (2018). Johnson's career in theatre started by winning a playwriting competition advertised in her local newspaper in Bristol where she was living as an unemployed single mother. She won and the play was staged at the Bristol Old Vic in 1987. She went on to achieve success for her theatre and television plays. *Mamma Mia!* was produced by Phyllida Christian Lloyd (b. 1967) whose theatre work includes directing production for the Royal Court Theatre, Royal National Opera, Opera North and the Royal Opera House at Covent Garden. Notably, Lloyd also directed *The Iron Lady* (2011) a film biopic of former British Prime Minister Margaret Thatcher with Meryl Streep in the Academy Award winning leading role.

Along with the screenplay for *Mamma Mia's* film adaptation, which was the highest grossing picture at the time in the UK and the biggest selling UK DVD of all time *Mamma Mia!* also received numerous awards and award nominations and has been one of the longest running productions on Broadway and in the West End.[17]

## Women's folk and protest song as popular music

Women have performed and written protest music in support of the suffragette movement, civil rights, worker rights and anti-war sentiment. Early exponents include Dame Ethel Smyth (1858–1944) who had an established career as a composer in England joining Emmaline Pankhurst's suffragette campaign and composing *Songs of Sunrise* (1911) with its rousing anthem 'The March of the Women'.

Miner's daughter Aunt Molly Jackson (Mary Magdalene Garland. B. 1880–1960) was jailed for union activities at ten years old and sang protest songs at picket lines arriving in New York in 1936 after being blacklisted in her home state of Kentucky. Her brother and husband died in mining accidents, her mother died of starvation and another brother was blinded in mining accidents. She sang about the trials of the men working in the coalmine. In 1939, 204 of her songs were recorded for the Library of Congress and she recorded one commercial single of her blues song 'Kentucky Miner's Wife'.[18] Ella May Wiggins (1900–1929) was a labour union organiser for the National Textile Workers Union who fought for maternity leave, African American union membership rights and sang ballads including her best known song 'A Mill Mother's Lament' (1929). Wiggins was shot dead in Gastonia following her protest balladeering in the Kentucky coalfields.[19]

Peggy Seeger (b. 1935) is one of the first women to become prominent in the 1950s for writing and singing folk songs from a feminist perspective. Her family were well-established folklorists in the United States and in 1956 Seeger went to study in England. Her engagement with left-wing singers resulted in her being blacklisted in several European countries along with threats from the US government. She joined the folk revivalist group The Ramblers in the late 1950s which expounded radical Marxist philosophy. Seeger wrote songs to document the activities of women's groups and peace organisations. She wrote the Greenham Common Women's Peace Camp anthem 'Carry Greenham Home' (1983) and became increasingly interested in feminist concerns. In 2002 she published 139 of her songs in Peggy Seeger, 40 years of songwriting.[20] In 2017 Seeger published her memoir accompanied by a double CD of songs.[21] She commenced her first farewell tour of Britain in 2022.

Protest songs drawing on South American folk traditions emerged in this era with women in rock and pop developing a more political voice.

Mercedes Sosa (b. 1935) and Joan Baez (b. 1941) were some of the leaders in this movement.

Argentine singer Mercedes Sosa, with her husband, started the Nuevo Cancionero, a fokloric musical movement expressing the voice of poor Argentines.[22] She began recording Argentine folksongs and concept albums of songs of Argentine women. Sosa performed with some of the most significant artists of her time in Argentina and on international stages receiving numerous awards. As a supporter of Péron she favoured leftist causes and after the military junta of Jorge Vileda in 1976 Sosa and her family faced death threats. In 1979, following a search and arrest on stage along with those attending her concert in La Plata, she was forced by the Argentine military dictatorship to abandon her country and she moved to Paris and then Madrid. On her return in 1982 she expanded her repertory to include 'rock nacional' that was developed by the resistance during the dictatorship. She began performing with rock musicians bringing her voice to different audiences and continued her hugely successful career into the 21st century. She was the recipient of six Latin Grammy awards (2000, 2003, 2004, 2006, 2009, 2011), including a Latin Grammy Lifetime Achievement Award in 2004 and two posthumous Latin Grammy Awards for Best Folk Album in 2009 and 2011. She won the Premio Gardel in 2000, the main musical award in Argentina. She served as an ambassador for UNICEF.

Joan Baez is a Scottish-Mexican self-taught singer and guitarist who won fame as a folk musician. Her first major professional success was at the Newport Folk Festival in 1959. She released six successful albums in the early 1960s which were accompanied by professional tours. She mainly recorded traditional songs, but introduced to the public works by contemporaries such as Phil Ochs and Bob Dylan. Her on-off relationship with Bob Dylan saw her incorporating many of his songs in her repertoire. She used her celebrity status to advocate for civil rights, social justice and had a significant impact on American popular music. Her appearance at Woodstock raised her international profile particularly following the successful release of the documentary Woodstock (1969). Her success continued into the 1970s with chart successes for songs such as 'The Night They Drove Old Dixie Down' (1971). Her Scottish and Mexican heritage influenced her perspective and as a Quaker she conveyed messages on non-violence, pathos and hope alongside songs performed in Spanish for her album *Gracia a la Vida* (1974). Her humanitarian profile was reinforced through her support for Martin Luther King and appearances at prominent events such as Live Aid (1987), as well as through her autobiography *And a Voice to Sing With* (1987).[23] Her political activism involved singing about and travelling to war-torn nations including Bangladesh (1971),

Vietnam (1972), Czechoslovakia (1989), the Middle East (1989) and Bosnia Herzegovina (1993). Some of the causes she championed through her performances and involvement with public protests include anti-war activism, civil rights, voting rights, opposing the death penalty, LGBTQI+ rights, human rights in Iran, environmental causes and Occupy Wall Street. She continued to perform throughout the 2000s at high-profile festivals including Glastonbury, UK (2008), Montreux Jazz Festival, Switzerland (2008) and the 50th Newport Folk Festival (2009). In 2007 she reissued her live album *Ring Them Bells* (1995) which featured her performing with other folk, rock and blues luminaries. In 2007 she received the Grammy Lifetime Achievement Award. In 2011 Baez was honoured by Amnesty International with the inaugural Amnesty International Joan Baez Award for Outstanding Inspirational Service in the Global Fight for Human Rights. The award would be given to any artist who has made a similar contribution to the advancement of human rights. On April 4, 2017, she released her first new song in 27 years, 'Nasty Man', a protest song against US President Donald Trump which became a viral hit. In 2017 she was inducted to the Rock and Roll Hall of Fame and in 2018 she released a new studio Album *Whistle Down the Wind* which was nominated for a Grammy and charted in many countries undertaking a 'Fare Thee Well Tour' to promote it. On July 28, 2019, she performed her final concert at Madrid's Tetro Real. She was to receive a 2020 Kennedy Centre Honour in 2020, but it was postponed because of the COVID-19 pandemic. Since stepping down from the music stage she has devoted herself to portraiture.[24]

Women began to express themselves through folk and soft rock on topics of personal relationships, the environment, politics and religion. Carole King (b. 1942), Joni Mitchell (b. 1943), Carly Simon (b. 1945) and Kate Bush (b. 1948) became extremely influential songwriters in folk, rock, jazz and pop idioms expressing ideas about womanhood, the environment and social justice with illustrious careers resulting in a string of classics.

Joni Mitchell trained in art in Calgary and moved to Detroit and New York via Toronto where she began recording albums at the age of 25. Her early albums, largely using voice and acoustic guitar, were in the contemporary folk style of the time. She addressed personal freedom from a female perspective and political themes. Her songs such as the environmental anthem 'Big Yellow Taxi' and 'Woodstock' recorded on her third album *Ladies of the Canyon* (1970) defined her era and her generation while her album *Blue* (1971) is often cited as one of the greatest albums of all time.[25] Her style is defined by a lyrical depth that has been described as demonstrating a visual imagination and sense of place and landscape.[26] In the late 1970s she began to explore jazz harmony resulting in a freer use of her voice and rhythmic inventiveness. She began working with noted jazz musicians famously collaborating with Charles Mingus on his final album *Mingus* (1979) being one of her most pure jazz releases. She later turned to pop and electronic music which was not as well received as her earlier work. She designed all her own album covers and described herself as a "painter derailed by circumstances".[27] Although she rejected being a feminist she represents a prominent women's perspective on cultural and political life.[28] She had control over the rights of all of her songs, but in the early 2000s she became critical of the music industry and expressed her desire for control possibilities by releasing her own music on the internet. She released her 17th and last album in 2017. She stopped touring and giving concerts in the late 2000s to concentrate on her painting, but made occasional appearances to speak on environmental issues. Mitchell has approved a number of archival projects including restored documentary footage of previous unseen interviews, photos, poetry and material from her personal vaults and remastering of her early recordings. On November 7, 2018, she attended the Joni 75: Birthday Celebration concert in Los Angeles. On January 28, 2022, Mitchell demanded that Spotify remove her songs from its streaming service in solidarity with her long-time friend, and fellow polio sufferer, Neil Young, in protest against COVID-19 misinformation on the streaming platform. On July 24, 2022, she gave her first full live performance since 2022 at the Newport Folk Festival where she performed alongside Brandi Carlile and a band of folk luminaries a complete 13-song set along with a guitar solo.

Mitchell's influence extends to her female listeners in the era of the male rock star. She also is considered one of the best guitarists and songwriters of her time. Her contemporaries have made chart hitting covers of her songs and she has influenced the next generation of artists including Taylor Swift, Björk, Haim and Lorde. She has received numerous honours from her home country including a star on Canada's Walk of Fame (2000) and a Companion of the Order of Canada (2002). She has received ten Grammy Awards and a Grammy Lifetime Achievement Award (2002). She was the first woman to receive the Les Paul Award (2020) and she receive the Kennedy Center Honour for lifetime achievement (2021).

American singer-songwriter and pianist Carole King wrote numerous hit songs with her husband Gerry Goffin and other songwriters in the 1960s before launching a solo career in the 1970s. As a child her mother taught her piano and she began song writing as a teenager. Her personal and professional relationship with Gerry Goffin resulted in the pair writing over one hundred songs that were recorded by major groups and solo artists. Following the disintegration of their marriage in 1967 King moved to Los Angele and started a recording career first with her band The City and then as a duo with James Taylor. The duo recorded songs reflecting environmental issues, politics, religion and dynamics of personal relationships. The album *Tapestry* (1971) reached No. 1 and won four Grammy Awards selling more than 24 million copies wordwide since its release. Her follow-up albums did not have such a broad impact, but were highly successful certifying gold and No. 1 on the charts. In the 1980s King became active in environmental affairs and restricted her performances to charity concerts. In 1993 *Tapestry* was adapted into a theatrical show with a tribute album released in 1995. Her collaboration with Céline Dion on the single 'The Reason' (1997) and the live album *The Living Room Tour* (2005) became her highest chart hitting album since the 1970s. In 2007 she reunited with James Taylor for the Troubadour Reunion Tour and in 2010 she released a live recording from the tour along with *The Essential Carole King.* King published her autobiography in 2012 and it reached No. 6 on *The New York Times* Best Seller list.[29] Along with her environmental activism King has also been politically active campaigning for the US Democratic Party since the early 2000s.

King is considered one of the most significant and influential women songwriters and musicians of her time. Her lyrics and pop/folk style captured the Zeitgeist of the 70s. She won four Grammy Awards and was inducted into the Songwriters Hall of Fame alongside being inducted twice into the Rock and Roll Hall of Fame, as a performer and songwriter. She is the recipient of the 2013 Library of Congress Gershwin Prize for Popular Song, the first woman to be so honoured. She received an Honorary Doctorate from Berklee College of Music (2013) and a Kennedy Center Honoré (2015). She was also the subject of the Broadway musical *Beautiful: The Carole King Musical* (2013).

Singer, songwriter and author Carly Simon performed in the early 1960s with her sister Lucy as the Simon Sisters and went on to launch her solo career in the 1970s. Her self-titled début album was released in 1971 and in 1972 she won a Grammy Best New Artist. She achieved international fame with her third album *No Secrets* (1972) which sat at No. 1 on the Billboard 200 for five weeks and was certified platinum. She enjoyed a string of hits including the Grammy nominated 'You're so vain' (1972) and the duet with her then husband James Taylor, 'Mockingbird' (1974). Simon's collection of greatest hits was released in 1975 and became her bestselling album. She recorded the international hit 'Nobody does it better' (1977) for the James Bond film *The Spy Who Loved Me*. The early 1980s was a struggle for her and she had little professional success until the hit 'Coming around again' written for the film *Heartburn* (1986) and 'Let the river run' for the film *Working Girl* (1988) which earned her an Academy Award, a

Golden Globe and a Grammy. Simon is the first artist to win all three major awards for a song composed, written and performed entirely by a single artist. Her collection of standards recorded for the album *Moonlight Serenade* (2005) was her highest charting album in nearly 30 years. She maintained her high profile on the charts for the rest of the decade with the release of several albums alongside promotional tours and appearances. In 2010 she performed for a new UK audience and her UK release of her album *Never Been Gone* reached the top UK 100 charts. In 2012 Simon contributed to the Bob Dylan tribute album Chimes of Freedom to raise funds for Amnesty International. In 2013 she performed 'You're So Vain' with Taylor Swift on her Red Tour with Swift claiming that the song was one of her favourites and Simon as a major musical influence on her.[30] In 2015 Simon published an autobiography *Boys in the Trees: A Memoir* along with a two-disc compilation album *Songs from the Trees* featuring two previously unreleased songs one co-written and performed with her son Ben.[31] Both were met with critical acclaim.

Simon is a recipient of all major US awards including two Grammys (from 14 nominations), an Academy Award and Golden Globe Award, plus BAFTA nominations (1990 and 1991). Simon was inducted into the Songwriter's Hall of Fame (1994) and received an Honorary Doctorate from Berklee College of Music (1998). Her song 'You're So Vain' was inducted into the Grammy Hall of Fame (2004) and she was nominated for a star on the Hollywood Walk of Fame (2005). She was also honoured with a Founders Award from the American Society of Composers, Authors and Publishers (2012). Amongst her awards are her rankings on music charts which include top billing songs including numerous gold and platinum certifications of her albums and singles. Her songs have been covered by major artists including Taylor Swift, Tori Amos and Natalie Maines from Dixie Chicks who have all claimed Simon to be a major musical influence.

Kate Bush's eccentric experimental pop was influenced by the London arts scene and incorporated folk influences of Ireland and Eastern Europe. While not overtly feminist or political Bush draws inspiration from themes such as the Vietnam War, motherhood, Indigenous Australians and LGBTQI+ stories. Her début single 'Wuthering Heights' (1978) reached No. 1 on the UK charts making her the first female songwriter to achieve a UK No. 1 and the accompanying album *The Kick Inside* featuring songs all written by Bush showcased her introspective almost hysterical lyrics. The single and album became international hits. The follow-up album *Never for Ever* (1980) featured the hit single 'Army Dreamers' which was a commentary on the Northern Ireland conflicts of the time. Bush has released 24 top 40 singles and ten top ten studio albums. She set up her own publishing and management company to maintain control of her works. For her performances she controlled every aspect of production, set, costume, lighting, sound and choreography. Dance and mime were central to her performance and required a newly engineered wireless headset radio mike so that she could dance and sing during her performances. She experimented with electronic synthesisers and drum machines and eventually for her album *Dreaming* (1982) took control of production where she could experiment with the soundscapes. Her only concert tour was in 1979 and she has been a reluctant performer. She returned in 2014 for a 22-night residency at the London Hammersmith Apollo which sold out in 15 minutes. In 2018 she published her first book, a compilation of lyrics and two box set remasters of her studio albums.[32] As a result of her 1985 single 'Running Up That Hill' being used for the Netflix series *Stranger Things* (2016–present) the song and its parent album had a huge resurgence on the pop charts surpassing its original charts success. Apart from her enormous influence and legacy the recurring 'Most Wuthering Heights Day Ever' sees an increasing number of flash mobs gathering in growing numbers of locations worldwide to recreate the dance routine from the music video of her 1979 hit 'Wuthering Heights' dressed in red and adorned with flowers. Her accolades include receiving the Edison Award (1979), Brit Award for Best Female Artist (1987), Ivor Novello Award (1979, 2002), Broadcast Music Incorporated Awards (2003), Companion of the British Empire (2013) and nominations for three Grammy Awards (1988, 1991, 1996). In 2020 Bush became a Fellow of the Ivor's Academy, the UK's independent professional association for songwriters and composers.

## Civil and human rights activism

Women musicians have played a significant role in civil rights activism often with retaliatory consequences such as blacklisting. Actress and singer Eartha Kitt (1927–2008) addressed anti-Vietnam War sentiments at a White House luncheon and believes she was censured.[33] Buffy Saint-Marie (b. 1941) a mixed blood Cree Indian who spoke about Native American Civil Rights and wrote the soundtrack for Mike Nichol's film *Soldier Blue* (1970) which was inspired by the 1864 Sand Creek massacre in Colorado. She was asked not to sing anything to do with the Indian people and she claims Lyndon Johnson sent a letter to radio stations not to work with civil rights activists.[34] Nina Simone was also cold shouldered when she began playing Student Non-violent Coordinating Committee (SNCC) benefits. Dusty Springfield was deported from South Africa when she included a 'no Apartheid' clause in her South African tour at a time when the propaganda for the Apartheid regime was at its height in the 1960s and 1970s. Her actions were condemned by government in England and fellow performers.[35] Miriam Makeba used her status to speak out against Apartheid and when she married civil rights activist Black Panther leader Stokely Carmichael she was effectively blacklisted.[36] White audiences in the United States stopped supporting her and she was under surveillance from the FBI and CIA.[37] The 1980 UN resolution supporting the cultural boycott of South Africa caused issues for Makeba when she supported Paul Simon's Graceland recording with African musicians without the permission of the African National Congress (ANC). He was considered a sell out for breaking the cultural boycott which weakened her position by association.[38] After Nelson Mandela's election victory artists could tour South Africa with Whitney Houston's large-scale promotion to townships, factories and the general outlets. Jazz singer Abbey Lincoln was outspoken and played benefits for Malcolm X, the NAACP and the black Muslims and was accused of exploiting her racial identity to gain fame.[39] Sister Souljar used rap for her message of radical Nation of Islam and was singled out for public censure by Bill Clinton for anti-white racism resulting in the phrase 'Sister Souljar moment' to describe a politician's repudiation of extremist views to have some association with their party views.[40]

American singer, actress, guitarist, lyricist Odetta (Holmes 1930–2008) was often referred to as 'The voice of the Civil Rights Movement'.[41] She was an important figure in the American folk music revival. She trained for a career in opera, but became increasingly interested in folk songs and ballads. She moved to New York and became involved with the 1960s urban folk song movement. She became a famous interpreter of folksongs and became involved in the civil rights movement. She was one of a few women who performed at the historic March on Washington in August 1963 where Dr Martin Luther King gave his 'I have a dream' speech. Odetta also campaigned against US involvement in Vietnam appearing alongside Joan Baez, Pete Seeger and Paul Simon at the free 'War Is Over' concert in New York's Central Park, after the last Americans were airlifted from Saigon in April 1975. In her later years she lent her voice to social causes and in 1999 she was awarded the National Endowment of the Arts' National Medal of Arts. She was also awarded the Winnipeg Folk Festival Lifetime Achievement Award (2006) and the International Folk Alliance Traditional Folk Artist of the Year (2007). In the final year of her life aged 77 she toured North America and her last major concert was at the Hardly Strictly Bluegrass Festival before an audience of thousands in San Francisco's Golden Gate Park on June 20, 2008. She was hoping to perform at President Barak Obama's inauguration but passed away before the event.

Odetta shared the bill at the March on Washington with Bernice Reagon (b. 1942) who was a founding member of SNCC's Freedom Singers in the Albany Movement in Georgia using the power of collective singing to unify the protest for change during the early 1960s civil rights movement. In 1973 Reagon founded the all-black female a capella ensemble 'Sweet Honey and the Rock' to sing about racism, sexism and environmental issues. She became a cultural historian at the Smithsonian Institution directing a programme on black American culture earning a PhD in music (1975) from Howard University. She held the appointment as Distinguished Professor of History at American University (AU) in Washington, DC, from 1993 to 2003. Reagon has since been named Professor Emerita of History at AU and holds the title of Curator Emeritus at the Smithsonian, scholar in residence at Stanford and honorary doctorate of music from Berklee College of Music.

Joan Armatrading (b. 1950) was born in the British colony of Saint Christopher and Nevis. Her family moved to Birmingham when she was three years old at which time she remained with her grandmother until her parents could afford to bring their children and she was reunited with her parents in the UK aged seven. She was self-taught on piano and guitar and began performing in clubs as a teenager. Her first two albums received critical success but she did not receive commercial success until hit single 'Love and Affection' and its parent album *Joan Armatrading* (1976). She became established in the United States with her fourth album *Me, Myself, I* (1980). Her style features blues, jazz and reggae with her distinctive smooth, contralto voice and uncluttered vocal lines. Armatrading became the first female black singer-songwriter to achieve success in Britain and has maintained a successful career of recording and touring. She was the first UK female artist to début at No. 1 on the US Billboard Blues Chart with her album *Into the Blues* (2007) which was also nominated for a Grammy Award making her the first UK artist to be nominated into the Grammy Blues category. She supported new music and talent and for her 2012 Starlight tour she invited 56 singer-songwriters to open for her tour to their respective home towns.[42] In 2013 Armatrading presented a two-part radio series showcasing these artists on BBC Radio Two. In 2016 she was commissioned to write the music for the all-female production of Shakespeare's *The Tempest* for the Donmar Warehouse for which she released the accompanying album *The Tempest Songs*. Apart from her ongoing recording and touring she has appeared as guest in high-profile concerts such as The Prince's Trust Rock Gala (1983). She has also made guest appearances in film and on television. In 2001 she earned a BA degree in history from the Open University of which she later became a trustee. Her numerous awards include the Ivor Novello Award (1996), honorary degrees from a number of universities, a Lifetime Achievement Award at the BBC Radio Two Folk Awards (2016) and a Commander of the Order of the British Empire (2020). She is recognised as one of the outstanding influences on British music and musicians.

Musical activist Suzanne Vega (b. 1959) was involved in the 1980s Greenwich Village folk-roots revival and her début self-titled album received critical acclaim and reached platinum in the UK. This was followed by *Solitude Standing* (1987) which featured her hit single 'Luka' expressing the point of view of an abused child. The album's success led to an invitation to be the first female artist to headline Glastonbury Festival. The event was additionally notable as she wore a bullet proof vest due to a fan sending death threats ahead of the festival. In 2008 Vega established her own recording label to gain control over her works. Vega's combination of folk-styled pop-rock opened up the industry to women in the 1990s.

Tracy Chapman (b. 1964) addressed black women's issues having experienced discrimination first hand. Chapman was raised in a working-class family in Cleveland, Ohio, before winning a music scholarship to liberal boarding school through the Kennedy programme for the disadvantaged after which she graduated from Tufts University. She became known in the Boston coffee house circuit performing her own songs expressing black women's issues through the folk idiom which had been considered a white idiom leading to some criticism from her black peers. Her first self-titled album *Tracy Chapman* (1988) was a certified multi-platinum success with songs addressing racism, poverty, domestic violence and love. Her appearance at the June 1988 Nelson Mandela 70th Birthday tribute concert at London's Wembley Stadium beamed to 63 countries rocketed her into fame. Her human rights activism includes her performance at the 40th Anniversary of the Universal Declaration of Human Rights with Amnesty International (1988), her aforementioned performance at Nelson Mandela's 70th Birthday (1988), her collaboration with Spike Lee on her 1989 Born to fight video with archival footage from the civil rights movements and performing in the AIDS/LifeCycle event (2004). Chapman has won six Grammy Awards commencing with Best New Artist (1988), Best Female Pop Vocal Performance (1988) and Best Contemporary Folk Album (1989). Her subsequent albums went on to receive critical and sales success. She is a rare early example of an African American woman working as an instrumentalist and singer in the mainstream pop industry.

Alternative rock singer, songwriter, pianist and record producer, Tori Amos (b. 1963) explored female sexuality, personal relationships, religion and sexual violence in her début solo album *Little Earthquakes* (1992) which earned her critical acclaim. The first single from this album 'Me and a Gun' (1991) referred to her rape at knifepoint at the age of 21 which resonated for many women. In June 1994 she was the first national spokesperson for the newly established Rape, Abuse and Incest National Network (RAINN), a toll-free help line in the United States connecting callers with their local rape crisis centre. Amos answered the ceremonial first call to launch the hotline. She has continued to be closely associated with RAINN and on August 18, 2013, a concert in honour of her 50th birthday raised money for RAINN. Her classically trained pianistic virtuosity was notable amongst the alternative rock set and featured in her acoustic-based album *Under the Pink* (1994) which sold more than one million copies. Her album *Strange Little Girls* (2001) interpreted songs written by men to offer a female perspective while *Scarlet's Walk* (2002) explored Native American values through the development of her subjective alter ego, Scarlet. *American Doll Posse* (2007) developed five personae projecting different modes of female identity. Her classically inspired *Night of Hunters* (2011) featured a collaboration with a wind quartet and her own daughter's voice. She has explored themes of gender, class, race, history, religion and politics in her music along with confronting misogyny and pornography. In 2012 Amos launched her own record label intended to develop new artists and she also records from her own home recording studio to distance herself from recording executive control. She continued to produce albums and undertake promotional tours in the first decades of the 21st century releasing her 16th studio album in 2021 produced during the COVID-19 lockdowns.

Texan-born Michelle Shocked (Johnston, b. 1962) adopted the name as a play on 'shell shocked' the war veterans' condition. She emerged from the San Francisco punk squat scene protesting against corporations and political parties. She campaigned at women's peace camps in Europe and the squatter's movements in Amsterdam and New York. The release of recordings of her protest songs performed late one night at the Kerrville Folk Festival. *The Texas Campfire Tapes* (1986) was a huge success leading to a major record deal. She was resistant to commercial control of the recording industry and following breaking her contract with her label she worked to establishing her own label, Mighty Sound, starting with the release of *Deep Natural* (2002). She reissued and expanded versions of her catalogue having retained complete ownership of her work. She was mistakenly drafted as a gay icon and in 2013, when during a concert in San Francisco, she made what was perceived to be an anti-same-sex marriage statement which caused audience members to walk out and the concert season cancelled.[43] She later clarified that she had been misinterpreted.[44] Shocked continues to record and tour as an independent artist with a devoted following.

Natalie Merchant (b. 1963) started out as lead singer and primary lyricist of alternative rock group 10,000 Maniacs for their first seven albums and left to pursue a solo career in 1993 releasing seven solo albums. Her activism includes speaking on issues ranging from the Contras and US policy in Central America to domestic violence and the environment. She turned to issues of female representation at music awards. She organised a concert in 2012 to protest oil and gas fracking in New York state with an accompanying documentary titled *Dear Governor Cuomo*. She directed a short documentary *Shelter: A Concert Film to Benefit Victims of Domestic Violence* (2013) calling for an end to violence against women. Merchant was an outspoken critic of then-President-elect Donald Trump and is a member of the Canadian charity Artists Against Racism.

Irish singer and songwriter Sinead O'Connor (b. 1966) reached the international carts with her début album *The Lion and the Cobra* (1987) and has continued to release chart-topping solo albums since then. She has also written songs for films and collaborated with other artists at charity fundraising concerts. Her memoir *Rememberings: Scenes from My Complicated Life* (2021) became an international bestseller.[45] Her shaven head image was a feminist statement against traditional views of women. Controversies surround her public stance on organised religion, politics in Ireland, sexual abuse of children in the Catholic Church, women's rights and withdrawing from award ceremonies and nominations. Her appearance on Saturday Night Live (October 3, 1992) was a protest against sexual abuse of children in the Catholic Church where she ripped up a photograph of Pope John Paul II while singing the words 'evil' during her a cappella cover of Bob Marley's song 'War'. This performance resulted in her rejection by the Vatican and criticism from fellow singer-songwriter, Madonna, who publicly condemned O'Connor's behaviour. It also led to jeers from the audience at her scheduled performance at the Bob Dylan 30th Anniversary performance in Madison Square Gardens (1992) where she was unable to continue with the performance so she turned up the microphone and screamed a rendition of 'War' stopping at the mention of child abuse and staring at her audience before departing the stage.[46] She also was engaged in public criticism of Miley Cyrus's music video for 'Wrecking Ball' (2013) and public remarks about being involved in a violent stoush with pop star Prince. In the late 1990s she became ordained as a priest and in 2017 she changed her name after converting to Islam, but continues to record under her birth name. In 2018 she lashed out on Twitter criticising non-Muslims. She shared her struggles with mental illness and depression on her social media platforms.[47] Since losing custody of her 13-year-old son, Shane, she posted that she had suicidal thoughts and following his death in early 2022 she posted that she would kill herself after which she was hospitalised of her own volition.[48]

Fellow Irish singer Dolores O'Riordan (1971–2018) represented Irish alternative rock with her recognisable voice featuring lilting yodel, use of keening and Limerick accent. She did not enjoy being compared to O'Connor and wished to differentiate herself.[49] O'Riordan began performing in her church choir and trained in piano before leaving secondary school to join alternative rock band The Cranberries in 1990 seeking a vehicle for her songs. The group recorded seven studio albums including four that reached No. 1 on the hit charts. She branched out on her own to record her first solo album *Are You Listening* (2007) with a follow-up album *No Baggage* (2009). She reunited with the Cranberries and recorded *Roses* (2012) and undertook a world tour. She released her last album with the group *Something Else* (2017). She wrote the protest song 'Zombie' (1994), the lead single from their second album, in memory of victims of the IRA Warrington bombings. The song is considered a masterpiece of alternative rock and became one of their most successful international hits. O'Riorden struggled with depression which has been attributed to sexual abuse that she endured for years as a child.[50] She struggled with the pressures of success and touring and this combined with substance abuse led to compounding mental health issues leading to her untimely death in 2018.[51] Her memorial service attracted tributes from around the world and digital sales of her songs skyrocketed. The Cranberries disbanded after the release of their final album in 2019. Her unique style had a lasting impact on popular music and she was also considered a leading activist advocating for children and peace. She received numerous awards throughout her career and posthumously including MTV Europe Music Award for best song 'Zombie' (1995), Ivor Novello Award (1997), Top Female Artist of All Time in Billboard's Alternative Song Chart (2018) and honorary doctorate from the University of Limerick (2020).

Ani Di Franco (b. 1970) is a prolific folk singer-songwriter, guitarist, label owner and political activist. Her songs feature messages about gender, identity, social institutions and politics. She addresses social issues including racism, homophobia, poverty and reproductive rights. She began busking aged nine and left home aged 15 to build her following. Refusing to bow to record label demands Di Franco founded Righteous Records in 1989 (renamed Righteous Babe Records in 1994), an independent record label to produce her music along with that of other non-mainstream artists. Di Franco has also published two volumes of poetry and a memoir *No Walls and the Recurring Dream* (2019) which made The New York Times Best Seller list. Her activism extends to lending her voice to numerous social movements, performing benefit concerts, speaking at rallies and creating her own charities. She has been involved in activism against the first Gulf War, supporting Green Party candidate Ralph Nader in 2000 US election, Burmese resistance movement, lobbying against nuclear power establishing a public school programme supporting student in Buffalo's schools, raising funds for musical instruments destroyed in the 2005 Hurricane Katrina in New Orleans and Gulf Aid following the Deepwater Horizon Oil spill in the Gulf of Mexico, supporting the preservation movement in Buffalo and supporting Toronto-based charity Artists Against Racism. Her accolades include winning a Grammy for her recording *Evolve* (2004) and she was awarded the Woman of Courage Award (2006), Outstanding Achievement for Global Activism Award from A Global Friendship (2017) and John Lennon Real Love Award (2021).

### Punk and experimental women

By the mid-1970s women in rock and pop began to express alternative feminist messages addressing discrimination and misogyny through punk rock and experimental music. Patti Smith (b. 1946) and Yoko Ono (b. 1933) entered the scene with avant-garde and experimental contributions. Punk opened the way for female instrumentalists and non-stereotyped singing styles along with all-female bands. Siouxsie Sioux (b. 1957) and Poly Styrene (1957–2011) were both exponents of the movement in Britain along with the all-girl bands the Slits and the Raincoats who addressed issues such as rape and sexual abuse and refused to perform according to record industry stereotypes. Deborah Harry (b. 1945) challenged the punk statement by representing the cartoon punk with her blow up doll image which was intended as an attack on the image of women in the pop scene.

Patti Smith became influential in the New York City punk rock movement fusing rock and poetry into her music. She moved to New Jersey aged nine and worked in a factory as a teenager. Smith won a scholarship to attend Glassboro State Teacher's College during which time she became interested in the poetry of Arthur Rimbaud, Albert Camus, William Burroughs and Allen Ginsberg along with the music of the Rolling Stones, John Lennon and Bob Dylan. She moved to New York and by the 1970s she became a key player in the avant-garde scene. In 1974 she secured a recording contract for her single 'Hey Joe' featuring her monologue for Patty Hearst the fugitive heiress and B-side 'Piss Factory' where Smith speaks of her factory experience. Her first album *Horses* (1975) recorded with her band the Patti Smith Group was provocative and combative capturing the mood of punk rockers. Her image on the album's cover was fashioned with her partner photographer Robert Mapplethorpe featuring Smith staring insolently into the camera. Her second album *Radio Ethiopia* (1978) continued to capture the punk mood and *Easter* (1978) which featured her collaboration with Bruce Springsteen for 'Because the Night' which became a hit single. Her fourth album *Wave* (1979) was slightly less successful, but received commercial airplay. She retreated from the world of rock in the 1980s only recording one album *Dream of Life* (1998) as a tribute to her husband who died several years earlier. In 1995 she toured briefly with Bob Dylan. In the 1990s she released a series of compilations featuring her works to date such as *The Patti Smith Masters* (1996), along with albums *Gone Again* (1996), *Peace and Noise* (1997) and *Gung Ho* (2000) which featured tributes to her father, songs about the invasion of Tibet and Vietnamese revolutionary Ho Chi Minh. Her next album *Trampin'* (2004) included several songs about motherhood and tributes to her mother who died two years earlier.

In 2005 Smith curated the Meltdown festival in London where she gave a live performance of *Horses* in its entirety which was recorded and released later in the year as Horses/Horses. On October 15, 2006, Smith performed at the closing of the CBGB nightclub in New York concluding with a tribute to the rock and punk musicians who had died in the previous years. She also turned her attention to exhibiting her photography participating in live performances and recordings and was the subject of a documentary film *Patti Smith: Dream of Life* (2008). She published her memoir of her relationship with Robert Mapplethorpe *Just Kids* (2010) which was republished in 2018 with added photographs and illustrations.[52] She also published several volumes of poetry. Throughout the next decade Smith released her 11th studio album *Banga* (2012), appeared on stage at benefit concerts, on tribute albums, made brief cameos in films and on television and at award ceremonies, notably performing at the 2016 Nobel Prize Award Ceremony in Stockholm accepting the Nobel Prize for Literature prize on behalf of Bob Dylan. In 2018 her concert-documentary film *Horses: Patti Smith and Her Band* received wide critical acclaim. Smith's activism includes contributing to the 1993 AIDS-Benefit Album, campaigning for the US Green Party, performing at protests against the Iraq War, premièring protest songs against US foreign policy in *London* (2006) and performing annually at Tibet House in the United States. On February 24, 2022, for her first performance at the Capitol Theatre, New York, Smith referred to the Russian invasion of Ukraine stating that "peace as we know it is over in Europe".[53]

Smith has received numerous awards for her music, poetry and books. She has been named a Commander of the Ordre des Arts et des Lettres by the French Ministry of Culture (2005), inducted into the Rock and Roll

Hall of Fame (2007), winner of the Polar Music Prize (2011), received an honorary doctorate in fine arts from the Pratt Institute (2012), was set to receive the International Humanities Prize from Washington University in St Louis (2020), but the ceremony was cancelled due to COVID-19, and was awarded an honorary Doctor of Humane Letters from Columbia University (2022).

Yoko Ono, American performance artist, composer, singer and peace activist of Japanese birth, was born in Tokyo and moved to New York to study philosophy and music at Sarah Lawrence College. She was a pioneer in the conceptual art movements and she performed her self-composed pieces featuring her virtuosic vocal expressions using screams, moans and multi-phonics. Ono became involved in the New York downtown artists' scene following her first marriage in 1956 with the couple's apartment in Manhattan hosting many performance events. Her high-profile second marriage to English musician John Lennon of The Beatles featured their staging a public protest Bed-In for Peace against the Vietnam War at their honeymoon. In 1969 they formed Plastic Ono Band which featured a flexible membership melding rock and avant-garde styles. The recording of the performance at the Toronto Rock 'n' Roll Revival was released as *Live Peace* in Toronto in 1969. This was followed up with *Yoko Ono/ Plastic Ono Band* (1970) featuring a collaboration with free jazz musician Ornette Coleman. Her music focuses on themes of social change and her commitment to feminism is found in her albums *Feeling the Space* (1973) and *Blueprint for a Sunrise* (2001). Ono contributed tracks featuring the new-wave punk sound of the time to the Ono/Lennon album *Double Fantasy* (1980) which won a Grammy Award for Album of the Year and in the single 'Walking on Thin Ice' Ono explored avant-garde and rock vocalisation. Upon their return from recording the single Lennon was murdered outside their Manhattan apartment. 'Walking on Thin Ice (for John)', which was released a month later, was Ono's first chart success. Ono expressed her support for the gay rights movement and continued her anti-war efforts contributing to Amnesty International's compilation album *Wake Up Everyone* (2004). She has preserved the legacy of Lennon who was murdered in 1980 funding the Strawberry Fields Memorial in Manhattan's Central Park, The Imagine Peace Tower in Iceland and the John Lennon Museum in Saitama Japan

Ono continued to record and develop a following as a pioneer in merging the avant-garde with pop. In 1994 she produced her own off-Broadway musical *New York Rock* a fictionalised account of her life with Lennon. DJs began remixing her songs in the early 2000s and her *Walking on Thin Ice* (Remixes) rated No. 1 on Billboard's Dance/Club Party chart. Her second no. 1 hit was on the same chart with 'Everyman

... Everywoman ...' reworking of her song 'Every Man Has a Woman Who Loves Him' which promoted gay love. Ono had more Dance/Club Play no. 1 hits including 'No, No, No' (2008), 'Give Peace a Chance' (2009) and 'I'm Not Getting Enough' (2009). With a new Plastic Ono Band line-up including her son Sean she recorded *Between My Head and the Sky* (2009). In 2010 her son organised the concert 'We Are Plastic Ono Band' where she performed alongside original band collaborators and guests such as Bette Midler, Paul Simon, members of Scissor Sisters and Sonic Youth. In October 2010 she performed with her band at the Orpheum Theatre in Los Angeles with guest Lady Gaga. With her son Sean she organised a benefit concert in New York City to aid the victims of tsunami-ravaged Japan and in the same year her hit 'Move on Fast' reached no. 1 on the Billboard Hot Dance Club songs. In 2013 the Plastic Ono Band released the LP Take me to the Land of Hell, and in June 2013 she curated the Meltdown festival in London where she played two concerts with the Plastic Ono Band. By the end of 2013 at the age of 80 she became one of three artists with two songs in the Top 20 Dance/ Club and two consecutive no. 1 hits on Billboards Hot Dance Club Party Charts beating Katy Perry, Robin Thicke and Lady Gaga. In 2016 she released *Yes I'm a Witch Too* featuring remixes by prominent DJs which received critical acclaim. In 2018 she released *Warzone* which included previous recorded tracks including 'Imagine'. In November 2021 it was reported that Ono had withdrawn from public life.

Ono has made philanthropic contributions to the arts, peace and international disaster relief and she inaugurated the biennial $50,000 Lennon Ono Grant for Peace. In 2012 she received the Dr Rainer Hildebrandt Human Rights Award and co-founded the group Artists Against Fracking. In 2011 she collected the 8th Hiroshima Art Prize for her contributions to love and peace whilst visiting Japan to perform at the Tokyo Art Museum to support the earthquake victims where she painted a large calligraphy piece 'Dream' to help raise funds for the orphans of the earthquake.

English singer, songwriter and producer Siouxsie Sioux (Susan Janet Ballion) with her bands the Banshees and Creatures was influential in punk and post-punk music and style. Her introduction to punk music was The Sex Pistols and she regularly followed them as a teenager. She defined gothic fashion with her black fetish/bondage, glam attire and cat-eye makeup, dark lipstick and black spiky hair. She wore fascist symbols such as the Swastika for shock value. Her music dealt with sexual abuse, mental illness, medical terrors, childhood disturbance, depravity, anxiety and solitude much of which stemmed from her own personal childhood experiences. She introduced exotic sounds to her performances and recordings such as tubular bells, ocean waves, Hawaiian choirs and percussion, taiko drums, accordion, strings, electronic sounds and oriental instruments. Her legacy is her influence upon a new generation of artists through her revolutionary approach to rock and punk which broadened the available musical options. She has particularly inspired women artists with her unique approach to musical experimentation opening up possibilities that moved away from stereotypical roles for women in rock. She ended a five-year hiatus from performing to appear in Yoko Ono's Meltdown Festival (2013) to critical acclaim and sang the final song 'Walking on Thin Ice' with Ono at the Double Fantasy Concert (2013).

Punk English singer and songwriter Poly Styrene (Marianne Joan Elliot-Said) formed the band X-Ray Spex after seeing the Sex Pistols perform. She joined the hippy trail as a teenager and had her first foray into music as a reggae singer. Her feminist punk image saw her rebelling against the archetypal female sex object wearing dental braces and gaudy coloured clothes. Her rejection of gender norms was represented in her signature tune 'Oh Bondage Up Yours!' (1977) which opens with her spoken line "Some people think little girls should be seen and not heard" which was considered a rejection of male punk bands and rock journalists.[54] Her unpolished vocals and her cries against consumerism, racism and environmental destruction featured in her performances. X-Ray Spex released one album *Germfree Adolescents* (1978) before they split up and she went on to record more subdued New Age solo albums *Translucence* (1980) followed by *Flower Aeroplane* (1980). She retreated from the music industry in 1983 to be initiated into the Hare Krishna movement living as a devotee at the Bhakti Vedanta Manor. She made a few guest appearances including Live @ The Roundhouse London (2007) and Rock Against Racism (2008). She released a free download of 'Black Christmas' a collaboration with her daughter Celeste and her final solo album *Generation Indigo* in 2010.

A number of female punk bands emerged in the late 1970s leading the way for creating a feminine response to rock and punk. Punk all-female band The Slits formed in 1976 forging a unique sound with their self-taught approach which corresponded to the punk aesthetic of amateurism.[55] The cover of their first album *Cut* (1979) featured three shirtless young women wearing loincloths and daubed with mud and included song titles such as 'Shoplifting'. Lead singer Ari Up (1962–2010) drew on ska, punk, reggae, rock and experimentalism with critiques of consumerism, romance and sexism. The Raincoats, another well-known female punk band formed in 1977, held a strong pro-women stance and also took advantage of the punk ideology of amateurism to create what has been argued to be 'feminine music'.[56] They incorporated exotic instruments, British folk, free jazz and influences from world music. The Raincoats took on feminist causes such as Rock against sexism, Rock against Racism and funding Women's Aid and Rape Crisis. In the United States the Runaways formed in Los Angeles in 1975 as one of the few all-female line-ups dedicated to the style of hard rock and are considered to be one of the first punk rock female bands.[57] They were less successful in the United States, but extremely popular in Japan. The Go-Go's, formed in 1978, were a West Coast US all-female band who had chart hitting punk hits and have been inducted into the Rock and Roll Hall of Fame (2021) being considered one of the most successful all-female bands of all time.

Deborah Harry established her name with the band Blondie but found it difficult to extract the band's name from her own identity as the band's name was often mistaken as her own. Her platinum blonde hair with exposed dark roots played with the stereotypical sexualised pop image. Through her association with the alternative Warhol Manhattan art scene, she critiqued the pop scene, but her irony was lost with some viewing her as a hypocrite to the cause. A natural beauty alongside daring clothing choices helped establish her success with Blondie and as a solo performer. She also appeared in a number of film noir and horror movie roles and was immortalised in a 1980 set of Andy Warhol artworks. She has continued to perform at high-profile festivals and concerts and her 11th studio album *Pollinator* (2017) débuted at no. 4 in the UK. She has taken on philanthropic causes devoted to fighting cancer and endometriosis.

Lydia Lunch (1959) began her career in music in Punk Band Teenage Jesus and the Jerks and was influential in the New York City no wave scene with her anti-commercial noise music.[58] In 1984 she launched her own production company Widowspeak Productions to release her work with collaborators such as Nick Cave, Rowland S. Howard and Sonic Youth. In 2009 she formed the band Big Sexy Noise which toured throughout Europe to promote their albums. Her music challenges taboos on sex, death and womanhood. She has been an environmental activist since the 1980s and a critic of the US Justice system and the big business conglomerates. She has performed on recording collaborations, spoken word recordings, films, plays and authored a number of bestselling books. Lunch is hailed by climate activists Greta Thunberg and the Extinction rebellion.[59]

### Women in country music

Country music was characterised by fundamentalism where women were subjected to the values of a male-dominated society. However, early women pioneers of country music began to address the gender imbalance and broke through the barriers in the country music recording industry. Aspiring women musicians such as Kitty Wells (Ellen Muriel Deason; 1919–2012), Patsy Klein (Virginia Patterson Hensley; 1932–1963) and Tammy Wynette (Virginia Wynette Pugh; 1942–1998) found it difficult to find promoters because they were women.[60] However, Maybelle Carter (1909–1978) always had a strong influence in songwriting and playing. Carter was famed for developing the 'Carter scratch' which turned the guitar into a lead instrument and became one of the most imitated of acoustic guitar techniques.[61] She featured autoharp in performances popularising an instrument which had previously been quite obscure in country music.

Kitty Wells became the first female singer to top the US country charts with her hit 'It Wasn't God Who Made Honky Tonk Angels' (1952) which addresses the male–female double standards with its lyrics "It's a shame that all the blame is on us women". The song was banned by many stations, but despite this it took off and in 1952 and it peaked at No. 1 for six weeks as well as crossing over to the Billboard's pop charts reaching No. 27. As a result, she was admitted as a member to the Grand Ole Opry which had originally banned the single.[62] Wells followed the blockbuster with a string of hits sung from a female point of view: 'Paying For That Back Street Affair' (1953), 'Cheatin's a Sin' (1954), 'There's Poison in Your Heart' (1955), 'Searching' (1956), 'Repenting' (1957), 'Jealousy' (1958), 'Your Wild Life's Gonna Get You Down' (1959), 'Heartbreak U.S.A.' (1961), 'Will Your Lawyer Talk to God' (1962) and more. She also sang memorable duets with fellow superstars. Country music labels were reluctant to issue albums by female artists, but Wells proved that female artists could sell and she became the first female country singer to issue a hit album with *Kitty Wells' Country Hit Parade* (1956).

Wells was the only artist to be awarded top female vocalist for 14 consecutive years and her chart-topping hits inspired a generation of female country singers. She was referred to as the 'Queen of Country Music'.[63] Her list of achievements include first solo female artist to have a No. 1 record on the charts, first woman to headline a major tour, first woman to headline a syndicated television show, first woman inducted to the Country Music Hall of Fame (1976), Academy of Country Music's Pioneer Award (1985) and first female country music artist to receive a Grammy Lifetime Achievement Award (1991).

Patsy Cline influenced the direction of country music with her successful cross over into pop music broadening the appeal of country music.[64] Her first recording contract led to success with her singles including 'A Church, a Courtroom, Then Goodbye' (1955) and 'I've Loved and Lost Again' (1956). She moved to Nashville to join the Grand Ole Opry and her single

'I Fall to Pieces' (1961) became her first to top the Billboard country chart. She went on to record successful hits in the early 1960s and headlined concerts in a busy touring schedule. At the height of her career, in 1963 she was killed in a plane crash. Her success contributed to paving the way for women in Nashville by selling records and headlining concerts. In 1973 she became the first female to be inducted into the Country Music Hall of Fame and the several remastered reissues of her greatest hits since her death have repeatedly hit sales records.[65] She has been the subject of films, television dramas, musical and theatre shows. Her choice of subjects to sing about also defied stereotypes and showed that women could project a strong image on hard topics through country music.[66]

Sentiments that were expressed in Tammy Wynette's hit 'Stand by Your Man' (1968) divided opinion with feminists finding it problematic for contradicting their cause despite the intended irony.[67] The song was an international hit and she went on to receive numerous accolades. Her major follow-up hit 'D-I-V-O-R-C-E' (1968) centres on the female challenges of marriage and she subsequently was married five times with four divorces. She became an international star with a string of hits, but suffered significant personal struggles and health problems resulting in an untimely death. Along with Patsy Cline, Wynette brought a woman's perspective to country music and expanded the record buying public to women who identified with her songs. She is considered one of the most successful country singers of her time and she has the honorary title 'The First Lady of Country Music'.[68] Wynette has won numerous posthumous awards including Living Legends Award (1991), indicted into the Alabama Hall of Fame (1993) and Country Music Hall of Fame (1998).

Country music star Dolly Parton (b. 1946) has led the way for capitalising on her music. Parton's early career success was as a songwriter and with her début album *Hello, I'm Dolly* (1967). She joined the business empire of Porter Wagoner which included a spot on his popular weekly television programme and together they recorded successful duets. He assisted her in winning recording contracts for solo single releases, but none were as successful as her duets with Wagoner. They were named Vocal Group of the Year (1968) by the Country Music Association. Wagoner became her co-producer and owned nearly half of the company she had formerly established with her uncle. The team worked throughout the 1970s together winning some chart hits with her solo releases and their duets with the biggest hit being her song 'Jolene' (1973). Parton left Wagoner's organisation in 1974 to pursue her solo career and her song about the professional break 'I will always Love You' (1974) reached No. 1 on the country charts. During the 1970s she continued to have success on the country charts and began to take an active role in producing mainstream pop music. Crossover artists such as Olivia Newton-John, Emmylou Harris and Linda Ronstadt began covering her songs. Her first million-selling album *Here You Come Again* (1977) won a Grammy Award for Best Female Country Vocal Performance (1978). Her success continued with major hits, television appearances, movie roles, covers of her songs and collaborations with major country music and pop artists. In 2007 her first single from her own record company Dolly Records was followed by her studio album *Blackwood Barbie* which reached No. 2 on the country charts. Amongst her accolades are 11 Grammy Awards including a Lifetime Achievement Grammy (2011), three American Music Awards, ten Academy of Country Music Awards, Entertainer of the Year (1978) plus two stars on the Hollywood Walk of Fame (1984 and 2018). She has been inducted into numerous halls of fame including Grammy (2007 and 2019), Gospel (2009), Country Music (2010) and Happiness (2016).

Parton established her pop-cartoon image with exaggerated womanhood as a parody of the long-suffering wife and dumb blonde. She capitalises on the image through the use of plastic surgery to maintain her public image and stunts such as appearing on the cover of Playboy (October 1978) in a bunny outfit. The image is sustained by references such as Dolly the sheep named after her after being cloned from an ewe's mammary gland along with other references to her breasts from military equipment to bridge arches.

Despite her play on the dumb blond image Parton is not only a significantly talented songwriter, producer and performer, but also a savvy businesswoman and an advocate for many public causes. As co-owner of the Dollywood Company, she oversees the operations of its theme park, dinner theatres, resort and waterpark. The Dolly Parton's Stampede business includes ventures in Missouri and South Carolina. Her philanthropic efforts have been central to her work since the 1980s with her Dollywood Foundation supporting literacy programmes and the disadvantaged. She has worked to raise money for numerous causes including the American Red Cross, HIV/ADIS-related charities, hospitals, the preservation of the American Eagle Foundation and the 2016 Great Smoky Mountain Wildfires. In 2020 she donated one million dollars towards research on the COVID-19 pandemic and encouraged others to do so. In March 2021 she publicly posted on her social media receiving the COVID-19 vaccination encouraging others to do so and performed her hit song 'Jolene' substituting the words 'Vaccine' along with the sentiment 'if you don't get vaccinated you will die'.[69] In February 2022 her company announced that it would cover the costs of tuition fees and books for employees who wish to further their education. She has turned down the Presidential Medal of Freedom twice due to her husband's illness and the ongoing pandemic.[70] Seeing it unfit to grandstand during the pandemic she refused a proposal by the Tennessee legislature to erect a statue of her.[71] Her musical influence on country and pop musicians remains central to her legacy with the numerous successful covers of her songs and collaborations as a cowriter, producer and performer. Her continual engagement with the industry through her performances on stage, television and in film has a strong following of fans and continual recognition through prestigious awards.

## Women in rock

The 1960s rock scene featured women expressing raw sexuality on stage, and like their male counterparts engaged in heavy drinking, playing hard and getting high. For most this led to tragic consequences and mirrored the fate of many of their blues women precedents. Early rock women such as Janis Joplin (1943–1970), Stevie Nicks (b. 1948), Suzi Quatro (b. 1950), Tina Turner (Anna Mae Bullock; b. 1939) and Cher (b. 1946) led the way for women in rock in the 1960s and 1970s.

Janis Joplin entered the 1960s psychedelic rock scene and grew up on the music of the blues women expressing raw emotions of pain, suffering, love and joy. She was a vital member of the 1970s Height Ashbury rebellious counterculture and she fashioned a new style of female R&B performance. The four albums released during her short career were highly successful including platinum and gold certifications in the United States, UK, Japan and Canada. She struggled with addiction while sustaining a professional career, a battle lost to a heroin overdose in 1970 aged 27. The posthumous release of her studio and live material was also highly successful. Her expression of the zeitgeist of the time was an inspiration for women who sought permission to join in the fun. She broke the mould for white women to express raw sexuality on stage, however, with tragic consequences that were repeated by a gallery of rock performers. Her seminal influence on women in rock has been recognised posthumously with numerous honours including being inducted into the Rock and Roll Hall of Fame (1995), awarded a Grammy Lifetime Achievement Award (2005) and a star on the Hollywood Walk of Fame (2013).

Inspired by Joplin, Stevie Nicks emerged on the rock scene as lead singer for Fleetwood Mac and later as a successful solo artist. Fleetwood Mac's second album *Rumours* (1977) featuring Nicks became a bestseller certified 20x platinum in the United States. She launched her solo career in 1981 and recorded her studio album *Bella Donna* which topped the Billboard 200 and reached multiplatinum status. Nicks has released eight solo studio albums and seven studio albums with Fleetwood Mac with more than 65 million copies sold in the United States alone. She has been named one of the 100 Greatest Songwriters of All Time and inducted into the Rock and Roll Hall of Fame twice. Her awards include a Grammy for Album of the Year (1978) for *Rumours*. She overcame her struggle with addiction to continue her successful recording and touring career into the 2000s and returned to the charts with her album *In Your Dreams* (2011) which débuted at No. 6 on the Billboard 200. Her DVD release of *In Your Dreams* (2013) hit the Billboard and UK video charts. In the 2000s her charity foundation was set up to support wounded service personnel providing them with digital downloads of music to raise their spirits. She has been an inspiration to a generation of rock musicians mentoring the likes of Courtney Love and including those who have made successful covers of her songs. In 2019 she was inducted into the Rock and Roll Hall of Fame making her the first woman to be inducted twice. In 2020 Nicks released her first new material in six years along with a video accompanying the track 'Show Them the Way' reflecting on the hopes and dreams of the civil rights movement in a prayer for peace. Her 2021 scheduled headline performances for the Shakey Knees Music Festival in Atlanta Georgia were cancelled due to her concerns about COVID-19.

Suzi Quatro's bass electric guitar and leather attire led the charge at the domination of male rock guitarists. A product of the Glam Rock scene of the 1970s, Suzi Quatro was originally engaged to fill the void left by Janis Joplin providing a new female image for rock of assertiveness, toughness and power generally associated with masculinity.[72] Dressed in a leather jumpsuit with low slung bass guitar, Quatro's diminutive androgynous figure belted her hits 'Can the Can' (1973), 'Daytona Demon' (1973), '48 Crash' (1973) and 'Devil Gate Drive' (1974). Her songs found greater success in Europe and Australia than in her homeland the United States. Since she released her début solo album in 1973, she has released 15 studio albums and ten compilation albums. She has been voted into the Michigan Rock Legends Hall of Fame (2010) and is reported to have sold over 50 million records. She continues to perform live and release recordings with her studio album *The Devil In Me* (2021). In 2013 Quatro received the Women of Valour Award from the Musicians for Equal Opportunities for Women for her role in inspiring and influencing generations of female musicians. In 2020 Quatro was awarded the Icon Award by the Women's International Music Network. Her work influenced Chrissie Hynde (Pretenders) Joan Jett (Runaways) and Pat Benatar.

Tina Turner is often referred to as the 'Queen of Rock and Roll' who began her career with Ike Turner's Kings of Rhythm in 1957 and made her début with the hit duet with Ike Turner's 'A Fool in Love' (1960).

The husband-and-wife duo Ike and Tina Turner went on to release hits such as 'River Deep Mountain High' (1966), 'Proud Mary' (1970) and 'Nutbush City Limits' (1973) before disbanding in 1976. Many of the songs they recorded were written by Tina Turner including 'Nutbush City Limits'. In 1984 Tina Turner returned to the spotlight to release her multi-platinum album *Private Dancer* (1984) which won the Grammy Award for Record of the Year containing her hit song 'What's Love Got to Do with It'. The album became her first and only No. 1 on the Billboard Top 100 making her the oldest female solo artist to do so. She continued to produce hits and became the first black woman stadium rock star characterised by her mini skirt dance routines with her 1988 Break Every Rule Tour setting a then Guinness World Record for the largest paying audience for a solo artist.[73] She became an icon of survival when she went public about the violent physical abuse that she suffered at the hands of her husband Ike Turner in her biopic *What's Love Got to Do with It* (1993), based on her 1986 autobiography.[74] Tuner retired after her 2009 *Tina!: 50th Anniversary Tour*. In 2018 she became the subject of the jukebox musical *Tina*. She remains one of the bestselling recording artists of all time and has received 12 Grammy Awards including three Grammy Hall of Fame awards and a Grammy Lifetime Achievement Award. Her involvement in film and television along with her musical career earned a star on the Hollywood Hall of Fame and the St. Louis Walk of Fame, has been inducted into the Rock and Roll Hall of Fame twice (1991 with Ike and 2021 as solo) and is a recipient of the Kennedy Centre Honours and Woman of the Year Awards (2005).

Cher elevated the pop-rock chick to another level. She has been named 'The Goddess of Pop', the queen of comeback, the ultimate pop chameleon and a feminist icon. Her career is based upon her determination not to be dependent on men and refusing to bow to the conventional role of a woman in an industry that fetishises youth.[75] Her early success was with wholesome folk hippiedom in the duo with her husband Sonny Bono and their hit 'I Got You Babe' (1965) which peaked at No. 1 in the UK and US charts. Following the split from her husband in the late 1970s she moved into disco for her album *Take Me Home* (1979) and took on a residency at Las Vegas. Cher acted in a series of movies in the 1980s and performed on Broadway. Her performance in *Moonstruck* (1987) won her Best Actress awards in both the Academy and Golden Globe Awards. In the late 1980s she returned to her music career releasing rock infused albums *Cher* (1987), *Heart of Stone* (1989) and *Love Hurts* (1991). Her performance on the MTV Video for the single 'If I Could Turn Back Time' (1989) from Heart of Stone cemented her rock chick image with her fishnet suspender stockings, rear end tattoos, leather jacket over skimpy leather thong performing on a US navy battleship for the ship's crew and straddling a cannon. The controversy surrounding the video brought considerable attention to Cher's ability to reinvent herself and her comeback reached to top 10 on charts in the United States, Belgium, Canada, Ireland, Netherlands, New Zealand and No. 1 in Australia.

Her next film *Mermaids* (1990) featured her soundtrack and generated her single 'The Shoop (It's in His Kiss)' which became No. 1 on the UK charts. In 1996 she made her directorial début in the abortion-themed anthology *If These Walls Could Talk*. In 1998 she reached another commercial peak with her dance-pop album *Believe* with its title track becoming the bestselling single by a female artist in the UK. It features the pioneering use of Auto-Tune to distort her vocals becoming known as the 'Cher effect' which has influenced pop music into the future. Her 2002–2005 *Living Proof: The Farewell Tour* became one of the highest grossing concert tours of its time. In the following decade Cher continued to appear on screen and stage and released studio albums *Closer to the Truth* (2013) and *Dancing Queen* (2018) both of which débuted at No. 3 on the Billboard 200.

Cher is one of the world's bestselling music artists and she has won over 300 prestigious awards including a Grammy (2000), an Emmy (2003), an Academy (1988), three Golden Globes (1974, 1984 and 1988), Cannes Film Festival Award (1985), the Billboard Icon Award (2017) and Kennedy Centre Honours (2018). She has been inducted into the Grammy Hall of Fame (2017). Back in 2002 she was awarded the 'Oldest Female Artist to Top the Billboard Hot 100 Chart' by the Guinness Book of World Records which also proclaimed her *Living Proof: The Farewell Tour* as the Highest Grossing Tour by a Female Artist of All Time (2007). She is the only artist to have a No. 1 single for over six decades.[76] She is also noted for her philanthropic work, political and social activism including LGBTQI+ rights and HIV/AIDS prevention. The Cher Charitable Foundation supports health research, anti-poverty initiatives, soldiers and veterans, and vulnerable children. Outside of the foundation she has lent significant support to environmental causes including animal rights, LGBTQI+ rights, elder rights and COVID-19. She has also been politically vocal and been outspoken in the media and social media to voice her opinions on political candidates, policies, war and LGBTQI+ discrimination.

### Girl power

By the mid-1980s women were no longer novelties on stage, but the music industry was still largely dominated by men. The 1990s ushered a new wave of feminism from which emerged all-female bands and female songwriters addressing contemporaneous feminist themes. Riot Grrrl is an underground feminist hardcore punk movement emerging from indie rock paving the way for women to express female empowerment. Using zines (a shortened version of fanzines) to promote a DIY musical culture to address topics such as rape, body image, self-harm, sexual empowerment to encourage women to speak out against abuse and sexism and their performances projected these messages. Leaders in this movement such as Bikini Kill, Alanis Morissette (b. 1974) and Courtney Love (b. 1964) represented the commercial music 'angry women' movement.

Bikini Kill pioneered the Riot Grrrl movement with feminist lyrics and hardcore music. Formed in 1990 the band encouraged a female-centric environment at their shows and produced fanzines to accompany their tours and embolden women to express themselves creatively. Canadian singer Alanis Morissette had early success with dance-pop albums, but it was her alternative rock/grunge-oriented *Jagged Little Edge* (1995) with its contemporary feminist themes that earned her a Grammy Award for Album of the Year (1996) which was then made into a Tony-nominated musical. In the 2000s she assumed creative control of her recordings and she has reached top 40 in major international charts. By 2022 she had won seven Grammy Awards, 14 Juno Awards, one Brit Award and sold more than 75 million records worldwide.

Courtney Love (b. 1964) and her band Hole led the female alternative rock and female grunge movement with stunts such as exposing her breasts on stage and stage dives as an expression of the right to control their bodies. The aggressive style of rock with the power drumming of Patty Schemel (b. 1967) has sold millions of records worldwide and Hole is considered one of the most successful bands of all time fronted by a woman.[77] Love has been outspoken in her advocacy for reform in the record industry and race relations in the music industry. She is also a supporter of LGBTQI+ causes, HIV/AIDS charities and is a member of the Sophie Lancaster Foundation.

The British girl group Spice Girls formed in 1994 divided feminists who criticised them for being a product of the record industry to capitalise on the young teenage market and for projecting oversexualised imagery. However, early in the group's development they parted with their management due to its unwillingness to listen to their ideas and they took control of their own work. Their 1996 release of the début single 'Wannabe' went to the top of international pop charts along with their début album *Spice* (1996) which became the bestselling album by a female group in history. Their follow-up album *Spiceworld* (1997) received similar success and both albums featured messages of female empowerment through the songs co-written by the band members. Based on dance-pop they infused their music with a feminist stance promoting female power, self-love and solidarity. The message was featured in their manifesto *Girl Power!* with its original print run of 200,000 copies sold out in one day and then was translated into 20 languages.[78] Apart from the international sales success of their tours and recordings the Spice Girls amassed a fortune through endorsements and merchandise making them one of the most successful music marketing enterprises to date. They received numerous awards including five Brit music awards, three American Music Awards, four Billboard music awards and four MTV awards. In 2000 they became the youngest recipients of the Brit Award for Outstanding Contribution to Music.

Madonna's (b. 1958) exploitation of her body in music videos caused division on whether she was conforming to cultural expectations or challenging them. She exploited the video medium to objectify her feminine image reviving the glamour of the Golden Age of Hollywood. She has generated both criticism and acclaim for her controversial use of shock value in her music videos on themes of sexual, religious and social topics. Madonna had success with chart-topping singles and albums and maintained control over every aspect of her career. Her multimedia company Maverick capitalised on the artistic talent of the people she surrounded herself with and became one of the most successful artist-run labels in history.[79] Her profile was enhanced by her appearances on screen and her lead role as Eva Peron in the musical film *Evita* won her a Golden Globe for best actress. Her other ventures include fashion brands, books, health clubs, skincare and filmmaking. Madonna was one of the earliest adopters of the hands-free radio frequency headset microphones with it becoming known as the 'Madonna mic'. She became the subject of post-modern academic theory and a feminist icon which was contradicted by her image driven by sex appeal. Her philanthropic commitments include the founding of the Ray of Light Foundation (1998) and Raising Malawi (2006). She rates as one of the bestselling artists of all time and the highest earning female touring artists of all time along with being named by Forbes as holding the record as the annual top-earning female musician across four decades from the 1980s.[80] According to the Recording Industry Association of America she is the bestselling female rock artist of the 20th century and according to Billboard she is the highest grossing female touring artist of all time. Her level of power and control in the entertainment industry are considered unprecedented for a woman.[81]

Australian-born Helen Reddy's (1941–2020) song 'I am woman' (1972) stemming from her involvement with the women's movement became a feminist anthem solidifying her international success by reaching No. 1 in the United States and earning a Grammy Award.[82] She went on to record more than a dozen US top 40 hits and won the award for Favourite

Pop/Rock Female Artist at the inaugural American Music Awards (1974). Reddy was the first Australian to host a one-hour weekly primetime variety show on an American network along with specials that were seen in more than 40 countries. She continued to record into the 1990s and retired from live performance in 2002 when she returned to Australia to earn a degree to practise as a hypnotherapist and motivational speaker. Since returning to Australia she made public performing appearances on rare occasions. One such occasion was for the 2017 Women's March in Los Angeles to promote women's rights following the inauguration of Donald Trump before a rally of 750,000 people where she sang an a capella version of 'I am woman'.[83]

Reddy was instrumental in supporting the career of her fellow Australian friend Olivia Newton-John (1948–2022) encouraging her to emigrate to the United States and, following a chance meeting at Reddy's house with film producer Allan Carr, Newton-John won the iconic role in the hit film version of the musical *Grease*. The film became the biggest box office hit of 1978 and yielded three Top 5 singles for Newton-John along with a Golden Globe for Best Actress in a Musical and a performance at the 1979 Academy Awards. The film's popularity endured and its re-release in 1998 ranked as the second highest grossing film after *Titanic* in its opening weekend. The soundtrack is one of the bestselling soundtracks of all time. Prior to this success Newton-John had represented the UK in the Eurovision Song Contest in 1974, coming fourth to the winning entry ABBA. Her first pop hit was 'I Honestly Love You' (1974) which became her signature song also hitting the country charts and earning her to more Grammys. Her success in country music caused a stir amongst purists who questioned whether a foreigner could be named Country Music Association Female Vocalist of the year defeating established Nashville-based singers, but she was eventually embraced by the country music community. Following her success in *Grease* she capitalised on the bad girl image that transformed her character in the movie and her next release *Totally Hot* (1978) which hit both the pop and country charts despite the de-emphasising of the country sound on the recording. Her most successful studio album *Physical* (1981) with its suggestive overtones reinforced her risqué image and the associated exercise themed video turned it into an aerobics anthem, pioneering the nascent music video industry. She became an advocate for health research upon her diagnosis with breast cancer in 1992 and she supported health initiatives alongside her other involvement in humanitarian and environmental causes including UNICEF, United Nations Environment Program and Children's Health Environmental Coalition. In 1994 she released *Gaia: One Women's Journey* chronicling her cancer ordeal in her first album on which she wrote all the lyrics and music. In 2008 she raised funds to support the building of the Olivia Newton-John Cancer and Wellness Centre in Melbourne, Australia, leading a 228 km walk along the Great Wall of China joined by celebrities and cancer survivors. She continued to have recording and touring success winning numerous high-profile awards including the Companion of the Order of Australia (2019).

Another fellow Australian who achieved international fame was Judith Durham (1943–2022) initially as lead singer of The Seekers and later as a solo artist. Her homespun image which she retained throughout her life and the folk influenced pop style of The Seekers appealed to a wide audience. They achieved a string of hits in the UK and United States in the 1960s with 'Georgy Girl' (1966), which was the theme song for a successful British film of the same name, becoming their most successful hit. The group was awarded the joint honour of Australian of the Year in 1968 after which Durham announced that she was leaving the group to pursue a solo career. Her career success continued with the release of several chart hitting albums. Her awards include Medal of the Order of Australia (1995), the Officer of the Order of Australia (2014) and Victorian of the Year (2015) for her support of many charities including the Motor Neurone Disease Association of Australia, the Small Miracles Foundation, Yooralla, the Aboriginal Literacy Foundation and the Australian Children's Choir.[84] In 2019 she was inducted into the honour roll for Australian Women in Music Awards.[85]

Through androgynous appearance and the wearing of suits, women performers such as Grace Jones (b. 1948) and Annie Lennox (b. 1954) adopted the image of power and the symbol of being in control. Grace Jones moved from Jamaica to New York with her family as a teenager and took up a modelling career. In 1977 she embarked on a music career initially in the disco scene centred around Studio 54 and moving into 1980s new wave styles. Her highly sexualised, androgynous and flamboyant stage shows led her to be named 'Queen of the Gay Discos' even though she never publicly identified as gay. She has performed for many AIDS benefits and she had a strong gay following. Much attention is given to her appearance and she has been represented in artworks and photography by major artists in the 1970s and 1980s arts scene in portrayals emphasising exotic, androgynous and hypersexualised features. Scottish singer, songwriter, political activist and philanthropist Annie Lennox appeared in the 1983 video for 'Sweet Dreams (Are Made of This)' with orange cropped hair wearing a man's business suit breaking the mould for female pop stars. Her successful recording career with the Eurythmics and solo career commencing in

1992 led to numerous international hits, four Grammy Awards, an MTV Video Music Award, a Golden Globe Award, an Academy Award to name a few. She won the Ivor Novello Award (2015) and was the first woman to be made fellow of the British Academy of Songwriters, Composers and Authors (2015). Along with her Eurythmics partner Dave Stewart, she was inducted into the Songwriter's Hall of Fame (2020) and the Rock and Roll Hall of Fame (2022). Alongside her highly successful career as a musician, Lennox is a political and social activist for feminist, LGBTQI+ rights and environmental causes. The profits from the late 1990 tour to promote Eurythmics album *Peace* were donated to Greenpeace and Amnesty International. In 2003 Lennox performed at the inaugural concert for Nelson Mandela's HIV/AIDS Campaign. Her experience in South Africa inspired her to found the SING campaign, supporting women and children affected by HIV/AIDS. A goodwill ambassador for UNAIDS, Oxfam, Amnesty International and The British Red Cross, she is also Special Envoy for Scottish Parliament and the City of London. In 2008 she founded The Circle of Women, a private charitable fund to network and fund-raise for women's projects around the world. She received the Woman of Peace Award at the 2009 World Summit of Nobel Peace Laureates, and in 2011 she was named an Officer of the Order of the British Empire (OBE) in recognition of her humanitarian work. She is also an advocate for LGBTQI+ rights and her stage persona has made her a gay icon. In 2017 she was appointed Glasgow Caledonian University's first female chancellor.

By the mid-1980s women musicians such as Phranc (b. 1957) and Holly Near (b. 1949) came out to provide a role for lesbian women. k.d. lang (Kathryn Dawn; b. 1961) achieved recognition as an openly gay artist in the conservative of genre of country music. Her androgyny and grey suits protected her from being defined by her sexuality just as did initialising her name.[86] She has collaborated with major musicians, such as her 2002 tour with Tony Bennett, and contributed songs to movie soundtracks as well as occasionally appearing on screen herself. She came out in 1992 as gay and has been active as a gay rights and animal rights and Tibetan human rights activist as a tantric practitioner of Tibetan Buddhism. She has supported HIV/AIDS research and as a vegetarian she has campaigned for animal rights which caused banning of her music on radio in cattle industry towns such as her hometown Alberta as well as Kansas, Oklahoma, Missouri, Monatana and Nebraska.[87] She has had major hits and has won numerous awards including Juno Awards (1985, 1989, 1990, 1993) and Grammy Awards (1989, 1990, 1993, 2004). She received the National Arts Centre

Award (2005), A star on the Canada's Walk of Fame (2008) and was appointed to the Alberta Order of Excellence (2018).

Women such as Melissa Etheridge (b. 1961) and Skin (Deborah Anne Dyer; b. 1967) OBE followed the lead in coming out with Skin becoming a role model for black women. Whitney Houston (1963–2012) was also a huge commercial success starting out as a backup singer in her mother Emily 'Cissy' Drinkard Houston's nightclub. She was a role model for black women soul singers by amassing power, money and influence that had not been possible before. Her appearance in the Hollywood movie *The Bodyguard* (1993) added to her fame and image as a pop diva. Her superstar status in soul music earned her millions for her No. 1 hits.

While the sexualisation of women in popular music has driven the commercial imperatives of the industry, women in pop in the 21st century demonstrate defiance through taking control of their image and business. Jennifer Lopez (b. 1969) started out in the music industry until she decided to pursue a film career. She has used her sexuality to build her commercial image overriding producers' decisions to slim-down. She promoted her curves as enviable and something to be proud of. She maintained control over her image and her wealth and became a leading Hispanic icon propelling the Latin pop movement. Female performers increasingly performed in outlandish costumes creating extravagant public images and creating their own feminine imagery.

The youngest member of the Jackson Five, Janet Jackson (b. 1966) emerged as a soloist known for her innovative socially conscious and elaborate stage shows. She has been credited for leading the development of contemporary R&B ushering the use of rap into mainstream R&B.[88] Her studio albums along with their promotional videos created an image of a public sex symbol and she became a highly successful recording artist. The backlash from the 2004 Superbowl half-time show controversy which revolved around her accidentally exposing one of her breasts led to industry blacklisting and reduced airplay. After release from her recording contract, she launched her own label Rhythm Nation and releases her music as an independent artist. Her success on the charts has made her one of the bestselling artists of her time. She has been one of the world's most awarded artists which include Grammys, American Music Awards and Guinness World Records. She has a star on the Hollywood Walk of Fame for her screen appearances and in 2019 she was inducted into the Rock and Roll Hall of Fame.

Pink (Alecia Beth Moore; b. 1979) is not only recognised for her songwriting hits, but also her acrobatic stage performances above the audience as she sings. She was originally a member of the all-female band Choice, but following being awarded a solo record contract in 1995 she achieved early success with her début solo album which reached double platinum sales. Her early albums continued to achieve chart success and award recognition and she is one of the world's bestselling music artists. Her tough girl, tomboy style features adventurous haircuts often with pink dreadlocks or flourescent colours and eschews the oversexualised pop image. She is an active campaigner for PETA and involved with numerous charities including Human Rights Campaign, The Prince's Trust, New York Restoration Project, Save the Children, Take Back the Night, UNICEF and World Animal Protection. She is also outspoken about LGBTQI+ rights and supports same-sex marriage. She also provided support for COVID-19 crisis funds.

Beyoncé (Beyoncé Giselle Knowles-Carter; b. 1981) rose to fame in the 1990s in the highly successful all-female band Destiny's Child and went solo in 2003. Her first group Destiny's Child was managed by her father and styled by her mother. Knowles grew up on the talent show and beauty pageant circuit taking on a major role in production, songwriting and marketing retaining most of the profits. Her work addresses feminist issues for black women alongside her own personal struggles resulting from her husband's infidelity. Her image has divided feminists with some considering her highly sexualised commercialised commoditisation removed from the women that she is addressing, while others applaud the impact of the sentiments expressed in her music. She is one of the bestselling recording artists of her time and her songs address issues that have resonated for women across the board. She has actively campaigned for gun control, 'Black Lives Matter', transgender youth and political candidates including Barak Obama and Hilary Clinton. Her success continues into the 21st century with her acclaimed and bestselling albums *Lemonade* (2016), which addresses themes of infidelity and womanism, and *Renaissance* (2022) taking its inspiration from ball culture. Her accolades include 28 Grammy Awards, 26 MTV Video Music Awards, 24 NAACP Image Awards amongst others making her the most awarded singer of all time. Beyoncé is the highest earning black musician of all time and she has maintained control of her empire making her one of the richest female musicians of her time. Beyoncé employs tributes to black culture for the theatrical performance of her songs and her headlining 2018 Coachella as the first black woman to do so was lauded as an inspiration to black women.[89]

Britney Spears (b. 1981) became a teen pop idol with her first two studio albums becoming some of the bestselling albums of all time. She became executive producer of her fifth studio album *Blackout* (2007) but during the promotion of the album she gained widespread media attention for personal problems including failed battles for custody of her children resulting in a public nervous breakdown which limited the promotion of her album. She was placed into an involuntary conservatorship which gave her father control of her earnings, relationships and fertility. During this time, she released several highly successful albums, music videos, embarked on bestselling world tours, released clothing lines including intimate apparel, released perfumes, appeared on television series and embarked on a four-year residency at Planet Hollywood Resort & Casino. Her legal challenge to the conservatorship led to the establishment of the #FreeBritney movement and in 2021 the conservatorship was terminated when she accused her management team and family of abuse. In 2021 Time named Spears one of the most influential people in the world.[90] She is recognised as a gay icon and has shown support for the DREAM Act, Hilary Clinton and the 'Black Lives Matter' movement. She has engaged with philanthropy early in her career through her charitable foundation which was closed during her conservatorship. She has contributed to fundraisers for AIDS/HIV programmes, children's charities and natural disasters. Her comeback from her personal trials has been an inspiration to other artists and has highlighted the public treatment of famous artists. She posted on her Instagram a lengthy message that she later retracted stating that she would likely not return to the stage due to the exploitation she experienced during her conservatorship; however, her struggles have yet to be fully resolved.[91]

Amy Winehouse (1983–2011) combined soul, rhythm and blues and jazz in her expressive contralto voice. Her jazz-styled début album *Frank* (2003) featured only two covers with the rest co-written by Winehouse. It was a critical success and the song 'Stronger Than Me' won her the Ivor Novello Award for Best Contemporary Song from the British Academy of Songwriters, Composers and Authors. Her follow-up album *Back to Black* (2006) became an international hit and one of UK's bestselling albums. Her song 'Rehab' from the album with the official music video for *Rehab* by Amy Winehouse, was directed by Phil Griffin and released in September 2006. This video was nominated for Video of The Year at the 2007 MTV VMAs. The track itself won the Ivor Novello Award for Best Contemporary Song in May 2007, as well as three Grammy Awards the following year for Record of the Year, Song of the Year and Best Female Pop Vocal Performance. The official music video for *Back to Black* by Amy Winehouse, was again directed by Phil Griffin. This track is the third single from the *Back to Black* album and was released on April 30, 2007, reaching the top 10 in the UK charts and going on to be certified platinum by 2015. At the 50th Grammy Awards in 2008, she won five awards, tying the then record for the most wins by a female artist in a single night and becoming the first British woman to win five Grammys, including three of the General Field 'Big Four' Grammy Awards: Best New Artist, Record of the Year and Song of the Year (for 'Rehab'), as well as Best Pop Vocal Album. She lost her battle with addiction and died of an alcohol overdose in 2011 aged 27. After her death, *Back to Black* briefly became the UK's bestselling album of the 21st century.

Katy Perry (Kathryn Elizabeth Hudson; 1984) rose to fame with her single 'I kissed a girl' (2008) and became the first artist to reach one billion views on YouTube videos for her singles from her fourth album *Prism* (2013). Like Pink she is known for her spectacular stage stunts such as the premièring of her single 'Wide Awake' at the 2012 Billboard Music Awards as an angel flying and spinning acrobatically whilst singing live in a vocally challenged performance and her 2015 Superbowl half-show appearance where she performed her song 'fireworks' floating above the audience on a platform that appeared to be propelled by a shooting star amongst a fireworks display. Her albums have each surpassed one billion streams on Spotify, and she is one of the most-followed women on Twitter and one of the bestselling artists of all time. Her songs deal with themes of self-empowerment, liberation, motherhood, self-help often with political subtexts. She has won numerous accolades including from Guinness World Records, Billboard Music Awards and a Juno Award. Her philanthropic work has focused upon improving the lives and welfare of children and in 2013 she became UNICEF Goodwill Ambassador. She has provided financial support for charities including supporting musical education for underprivileged children, improving childcare in Vietnam and providing support for underprivileged mothers. She has contributed to breast cancer and HIV/AIDS charities as well as prevention of cruelty to animals. Perry has performed in benefit concerts for victims of the 2017 Manchester Area bombing, 2017 California wildfires and 2018 Southern California mudflows. She was heralded as a gay icon for her song 'I Kissed a Girl' which was about her own bisexual experiences and she has been outspoken in her support of LGBTQI+ rights. She has added her voice to political campaigns through Twitter and performing at political rallies for Barak Obama, Hilary Clinton, Joe Biden and Kamala Harris. She has declared herself a feminist and has expressed her stance in her songs.

Lady Gaga (Stefani Joanne Angelina Germanotta; b. 1986) is known both for her versatility as a singer and her image reinventions. Like Madonna and Lopez, Gaga also started her career pursuing music and branched out into film. Her outrageous fashion statements gained attention and her performances highlighted the destructive nature of fame such as her 2009 Video Music Awards performance Paparazzi where she 'dies' on stage to flashing cameras and ends up bloodied hanging from the ceiling. Her studio albums have hit the pop and rock charts and she is one of the world's bestselling artists. Her accolades include multiple Grammy Awards, MTV Awards and Guinness World Records. Her fashion statements have been her trademark and the famous 'raw meat' dress attracted international attention. She has supported various campaigns including the victims of the Haiti 2010 earthquake, the 2011 Japan earthquake and tsunami, Artists Against Fracking in Iceland, Victims of Hurricane Sandy, HIV/AIDS research, COVID-19 response and as a bisexual woman she has actively supported LGBTQI+ rights. Her Born This Way Foundation was launched in 2012 focusing on youth empowerment, anti-bullying support and initiatives to support mental health.

In the 21st century, women have stepped up as performers as well as executives in contemporary music which will be discussed later in the book. Taylor Swift (b. 1989) took control of her music empire early in her career which began in country music with her first three albums establishing her as a crossover country/pop artist. Her feminist voice developed as she matured and by her fourth album *Red* (2012) she started to experiment with rock and electronic music. She writes her own songs in a narrative style and took over the production of her music through her own production house. She has challenged the music industry on several occasions and has made some ground-breaking moves such as taking control of her back catalogue and opposing low royalties from streaming services. Her commercial success including merchandise such as perfume and sustainable fashion has been fuelled by her success on Twitter leading her to be named Woman of the Year by the age of 25. She has won numerous industry awards including Grammy, Emmy, American Music, MTV Video and Guinness World Records. She has broken records for album sales, pursuing music and tour income. Her accolades include Time Person of the Year (2017) for speaking out against sexual assault, the youngest woman to reach *Forbes*' 100 most powerful women list and the most googled female musician of 2019. In 2022 she received an honorary doctorate from New York University for her artistic achievements. She has been involved in supporting numerous charities and has been recognised for her philanthropic efforts worldwide. Swift has performed at charity relief events and donated directly for victims of natural disasters including Iowa Floods (2008), Australian Bushfires (2008), Tennessee Floods (2010), Louisiana Floods (2016), Texas Hurricane Harvey (2017) and Tennessee Tornado (2020). She has also supported the arts with donations to support music and music schools in Nashville and children's literacy programmes. Swift has also contributed to campaigns to protect children from online predators, research into children's health and cancer research. She has donated and raised funds to support the National Health Service and UNICEF during COVID-19 and supported independent record stores during the pandemic. She has also lent her name to political and pro-choice campaigns, supports LGBTQI+ rights, the Black Lives Matter movement and identifies as a feminist.

British singer-songwriter Adele (Adele Laura Blue Adkins; b. 1988) has been credited for changing the way women are perceived in the music industry focusing upon music rather than sexuality. She is one of the bestselling female artists and has won numerous awards including Grammys, Brit Awards and Guinness Book of Records mentions. Her record-breaking No. 1 albums and singles have earned her industry accolades such as Songwriter of the year by the British Academy of Songwriters, Authors and Composers (2012, 2016). She was awarded a Member of the Order of the British Empire (MBE) (2013) and named UK's bestselling female artist of the 21st century.[92] Adele has championed LGBTQI+ rights and considers herself a feminist. She composes her own material and relates her personal experiences in her albums.

Miley Cyrus (b. 1992) has challenged numerous stereotypes having begun her career as a teen idol acting in Disney's Hannah Montana where she achieved success on the pop charts and on tour. She controversially broke free from her homespun child star image with her provocative highly sexualised music videos which upset the TV censors.[93] Her performance at the 2013 MTV Video Music Awards with simulated sex acts resulted in widespread media attention and her music video accompanying the release of her chart hitting single 'Wrecking Ball' (2013) which featured her swinging naked on a wrecking ball was viewed more than 19 million times in the first 24 hours of its release.[94] In response to criticism her Godmother Dolly Parton defended her decision to take control of her own image as a brilliant songwriter and performer.[95] Controversy also surrounded her personal life when she claimed that she was pansexual aged 14 and she has been a supporter of LGBTQI+ rights. She also supports same-sex marriage. She is founder of the Happy Hippie Foundation fighting injustices facing homeless youth and LGBTQI+ youth. A former vegan she received criticism for spreading misinformation when she abandoned her vegan diet due to her claim that it was affecting her mental performance. She has been open about her use of Cannabis and has invested in a Cannabis company.[96] Cyrus has supported various charities and performed in many benefit concerts. She has given support to hospitals, youth services, HIV/AIDS research, entertainment industry, environmental organisations and victims of natural disaster to name a few. Her successful transition from teen idol to provocative pop superstar with fluid sexuality has established Cyrus as a powerful female celebrity.

Sia (Sia Furler; b. 1975) who really only broke through as a solo artist with her hit 'Chandelier' (2014) drew attention to her mental struggle with fame by refusing to show her face in her public appearances. She struggled with fame early in her career and after earning gold for her studio albums and receiving attention in her home country Australia she turned to songwriting with some highly successful hits for other artists such as Rihanna, Christina Aguilera and Beyoncé. She refuses to use her image to promote herself hiding her face for her appearances with face covering wigs, face masks, paper bags and developing videos which feature actors and dancers to accompany her releases and performances. Sia started collaborating with child dancer Maddie Ziegler performing as a proxy Sia in bobbed blond wigs on her 'Chandelier' video and has continued collaborating on subsequent videos and performances. Sia's 2016 Coachella performance was highly acclaimed for its theatricality with the shift of focus to the music and the story through theatrical performance art incorporating interpretive dance featuring Zeigler and film as Sia sang with a large wig covering her face in the background to the main stage. Sia makes a point of maintaining a private image to promote a message of the effects of fame on mental health. She has achieved enormous success not only for her albums and singles, but also for her film music and collaborations with other artists. She has been highly awarded with accolades including ARIA Awards, MTV Video Music and Grammy nominations. She is an advocate for animals and adoption of rescue dogs.

Sia is another leader in the movement away from sexualisation of women in the music industry and women such as Lorde (Ella Marija Lani Yelich-O'Connor; b. 1996) and Billie Eilish (b. 2001) also seek to avoid hyper sexualisation of their image. Lorde and Eilish both rose rapidly to fame as teenagers with their early studio albums topping the charts. Both musicians exhibit unconventional musical styles that captured international attention. Lorde's single 'Royals' (2012) released on her sound cloud reached No. 1 on the US Billboard Hot 100. Her studio album *Pure Heroine* (2013) which featured the single 'Royals' hit the US pop charts receiving attention for its critiques of mainstream culture and suburban disillusionment. Her second studio album *Melodrama* (2017) débuted at No. 1 on the US Billboard 200. Lorde has performed at major international music festivals and continues to receive critical acclaim. Her release of *Te Ao Mārama* (2021) sung entirely in Te Reo Māori is a project to raise funds for New Zealand-based charities Forest & Bird and Te Hua Kawariki. Lorde identifies as a feminist and she is disinterested in sexualised performances.

Billie Eilish became the youngest artist in Grammy history to receive awards in all four general categories. Her multiple accolades include American Music Awards, Golden Globe, Grammys and her co-written theme song for the James Bond film *No Time to Die* (2021) won the academy award for Best Original Song in 2022. She wore baggy clothes to avoid hyper sexualisation of her image in her performances and videos and in 2020 she used her own social media platforms avoiding commercial avenues to make a statement about body shaming. In the short film titled *Not My Responsibility* she removes her baggy clothing to partly reveal her breasts under a fitted tank top stating in a voice-over that "your opinion of me not my responsibility" before disappearing from view. She is an advocate for environmental issues, world poverty, animal rights, abortion rights, mental health and lends her voice to political campaigns.

## Women in hip-hop

Since hip-hop's beginnings in the 1970s in the New York Bronx area, women have been involved in shaping the culture through rapping, break dancing and graffiti art. Rap took off commercially with an obsession with wealth, glamour and unadulterated objectification of women moving away from its social commentary roots. In the 1990s women began to produce rap and hip-hop in response to the sexist and misogynistic expressions by men in these genres.[97] Women moved into producing their own independent labels achieving commercial considerable success. Some of the women pioneers in this genre are Salt-N-Pepa, Queen Latifah, MC Lyte, Lauryn Hill, Missy Elliott, Erykah Badu, and Me'Shell Ndegeocello, who use hip-hop, as well as other genres of music, to empower not only black women, but people in general.

Salt-N-Pepa was formed in New York in 1985 as an all-female hip-hop group which became one of the bestselling rap acts of all time who have earned the honorific 'The First Ladies of Rap and Hip Hop'. To counter the sexist hip-hop scene at the time the group drew on their sexy image and thoughts about men. Their song 'Let's Talk About Sex' (1992) was a huge hit. In 1994 they won several MTCV Video Music Awards for 'Whatta Man' and in 1995 Grammy Awards for Best Rap Performance by a Duo or Group for 'None of Your Business'.

Queen Latifah (Dana Owens; b. 1970) expressed Afrocentric socially conscious concerns through rap focused, black feminism, sexual harassment, sexual violence and Afrocentric concerns for both men and women. Her name Queen is a tribute to her African ancestors and Latifa, Arabic for 'sensitive'. She was influential in raising awareness of violence against women and objectification of black female sexuality.[98] Her Grammy Award-winning hit 'U.N.I.T.Y.' spoke out against domestic violence and assault against women. Her work in music, film and television has been recognised by major awards including Grammy, Emmy, Golden Globe, Screen Actors Guild, NAACP Image and Academy

Awards. In 2006 she became the first hip-hop artist to receive a star on the Hollywood Walk of Fame. Although not a self-confessed feminist, which she considers white women's issues, she considers that her music was not exclusively for the female audience.[99] While for a long time she refused to address speculation surrounding her sexuality in 2021 during the acceptance speech for her Lifetime Achievement Award at the BET Awards she acknowledged her female partner and son ending her speech with 'Happy Pride!'.[100] She is credited for starting the conversation about positive body image and pioneering size inclusivity.

Me'Shell Ndegeocello (b. 1968) rapper and bassist incorporates a variety of influences in her music and is considered a significant influence on the revival of soul music. She has received critical acclaim and performed in successful collaborations with major artists. MC Lyte (Lana Michele Moorer; b. 1970) is also one of the pioneers of female rap being one of the first solo female rappers to release a full album *Lyte as Rock* (1988). She joined the Stop the Violence Movement which released the single 'Self-Destruction' (1989) in response to the violence in the African American communities which débuted at No. 1 on the rap charts. The proceeds were donated to the National Urban League. As a rapper she has addressed issues of racism, sexism and the drug culture affecting the African American community. She has lent her name to philanthropic causes and is founder of the Hip Hop Sisters Foundation which presented scholarships to college students and to the #EducateOurMen initiative.

Missy 'Misdemeanor' Elliott (b. 1971) introduced a new style of rap that was more optimistic, light-hearted and comic. She moved away from the oversexualisation of women artists and promoted female self-esteem by celebrating her size. Her songs have been based on themes of feminism, gender equality, body positivity and sex positivity. Following a series of early chart hitting collaborations she went solo in 1997 with her début album *Supa Dupa Fly* which coincided with the launch of her own label Gold Mind Inc (1997). It reached No. 3 on the Billboard 200 being the highest charting début for a female rapper at the time. Elliott has continued to top the charts with her subsequent collaborations and solo releases alongside establishing herself as a successful producer of new rap artists through her own label. Her performance with Katy Perry at the 2015 Super Bowl half-time show increased her reputation as a mainstream artist resulting in a huge boost in sales of her recordings.[101] She has sold over 30 million records in the United States and her accolades include five Grammy Awards. She is the bestselling female rapper of her time and became the first female rapper inducted into the Songwriters Hall of Fame (2019). She has also received awards for her innovative music videos with Billboard ranking her at No. 5 on the 100 Greatest

Music Video Artists of All Time 2020. In recognition of her pioneering work in rap and influence upon the new generation of rap artists, Elliott received an honorary Doctor of Music degree (2020) from Berklee College of Music. Her philanthropic efforts have focused on animal rights and, as a result of her early traumatic childhood which featured an abusive father, she has donated considerable funds to Break the Cycle campaign against domestic violence. Elliott received the Women's Entrepreneurship Day Music Pioneer Award at the United Nations in 2019 in recognition for her achievements in music and being a leader. In 2021, she was honoured with a star on the Hollywood Walk of Fame.

Erykah Badu (b. 1971) incorporates rap into her new soul sound which is influenced by R&B, 1970s soul and hip-hop. Her début album *Baduizm* (1997) and the singles issued from it became instant hits and the album was certified triple Platinum. Her success continued with her subsequent releases reaching top spots on the hit charts. Her music is influenced by her beliefs of the 'Five Percenters' and the exploration of her African heritage. In *Mama's Gun* (2000) she covers themes of hip-hop culture, ghetto life, social issues and gang culture. Her following albums turn to issues of religion, institutional racism, poverty, urban violence, cultural identity, drug addiction and nihilism. Her albums and singles have won multiple music accolades.

Nefertiti (Anglica Strong; b. 1973) expresses issues from ecology, genocide to love and birth in her album *L.I.F.E* (Living in Fear of Extinction, 1994) in a style that was more aligned with Queen Latifa and MC Lyte rather than pop-rap or gangsta rap. Like Badu, Nefertiti was also an advocate for the 'Five percenters', followers of the radical Black Five percent notion of Islamic faith. American rapper Yo-Yo (b. 1971) advocates for female empowerment through her music. Emerging from the 'gangsta' rap scene she introduced contrasting uplifting themes and positive messages. She established the Intelligent Black Women's Coalition and aimed to set up education campaigns for young women in every US city. She also worked with her mother as an assistant in a home for abused women and children. She founded the Yo-Yo School of Hip Hop to provide programmes for at-risk students.

Luaryn Hill (b. 1975) is credited for popularising melodic rap and hip-hop integrating soul, reggae and hip hop into what became known as 'organic soul'. She has won more Grammys than any other female rapper and was the first woman to win the Grammy Award for Best Rap Album as the lead singer of *The Score* (1996). She wrote, arranged and produced her début solo album *The Miseducation of Lauryn Hill* (1998) which earned ten Grammy nominations and five awards and propelled women's hip-hop into the mass market. Hill used rap to express views on motherhood, faith and self-respect, 'To Zion' was written while she was pregnant and expressed her feeling of pressure to have an abortion to avoid disrupting her career. Accompanied by Carlos Santana on guitar, she sings to her son about the empowerment she felt in proceeding with the pregnancy. Her songs symbolised a new era of anti-racism, motherhood with her natural appearance of denim and dreadlocks representing disregarded for showbiz glitz and glamour. She has been hugely influential upon the music scene in general and has opened the way for female performers of rap.

British rapper and singer M.I.A. (Missing in Acton; Mathangi 'Maya' Arulpragasam; b. 1975) combines elements of alternative, dance, electronic, hip-hop and world music with eclectic instruments and samples. Her songs contain evocative political and social commentary regarding immigration, warfare and identity in a globalised world. Born in London to Sri Lankan Tamil parents, M.I.A. and her family moved to Jaffna in northern Sri Lanka when she was six months old, but her family returned to London as refugees from the Sri Lankan War when M.I.A. was 11 years old. Her childhood experiences of the war and displacement had a defining influence on her artistry. She started out as a visual artist, filmmaker and designer, and began her recording career in 2002. One of the first acts to come to public attention through the internet, she saw early fame as an underground artist in early 2004 with her singles 'Sunshowers' and 'Galang'. M.I.A.'s first two albums, *Arular* (2005) and *Kala* (2007), received widespread critical acclaim for their experimentation with hip-hop and electronic fusion. The single 'Paper Planes' from Kala reached No. 4 on the US Billboard Hot 100 and sold over four million copies. Her third album *Maya* (2010) was preceded by the controversial single-short film *Born Free*. Maya was her best-charting effort, reaching the top 10 on several charts. Her fourth studio album, *Matangi* (2013), included the single 'Bad Girls', which won accolades at the MTV Video Music Awards. M.I.A. released her fifth studio album, *AIM*, in 2016. She scored her first Billboard Hot 100 No. 1 single as a featured artist on Travis Scott's *Franchise* (2020), and two years later, her sixth studio album *Mata*, featuring lead single 'The One'. M.I.A.'s accolades include two American Society of Composers, Authors and Publishers awards and two MTV Video Music Awards. She is the first person of South Asian descent to be nominated for an Academy Award and Grammy Award in the same year. She was named one of the defining artists of the 2000s decade by Rolling Stone, and one of the 100 most influential people of 2009 by Time. Esquire ranked M.I.A. on its list of the 75 most influential people of the 21st century. According to Billboard, she was one of the 'Top 50 Dance/Electronic Artists of the 2010s'. M.I.A. was appointed MBE in the 2019 Birthday Honours for her services to music.

Lizzo (Melissa Viviane Jefferson; b.1988) is a hip-hop artist who incorporates rap, soul, R&B, funk and pop. She was inspired by Missy Elliott and Lauryn Hill to become a rap singer for its power to be political.[102] She is also an accomplished flautist often incorporating it into her performances. Her recordings have had considerable chart success and won many music award nominations and accolades such as Grammy and Billboard Music Awards. Her struggles with body issues inspired her to become an advocate for body positivity, diversity, sexuality and race. Her back up dancers, the Big Grrls, consist of plus-size dancers and she has promoted plus-sized fashion as well as making plus-sized runway and performance fashion statements.[103] She has a strong LGBTQI+ following and has appeared at major Gay Pride events. She is a vegan and has supported political causes. In 2022 she donated to Planned Parenthood following the US Supreme Court's decision to outlaw abortion. She also has worked as an actor and in 2019 Time magazine named Lizzo 'Entertainer of the Year' for her contributions to music and screen.

Cardi B (Belcalis Marlenis Almánzar, b. 1992) who grew up in a low-income household in the Bronx has become one of the leading women in rap. She became an internet celebrity promoting herself on social media and with more than 100 million followers in the second decade of the 20th century. Her first studio album *Invasion of Privacy* (2018) was a No. 1 hit and became the first rap album by a woman to receive a Grammy (2019). As a previous stripper and Afro-LatinX woman her brand of feminism is irreverent in her approach to addressing issues for black women with sexually charged lyrics. She identifies as a feminist and has lent her name to political causes such as gun control, support for Democratic politicians including Hilary Clinton, social justice issues such as Medicare, police brutality and free college tuition. She has achieved a number of firsts including the female rapper with the most No. 1 singles, the most diamond certified songs, the female rapper with the most songs with a billion streams on Spotify and the most streamed female rap album on Spotify. Her accolades include a Grammy, Billboard Music Awards, Guinness World Records, American Music Awards, Hip Hop Awards and Songwriting awards. Outside of music she became the creative director of Playboy magazine in 2022.[104]

## Conclusion

As women in commercial music have gained increased success and control the possibilities for taking on leadership roles in popular music have expanded. In the latter part of the 20th century and into the 21st century women musicians have amassed huge fortunes due to their record sales, performance income and business management. They have written major hit songs imparting feminist messages ranging from women's rights, diversity, body positivity, social justice, sexual abuse, violence against women and sexual empowerment to name a few. They use their influence to empower other women to engage in music performance and production through providing role models and mentorship. Women are increasingly taking on control of the artistic management of their music businesses either as label managers or producers removing industry control which has been largely dominated by men in the past. Some have built fortunes through business empires such as Parton's Dollywood.

Accolades for women musicians are growing with many firsts for women in commercial music along with being awarded prestigious honours enhancing their influence. Many have used this influence to lend their support to political campaigns and social justice issues. This has resulted in their appearances at high-profile charity fundraisers, adding their voice to campaigns or directly providing philanthropic donations to support causes such as the environment, AID/HIV research, underprivileged children, music education programmes and COVID-19 research to name a few.

## Notes

1 Power, G. (2004). Yvette Guilbert: A career of public applause and personal disappointment. *Context: Journal of Music Research*, 27/28, 31–41.
2 Steane, J. (2001). *Guilbert, Yvette*. Grove Music Online.
3 Thomson, V. (1947, 9 November). La Môme Piaf. *New York Herald Tribune*.
4 Burke, C. (2011). *No Regrets: The Life of Edith Piaf*. Alfred A. Knopf.
5 Bell, A. (2011). Falling in love again and again: Marlene Dietrich and the iconization of non-native English. *Journal of Sociolinguistics*, 15(5), 627–656.
6 Gammel, I. (2012). Lacing up the gloves: Women, boxing and modernity. *Cultural and Social History*, 9(3), 369–390.
7 https://commons.wikimedia.org/wiki/File:Marlene_Dietrich_CBC_Interview_1960.ogg
8 Bach, S. (1992). *Marlene Dietrich: Life and Legend*. William Morrow and Company, Inc, 442.
9 Cohen, R. & Sherman, D. (2020). *Theatre: Brief*, 3rd ed. McGraw-Hill Education.
10 Everett, W. (2001). *Simon, Lucy*. Grove Music Online.
11 Gerard, J. (2016, 4 April). London Loves Lin-Manuel Miranda Too (and 'Kinky Boots' & Judi Dench) – Olivier Awards. Deadline.com.
12 Jones, C. (2012, 27 September). Cyndi Lauper working out The Kinks in Kinky Boots. *Chicago Tribune*.
13 Heyman, M. (2008, 30 November). Shrek's Theater Queen. *W Magazine*.
14 Purcell, C. (2015, 7 June). Fun Home Duo Make History as First All-Female Writing Team to Win the Tony, Playbill, and Finalist: Fun Home, by Lisa Kron and Jeanine Tesori. Pulitzer.org.
15 Jeanine Tesori at IMDb.

16 Pilkington, E. (2009, 30 April). The sweet revenge of a backwoods Barbie in '9 to 5: The Musical' *The Guardian*: Rooney, D. (2009, 30 April). *Review: 9 to 5: The Musical*. Variety, 22; Dziemianowicz, J. (2009, 30 April). Dolly Parton's tunes work in '9 to 5'. *New York Daily News*.

17 Irvine, C. (2008, 30 October). Mamma Mia becomes highest grossing British film. *The Telegraph*.

18 Kentucky Miner's Wife, Part 1-2 (Ragged Hungry Blues) – Columbia 15731-D (1931).

19 Howie, S. (1996). Review of Gastonia 1929: The story of the Loray Mill strike. *Appalachian Journal*, 23(3), 329.

20 Seeger, P. (2002). *The Peggy Seeger Songbook: Forty Years of Song Making*. Oak Publications.

21 Seeger, P. (2017). *First Time Ever: A Memoir*. Faber & Faber.

22 Fairley, J. (1984). La Nueva Canción Latinoamericana. *Society for Latin American Studies*, 3(2), 112.

23 Baez, J. (1988). *And a Voice to Sing With: A Memoir*. Century Hutchinson.

24 Thomson, E. (2020). *Joan Baez: The Last Leaf*. Palazzo Editions.

25 Tsioulcas, A. (2017, 24 July). The 150 Greatest Albums Made By Women. National Public Radio and The Rolling Stone 500 Greatest Albums of All Time (Blue is listed at No. 30). *Rolling Stone*.

26 Griffiths, D. (2001). *Mitchell, Joni*. Grove Music Online.

27 Kelly, D. (2000, 8 June). I sing my sorrow and I paint my joy. *The Toronto Globe and Mail*.

28 Ghomeshi, J. (2013, 10 June). The Joni Mitchell Interview. *CBC*.

29 King, C. (2012). *A Natural Woman: A Memoir*. Grand Central.

30 Adams, C. (2013, 16 May). Taylor Swift is happy to be your break-up musician. News.com.au.

31 Simon, C. (2015). *Boys in the Trees: A Memoir*. Flatiron Books.

32 Bush, K. (2018). *How to Be Invisible*. Faber and Faber.

33 Garcia E. (2022, 16 February). When Eartha Kitt Disrupted the Ladies Who Lunch: Scott Calonico's documentary short 'Catwoman vs. the White House' reconstructs an unexpected moment of activism during the Vietnam War. *The New Yorker*.

34 Paulsen, S. (2011, 24 September). An original rebel with a resonating voice. *Napa Valley Register*.

35 Gulla, B. (2008). *Dusty Springfield. In Icons of R&B and Soul: An Encyclopaedia of the Artists Who Revolutionized Rhythm*. Greenwood Press, 368.

36 Fleming, T. (2016). A marriage of inconvenience: Miriam Makeba's relationship with Stokely Carmichael and her music career in the United States. *Safundi: The Journal of South African and American Studies*, 17(3), 312–338.

37 Sizemore-Barber, A. (2012). The voice of (which?) Africa: Miriam Makeba in America. *Safundi: The Journal of South African and American Studies*, 13(3–4), 265.

38 Feldstein, R. (2013). *How It Feels to Be Free: Black Women Entertainers and the Civil Rights Movement*. Oxford University Press.

39 Porter, E. (2002). *What Is This Thing Called Jazz? African American Musicians as Artists, Critics, and Activists*. University of California Press.

40 Page, C. (2014). *Weaponized Umbrage. Culture Worrier: Selected Columns 1984–2014: Reflections on Race, Politics and Social Change*. Agate Publishing.

41 Weiner, T. (2008, 3 December). Odetta, Voice of Civil Rights Movement, Dies at 77. *The New York Times.*

42 Joan Armatrading presents 56 singer/song-writers of the Local Talent. Propermusic.com.

43 Avery, D. (2013, 18 March). Alt-Folk Singer Michelle Shocked Goes on Homophobic Rant, Tells Audience 'God Hates Fags'. Queerty.com.

44 Willman, C. (2013, 2 April 2). Michelle Shocked on 'Piers Morgan': Evasive, Incoherent, Says 'I'm Not Homophobic'. *The Hollywood Reporter.*

45 O'Connor, S. (2021). *Rememberings: Scenes from My Complicated Life.* Dey Street Books.

46 Mayhew, E. (2006). The Booing of Sinéad O'Connor: Bob Dylan 30th Anniversary Concert, Madison Square Garden, New York, 16 October 1992. In *Performance and Popular Music: History Place and Time.* Ed. Inglis, I. Routledge, 172–187.

47 Telegraph reporters. (2017, 8 August). Sinead O'Connor sparks fears for her mental health after posting tearful video online. *The Telegraph.*

48 Owoseje, T. (2022, 14 January). Sinead O'Connor hospitalized, days after teenage son's death. *CNN.*

49 Foege, A. (1995, 23 March). Dolores O'Riordan and the Cranberries: Strange Fruit. *Rolling Stone.*

50 Chiu, M. (2018, 15 January). Sexual Abuse, Depression and a Prior Suicide Attempt: Inside Dolores O'Riordan's Difficult Life. *People.*

51 Telegraph reporters. (2014, 22 November). The demons that linger in her life. *Belfast Telegraph.*

52 Smith, P. (2010). *Just Kids.* Ecco.

53 Benitez-Eves, T. (2022, 4 March). Smith Comforts New York, Plays First-Ever Show at Capitol Theatre. *American Songwriter.*

54 BBC news reporters. (2011, 26 April) Punk icon Poly Styrene dies at 53. *BBC News.*

55 Prinz, J. (2014). The aesthetics of punk rock. *Philosophy Compass*, 9(9), 583–593.

56 O'Meara, C. (2003). The raincoats: Breaking down punk rock's masculinities. *Popular Music*, 22(3), 299–313.

57 Waksman, S. (2001). *The Runaways.* Grove Music Online.

58 Masters, M. (2007). *No Wave.* Black Dog Publishing.

59 Andrews, C. (2019, 10 July). Punk hellraiser Lydia Lunch: 'I'm chronically misunderstood – but I get off on it'. *The Guardian.*

60 Bufwack, M., & Oermann, R. (2003). *Finding Her Voice: Women in Country Music: 1800–2000.* The Country Music Press & Vanderbilt University Press, 289.

61 Lilly, J. (2001). *The Carter Family.* Grove Music Online.

62 Friskics-Warren, B. (2012, 16 July). Kitty Wells, Trailblazing Country Singer, Dies at 92. *The New York Times.*

63 Oermann, R. (2012, 16 July). *Kitty Wells, The Queen of Country Music, Passes.* Music Row.

64 Jensen, J. (1998). *The Nashville Sound: Authenticity, Commercialization, and Country Music.* Vanderbilt University Press.

65 Jones, M. (1994). *The Life and Times of Patsy Cline.* Harper Collins.

66 Leppert, R. (2008). Gender sonics: The voice of Patsy Cline, musicological identities. In *Essays in Honor of Susan McClary.* Ed. Bauer, S., Knapp, R. & Warwick, J. Aldershot, 191–204.

67 Wolff, K. (2000). *Country Music: The Rough Guide*. Penguin Books Ltd, 334–337.

68 Bufwack & Oermann. Ibid., 286.

69 Porterfield, C. (2021, 2 March). Dolly Parton Gets The Moderna Coronavirus Vaccine Her $1 Million Donation Helped Fund. *Forbes*.

70 Kubota, S. (2021, 1 February). Dolly Parton turned down the Presidential Medal of Freedom twice. TODAY.com.

71 Payne, E. (2021, 18 February 18). Parton says no (for now) to statue at Tennessee Capitol. *WECT6 News*.

72 Auslander, P. (2006). *Performing Glam Rock: Gender and Theatricality in Popular Music*. Ann Arbor.

73 Nicholson, B. (1988, 17 January). *Mini-skirted Tina Turner Claims Record Audience*. United Press International.

74 Turner, T. (1986). I, *Tina. Loder, Kurt*. Morrow.

75 Tasker, Y. (2002). *Working Girls: Gender and Sexuality in Popular Cinema*. Routledge, 191.

76 Caulfield, K. (2011, 18 January). *Cher Shines with No. 1 in Sixth Consecutive Decade*. Billboard.

77 Carson, M., Lewis, T. & Shaw, S. (2004). *Girls Rock!: Fifty Years of Women Making Music*. University Press of Kentucky, 90.

78 Sinclair, D. (2004). *Wannabe: How the Spice Girls Reinvented Pop Fame*. Omnibus Press, 102–103.

79 Taraborrelli, J.R. (2002). *Madonna: An Intimate Biography*. Simon & Schuster, 85.

80 Saad, N. (2013, 28 August). Madonna is *Forbes*' top-earning celebrity thanks to MDNA tour. *Los Angeles Times*.

81 Gorlinski, G. (2010). *The 100 Most Influential Musicians of All Time*. Rosen Publishing Group, 330.

82 Arrow, M. (2007). It has become my personal anthem: I am woman, popular culture and 1970s feminism. *Australian Feminist Studies*, 22(53), 213–230.

83 'Protesters Pour Into Downtown LA For Women's March', *KCBS News*, 2017, 21 January.

84 Webb, C. (2015, 1 July). Judith Durham named 2015 Victorian of the Year. *The Age*.

85 Australian Women In Music Awards. (2019, 29 September). Judith Durham AO to be inducted into the 2019 AWMA Honour Roll. Media release. https://womeninmusicawards.com.au/wp-content/uploads/2019/09/AWMA_Honour-Roll_FINAL.pdf

86 O'Brien, L. (2002). *She Bop II*. Continuum, 285.

87 Harrington, R. (1990, 2 July). Cattle country's beef with k.d.lang. *The Washington Post*.

88 Ripani, R. (2006). *The New Blue Music: Changes in Rhythm & Blues, 1950–1999*. University Press of Mississippi, 130.

89 Dunbar, J. (2021). *Women, Music, Culture: An introduction*, 3rd ed. Routledge, 367.

90 Hilton, P. (2021, September 15). Britney Spears: The 100 Most Influential People of 2021. *Time*.

91 Vargas, R, (2022, 13 September). Britney Spears says she'll 'probably never perform again' after 'trauma'. *The Guardian*.

92 Adele named the UK's Official best-selling female album artists of the century as National Album Day returns for 2021. British Phonographic Industry.

93 Ziegbe, M. (2010, 9 October). Miley Cyrus 'Who Owns My Heart' Video Blasted By Parents Television Council. *MTV News*.

94 Gilman, G. (2013, 10 September). Miley Cyrus' 'Wrecking Ball' Smashes One Direction's VEVO Record. *The Wrap*.

95 Parton, D. (2014, 23 April). Miley Cyrus. *Time*.

96 Adams, B. (2019, 22 August). Miley Cyrus and Other Stars Invest in Cannabis Company. *Culture Magazine*.

97 Pough, G. (2004). *Check It While I Wreck It: Black Womanhood, Hip Hop Culture, and the Public Sphere*. Northeastern University Press; Morgan, J. (2000). *When Chickenheads Come Home To Roost: A Hip Hop Feminist Breaks It Down*. Simon & Schuster.

98 Chearis, K. (2005). Women, Feminism, & Hip Hop. Socialism.com.

99 Powell, C. (1991). Rap music: An education with a beat from the street. *Journal of Negro Education*, 60(3), 245–259.

100 Mercado, M. (2021, 28 June). A Very Happy Pride to Queen Latifah. *The Cut*.

101 McIntyre, H. (2015, 6 February). Missy Elliott Saw A 2,500% Sales Bump After The Super Bowl. *Forbes*.

102 Feeney, N. (2018, 1 June). The Miseducation of Lauryn Hill 20th Anniversary: 16 Artists on Its Legacy. *Billboard*.

103 Mann, A. (2018, 28 June). Lizzo Performs at Pride Island in FIT Graduate's Design. *FIT Newsroom*.

104 Freund, J. (2021, 3 December). Playboy Taps Cardi B for Creative Post in Brand Comeback Bid. *Bloomberg*.

# 7

# WOMEN IN ELECTRONIC MUSIC

## Introduction

Electronic music has been a field in which women are highly marginalised and women in electronic music at the end of the 20th century were not highly visible. Women have found themselves outnumbered at electronic music conferences and festivals.[1] In recent decades there have been attempts to redress this with projects such as Pink Noises (2000) led by Tara Roberts, which started as a website aimed at promoting women in electronic music and was expanded into a book featuring interviews with women electronic musicians.[2] Also, the film project *Sisters with Transistors* (2021), a documentary of electronic music's unsung heroines, tells the story of female pioneers in electronic music and narrated by one of its champions Laurie Anderson.[3] The low representation of women in electronic music participation has been attributed to the domination of the skill set by men in schools and universities.[4] It has been argued that this trend begins as early as secondary school.[5] Where it is a DIY community it is generally dominated by men, and women are generally only introduced to the band if they are a vocalist or a girlfriend of one of the boys.[6] This chapter addresses how women have responded to the sexism of the electronic music scene to take on leadership roles as successful composers and performers.

DOI: 10.4324/9781003183631-8

## Women in experimental electronic music and electroacoustic music

Recording technology that emerged at the turn of the 19th century opened up new sound possibilities for musical creators and composers and was adopted by composers as soon as it emerged. Composers would create new sounds using the new technologies and performers would use sound engineers to produce their music. The electronic music scene was dominated by men due to training and societal expectation of women, but some women did embrace electronic music.[7]

An early example is Clara Rockmore (1911–1998) who worked with the inventor of the Theremin to modify the machine for her performance demands, including increasing the range of the instrument.[8] Originally a violin prodigy, Rockmore developed tendonitis as a teenager and turned to the newly invented Theremin to express her musical objectives. She became one of the most popular performers on the instrument promoting its possibilities to concert audiences in the United States who were originally sceptical. She ultimately gained critical acclaim and released the commercially successful recording *The Art of the Theremin* (1977).

English composer, technician and inventor Daphne Oram (1925–2003) was a pioneer in sound manipulation through technology.[9] She began working as a sound balancer for BBC classical music broadcasts and in 1957 established the radiophinic unit at the BBC becoming one of its directors. She also set up her own studio in Kent. She developed her Oramics system which gave composers control of subtle nuances in all musical parameters. In the 1990s she converted her Oramics system to RISC[10] computer technology which was suitable for use at home. She thought this was a liberating tool for composers, particularly women.[11]

Developments in tape and synthesisers occurred in laboratories to which women had limited access. However, Bebe Barron (1927–2008) was an early pioneer in electroacoustic work along with her husband Louis (1920–1989). Together they established one of the earliest electronic studios in New York with Bebe involved in seeking musical material for her compositions.[12] They are credited for having written the first electronic score for commercial motion pictures, *Forbidden Planet* (MGM 1956).[13] Bebe became the first Secretary of the Society for Electro-Acoustic Music in the United States in 1985 and also served on the Board of Directors. In 1997 she was presented with an award from the Society for Electro-Acoustic Music in the United States for the Barrons' joint lifetime achievement in electro-acoustic music.

Composer and flautist Ruth Anderson (1928–2019) undertook postgraduate work at the Columbia-Princeton Electronic Music Center and at Princeton University, and privately studied composition with Boulanger and Milhaud. In 1968 she designed and became the director of the first electronic music studio within CUNY at Hunter College, where she taught composition and theory (1966–1989). She composed dozens of electro-acoustic works for a variety of ensembles. Among her many awards are two Fulbright scholarships to Paris (1958–1960), residencies at MacDowell Colony (1957–1973) and Yaddo (1969, 1982).[14]

American composer, poet and choreographer Lucia Dlugoszewski (1931–2000) performed primarily on invented instruments, including her own 'timbre piano', a conventional piano played by striking, bowing or plucking the strings, and the many percussion instruments created for her by sculptor Ralph Dorazio.[15] She was inspired by Haiku poetry and oriental philosophy. She was best known for her dance scores becoming the first woman recipient of the Koussevitzky International Recording Award for *Fire Fragile Flight* (1973), she also received the Tompkins Literary Award for poetry (1947) and an award from the National Institute of Arts and Letters (1966).

English composer Delia Derbyshire (1937–2001) developed a career as one of the BBC Radiophonic Workshops' most prolific and inventive creators.[16] She composed over 200 pieces for various radio and television dramas and features, many of which have subsequently appeared on commercial CD releases. She was interested in the physics of sound and she was inventive in the creation of new sounds from random objects and modified musical instruments. Derbyshire composed music for television, radio live theatre and is best known for her electronic realisation of Ron Grainer's music score for the 'Doctor Who' theme tune. She is still regarded today as a pioneer in electronic music making, and has influenced many contemporary popular artists.

Pauline Oliveros (1932–2016) was one of the leading post-war figures in electroacoustic music whose groundbreaking work continues to have an impact on the field. Her early interest in background noises and white noise was developed on a wire recorder that she was gifted by her mother.[17] Oliveros pushed the sonic envelope and her lessons on accordion led to her fascination with combination tones that the instrument produced. She used amplification to isolate tones and create new sounds from the instrument. She manipulated sound–time connections through tape delay and layered sounds through manipulating tape on reel-to-reel machines. Her experiments in 'Deep Listening' involved creative listening and improvisation often in resonant spaces. Her study of Asian and Native American cultures has led to incorporating different approaches to meditation aimed at greater awareness of the body, sound and the environment. Her preoccupation with feminism and queer identity is developed by her ♀ ensemble. As virtual reality (VR) technology emerged in the 21st century she developed music for virtual space through her Telematic Circle. Oliveros also experimented with cyber jamming over the internet through her Adaptive Use Music Instruments software along with exploring software to assist the physically and cognitively challenged participate in music making.[18] Her international appearances as a composer, improviser and accordionist resulted in residencies at institutions such as Stanford, Northwestern and Oberlin. Oliveros was Distinguished Research Professor of Music at Rensselaer Polytechnic and Milhaud Professor at Mill College. She won the Boon Beethoven Prize, Columbia University's William Schumann Award and Fellowships from Gaudeamus, Seamus, Fulbright, Guggenheim and NEA. She has been awarded several honorary doctorates and commissions.

French electronic music composer Eliane Radigue (b. 1932) studied in Paris with Pierre Schaeffer at the Studio d'Essai (1957–1958) and with Pierre Henry at the Apsone-Cabasse Studio (1967–1968). In 1970 she was artist-in-residence at New York University's School of Arts, and she has subsequently worked in the electronic music studios at the University of Iowa and the California Institute of the Arts (1973). In 1975 she became a disciple of Tibetan Buddhism which inspired her cycle of music based on the life of Tibetan Master Milarepa.[19] In 2000 she composed her last electronic work *L'Ile Re-sonante*, for which she received the Golden Nica Award (2006) at the Ars Electronica Festival.

Following studies in classical guitar at Oxford University and composition at Julliard School and CUNY, Laurie Spiegel (b. 1945) began to compose computer music at Bell Laboratories in the 1970s. She went on to establish the computer music studio at New York University (1982–1983), the Aspen Music Festival (1971–1973) and Cooper Union for the Advancement of Science and Art, New York (1980–1981). Spiegel helped to design the AlphaSyntauri and McLeyvier synthesisers. Her interactive music programme Music Mouse–An Intelligent Instrument (1985) for Macintosh computers allows selected aspects of composition to be automated, increasing the number of musical dimensions that can be controlled in real time and thus creating more spontaneous performances. Her works using this software highlight its expressive capabilities.[20] She has also composed music for acoustic instruments. Her honours include awards from the Institute for Studies in American Music (1973–1974), Meet the Composer (1975–1977, 1979–1980) and the New York Foundation for the Arts (1991–1992). Her numerous articles appear in such publications as *Computer Music Journal* and *Electronic Musician* magazine.

American composer Vivian Rudow (b. 1936) was the founding artistic director of Res MusicAmerica. Her music integrates electronic sounds with acoustic instruments and she also includes narration, dance and audience participation. In 1986 she became the first American woman to win the first prize in the Bourges International Electroacoustic Music Competition in France for her piece *With Love* for solo, cello and cello cases equipped with speakers. In 1987 she won her first ASCAP Standard Award; she won this award in every subsequent year into the 2010s.

New Zealand–born Annea Lockwood (b. 1939) studied at Canterbury University (BMus 1961) and went on to study at the RCM London (1961–1963) along with attending Darmstadt summer courses. After working in Europe for several years she went to the United States to work at the Hunter College, CUNY and Vassar College. Her electronic music experiments include recordings of sounds from nature, automation and musical instruments, some of her own invention. Among her controversial pieces are *Tiger Balm* (1973) incorporating sounds of a cat purring, a heartbeat, gongs, Jew's harps, tigers mating, an airplane and a woman's sexual arousal, her *Glass Concert* (1966–1973) featured glass being played and *Piano Transplants* (1968–1972) in which pianos were burnt, gradually drowned in a shallow lake, planted in a garden or anchored at a beach.

Two women were also prominent in the Columbia-Princeton Electronic Music Centre, Alice Sheils (b. 1943) and Pri Smiley (b. 1943), as studio instructors and composers. Their contribution to instrument testing, development and teaching is highly significant, but they have been to date somewhat overlooked for their significant contributions. Sheils was a technical instructor in the studios from 1965 to 1982, an Associate Director of the Centre from 1978 to 1982 and the Associate Director of Development at the independent Columbia Centre from 1994 to 1996. Smiley was appointed acting director of the Electronic Music Centre in 1984 and served as its associate director during the period 1985–1995.

French composer Françoise Barrière (b. 1944) is committed to the dissemination of electro-acoustic music and founded the Groupe de Musique Expérimentale de Bourges (GMEB) in 1970, which is known for its creation of electroacoustic instruments for broadcasting or performance ('Gmebaphone'), and for beginners ('Gmebogosse'). In the same year, she co-founded the Concours Internationaux de Musique.

With the advent of digital technology composers have engaged with complex mathematical analysis of waveform structures and sophisticated compositional techniques such as spectrum analysis. One of the leading proponents of post-spectral composition is Kaija Saariaho (née Laakkonen, b. 1952, in Helsinki). Following training at the Sibelius Academy and later studies at Freiburg, Germany, and the Institute de Recherche et de Coordination Acoustique-Musique (IRCAM), Paris, where she has been a leader in computer-assisted composition since the 1980s. In 2016 she became the second woman to have an opera performed by the Metropolitan Opera, New York, with her opera *L'Amour de lion* (Love from afar, 2000). The first woman to have this honour 113 years earlier was English composer and member of the women's suffragette movement, Ethyl Smyth with two performances of her *Die Wald*. Saariaho's *L'Amor de Lion* was also performed by the Santa Fe Opera in 2002 and the same company performed her opera Adriana Mater in 2008. The subsequent transmission of the opera to cinema on December 10, 2016, as part of the Metropolitan Opera Live in HD series marked the first opera by a female composer, and the first opera conducted by a female conductor (Susanna Mälkki), in the series. Her numerous awards include 2011 Grammy Award for Best Opera Recording (*L'Amour de loin*), Polar Music Prize (2013), BBVA Foundation Frontiers of Knowledge Award in Contemporary Music (2017) and Leone d'oro di Venezia, Biennale della Musica Contemporanea (2021). Apart from these accolades she has been commissioned in a range of genres by leading ensembles and has won numerous awards including being nominated the greatest living composer by *BBC Music Magazine* in 2019.

## Women in popular electronic music

Women have embraced technology in popular music to create unique innovative sounds and instruments. Laurie Anderson (b. 1947) has taken a leading position in technology and music, but does not come from a training in music, rather in visual arts. She challenges these separations and has risen to popularity amongst alternative music underground audiences distinguishing herself as a performance artist, composer and instrument inventor. She studied violin as a child and went on to study visual arts at Barnard College (BA, 1969) and Columbia University (MFA, 1972). She gained attention in the 1970s for her performances which included music, speech, electronic instruments, video, lighting and graphics. Her electronic music inventions include her tape bow violin (1977), her 'talking stick' which is used to replicate sounds, voice filters and to deepen her voice into the masculine range. Her work is characterised by experimentation with sound and vocal effects using a variety of electronic gadgets that she devises such as sensors placed on her body to send messages to drum machines, lights and speakers in her mouth, electronic distortion and multiplication of her voice to create a choir or creating a gender-neutral voice. She works across and blends multiple platforms such as film, dance, special lighting effects and VR. Her song 'O Superman' (1981) brought her international fame reaching number two on the UK singles chart. In

2003 she became NASA's first artist-in-residence and in 2004 she was part of the team that created the Athens Olympic Games opening ceremony. She continued to build on her success in the late 2000s and won high-profile residencies and commissions. In 2010 she was commissioned to write a new theatrical work for the Vancouver Olympics. For the next decade, she undertook commissions including the collaboration with her partner Lou Reed for Vivid Live Sydney (2010), River to River Festival New York (2013) and virtual reality collaborations with Taiwanese artist Hsin-Chien Huang *Chalkroom* (2017) and *To the Moon* (2019). She collaborated as narrator on the documentary film on pioneering women in electronic music *Sisters with Transistors* (2021).[21] Anderson has received numerous awards including an honorary doctorate from Aalto University School of Arts, Design and Architecture (2013), Grammy Award (2019) and in 2021 she was appointed Professor of Poetry at Harvard University.

Diamanda Galas (b. 1955) is the daughter of Anatolian and Greek Orthodox parents who distinguished herself in singing, although she was originally trained in piano. She performed Beethoven's Frist Piano Concerto with the San Diego Symphony Orchestra at the age of 14. She turned to jazz and as a teenager performed with African American drag queens in San Francisco. Whilst studying biochemistry at the University of Southern California she participated in biochemical experiments involving sadomasochism, acid and mental illness. She went on to study a master's in music at the university's Center for Music Experiment and took lessons in voice in the United States and Europe. She became known for her theatrical real-time electronic manipulation of her wide-ranging voice while exploring innovative techniques such as use of body resonance, vibrato, high sustained screams and harmonics. Her compositions explored dark themes emerging from first-hand experience of drug abuse, prostitution, manic depressions and her direct experience of her brother's battle with AIDs which he lost in 1986. Her first solo album, *The Litanies of Satan* (1982), included only two operatic compositions: 'Wild Women with Steak-Knives', a 12-minute tragedy-grotesque and 'Litanies of Satan', based on a section from Charles Beaudelaire's poem 'Les Fleurs du Mal'. Her second album, *Diamanda Galas* (1984), also contained two lengthy compositions, 'Panoptikon' and 'Tragoudia Apo To Aima Exoun Fonos' ('Song From the Blood of Those Murdered'), a Greek-language piece dedicated to those political prisoners who were either murdered or executed during the Greek military regimes in the years 1967–1974. When her brother died of AIDs she completed her *Masque of the Red Death* denouncing the cultural response to the illness and in her shorter live version she appears bathed 'blood' under red stage lights. Her later albums continue to explore mental trauma, homicide, sadomasochism and settings of poetry by P.P. Pasolini, Baudelaire, M.H.

Mixco and others. For her album *La serpenta canta* (The serpent sings 2003), she covers R&B standards bringing to the fore the dark sadness of these songs and in the same year she released *Defixiones, Will and Testament* which is an even darker dedication to the grieving of the 1914–1923 genocides of Armenian, Assyrian and Anatolian Greeks. After 2009 Galás focussed on regaining control of her catalogue, following the sell off to BMG, remixing her earlier works and releasing new work online. She established her own label Intravenal Sound Operations and released two new albums which she took on a world tour. In 2019 she regained rights to her back catalogue and remastered some of her earlier work. Her next release Broken Gargoyles was composed during the COVID-19 pandemic based on a sound installation at the Kapellen Leprosarium (Leper's Sanctuary) in Hanover, Germany. Through her exploration of original and novel vocal techniques Galas addresses topics of human suffering and grief giving voice to victims of unspeakable pain. Her artistry whilst based in a strong musical foundation, draws upon poetry, performance art and visual art.

Sussan Deyhim (b. 1958) combines Iranian music to take on leadership in addressing social justice for women. She received her early training in Iran studying with master folk musicians and dancers. In 1980 she moved to New York and collaborated with leading artists in the contemporary arts space. In 2006 she moved to Los Angeles. Her music draws on traditional musical sources of Iran to create a unique sonic language. She incorporates digital processing, extended vocal techniques, film and multimedia alongside ritual-based forms to create a personal style rooted in ancient Persian mysticism. She has performed with leading orchestras and ensembles, is regularly commissioned by leading international ensembles and records on her own label Venus Rising as well as Sony. Her activism has seen her perform at major international humanitarian events and benefits including the UN General Assembly 2001 Gathering of Spiritual Leaders, the first UN Gathering of Female Spiritual Leaders (2002), many fundraising galas for medical aid for Iraqi children and the 2009 UN General Assembly concert for misplaced children in Iran.

Björk (Guðmundsdóttir; b. 1965) is known for her eclectic musical style crossing over punk, experimental, avant-garde, electronic, pop and classical. Björk's unique experimental approach to music draws from diverse sources to create an innovative style that sets her apart from her precedents. Her collaborations with experimental musicians, classical musicians, inuit choirs and avant-garde artists have produced statements on challenging personal themes. Raised in Reykjavík, Iceland, in a commune with her political activist mother and guitarist stepfather, Björk began her studies of classical piano and flute at school. She gained international reputation as lead singer of the alternative rock band the Sugarcubes, before embarking on a successful solo career in the 1990s. Her albums have since been hits on mainstream music charts and over 30 of her singles have reached top 40 on international pop charts. Like Anderson, she has been involved in developing instruments for her projects such as the 'gamaleste', a celesta modified with gamelan for her first single 'Crystalline' from her 2011 *Biophilia* album. The album also featured an educational 'app album' exploring intersections between music and science designed for an education programme for school children. Her exploration of VR for *Björk Digital* (2016) featured the first virtual reality live stream broadcast on YouTube. Her 2022 album *Fossora* was inspired by the experience of the global pandemic, the death of her activist mother and environmental activism. Björk has received numerous accolades and awards including best actress at the 2000 Cannes Film Festival and named one of the 100 most influential people in the world by Time Magazine in 2015. She has been an environmental advocate and has raised money for the preservation of Icelandic natural resources, marine preservation and UNICEF for children affected by the tsunami that struck South East Asia in 2004. She has also lent her support to political liberation movements including independence for Kosovo, Greenland and the Faroe Islands, Catalan and Tibet.

## Women in sound production

Like other areas of the music industry, women have been underrepresented in sound engineering and access to the recording studio is male dominated with limited pathways for women in music production. Women are said to represent less than 5% of the people working in the production of music.[22] In addition, approximately 90% of music technology students are male.[23] Some women already discussed in the book worked their way into the studio through performing and taking over the production of their own work. Some tired of the music industry's control of their business formed their own labels. Notable examples mentioned in the earlier chapters are Mary Lou Williams, Marian McPartland, Jane Ira Bloom, Dolly Parton, Suzanne Vega, Tori Amos, Michelle Shocked, Ani Di Franco, Madonna, Janet Jackson, Diamanda Galas, Sussan Deyhim and the women in hip-hop such as Missy Elliott to name a few.

Since the 1940s women have been taking on the challenge of working in sound recording and production. Mary Shipman Howard (1911–1976) was one of the earliest female recording engineers who founded and owned Mary Howard Recording studio and MHR label in New York City. As a classically trained violinist she became interested in recording in the

1930s. She applied for a recording position at NBC, but the union did not allow women so she was hired as a secretary. Her break came when the NBC lost men to the war and she was given the opportunity to work in the studio.[24] Lillian McMurry (1921–1999) was also an early female record producer who founded Trumpet Records to record musicians from the Mississippi Delta.[25] McMurray's first releases were gospel music and she bagan to record blues artists for whom she also wrote songs. She produced many of the sessions and hired top musicians often freely mixing black and white musicians in defiance of the musician's union's segregationist policies.[26]

Another early pioneer in founding a record label was Cordell Jackson (1923–2004). Unable to break into the recording industry to release her music she founded Moon Records in Memphis Tennessee in 1956. She released and promoted the recordings from her home studio where she served as an engineer, producer and arranger. Her label became the oldest continuous label in Memphis operating up until the time of her death. Her innovative approach to marketing went against the trends of the day with the promotion of singles as opposed to albums.

Ethel Gabriel (1921–2021) was the first female A&R producer in the industry and the first female record producer for a major label. She produced over 2,500 music albums including 15 RIAA Certified Gold Records and six Grammy Award–winning albums. She studied trombone and performed with the Philadelphia Women's Symphony Orchestra from 1939 to 1940 and went on to study music education at Temple University. She joined RCA as a secretary with administrative duties and became familiar with a range of music as a tester listening for scratches.[27] She worked her way into producing where she achieved success as the A&R representative with her 'Living Strings' series of easy listening albums and producing major artists. She became Vice President of Pop Contemporary A&R being the first woman to achieve this position.[28] After retiring from RCA in 1984 Gabriel was President of JazzMania records, Vice President of Jade Panther Productions and President of Aurora Records as well as co-producing off-Broadway shows.

More women producers and engineers began to emerge in the 1960s such as Genya Ravan a.k.a. Goldie (b. 1940) who was a producer of punk rock acts as well as lead singer in a series of rock bands including the all-female Goldie and the Gingerbreads. Born in Poland, Goldie was a survivor of the Nazi Holocaust and migrated with her family to the United States in 1947. She had considerable success fronting rock bands in the 1960s and early 1970s recording a number of highly successful albums. She penned an autobiography and a retrospective of her career was the topic of the off-Broadway musical *Rock and Roll Refugee* (2016).[29] She worked as a producer for a number of labels launching the careers of punk rock and soul groups. She also hosted radio shows Chicks and Broads and Goldies Garage featuring women and new talent.

Canadian record producer Roma Baran (b. 1946) is an Oscar and Grammy Award–winning sound producer who along with her business partner Vivien Stoll owns and operates a production company in New York. Best known for her work with Laurie Anderson, Annabelle Chvostek (b. 1975) and Kate (1946–2010) & Anna McGarrigle (b. 1944). Tina Weymouth's (b. 1950) early career was as the bass guitarist for the American new wave group Talking Heads. After leaving the group she took over production of the group's side project the TomTom Club producing the work of independent artists, particularly female musicians.

Multiple Grammy Award–winning Leslie Ann Jones (b. 1951) was the first female engineer to be hired by ABC studios in Los Angeles before she moved to Automatt Studios in Northern California where she worked with Herbie Hancock, Bobby McFerrin, Holly Near and began her film score career mixing the Francis Ford Coppola film *Apocalypse Now* (1979). In 1987 she was hired as a staff engineer for Capitol Studios in Hollywood and moved to Skywalker Sound as Director of Music and Scoring in California where she has worked on film and television scores as well as video gaming scores. She worked with major artists and specialised in jazz and classical and was the first female National Officer on the National Academy of Recording Arts and Sciences. She serves on the advisory board of Women's Audio Mission dedicated to the advancement of women in the recording arts and has produced a number of recordings featuring women.[30]

Influential country music star Reba McIntyre (b. 1955) was dissatisfied with the lack of control over the choice and production of her material for her early albums and singles.[31] She moved into selecting her own material and producing which led to a breakthrough for her eighth studio album with her ninth album title track 'Whoever's in New England' (1986) winning her the Grammy Award for Best Female Country Vocal Performance and was certified platinum. In the late 1980s, she began making changes to her stage show implementing choreography and lighting taking more control over her artistry.[32] She fired her manager and formed her own entertainment company to produce and promote her material. She achieved Billboard success for her subsequent albums and mentored women in her company to help them break into the industry.

In the area of classical music working with contemporary composers Judith Sherman (b. 1942) is a leading audio engineer and record producer. She was nominated for 17 Grammy Awards and won 12 including Producer of the Year, Classical six times.[33] She graduated from the State University of New York with a Master of Fine Arts (1971) and joined WBAI radio in New York as an engineer graduating to producer and music director. In 1976 she established Judith Sherman Production where she has worked as a freelance producer.

In the 1970s emerging from the separatist lesbian feminist movement, women's music labels such as Olivia appeared to express topics that were outside of the dominant political discourse.[34] American feminist singer-songwriter Chris Williamson (b. 1947) was the catalyst for starting Olivia which she founded alongside Meg Christian (b. 1946) and Judy Dlugacz. The business catered mainly to white middle-class lesbians but later began to become more inclusive of women of colour.[35] Williamson's album *The Changer and the Changed* (1975) became one of the top-selling albums on any independent label at the time.[36]

## Women DJs

Another area where women have been underrepresented is as disk jockeys (DJs).[37] As in other areas of electronic music culture turntablism is highly male centric.[38] There are various projects dedicated to gender diversity in the industry such as DJs London and Discwoman, a New York–based collective.

Filipina DJ Dr Kuttin Kandi (b. 1975) defies stereotypes as a DJ who uses hip-hop, poetry and music to convey feminist activism responding to racism, sexism and social injustice. Raised in Queens, New York, to a Filipino working-class family who were early street vendors of Filipino food she was well acquainted with racism, underclass status and social injustice.[39] Kandi is a Queer gender fluid femme, disabled Filipinx–Pin[a/x]y–American writer, poet, theatre performer, educator, hip-hop feminist, public speaker and community organiser. She became the first woman to win a place in the Disco Music Club (DMC) in 1988. She has since toured and inspired countless other women in hip-hop. She is a founding member of the Anomalies Crew who shares hip-hop culture values and addresses social justice. She is also a volunteer with the Gabriela Network, a group that focuses upon the issue of sex trafficking of women and children. She has performed with Africa Bambaataa, LL Cool J and Jay-Z amongst others, and is one of the most sought-after hip-hop speakers in the United States addressing race, gender, power and privilege. In 2018, Kandi was titled a Global Cultural Ambassador by Next Level's Meridian International Center, the University of North Carolina at Chapel Hill and the US Department of State's Bureau of Educational and Cultural Affairs. She also serves as a Site Manager for Next Level. Kandi is the co-founder and Executive Director of Asian Solidarity Collective (formerly Asian for Black Lives San Diego) as well as the new Director of Campaigns and Organizing for the Partnership of Advancement for New Americans. Likewise, Kandi has co-founded several other local grassroots organisations such as Families for Justice in Education San Diego, the Intersectional Feminist Collective, the mutual aid–We All We Got San Diego, and the Dede McClure Bail Fund. Similarly, Kandi is involved with countless organisations such as the Asian Pacific American Labour Alliance–San Diego, the F.I.E.R.C.E. Coalition and the Filipino American Educators Association of California. Further, Kandi is a co-founder of national organisations, the People's Collective for Justice and Liberation and the University for Justice and Liberation (UJL). Newly appointed by The Board of Supervisors of the County of San Diego, Kandi serves on the Committee for Persons with Disabilities. More recently, Kandi received an Honorary Doctorate in Pinayism (2020) for her endless dedication to radical sisterhood, critical praxis, and transformative solidarity. Kuttin Kandy is leading the way with her musical skill and conscientious activism.

Women who began dominating the female DJ scene in the 21st century stem from diverse cultural backgrounds and include Grammy Award–winning Melbourne-born twin sister duo Olivia and Miriam Nervo, Belgian DJs Anouk Matton (known as 'MATTN'), Charlotte De Witte and Amelie Lens (b. 1990). Lens is also a producer and Lenske record label owner. DJ Mariana Bo is known as the only female musician and producer from Mexico. Soda from South Korea known for her exceptional electronic and hip-hop. Australian-born Alison Wonderland (b. 1986) earned New Artist of the Year at the Electronic Music Awards (2017). Isabelle Rezazadeh (Rezz) was born in Ukraine but is now a DJ and record producer based in Niagara Falls, Ontario. Also, Ukrainian-born and raised Miss K8 is the stage name of Kateryna Kremko, and has won The Juno Awards' Electronic Album of the Year twice. Nina Kraviz grew up in Siberia earned the title of Best Female Artist (Underground) in 2018 and has written music for Cyberpunk 2077, the video game and the PXO99: 100 Years of Columbia compilation. Belgian DJ Mandy Praet specialises in the hardstyle genre while South Korean Peggy Gou (b. 1991) who moved to Berlin has become an Asian leader in the industry. Her song, 'It Makes You Forget (Itgehane)', received the Best Track at the AIM Independent Music Awards and was selected to be part of the FIFA 2019 music list. RayRay is a Taiwanese native who has made a splash in the EDM world. Her extensive experience includes performing at well-known music festivals and venues, from The Sonar Music Festival in Barcelona to the Glastonbury UK Festival, as well as having her tracks used in a variety of films. Italian DJ Deborah De Luca (b. 1980) is the number one DJ in that country. Anna Lunoe is yet another Australian DJ who also sings, writes and produces her own songs. Although she was born in Sydney, Australia, she now resides in Los Angeles, California. Alongside these trailblazers are Johannesburg-born 'Nora En Pure' (Daniella Di Lillo), Ukrainian hardcore 'Juicy M' (Marta Martus), Tehran-born 'Lady Faith' who now resides in Los Angeles, California, and Mexican 'Le Twins' (Karla and Karen de la Garza) to name a few.

## Conclusion

This survey of women's participation in music technology has shown that they have not been silent. While the data indicates that women are still the exception in electronic music fields, there have been many women leading advances in music technology. Those listed in this chapter have been identified for their standout contributions, but they are by no means the only ones who have emerged in recent years. As more women become involved in the performance, mentoring and teaching of electronic music engagement in the genre has increased as can be demonstrated by the number of women who have become celebrated DJs on the international circuit in the 21st century.

## Notes

1 Abtan, F. (2016). Where is she? Finding the women in electronic music culture. *Contemporary Music Review*, 35(1), 53–60.
2 Rodgers, T. (2010). *Pink Noises: Women on Electronic Music and Sound*. Duke University Press.
3 Rovner, Lisa. Director. (2021), Sisters with Transistors, Documentary, Monoduo Films.
4 Born, G. & Devine, K. (2016). Gender, creativity and education in digital musics and sound art. *Contemporary Music Review*, 35(1), 1–20; Keefe, L. O. (2017, 4 October). Women in Sound: addressing the music industry's gender gap. The Conversation.
5 Keefe, L.O. (2017, 4 October). Women in sound: addressing the music industry's gender gap. The Conversation. See also Green, L. (2008). *Music, Gender, Education*. Cambridge University Press.
6 Oldenziel, R.A. (1997). Boys and their toys: The Fisher Body Craftsman's Guild, 1930–1968, and the making of a male technical domain. *Technology and Culture*, 38(1), 60–96.
7 Dunbar, J. (2021). *Women, Music, Culture: An Introduction* (3rd ed.). Routledge, 334.
8 Warshaw, D. (2011). Clara Rockmore: A legendary performer of an enigmatic instrument. *The Juilliard Journal*, 36(6).
9 Hutton, J. (2004). 'Daphne Oram: innovator, writer and composer'. *Organised Sound*, 8(1), 49–56.
10 RISC stands for Reduced Instruction Set Computer.
11 Oram, D. (1972). *An Individual Note – Of Music, Sound and Electronics*. Galliard.

12 Schrader, B. (2001). Barron, Bebe. Grove Music Online.

13 Brockman, J. (1992). The first electronic filmscore-forbidden planet: A conversation with Bebe Barron. *The Score*, 7(3), 5–13.

14 Petersen, B.A., revised by Rosen, J. (2001). Ruth Anderson. Grove Music Online.

15 Mattis, O., Highwather, J. & Jobin, S. (2001). Dlugoszewski, Lucia. Grove Music Online.

16 Winter, T. (2015). *Delia Derbyshire: Sound and Music for the BBC Radiophonic Workshop, 1962–1973*. PhD thesis, University of York.

17 Von Gunden, Heidi. (1983). *The Music of Pauline Oliveros*. Scarecrow Press.

18 Feisst, S. (2001). Oliveros, Pauline. Grove Music Online.

19 Weid, J. (2001). Radigue, Eliane. Grove Music Online.

20 Bosse, J. (2001). Spiegel, Laurie. Grove Music Online.

21 Rovner, L. Director. (2020). Sisters with Transistors. Metrograph Pictures.

22 Hernandez, K., Smith, S. & Piper, K. (2022, March). Inclusion in the Recording Studio?: Gender and Race/Ethnicity of Artists, Songwriters and Producers across 1,000 Popular Songs from 2012-2021. USC Annenberg Inclusion Initiative.

23 Born & Devine, Ibid., 3.

24 Sutton, A. (2021). *American Record Companies and Producers, 1888–1950: An Encyclopaedic History*. Mainspring Press.

25 Ryan, M. (1992). *Trumpet Records: An Illustrated History, with Discography*. Big Nickel Publications.

26 Ibid.

27 Whiteley, S. (2000). *Women and Popular Music: Sexuality, Identity and Subjectivity*. Routledge.

28 Gordon, C. (1992, 17 April). Ethel Gabriel has record of success. *The Express-Times*.

29 Ravan, G. (2004). *Lollipop Lounge, Memoirs of a Rock and Roll Refugee*. Billboard Books.

30 https://womensaudiomission.org

31 Wolff, K. (2000). *Country Music: The Rough Guide*. Penguin Books.

32 Carter, T. & McEntire, R. (1994). *Reba: My Story*. Bantam Books.

33 'Judith Sherman'. (2019, 15 February). GRAMMY.com.

34 Dolan, J. (2002). Feeling women's culture: Women's music, Lesbian feminism, and the impact of emotional memory. *Journal of Dramatic Theory and Criticism*, 26(2), 205–219.

35 Hayes, E. (2010). *Songs in Black and Lavender: Race, Sexual Politics, and Women's Music*. University of Illinois Press.

36 Peraino, J. (2005). *Listening to the Sirens Musical Technologies of Queer Identity from Homer to Hedwig*. University of California Press, 169.

37 Katz, M. (2007, 12 December). Men, women, and turntables: Gender and the DJ battle. *The Musical Quarterly*, 89(4), 580–599.

38 Farrugia, R. (2013). *Beyond the Dance Floor: Female DJs, Technology and Electronic Dance Music Culture*. University of Chicago Press.

39 Hisama, E.M. (2014). DJ Kuttin Kandi: Performing feminism. *American Music Review*, 43(2), 1–6.

# 8

# WOMEN IN NON-WESTERN MUSICAL CONTEXTS

## Introduction

Women's role in non-Western musical cultures has been addressed by researchers in the discipline of what has been termed ethnomusicology. This term is becoming increasingly redundant in the academy as it reinforces the binary of the one and the other, and for women in traditional music results in a further extension of this binary. As more research into ethnic and gender diversity emerges the study of non-Western cultural practises is becoming the mainstream in the academy. Koskoff's seminal contributions to women in cross-cultural contexts have shed light on the significance of women's contribution to traditional music.[1] Dunbar examines women's musical contributions in traditional and folkloric performance along with the role in contemporary cross-cultural music.[2] Research into women's role in First Nations people's music is linked to their leadership roles as society elders.[3] This chapter explores women from diverse cultural backgrounds and their leadership roles. It examines the diversity of leadership roles that women have undertaken in global music and the challenges faced by women in musical leadership in non-Western cultures.

## Cross-cultural contexts

Within cross-cultural and popular contexts, a number of significant studies on women's contribution to music emerged since the 1980s that have taken a feminist perspective as well as using tools drawn from anthropology and sociology. Feminist musicology has benefited from

DOI: 10.4324/9781003183631-9

the resulting interdisciplinary cross-fertilisation. Jane Bowers and Urban Bareis compiled the 'Bibliography on Music and Gender: Women in Music' which details ethnomusicological research into the cultural practices of women in folk and non-Western contexts.[4] The collection of essays edited by Ellen Koskoff in *Women and Music in Cross-Cultural Perspective* address women's musical activities across a range of cultures, with essays focusing on women's musical activities, genres, instruments and performance efforts that have hitherto been ignored.[5] Koskoff's collection demonstrates that women have not been silent in musical production and that music has often been used by women as a vehicle of challenge in a range of cultures. It reveals cross-cultural practices of women through the centuries that have resulted in the expression of alternative perceptions through women's cultural conceptions. The collection also addresses many common feminist themes, ranging from subversion of women through their social role in various societies to female musical practice as a form of expression of a feminine musical aesthetic. Koskoff revisits the theme in *A Feminist Ethnomusicology* creating a personal map of her excursions into women in music in diverse cultural contexts.[6] Along similar lines, the compilation *Music, Gender and Culture* focuses on the role of women in music in diverse cultural contexts highlighting the significant contribution made by women.[7] A recurring theme in academic feminism is that women's contributions in the private creative sphere have relegated their creative contributions to obscurity where value is attributed to public cultural contributions. The collections of essays on music making in cross-cultural contexts establishes that women have made significant cultural contributions through their ritual and domestic music making. In drawing attention to these contributions, researchers have uncovered a whole new area of creativity and commenced the process of providing recognition to women's music making in these contexts. These gender-specific compilations and analyses can be considered feminist, even when they do not draw directly upon feminist theory.

## The leadership role of women in music across cultures

Women's music in traditional cultures is primarily defined by their roles as mothers and in some societies as healers. Literature on women's music in folk or traditional settings focuses on music associated with women's life cycles and their roles in seasonal ceremonies or religious systems. Important genres that emerge in various societies are love songs, wedding songs, lullabies, laments or funerary songs. Women's songs have also accompanied agrarian cycles addressing women's role in planting, harvesting and preserving. Research into the role of women in religious systems and the musical rituals that accompany them indicates that women have contributed to in religious music outside of the Western tradition taking an important role in, for example, African American gospel music as discussed in Chapter 5. Outside of Christian traditions, women's musical roles in major religious systems worldwide still remains an area that has been largely overlooked. The role of female shamans who perform musical healing and spiritual rituals usually outside of the sanctioned religious system has been found in a range of cultures including Korea, Siberia, Haiti and the United States. Recording and documentation includes field work undertaken by ethnomusicologists for research purposes which is generally not available in commercial form with some exceptions.

## Music and women in contemporary non-Western cultural contexts

The technological advances of the commercial recording industry in the 20th century have seen the dissemination of music across the world, in particular music produced in the West. Increased access to international travel and improved global communication technologies have created opportunities for musicians to access musical styles from around the world. Musicians have drawn from the influences of Indigenous and folk music often collaborating to create fusions of international styles. This can create the risk of increasing musical homogeneity, the blurring of regional identities and the gradual extinction of traditional local music-making practices particularly where there are commercial imperatives.

In the 1960s, ethnomusicologist Robert E. Brown coined the phrase 'world music' for his program featuring concerts by musicians from Africa and Asia at Wesleyan University, Connecticut. In the early 1980s, 'world music' was adopted by British, American and French promoters, record companies, distributors, journalists and broadcasters to promote music from other countries, particularly Africa which sometimes became almost synonymous with the term. The aim was to bring together under one marketing genre diverse music from Africa, Eastern Europe, India, Asia, South America and the Caribbean. It became a widely accepted term for any music that was outside of the commercial popular music industry from non-Western countries including intercultural and quasi-traditional.

The term was considered by some as offensive and a marketing catch-all that did not represent a single genre. Nonetheless, industry recognition came with world music awards categories such as Billboard magazine introducing a world music chart and a Grammy Award world music category. In the 21st century, the genre was considered to have connotations of colonialism with the term 'global music' considered more politically correct and in 2020 the Grammy Award for best world music album was changed to best global music album with other institutions soon following suit. The genre has come to include other subgenres such as ethnic fusion, cross-over forms, new age and worldbeat.

The previous chapters (Chapters 5 and 6) on women in popular music genres outline how women have voiced their views through recordings, music videos and streaming. Women from non-Western countries found opportunities to record under the growth in interest in 'world music' performances and recording. Female precursors to the genre include Miriam Makeba, Millie Small and Lydia Canaan who in the 1960s and 1970s had hits on the US and UK charts.

In the Arab world, one of the most extraordinary female singers of the 20th century emerged from a Muslim society that is perceived as oppressive to women.[8] Umm Kulthum (1898–1975) cannot be categorised as a product of the commercial interest in world music but a product of Arab culture expressing the identity of Egypt and the Arab world during a time of tumultuous change.[9] Her family were poor villagers with her formal education consisting of reciting the Koran. Her father was an imam and she learned to sing from hearing her father teach her brother. She displayed exceptional singing talent at an early age singing in classic Arabic style and she became highly proficient in pronouncing the most difficult words in Quranic recitation for which she became famous. She joined her father's ensemble singing at religious celebrations dressed in boy's clothes to relieve her father's anxiety about her reputation and while her father did not think it appropriate for her to sing publicly, she was hugely popular. She earned large sums from their audiences and soon was invited to perform at the homes of wealthy families including those of royalty. Her family was helped by patrons to move to Cairo in the early 1920s belonging to the wave of peasants who moved to the city for work.

She became an exponent of classical Arab song tradition which involves audience engagement with the singer responding to requests for repetitions with subtle improvisations shifting the emotional emphasis. This resulted in improvisations lasting for up to five hours with no performance ever being the same. Her ability to subtly explore modal scales in her performance of ancient Arabic qasida would bring her audiences into an ecstatic state known as 'tarab'.[10] She brought the tradition into the modern era working with contemporary songwriters, composers and musicians to create a body of new repertoire.

The songs would be on topics of love, longing and loss and she believed that the beauty in Arabic song served the national revolutionary political agenda.[11] Her allusion to religious or historical events could be interpreted as political overtones all relevant to the contemporary turmoil in Egypt, but couched within the ancient tradition of love poetry.[12] She built her career upon the new technologies of her time bringing the new music songs by the best composers and poets of the day to her multitudes of fans through broadcasts, recordings, films and public performances. She embraced mass media and starred in numerous films, but maintained respectability in her modest dress and limited movement when singing to avoid negative moral connotations.[13] In 1934 she sang for the inaugural broadcast of Radio Cairo thereafter performing on the first Thursday of the month for over 40 years which brought the city to a standstill tuning into the broadcasts.[14] As the broadcast signal extended to other Arab nations her audience grew.

She supported the revolution against the British and raised money for the revolution in her 1932 tour of the Middle East and North Africa. She performed for the royal family who had ousted the British and was decorated with the highest honours normally reserved for the royal family by King Farouk. Following the 1952 revolution against the royals, her association with the family led to the musician's guild rejecting her and banning her broadcasts. President Nasser, leader of the Egyptian Revolution, was one of her biggest supporters, and reversed the decision recognising the influence she had over Egypt. He would coordinate his speeches with her radio broadcasts. Four million people attended her funeral when she died, and she is said to be responsible for helping to shape the modern state of Egypt.

South African singer Miriam Makeba (1932–2008) became the voice of political activism against apartheid. Known as 'Mama Africa', she toured the world to promote and educate about African culture and particularly her Xhosa roots through her click singing and telling stories about her songs. Her appearance in the anti-apartheid film *Come Back, Africa* (1959) brought her international attention and she toured Venice, London and New York.[15] She was subsequently banned from returning to South Africa for 30 years for her involvement in anti-apartheid activism. Her 1962 testimony for the United Nations Special Committee against Apartheid calling for sanctions against South Africa resulted in her South African citizenship being revoked along with her music being banned in South Africa and revoking her right to return. As a stateless person she was soon issued passports to nine countries and was granted honorary citizenship of ten countries.[16] Her music was also popular in Europe and she added songs to her repertoire from Latin America, Europe, Israel and other parts of Africa.[17] She was among the first African musicians to receive international fame and to promote African music to a Western audience making popular a number of songs critical of apartheid. Her collaboration with musician Harry Belafonte led to the recording of *An Evening with Belafonte/Makeba* (1965) dealing with the political plight of black South Africans including songs directly critical of the South African government. Her inclusion of lyrics in various African languages was considered the authentic voice of Africa and it won the Grammy Award (1966) for best folk recording.[18] Makeba became involved in the civil rights movement in the United States and her marriage to the leader of the Black Panther Party, Stokely Carmichael, in 1968 resulted in her losing support amongst white Americans with the US government revoking her visa. She and her husband relocated to Guinea for the next 15 years and she performed more frequently in African countries particularly at independence ceremonies as countries became independent of European colonial powers such as Kenya, Angola, Zambia, Tanganyika and Mozambique.[19] She became a diplomat for Ghana and was appointed Guinea's official delegate to the UN in 1975. Her participation in the Paul Simon's highly successful Graceland Tour was controversial for contravening the cultural boycott of South Africa, which Makeba herself endorsed, as it was recorded in South Africa. Nonetheless, the filmed version of the tour brought her back into the international spotlight. Her performance at the Nelson Mandela 70th Birthday Tribute at London's Wembley Stadium in 1988 was broadcast to millions worldwide and raised international support for the release of Nelson Mandela from prison. Upon Mandela's release in 1990 he persuaded Makeba to return to Africa which she did on her French passport. She continued recording, touring internationally and starred in the 1992 film *Sarafina!* based on the students involved in the 1976 Soweto uprising. She also campaigned for humanitarian causes including HIV/AIDS, child soldiers, the physically handicapped and established the Makeba home for female orphans. Amongst her honours are FAO Goodwill Ambassador (1999), Otto Hahn Peace Medal (2001) and Polar Music Prize (2001) along with several honorary doctorates. She is credited with bringing African music to a Western audience and popularising the concept of world music. She is also credited with influencing South African musicians such as kwaito musician Thandiswa Mazwai and her band Bongo Maffin, Simphiwe Dana and Angélique Kidjo. She was a style icon refusing to straighten her hair, wearing African jewellery, refusing to use skin lighteners and make-up and overall rejection of white standards of beauty. Since her death in 2008 she has been the subject of the musical *Mama Africa*, produced by Niyi Coker which premièred to a sold-out audience in Cape Town on May 26, 2016, along with other representations in films, concerts and tributes.

Singer-songwriter Lydia Canaan is a humanitarian activist and widely considered the first internationally successful Lebanese rock musician. She was recognised for her fusion Middle Eastern quarter notes and microtones with anglophone folk. She became active as a teenager in 1984 fronting a heavy metal band and singing in English during the Lebanese Civil War (1975–1990). In 1987 she embarked on a solo career performing her own songs and headlined major concerts and festivals in Lebanon in the late 1980s despite the associated risks during the Syrian occupation. Canaan left Lebanon and settled in Zürich, Switzerland, becoming a Swiss citizen. She began to receive airplay in Switzerland and soon won a London-based recording contract. Her release of her pop ballad 'Beautiful Life' (1995) gained critical acclaim and international attention. Her critically acclaimed début studio album *Sound of Love* (1997) was released in London, New York and the Middle East with supporting promotional tours. She is an active spokesperson for human rights as a United Nations delegate delivering speeches on Islamophobia and art, torture, human rights, civilian victims of counterterrorism and persecution of religious minorities. She has lent her name to numerous social justice campaigns including Human Rights Watch and the International Campaign to Prosecute War Crimes in Iraq. She has contributed to charity directly and performing at fundraisers particularly to those concerned with children, animals and the elderly. She was listed in the Rock and Roll Hall of Fame (2015) and won the award for Outstanding Achievement from the American Global Music Awards (2016). In 2019, Canaan was appointed as a member of the International Advisory Council of the Academic University for Non-Violence & Human Rights (AUNOHR).

Millie Small (1947–2020) was the Caribbean's first international recording star and one of its most successful performers. Her 1964 hit 'My Boy Lollipop' reached the top of the US and UK charts and was the first to record in the blue beat style directly based upon reggae. Her performances led her to becoming an international celebrity but by the early 1970s she stopped recording and performing staying out of the public eye. She claimed that she did not receive any royalties for her hits.[20] She received numerous distinctions for her contribution to the Jamaican music industry.

As the interest in world music developed in the latter part of the 20th century, more women emerged on the scene representing a diverse range of non-Western music to achieve major international mainstream success. Angelique Kijo (b. 1960) combines the styles of Bienese traditional music with global styles that have emanated from the African diaspora. She grew up in Ouidah, a village in Benin, in an artistic family. Her father was a musician and her mother a theatre director. Political conflicts at home led her to relocate to Paris in 1983 where she studied jazz and established her performing career.

Her homeland shores are where the Gate of No Return saw more than one million people boarding slave ships in the 17th–19th centuries. She combines in her music influences from Afropop, Carribean zouk, Congalese rumba, jazz, gospel and Latin along with her early influences including Miriam Makeba. She sings in Youba (her mother's language) and Fon (her father's language) combining them with Zilin vocal techniques while incorporating traditional instruments and costume in her performances and recordings. She also sings in other languages that she is fluent in such as French, English, Gen (Mina) and Swahili. She travelled through Benin to record the traditional rhythms to form the basis for her album *Fifa* (1996) and explored the African roots of music in the Americas in her trilogy of albums *Oremi* (1998), *Black Ivory Soul* (2000) and *Oyaya* (2004). She travelled from Benin to Kenya to record the songs of women's choirs as the basis of her album *Eve* (2014) which she dedicated to her mother and all women of Africa. Her 2015 release of her collaboration with the Luxembourg Philharmonic won her the Grammy for Best Global Music Album as did her 2019 tribute to Cuban singer Celia Cruz. In 2021 she released the album *Mother Nature* which featured collaborations with young African producers and singers. Since 2002 Kijo has been UNICEF goodwill ambassador and is one of the founders of the Batonga Foundation which aims to empower vulnerable women in Benin. She has participated in many social justice campaigns focussing upon issues including African women's rights, AIDS/HIV awareness, environmental matters and aid projects. She performed at high-profile events such as the Nobel Peace Prize, United Nations General Assembly, Nelson Mandela Foundation, FIFA World Cup and Olympic Games opening ceremonies. Her accolades include Commandeur de l'Ordre des Arts et des Lettres (France, 2019), the Legion of Honour (2021) and several Grammy Awards.

Oumou Sangaré (b. 1968) is a Malian musician performing the traditional song from the Wassoulou region from the south of the Niger River. Her parents were singers and exponents of the Wassoulou traditional songs. She began singing publicly at an early age to support her family after her father left. Her songs address social issues especially those concerning the low status of women African society. Her first album *Moussoulou* ('Women'; 1989) was a hit in West Africa and she joined the world music touring circuit in the mid-1990s promoting a number of successful follow-up recordings. In 1998 she was made Commander of the Order of Arts and Letters of France. She is an advocate for women's rights opposing child marriage and polygamy. She won the UNESCO Prize in 2001 and in 2003 was named ambassador for the UN's FAO. She is involved in the business world through hotels, agriculture and automobiles. In 2017 she won the Artist Award at WOMEX in recognition of her music and advocacy for women's rights.

Columbian singer Shakira (b. 1977; Shakira Isabel Mebarak Ripoll) established her career as a pop singer in Hispanic countries before entering the English language market with her fifth album, *Laundry Service* (2001), which sold over 13 million copies worldwide. She established a reputation as a leading crossover artist extending the global reach of Latino singers. Shakira is one of the best-selling music artists of all time and the top-selling female Latin artist of all time. She is credited with opening the doors to the international market for other Latin artists. Shakira has received numerous awards, including three Grammy Awards, 12 Latin Grammy Awards, four MTV Video Music Awards, seven Billboard Music Awards, 39 Billboard Latin Music Awards, six Guinness World Records and a star on the Hollywood Walk of Fame. She was named the Top Female Latin Artist of the Decade by Billboard twice (2000 and 2010). In 2011 she received recognition for philanthropic work with the Barefoot Foundation and her contributions to music winning the Latin Recording Academy Person of the Year and Harvard Foundation Artist of the Year awards. She was appointed to the President's Advisory Commission on Educational Excellence for Hispanics in the United States in 2011, and Chevalier of the Order of Arts and Letters by the French government in 2012. Shakira is a UNICEF Goodwill Ambassador and one of their global representatives. In 2020, Shakira was appointed by Prince William's Earthshot prize committee to support environmental pioneers tackling major problems impacting the environment and in the same year Shakira donated more than 50,000 face masks and ten respirators to combat the COVID-19 pandemic in her hometown of Barranquilla.

Cuban singer Addys Mercedes (b. 1973) began her career singing repertoire from Cuban son to American pop songs to support her family during the economic crisis of the periodo especial. In 1993 she moved to Germany where she began writing her own songs and produced her début album featuring musicians from Havana which became a European hit. Her second album *Nomad* (2003) featured the mixing electronic elements with Cuban son and her promotional tours saw her sharing the stage with international musical luminaries. She returned to the use of traditional Cuban instruments in her subsequent recordings which she often performed herself.

Indonesian-born Anggun (Anggun Cipta Sasmi; b. 1974) released her first studio album at the age of 14. Influenced by Western rock her singles 'Mimpi' (1989) and 'Tua Tusa Keladi' (1990) achieved some success along with her studio albums earning her the Most Popular Indonesian Artist 1990–1991 awards. In 1993 she became the youngest

Indonesian singer to found her own record company and took complete creative control of her work. By the age of 19 she had sold millions of albums in Indonesia, but dissatisfied with her achievement she sold her record company to fund her move to London to launch her career on the international stage. With limited success in London she moved to France where began to release songs in French and English. Her début single 'La neige au Sahara' (1997) from her first album fused electronic pop with Indonesian sounds and became a hit in France. The English version of the album was released with additional songs including 'Kembali' for the South East Asian market. It was a huge international success and launched her onto the world stage. Her subsequent recordings established her high-profile international career and her single 'Être une femme' (2004) addressing women's empowerment, became a top-selling hit. She has won numerous accolades including French Government Knight of Arts and Letters (2002) and Best International Singer (2018) European Latin Awards. She has been active in supporting charitable causes including AID/HIV, environmental preservation, tsunami victims in Asia, women's empowerment, LGBTQI+ awareness, artists rights and child welfare. She was appointed goodwill ambassador to the United Nations FAO (2009) and has actively campaigned for eradicating world hunger.

Not actually fitting into the context of the blues, world music or any other mainstream genre, the work of women in Indigenous contexts brings a new, but at the same time ancient voice to musical leadership. Indigenous voices do not consider themselves as a part of a conglomerate of world music or global music cultures, but a distinct cultural expression of people and place. The convergence of women's leadership roles in traditional cultures and the leadership role of contemporary Indigenous women in cultural restoration and healing signifies the importance of the role of women in musical leadership. Ethnomusicological research into Indigenous music from the anthropological stance has informed the academy on women's musical roles in pre-colonial societies, but as post-colonial Indigenous societies' cultural expressions locate a musical response a modern genre of Indigenous music emerges. Whilst the discussion of Indigenous women's musical leadership does not have an automatic fit into the genre of world music, the incarnation of global music may provide for a more inclusive space for the discussion of contemporary developments in Indigenous musical composition.

In Chapter 2 on women composers, I included a discussion of the work of Deborah Cheetham Fraillon. Whilst her work provides a new Indigenous perspective on classical structures such as opera and choral works, categorising her work as such highlights the associated pitfalls of categorising musical forms and approaches. Driven by a social-political objective of revival of Indigenous language and celebrating Indigenous culture in Australia brings her work closer to that of other musicians working in the First Nations space. However, despite the dangers of the associated binaries with both the music of women and that of women working in diverse cultural contexts, it is nonetheless important to highlight the significance of the leadership role of women in music in a range of endeavours.

Like Cheetham Fraillon, Australian singer-songwriter Gina Williams (b. 1969) sings in the Indigenous Noongar language of the South West corner of Western Australia. She is a passionate advocate for the preservation of Noongar language and culture and is a Balladong daughter, which is one of the 14 clan groups making up the Noongar nation. Noongar language is critically endangered and her mother and grandmothers, who both were of the Stolen Generations, were not permitted to speak their language as they were growing up.[21] The assimilation policies of the Australian government extended to 1969. Williams was not stolen from her family but was relinquished by her mother for adoption as a baby. Her journey through various foster homes and misinformation about her heritage led her to the rediscovery of her Noongar roots and language. In 2001 she won her first West Australian Music Industry Award for Indigenous Song of the Year and Most Popular Local Original Indigenous Act. In the same year, at age 40, she enrolled into a Noongar language course and wrote her first song in Balladong 'Iggy's Lullaby' whilst studying and pregnant with her first child. In 2010 Williams performed her cabaret 'Gina Williams and the Lubbly Sings' telling her story and the story of her people. In 2014 with her duo partner Guy Ghouse, she released Kalyakoori (Noongar 'Forever') which was entirely sung in Noongar. The partnership collaboration continued for 'Bindi Bindi' (The Butterfly; 2018) and 'Koorlangka' (Children's Legacy; 2020) along with the publication of their first music book for voice, guitar and piano, *Kalyakoorl, Ngalak Warangka* (Forever, we sing; 2021) through Magabala Books. In 2021 the partnership composed the Noongar Opera *Koolbardi Wer Wardong*, a story of Koolbardi the Magpie and Wardong the Crow for a sell-out season at the West Australian Opera with a follow-up tour in regional Western Australia (WA) in 2022. Williams' accolades include numerous West Australian Music Industry Awards and Inductee, West Australian Women's Hall of Fame (2018). She was appointed a Member of the Order of Australia for her services to the performing arts, Indigenous music and the media in the 2021 Queen's honours.

Canadian Aboriginal singer-songwriter Tanya Tagaq (b. 1975) developed a unique solo form of singing that is rooted in Inuit throat singing, but expands well beyond traditional culture to incorporate electronic, industrial and metal influences. She does not claim to represent traditional culture as her music is removed from the traditional context, however, her inclusions of animal sounds and sounds of nature stem from the original practise leading the way for a new form of gendered expression. Originating from Cambridge Bay, Nunavut, she is a popular performer in Canada and has received international recognition including her collaborations with Björk, the Kronos Quartet and Celtic fusion band Shooglenifty to name a few. Her recordings have earned her numerous awards including winning the Polaris Music Prize (2014 and 2017), Canadian Folk Music Pushing the Boundaries Award (2014), Western Canadian Music Award, Aboriginal Recording of the Year (2015) and Member of the Order of Canada (2016). As an Inuit, Tagaq is active in bringing Aboriginal concerns to her audiences and on social media. She is vocal about Indigenous land rights and her support of sealing as a cultural preservation practice has received considerable backlash from animal rights activists. Her abuse of PETA during her 2014 Polaris Award speech enraged animal rights activists.[22] She has voiced her activism surrounding missing and murdered Indigenous women and systematic racism in governments and in 2020 she provided narration for the music video 'End of the Road', a protest song about the missing and murdered Indigenous women by rock group Crown Lands.[23] Her 2022 album *Tongues* was recorded before the COVID-19 pandemic and is based on her novel *Split Tooth* (2018) relating her own personal story about an Indigenous woman growing up in the Arctic.

Just as in the West, leading women in the global music genres to date have been predominantly vocalists. In traditional music there are many instruments that are forbidden for women with performance barriers based upon gender. Access to training on these instruments breaches traditional mores which are still upheld in some contexts.

Sona Kobareth (b. 1983) is the first female professional kora player representing an advance for women in traditional African instrumental music. She is a British instrumentalist singer and composer of Gambian background from one of the five kora-playing griot families of West Africa. The playing of this instrument was passed down from father to son in selected families called groit. She was taught the instrument by her brother and then father alongside her study of cello, piano and harpsichord at the Royal College of Music in London. She began performing at an early age and as a music student worked on several projects with leading musicians and orchestras including the Evelyn Glennie, Irish Chamber Orchestra, Royal Philharmonic Orchestra and Britten Sinfonia. She went on to perform with African musicians including Oumou Sangaré and toured with her brother's African classical music ensemble. She has recorded several albums and appeared in collaborations with other

African musicians. She made her début as a film composer writing the soundtrack for the film on Africa titled *Motherland* (2009).[24] She has performed internationally at WOMAD festivals. She is also an activist who has spoken at high-profile international events including summits for the UN and World Trade Organisation (WTO). In 2015 she established the Gambia Academy to bring cultural traditions into the mainstream education curriculum in Africa.[25]

## Conclusion

Just as the women discussed in the previous chapters have used their influence to promote social justice concerns through musical narratives and direct philanthropic support, women from global cultures have been active in bringing their voices to the world stage addressing a range of issues particular to their concerns. Some have earned their commercial success from humble beginnings and recognise the plight of women in poverty particularly those from African nations. Their own direct experience of marginalisation, discrimination and dispossession have driven their commitment to social activism. Similar to the women in other contexts discussed in this book as women attain success through their musical achievements, they create opportunities for women's empowerment and emancipation providing inspiration and leadership for other musical women in global contexts.

## Notes

1 Koskoff, E., ed. (1987). *Women and Music in Cross-cultural Perspective.* Vol. 79. University of Illinois Press; Koskoff, E. (2014). *A Feminist Ethnomusicology. Writings on Music and Gender.* Illinois University Press.
2 Dunbar, J.C. (2020). *Women, Music, Culture: An Introduction.* Routledge.
3 Sinclair, A. (2013). Not just 'adding women in': Women re-making leadership. *Seizing the Initiative: Australian Women Leaders in Politics, Workplaces and Communities*, 15, 15–34; Coates, S.K., Trudgett, M. & Page, S. (2021). Examining Indigenous leadership in the academy: A methodological approach. *Australian Journal of Education*, 65(1), 84–102; Ryan, T. (2016). Seen but unseen: Missing visible Indigenous women and what it means for leadership in Indigenous Australia. *Platform: Journal of Media and Communication*, 7. ANZCA Special Issue, 26–34; Damousi, J, Rubenstein, K. & Tomsic, M. (2014). *Diversity in Leadership: Australian Women, Past and Present.* ANU Press.
4 Bowers, J. & Bareis, U. (1991). Bibliography on music and gender-women in music. *The World of Music*, 33(2), 65–103.
5 Koskoff (1987). Ibid.
6 Koskoff (2014). Ibid.

7 Herndon, M. & Ziegler, S. (1990). Music, gender, and culture. Ictm Study Group on Music and Gender & International Council for Traditional Music C F Peters Corporation.

8 Danielson, V. (2004). The voice of Egypt: Umm Kulthum. In Bernstein, J.A. *Women's Voices across Musical Worlds*. Northeaster University.

9 Ibid.

10 Scott, M. (2007). *Music in Egypt*. Oxford University Press.

11 This sentiment in her recorded statement in the DVD, Umm Kulthum: A Voice like Egypt, Dir. Michal Goldman. Narr. Omar Sharif. Arab Film Distribution, 1996.

12 Danielson. Ibid.

13 Dunbar. Ibid., 65.

14 Ibid.

15 Allen, L. (2008). Remembering Miriam Makeba. *Journal of Musical Arts in Africa*, 5(1), 89–90.

16 Ravell-Pinto, T. & Ravell, R. (2008). Obituary: African Icon: Miriam 'Mama Africa' Makeba, dies at age 76. *Journal of the African Literature Association*, 2(2), 274–281.

17 Sizemore-Barber, A. (July–October, 2012). The voice of (which?) Africa: Miriam Makeba in America. *Safundi: The Journal of South African and American Studies*, 13(3–4), 251–276.

18 Ibid.

19 Redmond, S.L. (2013). *Anthem: Social Movements and the Sound of Solidarity in the African Diaspora*. New York University Press.

20 Beaumont-Thomas, B. (2020, 6 May). Millie Small, My Boy Lollipop singer, dies aged 73. *The Guardian*. London.

21 Monica Tan (2015, 28 March). Gina Williams on why every Australian should know some Indigenous words. *The Guardian*.

22 Tanya Tagaq wins 2014 Polaris Prize, says 'Fuck PETA'. (2014, 22 September). Stereogum.

23 Anita Tai, Canadian Band Crown Lands Honours Missing Indigenous Women With New Single 'End Of The Road'. (July 16, 2020). *Entertainment Tonight Canada*.

24 Shahadah, Owen 'Alik. Director. (2010), Motherland. Halaqah Media Distribution Co.

25 https://sonajobarteh.com/the-gambia-academy

# 9

# WOMEN IN THE MUSIC INDUSTRY

## Introduction

The music industry remains very much a 'boys club' which is supported by research into the gender imbalance in the music industry. It indicates that while there is an increase in participation of women in music education with women often achieving better results which has not translated to increased success in the music industry. The barrier appears to occur when women enter the professional music industry.

The 2019 UK Counting the Music Industry report provides data on the gender gap in women signed to labels, in management and in music publishing revealing the deficit of women in the UK music industry which affects the professional and economic support required to nourish careers.[1] It finds that of the writers signed to UK music publishers 14.18% are female, of the artists signed to UK labels 19.69% are female and of those working for UK music publishers 36.67% are female. It also provides data on leadership in music publishing showing 82% of CEOs in UK music publishing companies are men with women in leadership positions at 10% in pop, 25% in classical and 30% in screen companies. The study of the music education pipeline finds that just under half the number of females participated in music specialisations through to postgraduate level with the smallest percentage of women studying music composition (14.45%) and music technology (12.88%) at the undergraduate level. At the postgraduate level, the percentages increase across all areas, but this does not translate to being signed as professional performers or songwriters. In big-budget rock and pop music festivals,

DOI: 10.4324/9781003183631-10

men still predominate and at major electronic music festivals female DJs on the line-ups range from 2.7% to 9.6%. Until recent years, the number of women receiving music industry awards has been exceptionally low with less than 10% of women receiving major awards in the UK. This has been partly attributed to record labels and publishers being the primary gatekeepers in selecting award entrants. Counting the Music seeks to address the barriers to the gender imbalance in the music industry, many of which have already been discussed in earlier chapters. These include the historical exclusion of musical women from the public sphere, the unpaid labour role of women as mothers and carers, the working hours, the touring schedules and the gender pay gap. Other contributing factors include the imbalance of female singers to female instrumentalists resulting in the gender and power imbalance in performing groups. Technical roles in music are also dominated by men as discussed in Chapter 8 and sexism and harassment pervades in the music industry. The imbalance can also be attributed to women choosing music careers such as education and marketing, unconscious bias in the industry, lack of role models and self-confidence.

The Annenberg initiative, a 10-year study of women in the United States, released in 2022 found that female representation in recording studios and the charts had not significantly increased over the previous ten years.[2] The study was performed by examining the artists, songwriters and producers credited on each of the 1,000 songs on Billboard Hot 100 Year End Chart from 2012 to 2021, along with the gender and race/ethnicity of every person in those three roles. In 2021, there were 180 artists on this chart, 76.7% of them were men and 23.3% were women. (No artists identified as gender non-conforming or non-binary in 2021.) Across all ten years, 78.2% of artists were men and 21.8% were women.

In Australia, research indicates similar outcomes with women underrepresented at senior levels in industry. In 2017, the University of Sydney's Women, Work and Leadership Research Group found that women in the music industry were 'chronically disadvantaged' against their male counterparts with women paid less than men, female artists outnumbered on festival line-ups, held less industry roles and were underrepresented on the boards of all peak industry bodies.[3] These figures are shown to have a poor correlation with the performance of women in schools and university music with females making up 45% of all qualified musicians and music students.

Initiatives such as government policies, inclusion of female directors on boards, stronger representation of women at festivals and women broadcasters promoting women musicians on the national music networks have been introduced, but while the situation for women is improving the data yields results that indicate the challenges for women in music industry have not yet been overcome.

Sexism and harassment have played a major role in women leaving the industry.[4] Surveys and first-hand reports of sexism in the industry reveal rampant sexual harassment in the music industry with respondents often being afraid to officially report cases due to fear of losing work or not being taken seriously. The #MeToo movement has highlighted how pervasive sexual harassment is in the creative industries which has resulted in many women ending promising careers.

## Women in the recording industry

Some women have broken into the executive level of the recording industry such as Sylvia Rhone (b. 1952). As chair and CEO of Epic Records, a subsidiary of Sony Music Entertainment, she is regarded as the most influential female executive in history and the first African American to attain such an influential position in the industry. Raised in Harlem, Rhone had early exposure to the R&B shows at the Apollo Theatre and found music an inspirational force.[5] She graduated with a Bachelor in economics from the Wharton School, University of Pennsylvania. Upon graduating she took a job in banking, but soon pursued her passion for music and joined Buddha Records in 1974. A series of promotions soon saw her holding positions at ABC Records, Ariola and Elektra Records and became director of national black music marketing for Atlantic Records. She began to take on broader responsibilities in Artists and Repertoire (A&R) and in 1986 was promoted to senior vice president and general manager at Atlantic Records. In 1990 she became the first African American woman to head a major record company when she was named CEO and president of Atlantic's EastWest Records America division. In 1991 when EastWest merged with Atco Records she became CEO of East West Record America and in 1994 she was appointed chairwoman and CEO of Elektra. She was involved in the merger of Elektra, EastWest and Sire Records to create one of Warner music's most diverse labels. In 2004 she was appointed president of Motown Records and executive vice president of Universal Records. At Motown she reinvigorated both the roster and staff along with building social media fan networks. In 2012 she established the label Vested in Culture which was distributed through Epic Records and in 2014 she was named President of Epic Records. She was promoted to Chairwoman and CEO of Epic Records in 2019 and has brought unprecedented hip-hop success to the label. She has actively promoted women in management for their collaborative skills and supported a safe work environment for women represented by the

#MeToo movement.[6] Her accolades include an honorary doctorate from Berklee College of Music (2019), Cultural Creators Icon Award (2018) and member of the Board of Directors of the Rock and Roll Hall of Fame.

Spring Aspers was promoted to President of Music for Sony Pictures in 2019 where she had worked for the past decade. She joined Sony Pictures Entertainment in 2009 as Executive Vice President of Music Creative Affairs where she assisted Diane Warren to win a Golden Globe for her song 'You Haven't Seen the Last of Me' from the movie *Burlesque* as well as assist John Legend receive a Grammy nomination for his song 'Tonight (Best You Ever Had)' from *Think Like a Man*. She has worked as a composer arranger, and conductor, but her primary role has been in production and management for over 60 motion pictures and soundtracks. Aspers' career started as an independent music supervisor working on *The Big Lebowski* (1998). At Sony, her credits include *Passengers* (2016), *Baby Driver* (2017) and *Venom* (2018) for which she recruited Eminem to create an original song. Since becoming President of Music at Sony she is credited with assembling all-star music collaborations for the Oscar-winning animated film, *Spider-Man: Into the Spider-Verse* (2019) including the song 'Sunflower' by Swae Lee and Post Malone, which has been certified Diamond by the RIAA with over 10 million record sales and over 2 billion streams. For *Charlie's Angels* Aspers teamed with Ariana Grande to executive produce the soundtrack and first single, 'Don't Call Me Angel,' with Miley Cyrus and Lana Del Rey.

In 1919 Deborah Dugan became the first female president and CEO of the Recording Academy, which presents the Grammy Awards. Formerly president of Disney Publishing Worldwide (2002–2006), CEO of Entertainment Rights North America (2007–2009) and CEO of (RED) (2012–2019), since 2020 she has been undertaking strategy work for social impact agency Handshake. Her appointment to the Recording Academy was in response to the low female representation at the 2018 Grammys and the then CEO Neil Portnow's comments that women musicians needed to "step up" in order to achieve parity which led to calls for his replacement.[7] A task force was set up by Time's Up co-founder Tina Tichen to address the Recording Academy's gender representation and make recommendations for the incoming CEO to implement.[8] Dugan was appointed to implement the recommendations and in the process made claims of sexual harassment and irregularities within the organisation. Her employment was terminated for misconduct after sending an email to the Academy's director of human resources outlining allegations of male domination in the organisation. She alleged that she was dismissed for raising concerns of conflicts of interest made possible by the 'boys' club, mentality'. The Academy claimed that her allegations were in response to a bullying claim against her from within the organisation and launched two independent investigations of Dugan after which she was fired.[9] The parties settled on an undisclosed amount and the whole incident has shed some light on the perils of 'stepping up' in the Academy.

In 2021 Natalie Waller became the first female chair of the Australian Recording Industry Association (ARIA) following the organisation coming under fire for failing to reflect cultural diversity in the music industry and the contribution of female artists at its industry awards.[10] As recently as 2019, the board was made up of entirely male executives. Waller joined the board in 2019 when the number of female board members increased following the investigation into the culture of the Australian music industry.[11] Waller has over 20 years' experience in broadcasting through the ABC and at the time of her appointment was Head of ABC Music & Events. Earlier in 2021 ARIA also appointed Annabelle Herd as CEO after 16 years in the position of Chief Operating Officer at the Channel 10 television network. Prior to that she was Senior Officer (Broadcasting and Copyright) for the Government of Australia, Acting Chief of Staff for the Minister of Communications and Government Lawyer for Intellectual property within the Attorney General's department. The appointment of both senior executives at ARIA along with the increase in female board representation is designed to address the issues of discrimination and harassment that have been revealed in the Australian music industry.

Cindy Charles works in the digital media space as an advisor on content acquisition and distribution and has advised many companies on the risks and rewards of entering this space. She is co-founder of She Is the Music (SITM), a non-profit organisation dedicated to increasing the number of women working in music including songwriters, engineers, producers, artists and industry professionals.[12] Charles is also co-founder of Women in Digital Media, and is on the advisory boards of Qwire, Hi5 and Women in Music. As head of music licensing and label relations at Twitch, Charles works with artists and producers to create music opportunities for women on the popular gaming platform.

Janet Billig Rich (b. 1968) is an artists' manager, producer and record label executive who founded the Los Angeles entertainment company Manage This! in 1996. In her early career she worked in A&R managing bands including Pussy Galore, Smashing Pumpkins and Nirvana. She became the youngest senior executive at Atlantic Records in the mid-1990s. Through Manage This! she manages a number of leading women artists including the Grammy Award–winning singer–songwriter Lisa Loeb, Courtney Love and Hole. She has provided music supervision for numerous television and film projects and in 2018 earned the prestigious Boss Lady Award from the Women in Music Network.

Ty Stiklorius (b. 1975) is a high-profile music executive as well as an accomplished film and television producer, entrepreneur, social impact leader and businesswoman. Prior to her MBA studies at Wharton Business School, she worked on the development of music notation software to allow musicians to collaborate on line. After completing her MBA, she worked in content distribution and talent management. Stiklorius served as Executive Producer on the Oscar-winning film *La La Land*, WGN's hit series Underground, NBC's A Legendary Christmas with John and Chrissy and the hit Netflix hip-hop competition show Rhythm + Flow starring Cardi B, T.I. and Chance the Rapper. In 2015 Stiklorius founded her female-backed music management, media and social impact company, Friends At Work (FAW). She supports social justice initiatives that impact women and people of colour in the entertainment industry as well as driving philanthropic initiatives for quality education and criminal justice reform. She specifically targets change-making artists with ambitious social impact goals.

In March 2019, Annie Lee was named the chief financial officer of Interscope Geffen A&M. Lee, who joined Interscope in 2006, is the daughter of Taiwanese immigrants and has been a leading advocate for diversity and inclusion at her company. She also is a mentor for emerging music industry executives.

## Women in music management

Whilst the study of arts management is popular amongst women, few of them end up in leadership positions. The gender imbalance is being somewhat redressed as women take on more senior traditional management positions, but it is still not proportional to the number of women in lower-level positions in arts organisations. As discussed in Chapter 1, women are largely invisible in leadership in arts organisations with the persistent pattern of women leading smaller organisations, but as they become larger and more significant the presence of women at the top diminishes.[13] This is also true for women in music organisations. However, more women are emerging in the music management leadership space.

In 2018 Vanessa Reed was recognised by the BBC Women's Hour as the third most powerful woman in music after Beyoncé and Taylor Swift, ahead of Adele.[14] In 2019 Reed was appointed President and CEO of New Music USA following her tenure as Chief Executive of the PRS Foundation, UK's leading charitable funder of new music. In the same year, she was awarded an Ivors Academy Gold Badge award for her contribution to the music industry in the UK. Following honours studies in French and music, Reed worked in music promotions, grant administration and as a strategic leader in the music industry in the UK and Europe. She is founder and Honorary Chair of the award-winning Keychange program for gender balance in the music industry.[15] Reed is also a Fellow of Leeds College of Music and a Fellow of the Royal Society for the Arts. She is on the board of the Performing Arts Alliance and serves as an advisor on the NY Chapter of the Recording Academy.

Mary Vallentine is one of Australia's most experienced arts managers who has had a significant leadership role in major music organisations. Following drama and music studies she trained in arts management. She was administrator of the Adelaide Festival in 1980 and 1982 and Managing Director of the Sydney Symphony Orchestra from 1986 to 2009. In 2010 she was appointed Managing Director of the Melbourne Recital Centre until 2016. She was recognised for her services to the arts as Officer of the Order of Australia (1996), Sydney Myer Performing Arts Facilitators Prize (2002) and Vice Chancellor's Professorial Fellow of Monash University (2017–2020).

Top Job, a 2022 documentary by Miriam Gordon Stewart laments the lack of women employed in opera leadership roles in Australia.[16] This has been somewhat addressed by the appointment of Fiona Allen as CEO of Opera Australia who in the documentary argues for the importance of a gender balance in artistic teams. A former clarinettist who received her BA (Hons) from the University of Sydney and went on to study Arts Management and an MBA. She has worked since with Sydney Opera House, Wales Millennium Centre and in 2015 was appointed as the first women Artistic Director and Chief Executive of Birmingham Hippodrome. Her honorary roles include President of UK Theatre, Chair of the Midlands Regional Tourism Board, a Director of Women of the Year and member of the Midlands Regional Council, Creative Industries Federation Council and Midlands Engine Business Council. She was presented with the Inaugural Woman of the Year, Women with Edge Award (2018), Outstanding Business Woman of the Year Awards by the Asian Business Chamber of Commerce (2019) and Deputy Lieutenant for the West Midlands (2021).

## Women in music journalism

Unsurprisingly music journalism is male dominated across all musical areas with some major newspapers employing no female music critics. Music criticism can have a significant influence on who and what is programmed along with informing public opinion on musical performances. However, some women have broken through the ranks to achieve success. In the area of classical music, Anne Midgette (b. 1965) was the first female music critic for the *New York Times* from 2001 to 2007 and was the chief classical music critic for *The Washington Post* from 2008 to 2019. She also maintained a classical music blog along alongside publishing articles and books on music, dance, theatre, film and the visual arts. Following studies in Classics at Yale University where she graduated with a BA (1986) Midgette moved to Münich, Germany, and travelled throughout Europe as a freelance arts critic. In 1988 she returned to the United States where she continued her freelance writing before taking on the role of classical music critic for the *New York Times*.[17] Wynne Delacoma was the first female classical music critic for the *Chicago Sun-Times* from 1992 to 2006. She was replaced by freelance critics and she continued to work as a freelance critic and academic. Marion Rosenberg (1961–2013) was a freelance music critic who contributed features, essays and reviews to US newspapers and magazines. She was noted for her award-winning writings on Maria Callas.[18]

In popular music, female critics are rare but nonetheless a number of women have broken through the ranks to become influential in this field. Linda Solomon (b. 1937) was a prolific columnist for *The Village Voice* and has critiqued folk music, blues, R&B, jazz and country music. She contributed to most major music magazines along with writing liner notes for music recordings by major folk, jazz and blues artists. Activist and feminist Ellen Willis (1941–2006) was the first pop music critic for *The New Yorker* and went on to write for major music magazines including *Village Voice* and *Rolling Stone*. Her articles contributed to the anti-pornography movement known as the sex wars and she coined the term 'pro-sex feminism' in her 1981 essay 'Lust Horizons: Is the Women's Movement Pro-Sex?'.[19] In the UK, Penny Valentine (1943–2003) became one of Britain's most influential reviewers of pop singles during her time.[20] She worked for a number of magazines in the UK and spent a period working in New York City as well as working as press officer for her friend Elton John. She was active in Women in Media and the National Union of Journalists and in 1980 founded the politically radical publication City Limits. She supported soul singers such as Aretha Franklin and co-wrote a biography of Dusty Springfield.[21]

The domination of men in rock music criticism followed the general state of the genre itself, but Lillian Roxon (1932–1973) was a noted Australian journalist and is best known for her 1969 *Rock Encyclopaedia*.[22] Her family was Jewish, originally from Ukraine and Poland and to escape from fascism they moved to Australia via Italy where she was born. Following her university studies in Queensland and Sydney she worked for tabloid magazines before becoming the first female overseas correspondent for *The Sydney Morning Herald* when she moved permanently to New York in 1959. She became interested in popular music and became one of the leading critics in the burgeoning rock scene. In the 1970s, she adopted a stronger feminist stance in her writing and became good friends with other feminists including Australian singer Helen Reddy and Australian academic Germaine Greer.[23]

The next generation of female music critics includes Ann Powers (b. 1964) working for NPR and a regular contributor at *The Los Angeles Times* where she previously served as chief pop critic. She also was an editor at *The Village Voice*. Her work often critiques perceptions of race, gender and social issues in the music industry and has written on feminism, film and music. She co-edited the anthology *Rock She Wrote: Women Write about Rock, Pop, and Rap*[24] and was guest editor for *Best Music Writing 2010.*[25] She has also written a memoir of her time living in northern US bohemian music culture[26] along with a book co-authored with Tori Amos who relates her experience of being a woman in the music industry.[27] In 2017 she published a history of American popular music through the lens of sexuality and eroticism.[28]

Joy Press (b. 1966) was the music critic for a number of American magazines and for the English weekly music paper *Melody Maker*. In 1996 she became editor of *The Village Voice* literary supplement and later becoming its culture editor. In 2010 she became culture editor for *The Los Angeles Times* and continued to contribute to other major US magazines. Press has written on the topic of gender and co-authored *The Sex Revolts: Gender, Rebellion and Rock'n'Roll.*[29] In 2018 Press published *Stealing the Show: How Women Are Revolutionizing Television.*[30] Journalist, critic and film-maker Raquel Capeda (b. 1973) is of Dominican descent and found herself challenging the narratives of American history as a student. She became one of the hip-hop community's leading writers and documentary film-makers. She was editor of the award-winning anthology *And It Don't Stop: The Best American Hip-Hop Journalism of the Last 25 Years*[31] and author of *Bird of Paradise: How I Became a Latina* which explores her own history and genealogy.[32]

Broadcasting has an impact on what music is heard and sold. As more females take on roles as broadcasters there is potential for playlists to become more inclusive. International Women's Day dedicates broadcasts to women and playlists are drawn up of significant women contributors to music performance and production in both classical and popular music. The efforts to increase the quotas of women's music by public broadcasters across the board have increased the amount of music by women being heard resulting in firsts for women such as heading up broadcasting popularity polls.[33] Efforts to create stations which include music only by women such as Scala Radio's digital station devoted to classical music entirely by women seeks to highlight women composers.[34] Scala has allied with charity Donne which is dedicated to gender equality in the music industry. These types of initiatives compounded with changes in the gender balance in the music industry have contributed to the recognition of leading women musicians in the early decades of the 21st century.

## Women's music festivals

Professional music organisations have been established by women since the 19th century as discussed in Chapter 4. The second wave of feminism saw a spike in women composers' festivals and conferences internationally. In popular music, women began organising all-women's festivals in the 1970s to increase opportunities for women musicians and artists who were being overlooked by mainstream promoters. Sometimes called womxn's music festivals and occasionally organised for lesbians or diverse communities with the aim of providing a safe and inclusive environment for creative women and musicians.

One of the first women's festivals in the United States was held in 1973 at Sacramento State University and in May 1974 the first National Women's Music Festival with a folk music focus was held in Illinois led by graduate student Kristin Lems who was tired of the lack of programming women at major festivals.[35] In 1976 sisters Lisa and Kristie Vogel and friend Mary Kindig founded Michigan Womyn's Music Festival as an event for lesbians providing an opportunity for women to meet and collaborate.[36] Apart from the all-female line-up, the entire festival was produced and managed by women ranging from lighting, sound, electrical, medical, catering, childcare and workshops. Since the mid-1970s, many women's music festivals have been established and vary in size from a few hundred to thousands of attendees such as The Los Angeles Women's Music Festival, the Sappho Lesbian Witch Camp, near Vancouver, Canada, and the Sistajive Women's Music Festival in Australia. The all-female Lilith Fair tour, taking Lilith from the medieval Jewish legend that Lilith was Adam's first wife, was co-founded by Sarah McLachlan (b. 1968) and was one of the highest-grossing touring festivals of its time taking place in the summers of 1997, 1998 and 1999.

Examples of festivals celebrating the contributions of women to composition, performance and teaching in the United States include the Women in Music festival established in 2005 at the Eastman School, New York. Women composers' conferences and festivals were held in Australia with the first being held in Adelaide, South Australia, in 1991 instigated by composer Becky Llewellyn (b. 1950), which drew attention from the national broadcaster and feminist musicologists. This was followed up by a series of women composers' conferences and festivals during the next decade in Australia.

## Women in artistic leadership, programming and curating

Increasing numbers of women are becoming involved in programming for concerts and festivals with some taking on leadership positions in major international festivals. Australian singer and songwriter Robyn Archer (b. 1948) began her career in feminist cabaret and devising stage works. She became artistic director of arts festivals internationally commencing with the National Festival of Australian Theatre from 1993 to 1995. She then became Artistic Director at the Adelaide Festival of Arts (1998 and 2000), The Melbourne International Arts Festival (2002–2004), founded Ten Days on the Island Festival in Tasmania (2001), Artistic Director at the Liverpool European Capital of Culture 2008 (2004–2006) and advised on the start-up of Luminato in Toronto. In 2007 she created The Light in Winter for Federation Square in Melbourne and in July 2009 was appointed Creative Director of the Centenary of Canberra 2013. She is in demand as a speaker and public advocate for the arts and cultural diversity and was the commentator for the inaugural broadcast of the Sydney Gay and Lesbian Mardi Gras for the ABC. Alongside her numerous artistic leadership roles and speaking engagements, she maintains her musical career devising shows such as the 2023 touring show Robyn Archer: An Australian Songbook. Her honours include Officer of the Order of Australia (2000), Chevalier of the Ordre des Arts et des Lettres (France, 2001) and Officer of the Order of the Crown (Belgium, 2008).

In 2022 The Edinburgh Festival appointed its first female artistic director, the award-winning Scottish violinist Nicola Benedetti (b. 1987). In 2002 she won the UK's Brilliant Prodigy Competition and in 2004 she won the BBC Young Musician of the Year. She has performed with major UK orchestras and has been awarded a number of honorary degrees from UK universities. She became a member of the Order of the British Empire (2013), honorary fellow of the Royal Society of Edinburgh (2017), was the youngest recipient of the Queen's Medal for Music (2017) and was made a Commander of the British Empire (2019). In 2019 she was awarded the annual Medal of the Royal Society of Edinburgh for improving the lives of deprived Scottish children through Sistema Scotland and the Big Noise Orchestras. She won the Grammy for best classical music performance (2020), the ISM Distinguished Musician Award (2021) and was appointed the honorary president of the Royal Conservatoire of Scotland. Her appointment as director of the Scottish Festival has been attributed to the recognition of her musical leadership and advocacy as well as the current board of the festival having a majority female membership.[37]

## Conclusion

While women still are a minority in many areas of the music industry, the presence of influential women who have taken on senior leadership roles has contributed to the growth of women's power in the music industry. Other areas that need to be researched are women in publishing, broadcasting and band management which all have a direct influence on women's visibility in music. The visibility of women in leadership provides role models for future generations of performers and musical leaders.

## Notes

1 Bain, V. (2019). Counting the Music Industry: The Gender Gap. https://vbain. co.uk/research/

2 Hernandez, K., Smith, S. & Piper, K. (2022, March). Inclusion in the Recording Studio?: Gender and Race/Ethnicity of Artists, Songwriters and Producers across 1,000 Popular Songs from 2012-2021. USC Annenberg Inclusion Initiative.

3 Cooper, R., Coles, A. & Hanna-Osborne, S. (2017). *Skipping a Beat: Assessing the State of Gender Equality in the Australian Music Industry.* University of Sydney.

4 Crabtree, J.R. (2020). Tunesmiths and Toxicity: Workplace Harassment in the Contemporary Music Industries of Australia and New Zealand. Open Publications of UTS Scholars.

5 Mitchell, G. (2018, 28 June). How Sylvia Rhone became Sony Music's most powerful African-American woman: 'Many questioned my ability'. *Billboard.*

6 Variety staff. (2019, 23 April). Sylvia Rhone promoted to Chairman & CEO of Epic Records. *Variety.*

7 Aswad, J. & Halperin, S. (2019, 18 March). Recording Academy narrows search to replace Neil Portnow. *Variety.*

8 Lewis, R. (2020, 18 January). Sexism? Cronyism? Mismanagement? After sudden ouster of Grammys chief, spin and finger-pointing begin. *Los Angeles Times.*

9 France, L.R. (2020, 2 March). Recording Academy fires Deborah Dugan. CNN.

10 Burke, K. (2021, 13 July). Music industry shake-up: Aria appoints Natalie Wallers as first female chair. *The Guardian.*

11 Burke, K. (2021, 21 June). Revealed: Multiple allegations of toxic culture at Sony Music Australia as CEO Denis Handlin leaves. *The Guardian.*

12 sheisthemusic.org

13 Caust, J. (2018). *Arts Leadership in Contemporary Contexts.* Routledge.

14 Murray, K. Host. (2018, 28 September). Beyoncé, Taylor Swift and Vanessa Reed top the fifth Woman's Hour Power List on BBC Music Day. https://bbc. in/2xI7q2y

15 www.keychange.eu

16 Gordon-Stewart, M. Soprano and director. (2022, 22 October). Top Job. Documentary. miriamgordon.com.

17 Helgert, L. (2013). Criticism: 5. Since 1960. Grove Music Online.

18 The essay 'Re-visioning Callas', published in (the now-defunct) USItalia, won a Front Page Award from the Newswomen's Club of New York.

19 A slightly revised version of the original 'Lust Horizons' essay can be found in Willis, E. (1992). *No More Nice Girls: Countercultural Essays*. Wesleyan University Press, 3–14.

20 Williams, R. (2003, 13 January). Penny Valentine. *The Guardian*.

21 Valentine, P. & Wickham, V. (2000). *Dancing with Demons: The Authorised Biography of Dusty Springfield*. Hodder & Stoughton.

22 Roxon, L. (1969). *Lillian Roxon's Rock Encyclopaedia*. Grosset & Dunlap/ Workman Publishing.

23 Milliken, R. (2002). Roxon, Lillian (1932–1973). *Australian Dictionary of Biography*. National Centre of Biography, Australian National University. 16.

24 McDonnell, E. & Powers, A., eds. (1995). *Rock She Wrote: Women Write about Rock, Pop, and Rap*. Plexus.

25 Powers, A., ed. (2010). *Best Music Writing 2010*. Da Capo Press.

26 Powers, A. (2000). *Weird Like Us: My Bohemian America*. Simon & Schuster.

27 Amos, T. & Powers, A. (2005). *Tori Amos: Piece by Piece. A Portrait of the Artist: Her Thoughts, Her Conversations*. Broadway Books.

28 Powers, A. (2017). *Good Booty: Love and Sex, Black & White, Body and Soul in American Music*. William Morrow.

29 Reynolds, S. & Press, J. (1995). *The Sex Revolts: Gender, Rebellion, and Rock'n'roll*. Harvard University Press.

30 Press, J. (2018). *Stealing the Show: How Women Are Revolutionizing Television*. Faber & Faber.

31 Capeda, R. (2004). *And It Don't Stop: The Best American Hip-Hop Journalism of the Last 25 Years*. Faber & Faber.

32 Capeda, R. (2013). *Bird of Paradise: How I Became Latina*. Atria Books.

33 Jeffrey, J. & Donoughue, M. (2020, 25 January). Hottest 100 sees Billie Eilish become first solo woman to top the poll ahead of Tones and I, Mallrat and Flume. Abc.net.au.

34 Moss, S. (2022, 10 January). From Mendelssohn to mush: A day tuned to Scala Radio's Women Composers. *The Guardian*.

35 Buttel, R. (1974, 26 March). UI grad students organising national women's folk festival. *The Daily Illini*.

36 Morris, B.J. (1999). *Eden Built by Eves: The Culture of Women's Music Festivals* (1st ed.). Alyson Publications. p. 60. See also by Morris, B.J. (2003). Music: Women's Festivals. In *Encyclopedia of Lesbian, Gay, Bisexual and Transgender History in America*. Ed. Stein, M.. Charles Scribner's Sons; Morris, B.J. (2005). Negotiating Lesbian worlds. *Journal of Lesbian Studies*, 9(1–2), 55–62.

37 Carrell, S. & Khomami, N. (2022, 1 March). Nicola Benedetti becomes first woman and first Scot to lead Edinburgh international festival. *The Guardian*.

# CONCLUSION

The preceding chapters indicate that women have participated in music from the beginning of time across nations as performers, composers, managers and leaders in all musical styles and genres. However, preconceptions about women in musical leadership such as sexism and patriarchal histories have limited opportunities for women in music up until the present day. Women's struggle to wrest control of their careers mirrors that of women in other industries and gender parity in music is still a distant aspiration. The glass ceiling still exists for women in business and politics and my allusion to the glass harmonica in music aims to address the multifaceted and labyrinthine path of musical leadership. Despite the remaining imbalance, opportunities for women to realise their potential and take on leadership roles in music are increasing. The case studies of contemporary women in music leadership outlined in this book demonstrate that the future of women in musical leadership is bright. Efforts to address the gender imbalance in the music industry have been reinforced by successful role models and women in leadership positions. The women who have set the scene for women in musical leadership have opened up the possibilities for more women to be represented on the stage and in musical leadership contributing to the possibility of a gender balance in music. The engagement of women in musical leadership contributes to the removal of limitations for women's equal participation in music and allows for the women's voice to be heard in music.

DOI: 10.4324/9781003183631-11

# BIBLIOGRAPHY

Abbott, L. & Seroff, D. (2009). *Ragged but Right: Black Traveling Shows, Coon Songs, and the Dark Pathway to Blues and Jazz*. University Press of Mississippi.

Abtan, F. (2016). Where is she? Finding the women in electronic music culture. *Contemporary Music Review*, 35(1), 53–60.

Adkins Chiti, P. (2003). Cultural diversity-musical diversity: A different vision – women making music, 1–9 www.imc- cim.org/mmap/pdf/prod-chiti-e.pdf

Adler, N. & Osland, J. (2016). Women leading globally: What we know, thought we knew, and need to know about leadership in the 21st century. *Advances in Global Leadership*, 9, 15–56.

Albertson, C. (2003). *Bessie*. Yale University Press.

Allen, L., (2008). Remembering Miriam Makeba. *Journal of Musical Arts in Africa*, 5(1), 89–90.

Amero, R. (1991). Madame Schumann-Heink: San Diego's Diva. *Southern California Quarterly*, 73(2), 157–182.

Amos, T. & Powers, A. (2005). *Tori Amos: Piece by Piece. A Portrait of the Artist: Her Thoughts, Her Conversations*. Broadway Books.

Anderson, M. (1956/Revised 2002). *My Lord, What a Morning with intro.* by J.A. DePriest. Urbana.

Armstrong, J. (2021). *When Women Invented Television: The Untold Story of the Female Powerhouses Who Pioneered the Way We Watch Today*. Harper Collins.

Arnold, K.A. & Loughlan, C. (2018). Continuing the conversation: Questioning the who, what, and where of leaning in. *Academy of Management Perspectives*. 33(1), 94–109.

Arnold, D. (1988). Music at the ospedali. *Journal of the Royal Musical Association*, 113(2), 156–167.

Arrow, M. (2007). It has become my personal anthem: I am woman, popular culture and 1970s feminism. *Australian Feminist Studies*, 22(53), 213–230.

Arsenault, R. (2010). *The Sound of Freedom: Marian Anderson, The Lincoln Memorial, and the Concert that Awakened America*. Bloomsbury Publishing USA.

Auslander, P. (2006). *Performing Glam Rock: Gender and Theatricality in Popular Music*. Ann Arbor.

Avolio, B. & Bass, B. (2002). *Developing Potential Across a Full Range of Leadership: Cases on Transactional and Transformational Leadership*. Lawrence Erlbaum Associates.

Bach, S. (1992). *Marlene Dietrich: Life and Legend*. William Morrow and Company, Inc.

Baez, J. (1988). *And a Voice to Sing With: A Memoir*. Century Hutchinson.

Baird, I. (2015). Capturing the song of the nightingale. *Science Museum Group Journal*, 4(4).

Baldauf-Berdes, J.L. (1996). *Women's Musicians of Venice: Musical Foundations, 1525–1855*. Clarendon Press.

Barkin, E. (1980–1981). Questionnaire. *Perspectives of New Music*, 19, 460–462.

Barlow, W. (1989). *Looking Up at Down: The Emergence of Blues Culture*. Temple University Press.

Bartleet, B. (2002). Re-embodying the 'gendered podium'. *Context: Journal of Music Research*, 23, 49–57.

___. (2005). 18 Reflections on females conducing. In *Aesthetics and Experience in Music Performance*. Ed. Mackinlay, E. Collins, D. & Owens, S. 235–242.

___. (2006). Conducting motherhood: The personal and professional experiences of women orchestral conductors. *Outskirts: Feminisms Along the Edge*, 15.

___. (2008a). Women conductors on the orchestral podium: Pedagogical and professional implications. *College Music Symposium*, 48, 31–51. College Music Society.

___. (2008b). You're a woman and our orchestra just won't have you: The politics of otherness in the conducting profession. *Hecate*, 34, 6–23.

Bass, B. & Stogdill, R. (1990). *Bass & Stogdill's Handbook of Leadership: Theory, Research, and Managerial Applications*. Free Press.

Beer, A. (2016). *Sounds and Sweet Airs: The Forgotten Women of Classical Music*. Simon and Schuster.

Bell, A. (2011). Falling in love again and again: Marlene Dietrich and the iconization of non-native English. *Journal of Sociolinguistics*, 15(5), 627–656.

Bennett, D. (2008). A gendered study of the working patterns of classical musicians: Implications for practice. *International Journal of Music Education*, 26, 89–100.

Bertrand, M., Black, S., Jensen, S. & Lleras-Muney, A. (2019). Breaking the glass ceiling? The effect of board quotas on female labour market outcomes in Norway. *The Review of Economic Studies*, 86, 191–239.

Block, A.F. (1992). Two virtuoso performers in Boston: Jenny Lind and Camilla Urso. In *New Perspectives on Music: Essays in Honor of Eileen Southern*. Ed. Wright, J. & Floyd, S.A. Harmonie Park Press, 355–372.

Blyth, A. (2001). *Price, (Mary Violet) Leontyne*. Grove Music Online.

Bogin, M. (1980). *The Women Troubadours*. W.W. Norton.

Bogle, D. (2001). *Primetime Blues: African Americans on Network Television*. Farrar, Straus and Giroux.

___. (2007). *Brown Sugar: Over One Hundred Years of America's Black Female Superstars*. Continuum International Publishing Group.

___. (2011). *Heat Wave: The Life and Career of Ethel Waters*. HarperCollins.

Born, G. & Devine, K. (2016). Gender, creativity and education in digital musics and sound art. *Contemporary Music Review*, 35(1), 1–20.

Bosse, J. (2001). *Spiegel, Laurie*. Grove Music Online.

Bourne, S. (2007). *Ethel Waters: Stormy Weather*. Scarecrow Press.

Bowers, J. & Bareis, U. (1991). Bibliography on music and gender-women in music. *The World of Music*, 33(2), 65–103.

Bowers, J. & Tick, J. (1987). *Women Making Music: The Western Art Tradition, 1150–1950*. University of Illinois Press.

Braun, W. (2015). Jessye Norman & Mark Markham; New York City, Carnegie Hall, 2/14/15. *Opera News*, 79(11).

Bridges, T. (2001). *Casulana [Mezari], Maddalena*. Grove Music Online.

Briscoe, J. (2011/2012). *Jolas, Betsy*. *Grove Dictionary of American Music*, 2nd ed. Oxford Music Online.

Broadbent, M. & Broadbent, T. (n.d.). *Leginska: Forgotten Genius of Music. The Story of a Great Musician*. Leginska.org. Leginska.org.

Brockman, J. (1992). The first electronic filmscore-forbidden planet: A conversation with Bebe Barron. *The Score*, 7(3), 5–13.

Brown, H.M. (1986). Women singers and women's songs in fifteenth-century Italy. In *Women Making Music: The Western Art Tradition, 1150–1950*. Ed. Bowers. J. & Tick, J. University of Illinois Press , 62–89.

Bufwack, M. & Oermann, R. (2003). *Finding Her Voice: Women in Country Music: 1800–2000*. The Country Music Press & Vanderbilt University Press.

Burke, C. (2011). *No Regrets: The Life of Edith Piaf*. Alfred A. Knopf.

Bush, K. (2018). *How to Be Invisible*. Faber and Faber.

Caldwell, J. (2010). *Essays on the History of English Music in Honour of John Caldwell: Sources, Style, Performance, Historiography*. Boydell & Brewer.

Campbell, M. (2011). *The Great Cellists*. Faber & Faber.

Capeda, R. (2004). *And It Don't Stop: The Best American Hip-Hop Journalism of the Last 25 Years*. Faber & Faber.

___. (2013). *Bird of Paradise: How I Became Latina*. Atria Books.

Carson, M., Lewis, T. & Shaw, S. (2004). *Girls Rock!: Fifty Years of Women Making Music*. University Press of Kentucky.

Carter, T. & McEntire, R. (1994). *Reba: My Story*. Bantam Books.

Catalyst. (2020). The Detrimental Impact of COVID-19 on Gender and Racial Equality. www.catalyst.org/research/covid-effect-gender-racial-equality

Caust, J. (2018). *Arts Leadership in Contemporary Contexts*. Routledge.

Chapman, E. (2012). *From Russia to Love: The Life and Times of Viktoria Mullova*. Robson Press.

Chearis, K. (2005). *Women, Feminism, & Hip Hop*. Socialism.com.

Chilton, J. (2004). *Who's Who of British Jazz*, 2nd ed. Continuum.

Citron, M. (1993). *Gender and the Musical Canon*. University of Illinois Press.

Cixous Hélène, Cohen K. & Cohen P. (1976). The laugh of the medusa. *Signs* 1(4), 875–893.

Clinton, H. (2017). *What Happened.* Simon & Schuster.

Coates, S.K., Trudgett, M. & Page, S. (2021). Examining Indigenous leadership in the academy: A methodological approach. *Australian Journal of Education*, 65(1), 84–102.

Cohen, R. & Sherman, D. (2020). *Theatre: Brief*, 3rd ed. McGraw-Hill Education.

Cohodas, N. (2010). *Princess Noire: The Tumultuous Reign of Nina Simone.* Pantheon Books.

Comi, S., Grasseni, M., Origo, F. & Pagani, L. (2020). Where women make a difference: Gender quotas and firms' performance in three European countries. *ILR Review*, 73(3), 768–793.

Cooper, R., Coles, A. & Hanna-Osborne, S. (2017). *Skipping a Beat: Assessing the State of Gender Equality in the Australian Music Industry.* University of Sydney.

Cox, R. (1991). Rediscovering jouissance: An introduction to feminist musical aesthetics. In *Women & Music: A History*. Ed. Pendle, K. Indiana University Press. 331–340.

Crabtree, J.R. (2020). *Tunesmiths and Toxicity: Workplace Harassment in the Contemporary Music Industries of Australia and New Zealand.* Open Publications of UTS Scholars.

Craig, L. & Churchill, B. (2020). Dual-earner parent couples' work and care during COVID-19. *Gender, Work & Organization*, 28(1), 66–79.

Cusick, S. (2004). Francesca Caccini. In *New Historical Anthology of Music by Women*. Ed. Briscoe, J.R. Indiana University Press, 48–59.

Dahl, L. (1984). *Stormy Weather: The Music and Lives of a Century of Jazzwomen.* Hal Leonard Corporation.

___. (2000). *Morning Glory: A Biography of Mary Lou Williams.* Pantheon Books.

Damousi, J, Rubenstein, K. & Tomsic, M. (2014). *Diversity in Leadership: Australian Women, Past and Present.* ANU Press.

Danielson, V. (2004). The voice of Egypt: Umm Kulthum. In *Women's Voices Across Musical Worlds*. Ed. Bernstein, J.A. Northeaster University. 147.

De Barros, P. (2012). *Shall We Play That One Together?*. St. Martin's Press.

De Beauvoir, S. (1971). *The Second Sex.* Alfred A. Knopf.

DeCurtis, A., Henke, J. & George-Warren, H. (1992). *The Rolling Stone Illustrated History of Rock & Roll.* Random House.

Del Boca, D., Oggero, N., Profeta, P. & Rossi, M. (2020). Women's work, housework and childcare, before and during COVID-19. *Review of Economics of the Household*, 18, 1001–1017.

Denny, G. (1962). *Jenny Lind, the Swedish Nightingale.* Lippincott.

Derrida, J. (1967. Reprinted 2001). *Writing and Difference.* Routledge.

Dickerson, J.L. (2002). *Just for a Thrill: Lil Hardin Armstrong, First Lady of Jazz.* Cooper Square Press.

Dolan, J. (2002). Feeling women's culture: Women's music, lesbian feminism, and the impact of emotional memory. *Journal of Dramatic Theory and Criticism*, 26(2), 205–219.

Dunbar, J. (2021). *Women, Music, Culture: An Introduction*, 3rd ed. Routledge.

Dunoyer, C. (1993). *Marguerite Long: A Life in French Music, 1874–1966.* Indiana University Press.

Du Pré, P. & Du Pré, H. (1997). *A Genius in the Family: An Intimate Memoir of Jacqueline du Pré.* Sinclair-Stevenson.

Eagly, A. & Carli, L. (2007). Women and the labyrinth of leadership. *Harvard Business Review,* 85, 62.

Easton, C. (2000). *Jacqueline du Pré: A Biography.* Da Capo Press.

Einstein, A. (1962). *Mozart, His Character, His Work.* Oxford, 303.

Everett, W. (2001). *Simon, Lucy.* Grove Music Online.

Fairley, J. (1984). La Nueva Canción Latinoamericana. *Society for Latin American Studies,* 3(2), 107–115.

Farrugia, R. (2013). *Beyond the Dance Floor: Female DJs, Technology and Electronic Dance Music Culture.* University of Chicago Press.

Fauser, A. (2004). Lili Boulanger. *New Historical Anthology of Music by Women,* Ed. Briscoe, J.R. Indiana University Press. 275.

Feisst, S. (2001). *Oliveros, Pauline.* Grove Music Online.

Feldstein, R. (2013). *How It Feels to Be Free: Black Women Entertainers and the Civil Rights Movement.* Oxford University Press.

Ferrari, G., Ferraro, V., Profeta, P. & Pronzato, C. (2022). Do board gender quotas matter? Selection, performance, and stock market effects. *Management Science,* 68(8), 5618–5643.

Fétis, F. (1860–1868). Biographie universelle des musiciens et bibliographie générale de la musique, vol VII. Firmin-Didot.

Fillmore, J.C. (1877). Piano teachers and concert pianists. *Dwight's Journal of Music,* 37, 84–85.

Flabbi, L, Macis, M., Moro, A. & Schivardi, F. (2019). Do female executives make a difference? The impact of female leadership on gender gaps and firm performance. *The Economic Journal,* 129, 390–423.

Fleming, T. (2016). A marriage of inconvenience: Miriam Makeba's relationship with Stokely Carmichael and her music career in the United States. *Safundi: The Journal of South African and American Studies,* 17(3), 312–338.

Foulkes-Levy, L. & Levy, B. (2005). *Journeys Through the Life and Music of Nancy van de Vate.* Scarecrow Press.

Frazes Hill, C. (2022). *Margaret Hillis: Unsung Pioneer.* Carroll Lee Gonzo.

Friedan, B. (2010). *The Feminine Mystique.* W.W. Norton.

Fuller, S. (2001a). *LeFanu, Nicola.* Grove Music Online.

___. (2001b). *Smyth, Ethel.* Grove Music Online.

Fussi, F., & Paolillo, N. (2011). Analisi spettrografiche dell'evoluzione e involuzione vocale di Maria Callas alla luce di una ipotesi fisiopatologica. *La voce del cantante,* 7, 33–51.

Gaar, G. (1992). *She's a Rebel: The History of Women in Rock & Roll.* Seal Press.

Gammel, I. (2012). Lacing up the gloves: Women, boxing and modernity. *Cultural and Social History,* 9(3), 369–390.

Garon, P. & Garon, B. (1992). *Woman with Guitar: Memphis Minnie's Blues.* Da Capo Press.

George, A., Weiser, M.E. & Zepernick, J. (2013). *Women and Rhetoric between the Wars.* Southern Illinois University Press.

Gillard, J. & Okonjo-Iweala, N. (2020). *Women and Leadership: Real Lives Real Lessons*. Penguin Random House.

Gioia, T. (2012). *The Jazz Standards: A Guide to the Repertoire*. Oxford University Press.

Glixon, B. (1999). More on the life and death of Barbara Strozzi. *The Musical Quarterly*, 83, 134–141.

Goldin, C., & Rouse, C. (2000). Orchestrating impartiality: The impact of 'blind' auditions on female musicians. *American Economic Review*, 90, 715–741.

Gorlinski, G. (2010). *The 100 Most Influential Musicians of All Time*. Rosen Publishing Group.

Gourse, L. (1995). *Madame Jazz: Contemporary Women Instrumentalists*. Oxford University Press.

___. (2000). *The Billie Holiday Companion: Seven Decades of Commentary*. Schirmer Trade Books.

Green, L. (2008). *Music, Gender, Education*. Cambridge University Press.

Griffiths, D. (2001). *Mitchell, Joni*. Grove Music Online.

Grolman, E. (2001). *Tower, Joan*. Grove Music Online.

Grout, D.J. & Palisca, C. (2009). *A History of Western Music*, 8th ed. W.W. Norton.

Gulla, B. (2008). *Icons of R&B and Soul: An Encyclopaedia of the Artists Who Revolutionized Rhythm*. Vol 1. Greenwood Press.

Hallman, D. (2001). *Bloomfield Zeisler [née Blumenfeld], Fannie*. Grove Music Online.

Halstead, J. (1997. Revised 2017). *The Woman Composer: Creativity and the Gendered Politics Of Musical Composition*. Routledge.

Harrison, D.D. (1988). *Black Pearls: Blues Queens of the 1920s*. Rutgers University Press.

Hayes, E. (2010). *Songs in Black and Lavender: Race, Sexual Politics, and Women's Music*. University of Illinois Press.

Helgert, L. (2013). *Criticism: 5. Since 1960*. Grove Music Online.

Hernandez, K., Smith, S. & Piper, K. (2022, March). *Inclusion in the Recording Studio?: Gender and Race/Ethnicity of Artists, Songwriters and Producers across 1,000 Popular Songs from 2012–2021*. USC Annenberg Inclusion Initiative.

Herndon, M. & Ziegler, S. (1990). Music, gender, and culture. ICTM Study Group on Music and Gender & International Council for Traditional Music C F Peters Corporation.

Hetherington, J.A. (1967/2013). *Melba*. Melbourne University Publishing.

Higgins, P. (1993). Women in music, feminist criticism, and guerrilla musicology: Reflections on recent polemics. *19th Century Music*, 27(2), 174–192.

Hisama, E.M. (2006). *Gendering Musical Modernism: The Music of Ruth Crawford, Marion Bauer, and Miriam Gideon*. Cambridge University Press.

___. (2014). DJ Kuttin Kandi: Performing feminism. *American Music Review*, 43(2), 1–6.

Hisama, E.M. & Tick, J. (2001). *Crawford (Seeger), Ruth*. Grove Music Online.

Howie, S. (1996). Review of Gastonia 1929: The story of the Loray Mill strike. *Appalachian Journal*, 23(3), 326–331.

Hutton, J. (2003). Daphne Oram: Innovator, writer and composer. *Organised Sound*, 8(1), 49–56.

James, E. & Ritz, D. (1998). *Rage to Survive: The Etta James Story*. Da Capo Press.

Jensen, J. (1998). *The Nashville Sound: Authenticity, Commercialization, and Country Music*. Vanderbilt University Press.

Jezic, D. & Wood, E. (1994). *Women Composers: The Lost Tradition Found*. Feminist Press at CUNY.

Jones, M. (1994). *The Life and Times of Patsy Cline*. Harper Collins.

Kagan, S. (1977). Camilla Urso: A nineteenth-century violinist's view. *Signs: Journal of Women in Culture and Society*, 2(3), 727–734.

Katz, M. (2007, 12 December). Men, women, and turntables: Gender and the DJ battle. *The Musical Quarterly*, 89(4), 580–599.

Kelly, G. (2017). *Live, Lead, Learn: My Stories of Life and Leadership*. Penguin Group.

Kendall-Davies, B. (2012). The life and work of Pauline Viardot-Garcia. Vol. 2, *The Years of Grace, 1863–1910*. Cambridge Scholars.

Kendrick, R. (2002). Intent and intertextuality in Barbara Strozzi's sacred music. *Recercare. Rivista per lo Studio e la Practica della Musica Antica*, 14, 65–98.

Kimber, M.W. (2004). *The Cambridge Companion to Mendelssohn*. Ed. Mercer-Taylor, P. Cambridge University Press.

King, C. (2012). *A Natural Woman: A Memoir*. Grand Central.

Kisby, F. (2001). Urban history, musicology and cities and towns in renaissance Europe. In *Music and Musicians in Renaissance Cities and Town*. Ed. Kisby, F. Cambridge University Press, 1–13.

Klenke, K. (2011). *Women in Leadership: Contextual Dynamics And Boundaries*. Emerald Group Publishing.

Koskoff, E., ed. (1987). *Women and Music in Cross-cultural Perspective*, Vol. 79. University of Illinois Press.

___. (2014). *A Feminist Ethnomusicology. Writings on Music and Gender*. Illinois University Press.

Kottick, E. (2003). *A History of the Harpsichord*, Volume 1. Indiana University Press.

Lassemonne, D. & Ferguson, H. (1966). *Myra Hess, By Her Friends* (First American ed.). Vanguard Press.

Lazarou, L. (2017). *Women Conductors: A Qualitative Study of Gender, Family, 'The Body' and Discrimination*. Durham University.

Leonard, K. (2014). *Louise Talma: A Life in Composition*. Ashgate.

Leppert, R. (2008). Gender sonics: The voice of Patsy Cline, musicological identities. In *Essays in Honor of Susan McClary*. Ed. Bauer, S., Knapp, R. & Warwick, J. Aldershot, 191–204.

Leung, E., Brown, V., Blackshaw, J., Shapiro, A., Snyder, C., Taylor, R. & Watkins, A. L. (2021). *The Horizon Leans Forward: Stories of Courage, Strength, and Triumph of Underrepresented Communities in the Wind Band Field: With an Annotated Bibliography of Works by Underrepresented Composers*. GIA Publications Inc.

Lieb, S. (1983). *Mother of the Blues: A Study of Ma Rainey*, 3rd ed. University of Massachusetts Press.

Lilly, J. (2001). *The Carter Family*. Grove Music Online.

Lukomsky, V. (1999). 'Hearing the subconscious': Interview with Sofia Gubaidulina. *Tempo*, 209, 27–31.

Lutyens, E. (1972). *A Goldfish Bowl*. Cassell.

Macarthur, S. (2010). *Towards a Twenty-First-Century Feminist Politics of Music*. Ashgate.

Macarthur, S., Bennett, D., Goh, T., Hennekam, S. & Hope, C. (2017). The rise and fall, and the rise (again) of feminist research in music: What goes around comes around. *Musicology Australia*, 39(2), 73–95.

Macleod, B. (2000). *Women Performing Music: The Emergence of American Women as Classical Instrumentalists and Conductors*. McFarland.

Masters, M. (2007). *No Wave*. Black Dog Publishing.

Mattis, O., Highwather, J. & Jobin, S. (2001). *Dlugoszewski, Lucia*. Grove Music Online.

Matushita, H. (2004). Maria Theresa von Paradis. In *New Historical Anthology of Music by Women*. Ed. Briscoe, J.R. Indiana University Press. 121.

Mayhew, E. (2006). The Booing of Sinéad O'Connor: Bob Dylan 30th Anniversary Concert, Madison Square Garden, New York, 16 October 1992. In *Performance and Popular Music: History Place and Time*. Ed. Inglis, I. Routledge, 172–187.

McClary, S. (1991). *Feminine Endings: Music, Gender, and Sexuality*. University of Minnesota Press.

McDonnell, E. & Powers, A., eds. (1995). *Rock She Wrote: Women Write about Rock, Pop, and Rap*. Plexus.

McKeage, K. (2014). Where are all the girls? Women in collegiate instrumental jazz. *GEMS (Gender, Education, Music, and Society)*, the on-line journal of GRIME (Gender Research in Music Education), 7(3), 12–19.

Melba, N. (1925/2011). *Melodies and Memories*. Cambridge University Press.

Mercier, A. (2017). *Guilhermina Suggia: Cellist*. Routledge.

Milliken, R. (2002). *Roxon, Lillian (1932–1973)*. *Australian Dictionary of Biography*. National Centre of Biography, Australian National University, 16.

Monsaingeon, B. (1985). *Mademoiselle: Conversations with Nadia Boulanger*. Carcanet Press.

Moran, W.R., ed. (1984). *Nellie Melba: A Contemporary Review*. [with bibliography and discography]. Greenwood Press.

Morgan, J. (2000). *When Chickenheads Come Home To Roost: A Hip Hop Feminist Breaks It Down*. Simon & Schuster.

Morris, B.J. (1999). *Eden Built by Eves: The Culture of Women's Music Festivals*. Alyson Publications.

___. (2003). Music: Women's festivals. In *Encyclopedia of Lesbian, Gay, Bisexual and Transgender History in America*. Ed. Stein, M. Charles Scribner's Sons, 12–19.

___. (2005). Negotiating lesbian worlds. *Journal of Lesbian Studies*, 9(1–2), 55–62.

Myers, R. (1947). *Music Since 1939*. British Council.

Neuls-Bates, C. ed. (1996). *Women in Music: An Anthology of Source Readings from the Middle Ages to the Present*, revised ed. Northeastern University Press.

Nicholson, S. (1995). *Billie Holiday*. Victor Gollancz Ltd.

Nixon, C. & Sinclair, A. (2017). *Women Leading*. Melbourne University Publishing.

Oakley, G. (1997). *The Devil's Music*. Da Capo Press.

O'Brien, L. (2002). *She Bop II*. Continuum.

O'Connor, S. (2021). *Rememberings: Scenes from My Complicated Life*. Dey Street Books.

Oldenziel, R.A. (1997). Boys and their toys: The Fisher Body Craftsman's Guild, 1930–1968, and the making of a male technical domain. *Technology and Culture*, 38(1), 60–96.

O'Meara, C. (2003). The raincoats: Breaking down punk rock's masculinities. *Popular Music*, 22(3), 299–313.

Oram, D. (1972). *An Individual Note – Of Music, Sound and Electronics*. Galliard.

Orledge, R. (2001). *Tailleferre, Germaine*. Grove Music Online.

Orr, M. (2019). *Lean Out: The Truth About Women, Power, and the Workplace*. HarperCollins.

Page, C. (2014). *Weaponized Umbrage. Culture Worrier: Selected Columns 1984–2014: Reflections on Race, Politics and Social Change*. Agate Publishing.

Payne, A., & Calam, T. (2001). *Lutyens, (Agnes) Elisabeth*. Grove Music Online.

Pelic, B. (2018). *Music and Leadership: Empowering Global Leaders for the New Millenia*. Books on Demand.

Pendle, K., ed. (1991). *Women and Music: A History*. Bloomington.

___. (2004). Mariana von Martines. In *New Historical Anthology of Music by Women*. Ed. Briscoe, J.R. Indiana University Press, 113.

Peraino, J. (2005). *Listening to the Sirens Musical Technologies of Queer Identity from Homer to Hedwig*. University of California Press.

Pescerelli, B. (1979). I madrigali di Maddalena Casulana. *LS Olschki*.

Petersen, B.A., revised by Rosen, J. (2001). *Ruth Anderson*. Grove Music Online.

Petsalis-Diomidis, N. (2001). *The Unknown Callas: The Greek Years*, Vol. 14. Hal Leonard Corporation.

Petteys, M. (2001). *Rivé-King [née Rivé], Julie*. Grove Music Online.

Pettigrew, R. & Duncan, K. (2021). Fathers use of parental leave in a Canadian law enforcement organization. *Journal of Family Issues*, 42(10), 2211–2241.

Phelps, A. (2010). Beyond auditions: Gender discrimination in America's top orchestras. DMA Dissertation, University of Iowa, USA.

Pita, L. (2015). *Carreño, (María) Teresa*. Grove Music Online.

Porter, E. (2002). *What Is This Thing Called Jazz? African American Musicians as Artists, Critics, and Activists*. University of California Press.

Potter, C. (2001). *Boulanger, (Juliette) Nadia*. Grove Music Online.

Pough, G. (2004). *Check It While I Wreck It: Black Womanhood, Hip Hop Culture, and the Public Sphere*. Northeastern University Press.

Powell, C. (1991). Rap music: An education with a beat from the street. *Journal of Negro Education*, 60(3), 245–259.

Power, G. (2004). Yvette Guilbert: A career of public applause and personal disappointment. *Context: Journal of Music Research*, (27/28), 31–41.

Power, K. (2020). The COVID-19 pandemic has increased the care burden of women and families. *Sustainability: Science, Practice and Policy*, 16(1), 67–73.

Powers, A. (2000). *Weird Like Us: My Bohemian America*. Simon & Schuster.

___. ed. (2010). *Best Music Writing 2010*. Da Capo Press.

___. (2017). *Good Booty: Love and Sex, Black & White, Body and Soul in American Music*. William Morrow.

Press, J. (2018). *Stealing the Show: How Women Are Revolutionizing Television*. Faber & Faber.

Prinz, J. (2014). The aesthetics of punk rock. *Philosophy Compass*, 9(9), 583–593.

Rabaka, R. (2012). *Hip Hop's Amnesia: From Blues and the Black Women's Club Movement to Rap and the Hip Hop Movement*. Lexington Books.

Radic, T. (1986). *Melba: The Voice of Australia*. Springer.

Ravan, G. (2004). *Lollipop Lounge, Memoirs of a Rock and Roll Refugee*. Billboard Books.

Ravell-Pinto, T. & Ravell, R. (2008). Obituary: African Icon: Miriam 'Mama Africa' Makeba, dies at age 76. *Journal of the African Literature Association*, 2(2), 274–281.

Redmond, S.L. (2013). *Anthem: Social Movements and the Sound of Solidarity in the African Diaspora*. New York University Press.

Reed-Jones, C. (2004). *Hildegard of Bingen: Women of Vision*. Paper Crane Press

Reich, N. (2001). *Clara Schumann: The Artist and the Woman*. Cornell University Press.

Reynolds, S. & Press, J. (1995). *The Sex Revolts: Gender, Rebellion, and Rock'n'roll*. Harvard University Press.

Rieger, E. (1985). 'Dolce semplice'? On the changing role of women in music. In *Feminist Aesthetics*. Ed. Ecker, G. Beacon Press, 135–149.

___. (1992). 'I recycle sounds': Do women compose differently? *Journal of the International League of Women Composers*, March 1992, 22–25.

Ripani, R. (2006). *The New Blue Music: Changes in Rhythm & Blues, 1950–1999*. University Press of Mississippi.

Rodgers, T. (2010). *Pink Noises: Women on Electronic Music and Sound*. Duke University Press.

Rosand, E. (1978). Barbara Strozzi, 'virtuosissima cantatrice': The composer's voice. *Journal of the American Musicological Society*, 31, 241–281.

___. (2001). Vivaldi's stage. *Journal of Musicology*, 18(1), 8–30.

Rosand, E. & Glixon, B.L. (2001). *Strozzi, Barbara*. Grove Music Online.

Rosenstiel, L. (1998). *Nadia Boulanger: A Life in Music*. W.W. Norton.

Roxon, L. (1969). *Lillian Roxon's Rock Encyclopaedia*. Grosset & Dunlap/Workman Publishing.

Rusak, H. (2005). Simply Divine: Feminist aesthetics in three music theatre works of Elena Kats-Chernin. Phd Dissertation, University of Adelaide.

___. (2010). Operas by women in Australia: Some data. *Asia Pacific Journal of Arts and Cultural Management*, 7(1), 557–568.

___. (2019). Wild Swans by Elena Kats-Chernin: The journey from the Australian Ballet to the UK dance charts. *Sound Scripts*, 6(1), 17.

___. (2020). The Divorce: A soap opera. In *Opera, Emotion, and the Antipodes*, Volume II. Ed. Davidson, J., Halliwell, M. & Rocke, S. Routledge, 90–112.

Russell, T. (1996). *The Blues: From Robert Johnson to Robert Cray*. Carlton Books.

Ryan, M. (1992). *Trumpet Records: An Illustrated History, with Discography*. Big Nickel Publications.

Ryan, T. (2016). Seen but unseen: Missing visible Indigenous women and what it means for leadership in Indigenous Australia. *Platform: Journal of Media and Communication*, 7. ANZCA Special Issue, 26–34.

___. (2018). *Deadly Women: An Analysis of Indigenous Women's Leadership in Australia*. University of Canberra.

Rye, H. (2001). *Snow, Valaida*. Grove Music Online.

Saarikallio-Torp, M. & Miettinen, A. (2021). Family leaves for fathers: Non-users as a test for parental leave reforms. *Journal of European Social Policy*, 31(2), 161–174.

Sandberg, S. (2013). *Lean In: Women, Work, and the Will to Lead*. Random House.

Sayrs, E. (1993). Deconstructing McClary: Narrative, feminine sexuality, and feminism in Susan McClary's feminine endings. *College Music Symposium*, 33, 41–55.

Schiller, J. (2006). *Camilla Urso: Pioneer Violinist (1840–1902)*. University of Kentucky.

Schonberg, H. (1987). *The Great Pianists*. Simon & Schuster.

Schrader, B. (2001). *Barron, Bebe*. Grove Music Online.

Schuller, G. (1986). *Early Jazz: Its Roots and Musical Development*. Oxford University Press.

Schwartz, K.R. (2001). Zwilich, Ellen Taaffe. Grove Music Online.

Scott, M. (2007). *Music in Egypt*. Oxford University Press.

Seeger, P. (2002). *The Peggy Seeger Songbook: Forty Years of Song Making*. Oak Publications.

___. (2017). *First Time Ever: A Memoir*. Faber & Faber.

Seeger, R.C., Crawford, R. & Polansky, L. (2001). *'The Music of American Folk Song' and Selected Other Writings on American Folk Music*, Vol. 17. University Rochester Press.

Sergeant, D. & Himonides, E. (2019). Orchestrated sex: The representation of male and female musicians in world-class symphony orchestras. *Frontiers in Psychology*, 10, 1760.

Sevilla, A. & Smith, S. (2020). Baby steps: The gender division of childcare during the COVID-19 pandemic. *Oxford Review of Economic Policy*, 36(Supplement_1), S169–S186.

Shaffer, K. & Greenwood, G. (1988). *Maud Powell: Pioneer American Violinist*. Maud Powell Foundation.

Shapiro, R. (2011). *Les Six: The French Composers and Their Mentors, Jean Cocteau and Erik Satie*. Peter Owen.

Shawe-Taylor, D. (1997). Schumann-Heink, Ernestine. In *The New Grove Dictionary of Opera*, Vol. 4. Ed. Stanley, S. Oxford University Press, 255.

Shepherd, J. (1993). Power and difference in music. In *Musicology and Difference: Gender and Sexuality in Music Scholarship*. Ed. Solie, R. University of California Press, 46.

Sheridan, A., Pringle, J. & Strachan, G. (2009). Doing scholarship differently: Doing scholarship that matters: An interview with Amanda Sinclair. *Journal of Management and Organization*, 15, 549–554.

Sicherman, B. & Green, C. (1980). *Notable American Women: The Modern Period: A Biographical Dictionary*. Belknap Press of Harvard University Press.

Simon, C. (2015). *Boys in the Trees: A Memoir*. Flatiron Books.

Sinclair, A. (1994). *Trials at the Top: Chief Executives Talk About Men, Women and the Australian Executive Culture*. University of Melbourne.

___. (1998). *Doing Leadership Differently: Gender, Power, and Sexuality in a Changing Business Culture*. Melbourne University Press.

___. (2005a). Body and management pedagogy. *Gender, Work & Organization*, 12, 89–104.

___. (2005b). *Doing Leadership Differently: Gender, Power and Sexuality in a Changing Business Culture*. Melbourne University Press.

___. (2007). Leadership for the disillusioned. *Melbourne Review: A Journal of Business and Public Policy*, 3: 65–71.

___. (2009). Seducing leadership: Stories of leadership development. *Gender, Work & Organization*, 16: 266–284.

___. (2013). Not just 'adding women in': Women re-making leadership. *Seizing the Initiative: Australian Women Leaders in Politics, Workplaces and Communities*, 15, 15–34.

Sinclair, D. (2004). *Wannabe: How the Spice Girls Reinvented Pop Fame*. Omnibus Press.

Sizemore-Barber, A. (2012). The voice of (which?) Africa: Miriam Makeba in America. *Safundi: The Journal of South African and American Studies*, 13(3–4), 251–276.

Smith, P. (2010). *Just Kids*. Ecco.

Solie, R. (1991). What do feminists want? A reply to Pieter van den Toorn. *The Journal of Musicology*, 9, 399–410.

___. ed. (1995). *Musicology and Difference: Gender and Sexuality in Music Scholarship*. University of California Press.

___. (2001). *Feminism*. Grove Music Online.

Solomon, M. (1995). *Mozart: A Life*, reprint ed. Harper Collins.

Steane, J. (2001). *Guilbert, Yvette*. Grove Music Online.

Stoneman, T. (2017). International economic law, gender equality, and paternity leave: Can the WTO be utilized to balance the division of care labour worldwide. *Emory International Law Review*, 32, 51.

Story, R.M. (1990). *And So I Sing: African American Divas of Opera and Concert*. Amistad.

Sutton, A. (2021). *American Record Companies and Producers, 1888–1950: An Encyclopedic History*. Mainspring Press.

Taraborrelli, J.R. (2002). *Madonna: An Intimate Biography*. Simon & Schuster.

Tasker, Y. (2002). *Working Girls: Gender and Sexuality in Popular Cinema*. Routledge.

Tharp, D. & Parks-Stamm, E. (2021). Gender differences in the intended use of parental leave: Implications for human capital development. *Journal of Family and Economic Issues*, 42(1), 47–60.

Thomson, E. (2020). *Joan Baez: The Last Leaf.* Palazzo Editions.

Throsby, D. & Petetskaya, K. (2017). *Making Art Work: An Economic Study of Professional Artists in Australia.* Australia Council for the Arts.

Thurlow, J. (2001). *Jolas, Betsy.* Grove Music Online.

Tick, J., Ericson, M. & Koskoff, E. (2001). *Women in Music.* Grove Music Online.

Tick, J., Margaret E. & Koskoff, E. (2001). *Women in Music.* Grove Music Online.

Tirro, F. (2007). *Historia del jazz clásico.* American Bar Association.

Tunley, D. (2014). *Joyce, Eileen Alannah (1908–1991).* Australian Dictionary of Biography, National Centre of Biography, Australian National University.

Turnbull, M. (1997). *Mary Garden.* Scolar Press.

Turner, T. (1986). *I, Tina. Loder, Kurt.* Morrow.

Tyrefors, B. & Jansson, J. (2017). Gender quotas in the board room and firm performance: Evidence from a credible threat in Sweden. IFN Working Paper. No. 1165.

Valentine, P. & Wickham, V. (2000). *Dancing with Demons: The Authorised Biography of Dusty Springfield.* Hodder & Stoughton.

Van den Toorn, P. (1991). Politics, feminism, and contemporary music theory. *The Journal of Musicology,* 9(3), 275–299.

___. (1996). *Music, Politics, and the Academy.* University of California Press.

Von Gunden, H. (1983). *The Music of Pauline Oliveros.* Scarecrow Press.

Waksman, S. (2001). *The Runaways.* Grove Music Online.

Wehr-Flowers, E. (2006). Differences between male and female students' confidence, anxiety, and attitude toward learning jazz improvisation. *Journal of Research in Music Education,* 54(4), 337–349.

Weid, J. (2001). *Radigue, Eliane.* Grove Music Online.

White, J.D. & Christensen, J. (2002). *New Music of the Nordic Countries.* Pendragon Press.

Whiteley, S. (2000). *Women and Popular Music: Sexuality, Identity and Subjectivity.* Routledge.

Willis, E. (1992). *No More Nice Girls: Countercultural Essays.* Wesleyan University Press.

Wilson, E. (1999). *Jacqueline du Pré: Her Life, Her Music, Her Legend.* Faber and Faber.

Winter, T. (2015). *Delia Derbyshire: Sound and Music for the BBC Radiophonic Workshop, 1962–1973.* PhD thesis, University of York.

Wolff, K. (2000). *Country Music: The Rough Guide.* Penguin Books Ltd.

Wood, E. (1980). Women in music. *Signs: Journal of Women in Culture and Society,* 6, 283.

Worthey, D. & Wallace, M. (2020). *In One Ear and Out the Other: Antonia Brico and Her Amazingly Musical Life.* Penny Candy Books.

Yanow, S. (2003). *Jazz on Record: The First Sixty Years.* Backbeat Books.

# INDEX

Printed in the United States
by Baker & Taylor Publisher Services